Posthumanist Nomadisms across Non-Oedipal Spatiality

Edited by

Java Singh
Doon University, India

Indrani Mukherjee
Jawaharlal Nehru University, India

Series in Anthropology

VERNON PRESS

In the Americas:	*In the rest of the world:*
Vernon Press	Vernon Press
1000 N West Street, Suite 1200,	C/Sancti Espiritu 17,
Wilmington, Delaware 19801	Malaga, 29006
United States	Spain

Series in Anthropology

Library of Congress Control Number: 2021943151

ISBN: 978-1-64889-451-0

Also available: 978-1-64889-113-7 [Hardback]; 978-1-64889-391-9 [PDF, E-Book]

Cover image by Tomislav Jakupec from Pixabay.

Cover design by Vernon Press.

Table of contents

List of figures and table

Figures

Table

Acknowledgement

We would like to acknowledge that this project would not have taken off without our participation in the 50th Northeast Modern Language Association held in Washington DC from March 21 to 24th, 2019. The theme of the conference was "Transnational Spaces: Intersections of Cultures, Languages, and Peoples" where our session proposal entitled, "Nomadisms across non-Oedipal Spatiality in Contemporary Narratives of Becoming" was accepted. We had a very positive response from researchers working on diverse literary and cultural representations. Thereafter, when the Vernon Press offered to publish our proceedings, we sent out our CFP once again and finally chose the articles which appear here.

The articles selected in this book have been double blind peer reviewed by a distinguished team of experts, some of whom are also our authors. We would like to thank all of them. We would also like to acknowledge colleagues who have helped us give the book its present shape, especially Prof. Didier Coste (Bordeaux, Montaigne), Prof. Debra Castillo (Corneille, New York) and Prof. Elena Losada Soler (Universidad de Barcelona).

Preface by Walter Mignolo
What does it mean to be human?
Border thinking on racism and migrations

It is a rare occasion, and a welcome one, when the person receiving thankful appreciation from the authors is invited to preface their book, giving him the opportunity to express his dissenting opinion. I am pleased to return the appreciation and continue the conversations initiated at Hyderabad in December of 2019 and followed up via email since. Indeed, the friendly conversations started and unfolded on a divergent understanding of what is meant and understood when the word 'human' is articulated in a given modern European vernacular and imperial language (*humano* in Spanish; *humaine* in French; *Mensch* in Germany; *umano* in Italian; *humano* in Portuguese). The following reflections are neither intended to correct the summary of my words that Professors Indrani Mukherjee and Java Singh offer in the introduction, nor to comment on subsequent chapters. My reflections provide a background of what I thought and said during the conversations summarized in the introduction.

Since the volume underscores both the posthuman and nomadism, I divided this preface into two sections, one in conversation with the posthuman and the second with nomadism. Section three is a conclusion connecting the threads of parts one and two. My reflections on the posthuman are based on Sylvia Wynter's distinctive approach to the question. As a Black woman, scholar, and activist from the Caribbean, she pursued a basic question: what does it mean to be human? The question is engrained in the lived African diaspora in the Caribbean. She cast her argument in the expression "after man," a radical starting point away from the 'post-' and from the 'human'.[I] The second part is based on my own immigrant experience. All my grandparents migrated from Italy to Argentina. I then migrated from Argentina to France and later to the US. 'Nomadism' is a very alien word in my experience and my decolonial articulation of that experience. 'Immigrant consciousness' is a concept that I sense in my body, and immigration consciousness presupposes border dwelling and border thinking.[1]

---

[1] Walter D Mignolo, "Introduction. Immigrant Conscousness. » In Rodolfo Kusch, *Indigenous and Popular Thinking in America* [1970]. Translated by María Lugones and Joshua M. Price. Durham: Duke University Press, 2010, xiii-xl.

I

'Human' is a regional word to name one species of living organism that, among other features, walks on the two lower extremities and that, in so doing, liberates their hands to provide themselves with food and shelter. Once the mouth was liberated from the necessary task of providing nutrition, the organ began to be used to expand its capacity to emit sound and expand the coordination of activities with other organisms of the same species co-existing in the same space. Like any other mobile living organisms (what we call animals (including insects) and aquatic vertebrates, etc.) they group with members of the same species living in the same surroundings. Over time, millions of years, our ancestors expanded their ability to coordinate their activities through sounds and scratching symbols on flat surfaces (what is generally called writing).

To make the story short, languaging became a distinctive feature of one species of living organisms that allowed the members of said species to tell stories about the origination of the cosmos (to use a common word), of planet earth, of all living organisms, and about the conditions that makes living organisms on earth possible. The particular genus of the species telling the story of the origination of the universe (of planet earth, of all living organisms) were and are the genus of the particular species of living organisms walking on only the lower extremities, thereby liberating the mouth from the task of food provision and allowing them to engage in languaging. Furthermore, liberating the upper extremities from walking meant that they could be used to provide themselves with food, shelter, and to build instruments to extend the uses of the hands. Languaging and storytelling emerged to coordinate and reflect on the meaning of their actions, their memories, and, briefly, the constitution of the communal organization.

The point here is that, in modern vernacular European languages, the term 'human' and the meanings attached to the word, is neither the word nor the meaning common to the speaker of non-European languages. That is until colonial invaders came with their own image of themselves, their own storytelling that ignored, destituted and silenced the invaded people's ways of thinking of themselves as well as their own judgements of the invaders. For example, the word *Runa* in Quechua cannot be properly translated as 'human'. *Runa* implies the weaving of life in the planet and cosmos (all the living energies and water, sun, light, winds, and organisms and their constant flow), of which *Runa* are just one particular type of organism. 'Human', according to

Western vocabulary (Man1 in Wynter's argument),[2] separated itself from all the living which was, in turn, reduced to a single noun: *Nature,* an object as it were. Western civilisation is one populated with objects, not with relations and flows. Andean cosmology was destituted (I am using it as a verb, to enact destitution in the same movement of self-constitution). The intrusion and self-constitution of Western cosmology, and the concept of the 'human' did not destitute the concept of *Runa.* Both concepts co-exist in conflict and power differential. The same applies with the Chinese *Ren. Ren* cannot be translated as 'human' since *Ren* is integrated to *Tianxia (All under heaven),* while 'human' is localized in the frame of Western cosmology (theological and secular (e.g. the Big-Bang story replacing the Biblical narrative)).

The thousand years old Andean civilizations was not only dismantled in its current stage (e.g. the Inca Civilization) but it was conceptually destituted, ignored and demonized: contrary to the European missionaries who honored their own ancestrality, Andean people needed to forget their own past and to be saved from the kingdom of the Devil, which was, of course, unknown in the Andes. The Devil was a Christian invention. The Renaissance Man1´s storytelling conceived of itself as *Human* and relegated the Andean people to lesser, deficient humans, ignoring the Andean´s self-conception based on their own cosmological storytelling. The rhetoric of the *Human* persisted and was the foundation of racism, sexism, and the objectification and commodification of Nature. Man2 appeared with secularization that 'de-goded' God and replaced it with Reason. Man3 emerged after World War Two with cybernetics and two of its consequences: the modelling of the life and deeds of the consumer by the invasion of advertising and, more recently, by the use of artificial intelligence to program our lives. Both consequences accentuate the separation, not only of the 'human' with living energies in the planet and the cosmos, but of the flow of life energies, replacing it with the sacralization of the *Instrumentality* of life. Man3, following Wynter's chronology, would be the *Posthuman.* Man1 and Man2 were tantamount to the invention of the *Individual,* a distinctive feature of Western civilization with its splendors and misery. Man3 is tantamount to the sanctification of the *Individual* and its elevation to the Ego as the the game of life: a model of *man* (Man3) that was developed by economists and the military which consisted in an egotistical being interested only in his own benefit and in duping his opponents to achieve

---

[2] Sylvia Wynter, "Unsetling the Coloniality of Being/Power/Truth/Freedom: Towards the Human, After Man, Its Overrepreesentation—An Argument." *CR: The. Ew Centennial Review.* 3/3, 2003, 257-337. Katherine McKittrick, editor. "Sylvia Winter: On Being Human as a Praxis. Durham: Duke University Press, 2015.

his ends: a modern homo oeconomicus. [3] I am talking about two trajectories: the trajectory that leads to the post-human and the trajectory that lead to Man3, the consolidation of a game of life that prevents asking what does it mean to be human.

This is also, in my understanding, the territory of the posthuman. But, as the dictum goes, and as Jorge Luis Borges parodied, the map is not the territory. There are other territories. One of them is "After Man" irreducible to the genealogy of Man1 to Man3. "After Man" is the humanness reclaimed by the descendant of the long history of racialized and sexualized peope, since he sixteenth century. Classified as ontologically (lesser humans) inferior and epistemologically deficient (irracionals or not quite rationals) who precisely because of their inferiority and their deficiencies were not supposed to think. They/we are now thinking and reducing the posthuman and Eurocentrism (Eurocentrism is an epistemological and aesthetic phenomenon whose enunciation is located in Western Europe but whose tentacles reached diverse points of the planet) to its own size. "After Man" emerge from the mayority of non-European population who have been left out from the trajectories Human to post-Human and from Man1 to Man3. The post-Human is not universal. Is the eurocentric critique of Eurocentrism while Wynter's Man1 to Man3 outlines a decolonial critique of eurocentrism. The decolonial option illuminate the paths toward the humanness of the After Human, co-existing with the post-Human.

I am aware that promoters of the 'post-human' are driving towards escaping the trends of anthropocentrism. And I do not have a problem with that. It is one way to go. I am describing a different path to delink from anthropocentrism. I am not trying to supersede what, in a different frame, is conceived as 'post-human'; I am not interested in disqualifying it. I am just saying that I do not and cannot fully accept it. And I am saying that there is one path to go and that path is to add a prefix 'post-' to whatever you would like to supersede. I am talking about co-existences in diversity (that is pluriversality). In a pluriversal ecumene, 'post-' means one temporal and conceptual line and the assumption that there is one, universal, time. It is generally assumed that all 'after' has to be 'post-', and that all dissension and attempts to supersede something in the prison of North Atlantic Universals (in the apt description offered by Michel Rolph-Trouillot)[4] has to be referred to with 'post-'. There is no way out of

---

[3] Frank Shiffmacher, *Ego: The Game of Life*. London: Polity Press, 2015

[4] Michel-Rolph Trouillot, "North Atlantic Universals. Analytical Fictions 1492-1945." *South Atlantic Quarterly*, 2002, 101/4, 839-858/

capitalism - so the dictum goes - because there is no way out of Western Abstract Universals. Many of us disagree.

II

When I arrived in Paris (in mid 1969) to work on my *doctorat d'état*, I had a better grasp of what it might have meant to my grandparents to move to Argentina in adverse conditions, belonging to generations at the end of the nineteenth century when thousands of Italian migrants moved from Buenos Aires to New York. Now I was moving in the reverse direction, from the West (Indias Occidentales) to the East (Europe), but with the support of a fellowship granted by the University of Córdoba, Argentina.

When I migrated to the US in 1973, the feeling of being a foreigner had already settled. No complaints, no nostalgia. It was what I was. I accepted it and left with it. That lived experience took me where I am today, thinking the way I do and saying the things I say. Disciplines are secondary. They are just tools. I do not follow disciplinary regulations, although I have an academic title. I first studied philosophy and literature and I then got a PhD in semiology. On another day of the journey (metaphorically, since it has not been in one particular day and month and year), salvation came from an encounter with the LatinX population in the US (at that time referred generally as Hispanics, Chicanos and Latinos, no 'a' or 'X' was used at that time). A '*eureka*' feeling and salvation came when I read Gloria Anzaldúa's *Borderland/La Frontera: The New Mestiza* (1987). I understood what being Italo/Argentinian meant, although the particular meaning of being a heterosexual Italo/Argentinian male was quite different from that of being a homosexual Mexican/American female. I understood what dwelling in the borderland and borderline means. That experience nourishes border thinking and border gnoseology (a key concept in *Local Histories/Global Designs. Literacy, Territoriality and Border Thinking,* 2000). Nevertheless, I understood that there was something deeper, a deeper logic to common differences that are culturally perceived at the surface. Superficial differences, literally, hide the deeper logic: the colonial difference.

But let's go back to Anzaldúa. *The Darker Side of the Renaissance: Literacy, Territoriality and Colonization* (1995) came from the gift that Anzaldúa´s book offered. The book is really an autobiographical journey to account for the immigrant consciousness that was growing in me, and myself with it. It was making sense of the Italian Renaissance, the Italian migrants moving to Argentina, and the history of Spanish colonization of the Americas. Anzaldúa's local history (personal and geo-political) had to do with the place of Mexico in colonial history, first in the hands of Spaniards, and later in the hands of the US. The Mexican-American war of 1848 allowed the US to move the 'border' south and leave inside the territorial States a significant number of Mexicans who lost their original nationality.

They did not move; they were not nomads. The frontier moved beyond them. The second connection with Anzaldúa was her signpost sentence: "The U.S-Mexican border es una herida abierta where the Third World grates against the first and bleeds. And before a scab forms it hemorrhages again, the lifeblood of two worlds merging to form a third country — a border culture".[5] Despite different generations, different sexual preferences, and different geopolitical local histories (Mexico on the one hand, Argentina on the other), Anzaldúa and myself both lived the Third World experience. Paraphrasing Anzaldúa I would have said at that time that "The modern/colonial borderlines are heridas abiertas where the Third World grates against that first and bleeds" and these borders and wounds are today planetary. They are the territories where "border cultures" emerge, are formed and persist. Border thinking sprouts from lived experiences in the borderland and borderlines (racial, sexual, nacional, civilizational) It means that coloniality is everywhere, even when settler colonialism ended, coloniality persisted. 'Border cultures' are entangled in power differentials (they are not equal on both sides), and that power differentials are dictated by one of the border cultures. That dictation consisted in the invention of the 'colonial difference': cultural differences are never of equal weight, they are always entangled in power differentials.

I am telling you this story to make more explicit my thoughts on nomadism, migrations, immigrant consciousness, and border thinking. After I finished the manuscript of *The Darker Side of the Renaissance*, I continued what I had started in writing that book but brought my reflections to the end of the twentieth century. Out of this research, teaching, workshops and published articles came *Local Histories/Global Designs*. During that process I was asked many times in graduate seminars, workshops and lectures, why I was not referring to or quoting Deleuze and Guattari´s concept of 'nomadism' since, in the understanding of the person asking the question, there were obvious similarities. I addressed the tenor of these questions in several pages of *Local Histories/Global Designs* (66-77). I explained there why Deleuze and Guattari´s nomadism was irrelevant to my own experience and thinking. Decolonially, we (those of us who follow the path opened by Aníbal Quijano and Gloria Anzaldúa, followed up by María Lugones at the crossroads of Quijano´s coloniality and Anzaldúa geopolitical (Mexico / US) and body-political borderlands (women / lesbians of color)), do not begin from ethereal concepts but from the grounding from where such and such concepts emerge. Concepts are connected to feelings

---

[5] Gloria Anzaldúa. *Borderland/La Frontera. The New Mestiza*. San Franciso: Aunt Lutte, 1987, 25

and emotions, rather than floating in disciplinary clouds. That is why I (and others working on these assumptions) do not follow disciplinary regulations, even less any top-down orientation. Decoloniality is not deconstruction, it is alien to the postmodern and it is undisciplined.

We (the same as above) do not start from the enunciated but from the enunciation which presupposes lived experience rather than disciplinary regulations; the life-world if you wish (not Husserl´s life-world in Freiburg, but Quijano's life-world in the South American Andes or Anzaldúa's on the border between the First and the Third Worlds), which I explained in countless occasions in public talks and writing. In this regard, Deleuze and Guattari's experience (like that of Husserl, there is no personalization here)[6] is alien to us (the same as above and many others as well). Their thinking, rooted in their implicit geo-and body-political grounding in Western modernity, is not the experiential grounding of people dwelling in the borderland, borderline of modernity/coloniality. I am not saying that they are wrong or that we are superseding them, or critiquing them. I am just saying that they are irrelevant to our living and thinking and that they have the right to their own opinion and their ethical responsibility.

Migrations in the past two hundred years (since the creation of the nation-state, the territorial border of the state and the regulation of citizenship), disturb the homogeneity of one state/ one nation (e.g. the nation state) and reveal the power border differential. They reveal the colonial difference' (which is the concept that links to my entire argument in *Local Histories/Global Designs* and essays and speeches I delivered before the publication), the *irreducible difference* that divides and unites modernity/coloniality. Here is a paragraph which summarizes the point I made in *Local History* addressing the similarities perceived by readers or listener. I made the point by building my argument on that of Moroccan philosopher, writer, and thinker Abdelkebir Khatibi and Martinican writer, poet, and thinker Edouard Glissant (and Gloria Anzaldúa in the previous pages):

> Glissant and Khatibi arrive, in fact at a similar view, but not from the local history of knowledge built from the perspective of modernity, as it is the case of Deleuze and Guattari, but from local histories of knowledge built from the perspective of coloniality. It is the coloniality of power and knowledge as articulated in languages that lead Khatibi and Glissant to a critique of Western epistemology and to the articulation of the irreducible difference with their "alias." European thinkers practicing

---

[6] Walter D. Mignolo, "Decoloniality and Phenomenology.The Geopolitics of Knowing and the Epistemic/Ontologial Difference." *The Journal of Speculative Philosophy.* 32/3, 2018, 360-387.

monotopic critique of modern epistemology [while] Glissant version of "Creolization of the world" in this context moves along the lines of Khatibi "another thinking", both complementary [clashing] and irreducible to a "nomadic" of "minor science." (2000, pp. 77).

III

A significant sector of the population of the planet has been, for five hundred years, classified as lesser humans. It is meaningless to think of the *Posthuman* from the experience of people who are yet not considered human enough. Racism and sexism are intermingled with the language you speak, the nation-state you belong to (or do not belong to), the religion you have chosen. *Human* is a category that serves well to maintain classifications and hierarchies. Decolonially speaking, *Human* has to be called into question. Wynter's "after human" does it. She is not proposing to supersede the *Human* with the *Posthuman*. It is in fact a different option, the option that is coming from those lesser humans that were not supposed to think and that, therefore, had to follow North Atlantic Abstract Universals.

Classifications are not a 'representation' of what there is, but are the framing that creates the illusion that what we see is what there is rather than simply what we see. The classification was an invention that 'succeeded' in making people believe in such hierarchies, including those who were ranked inferior. The principle of classification was the concept of 'race'.[7] And the concept of race was (and is?) supported and managed by institutions, actors, and languages. Today, people classified as lesser human are taking the field and revealing that the concept of race was an invention uttered, pronounced, and enunciated in modern vernacular European languages, and maintained by North Atlantic institutions and actors. Of course, there were hierarchies in co-existing languages and civilizations (say Chinese, Indian, Persian, Mayan, Incas) before the advent of racism, colonialism, and the historical foundation of capitalism in the sixteenth century, but not all hierarchies are equivalent to the modern/colonial concept of race and the ideological consequence, racism. Pre-existing sexism and patriarchies had acquired a new meaning in their intersection with racism. Racism is not ontic, but epistemological and ontological: He who controls and manages institutional knowledge and imperial languages, has the privilege to identify himself with the essence of the *Human* and relegates to lesser humans whomever does not conform with the

---

[7] Anibal Quijano, "Coloniality and Modernity/Rationality." [1992]. *Cultural Studies*, 21, 2/3, 168-178.

invention of the essence of the *Human*. That invention was a modern/colonial invention of the European Renaissance.[8]

Lesser humans were and still are (as we have been witnessing the increasing manifestations of racism in Western Europe and the US) ontologically inferior and epistemological deficient. Explicitly, during four hundred years more or less, and implicitly in recent times, the ingrained idea has been that non-Western people cannot think.[9] No longer. However, the irreducible difference remains in place and will remain until the hegemony of Western epistemology is reduced to its own well-deserved, regional size. Works like that of Khabiti, Glissant, and many others since then, are not moving toward the 'post-human' (that is a modern/postmodern concern), but exploring the very concept of *Human*: what it means to be *Human* is the fundamental question. When was the concept of the *Human* put in place, where, by whom, why, and with what purpose? These questions lead us to a change of terrain: beyond the Eurocentric critique of the Eurocentrism of the *Human* (e.g the post-human), emerge decolonial critiques, from the memories and praxis of living of former settler colonies, critiques of both Eurocentrism of the *Human* and its Eurocentric critiques (post-human). The implications are large: we on the planet are living and experiencing a change of era. The era of changes in which change could be understood by adding the prefix 'post-' to an abstract universal is ending. There is no *transition to the new era* but the *explosion of the edifice of unilinear time and of the time of history.*

In the change of era there is no room for the prefix 'post-'. Resurgence, re-existence, and self-governance imply the restitution of local temporalities. The idea of a universal time of history is reduced to its own size: a regional belief in abstract universals is integrated in the explosion of pluriversal temporalities and the temporalities of the "after human." The pluriversal that is emerging in the public spheres (independent from the states, the corporations and the official mass media), is one dimension of the change of era. The other is the explosion of the unipolar inter-state world order into the multipolar world order. The abstract universal category of the *Human* (and its sequel, the post-human, even in their cyborg and AI versions) is losing its grip in the explosion, the change of era in which pluriversality and multipolarity are not superseding the *Human* and the post-human but rather re-locating them, that is, recognizing

---

[8] Margaret R. Greer, Walter D. Mignolo and Maureen Quilligan, editors. Chicago: The University of Chicago Press, 2007.

[9] Kishore Mahbubani, *Can Asian Think?* Understanding the Divide Between East and West. London: Times Book, 1998. Hamid Dabashi, *Can Non-European Think?* London: Zed Books, 2015, Walter D. Mignolo, "Yes, We Can. (Introduction to Hamid Dabashi's book), *op.cit,* i-xxxvi.

their regional dimension. 'Nomadism' is caught in the co-existing turmoil and the political differential webs of the pluriversal and multipolar coming into being, and for the time co-existing with Western abstract universals.

Walter D Mignolo
Nov 2021

Introduction

In a casual conversation that we had with Prof. Walter Mignolo on the sidelines of an international conference in Hyderabad last year, we chanced upon a discussion of the posthuman in the context of our forthcoming book. This dialogue continued over email. He explained his main issue with the posthuman as, "I have difficulty in understanding that concept in general, beyond the concern of a small group of intellectuals in the North Atlantic. Therefore [it is] less clear what posthuman could mean in India. Or for that matter in South Africa or in Bolivia if there were conversations in those places on the posthuman."[1] In another email on the same day, he continues his provocations against the concept of the posthuman where he says,

> It was only relevant to some sectors of the Commonwealth [...] [e]specially [to] those who adhere to the postmodern ideological option or frame and believe that postmodernity is universal [...] But many, perhaps the majority of us, are out of that game, playing different ones. And that includes white feminists for white feminists never questioned humanity but wanted to be equal with white males. For the rest of the world, which are not yet human in different ways and scales, the posthuman seems to be another slap on the face.[2]

Our introduction begins, very significantly, in response to Mignolo's *pretensions* of a *hominem indocte*, that is, the unskillful person. He was actually pushing us to *see* from our location as we had been reading the European and American schools of posthuman thinking. However, we had indeed also been reading others like Edouard Glissant, Hamid Dabashi, and Jasbir Puar. Our understanding of posthumanism springs from, among many others, Mignolo's own critique of the enlightened human who is a white male, rational being suffering from colonial blindness, from the purity of blood syndrome, and from the civilizing mission.[3] Further, Mignolo's understanding of deep ecology in his conception of "*vincularidad*" (converging with the assemblage of Deleuze and Guattari, a poetics of relation of Edouard Glissant), splinters any scope of human

---

[1]. In a personal communication with the editors, 08:04, May 16, 2020.
[2]. In a personal communication with the editors, 19:43, May 16, 2020.
[3]. Walter Mignolo, *Local Histories/Global Designs: Coloniality, Subaltern Knowledges, and Border Thinking* (Duke University Press, 2000), 27, 49, 54.

privilege.[4] Our stand on the posthuman, therefore, is distinctly de-centering of the human overall other non-human species and things. Indigenous cultural practices and episteme had already been living the organic multi-polar world view where the human and the non-human species and planetary forces are in a state of continuous pluri-vocal discursivity. Why, then, should we aspire to anything human from the tradition of enlightenment's humanism? Mignolo has seen it as the underside of modernity, which is dark, exploitative, and deeply violent. Our posthuman understanding is, therefore, not a slap on the face of our indigenous-cosmopolitan-postcolonial-feminist-mestiza-chicana-black-minoritarian thinking. Instead, it aims to problematize the human couched in the humanist tradition of their thinking. This other human is a new order of global posthuman that is not polite, not white, not rational, and surely not exploitative. It re-routes entanglements of the human and non-human into a non-European perspective on the human. This is another humanism, as one imagined by an Andean Indian, a Caribbean creole, and a Dalit Indian that highlights a nomadic ontology of spatiality, that is problematically hybrid, interstitial, or intersectional.

Mignolo's submission on *vincularidad* entails a relationship between all living beings with the land and the cosmos. He draws this concept from the Andean indigenous vision of the integral nature of all life forms and their material surroundings. Edouard Glissant's relation language is made of rocks; in which words, verb, noun, subject, object, are not fixed in their places, and "in Relation every subject is an object, and every object is subject."[5] He also takes cognizance of the Deleuzean rhizome as "an enmeshed root system, a network spreading either in the ground or in the air, with no predatory rootstock taking over permanently. The notion of the rhizome maintains, therefore, the idea of rootedness but challenges that of a totalitarian root."[6]

The present volume is an attempt to further the posthuman interrogations of nomad spatiality in general and explore especially the scope and ethics of an alternative way of thinking involved in a constant tussle with the institutional striations of the state, its so-called rationalism, its view of knowledge as universal truth and its monolithic thinking which normalizes any difference with its colonial blindness. It exposes that the non-human and the human other can be materially agency-laden and often non-governable in its potential

---

[4]. Walter Mignolo and Catherine Walsh, *On Decoloniality: Concepts, Analytics, Praxis* (Duke University Press, 2018), 1.
Edouard Glissant, *Poetics of Relation* (Michigan University Press, 1997), xx and 11.
[5]. Glissant, *Poetics by Relation*, xx.
[6]. Ibid., 11.

to territorialize through nomad space. Hence it is always a threat to the rational order of things and labeled as savage and barbaric. The non-human is about another way of being human/non-human in a relationality of "becoming" minoritarian, animal, woman, and marginal.[7] This way of becoming is about horizontal networking of the non-human with its/his/her biodiversity and ecology in such a way that none is central, rather all are dots in a chain of processual sustainability which is not exploitative nor genocidal. It is how the indigenous peoples of the world continue to think today as they struggle against dire situations of dispossession, displacement, and modernization. In fact, it was modernity and coloniality that wrenched all humans out from any organic understanding of the planet in order to conquer, contain, and control other spatiality. Rigoberta Menchu, Vandana Shiva, and Gloria Anzaldúa, among many others, have invested their entire lives in bringing this world vision to the fore. The posthuman understanding is, therefore, not a dismissal nor a disapproval of the *humanitarian* rather a problematizing and contestation of *enlightened* humanism. Hence posthumanism is also decolonial from within the ethics of Mignolo's concept of epistemic disobedience and Glissant's right to opacity to build solidarities through different posthuman possibilities of another thinking.

Posthumanist Nomadisms affirms multiplicities, mutations, and materiality of human and non-human entanglements. It negates the privilege of fixity over mobility, of roots over routes, of tracings over maps, and of writing over memory.[8] In addition to freeing itself of a binary bind, it also contests the vertical accumulations enabled by the neoliberal structures of global capitalism. Financial capital agglomerates in steep pyramids, factories are uprooted and re-rooted in a matter of days and, high-skilled individuals move up a professional conveyor belt as they repeatedly cross national frontiers at a meteoric pace. All movement is not nomadic. The hypermobility coded into the operative manuals of multinational entities or the mass mobilizations of colonial empires—multinational juggernauts from an earlier era—does not

---

[7] . Gilles Deleuze and Félix Guatarri, *A Thousand Plateaus* (London and Minneapolis: University of Minnesota Press, 1987), 106.

[8] . Brian Massumi, "Translator' Note," in *A Thousand Plateaus* (London and Minneapolis: University of Minnesota Press, 1987), xvi.

Rosi Braidotti, *The Nomadic Subject* (New York: Columbia University Press, 2002), 14.

Massumi explains that "The French word tracer [...] has all the graphic connotations of "to draw" in English but can also mean to blaze a trail or open a road. "To trace" (d'ecalquer), on the other hand, is to copy something from a model."

Rosi Braidotti evokes the sense of the French *tracer*-to draw, and not d'ecalquer, when she says, "the nomad stands for movable diversity, the nomad's identity is an inventory of *traces*," emphasis ours.

constitute a nomadic movement. The neo-nomadism of neoliberal global nomads lacks a nomadic consciousness because they never disavow their structural coordinates. The vertical movement of emigrants from the Global South to the Global North in search of better financial remuneration alone is not nomadic; it presents a vertical movement, not a vortical movement. Unlike a vortical movement, their relocation does not allow them to break away from the striated spaces where they remain at the bottom of the hierarchical socio-cultural-political pyramid.

The articles in the present volume examine the compositional multiplicities of nomadic movements. Collectively, they also foreground discursive traces of a system of ethical values that move away randomly from any steady and unified vision of the human and grapples instead with a non-unitary, nomadic view. Nomads include im - migrants - exiles - refugees - homeless - stateless-peoples, travelers - Voyagers - cartographers - mappers of counter-discourse, the dispossessed - displaced - disenfranchised, insiders-outsiders, border bearers, global - local dwellers, animals - birds - jungles - deserts - deltas - spaces-oceans, forgotten or reclaimed cultures - housekeeping manuals - languages - crops - paths, dacoits - criminals, and ever - increasing numbers of earth - others with whom we inhabit the planet. From the minoritarian nomadic perspective, a non-Oedipal relationship with space is implicit in such co-habitation. When we look closely, Oedipal semiotics are shot through with multiplicities and identity fracturing alterities. Non-Oedipal spatiality of margins, borders, and no-man's lands lies along the same plane as Oedipal territoriality. The nomad cannot inhabit the territory, and non-oedipal spatiality is unsuited to permanent occupation. Therefore, the nomad can / not remain, can/not locate, and can/not de/reterritorialize. As the unstable moorings of socio-political-economic structures elude them, the nomads slip in and out of interstices of unbelonging and schizophrenia. Their interstitial flights map a non-unitary discursivity wherein any structure sustaining verticalities and binaries collapse and wherefrom multi-directional lines of flight emerge.

The book contains fifteen articles that have gone through the process of double-blind peer review. The articles are organized into three sections called "Nomadic Assemblages," "Maps in Non-Oedipal Cartographies," and "Space-Time Montages." It was not a sheer coincidence that they could be organized thus. By making these sections, we put together a war machine that negates absorption into the interiority of sovereign territory. The sections are not an attempt at corralling the nomadic spirit into separate enclosures. Instead, the sections are bands of warriors that operate the violence of the hunted animal, dehumanized human others, and earth others. We struggle to sustain our nomadic sensibilities and sensitivities against forces considered to be of a normalizing order and consistency that threaten to condemn us to panoptical imprisonments. The articles are in constant multi-vocal conversations with narratives that camp on the turbulent weathers of global transitory spaces. They charter real or intellectual turfs of interstitial/ rhizomatic nomadic epistemologies as political resistance to the exclusionary practices of a violently wired world.

The first section, "Nomadic Assemblages," contains articles which conjure real nomad objects-as-subjects-as-objects which/who may be nomads—seeds, animals, and spaces as floating signifiers—open-ended and maze-like in the way they configure. Deleuzian assemblages are fundamentally territorial, but even as territoriality is configured through given assembled behaviors, amorphous assemblages emerge in chaotic, organized, escape passages.[9] Birds generate assemblages with the territory they inhabit, through birdsong, mating dances, nests, and foraging expeditions.[10] Similarly, other non-human and human inhabitants arrange themselves and other territorial elements in mutually specifying relations of assemblage. The articles in the first section examine some actualizations of such assemblages.

Didier Coste's article tracks "ambiguous mobilities" across different disciplines, identities, and spatiality, either physically, metaphorically, or intellectually, through globalized or localized or anarchistic dispositions. He negotiates the exotic orientalist nomadism with its romanticism while also addressing the modern and contemporary notions of nomadism that hang between biographies, travel narratives, and real tales by nomads. His final aim is to read, especially the writing by Isabelle Eberhardt, a Russian Francophone expatriate in North Africa, through her continuous crossing over of religious, cultural, sexual, and linguistic borders. The uniqueness of this article lies in the blurring of imaginary and real frontiers of the state and the war machine, which are in a constant tussle in order to devour the other cannibalistically. Didier Coste's article makes transversal connections with all the others as it carries out detailed excavations from anthropology, molding the excavated material by contemporary manoeuvrings of the concept of the nomad.

Java Singh, in her article, shows how amaranth, which was important in Aztec religious rituals, becomes and survives as a banned crop under Spanish colonization. The amaranth's endurance helps it overcome and outlive colonization and the ensuing coloniality of power. However, any attempt at managing cultivation and promotion of the traditionally indigenous crop through modern technoscientific knowledge is the colonial mercantile equivalent of colonizing salvation missions. Amaranth has repeatedly refused to occupy the

---

9. Deleuze and Guattari, *A Thousand,* 323.
10. Ibid., 312.

time and space allocated to it, striking up new relationships instead, with the changing habits and habitats around it.

Olivia A. Kurajian tracks the Serengeti-Mara's ecosystem extensively to look at how animal routes crossing Tanzania and Kenya are affected by increasing human activity, such as erecting physical fences, drawing imaginary national borders, and deforestation. Conservation becomes a political ball in the courts of the pastoralists and capitalist farmers. The Serengeti-Mara ecosystem, however, cannot be managed without community-based local knowledge of sustainable co-habitation within the given milieu of that ecosystem.

Prantik Bannerjee configures the adda as a safe socio-political space for elite conversations among the upper caste Bengali bhadrolok, who were nonetheless colonized subjects. It allowed them to flaunt global and local knowledge in an identitarian fervor to aspire to belong so that they could be redeemed from their status of a colonized un-belonging. Decolonial thinking around modernity and the Bengal Renaissance sprung in this space. In postcolonial Bengal, the adda continued as a local marker of liberal thinking towards a global cosmopolitanism.

The last article in the section by Swagata Basu looks at the assemblage of language, profession, aspiration, and gender. The researcher, a native Bengali speaker, spent three months in Barcelona, conducting detailed interviews and focus group discussions with South Asian women immigrants, mainly from Bangladesh. The women who participated in the study reveal nomadic transversality as they attempt to reconcile traditional ways of living with the globalized spatiality into which they have been inserted.

The second section, entitled "Maps in Non-Oedipal Cartographies," takes cognizance of maps and their multiple entryways, as they work to move away from the anomalies of representation, thus allowing creative processes of perception and thinking. The map, as part of a rhizome, is detachable, reversible, and malleable, fostering exploration of unknown territories. Each article of this section deals with texts which overlap with real or imagined cartographies of travel narratives that lead the nomad in an outward or in an inward journey, though sometimes confusingly both.

Tonisha Guin's article on Atin Bandopadhyay's short story for children, "Atapurer Bagh," interrogates an elitist Bengali *bhadrolok* representation of the Sunderbans, through Radhamohon Babu's urban sensibilities. The story traverses the upper-caste widower's horrifying wanderings with a tiger and Bagharu, his domestic help's son, through the wilderness of the mangrove delta. Bagharu's opaque resistance to refuse to explain anything to an outsider completely dislodges Radhamohon Babu's pre-conceived notions of the indigenous peoples' habitat and their understanding of deep ecology. The story maps the journey of Radhamohon Babu as an identitarian faux pas through nomad space.

Shelby Ward shows how Jean Arasanyagam's "Geography Lessons" and Ramya Chamalie Jirasinghe's "Sri Lankan Nights in L.A." become the very theoretical lens that serves to read the language and the geography of colonialism critically to reclaim authentic ethnic Sri Lankaness. The poems map the processes of authentic knowledge production, in relation to fluid identities and bodies, through myths and memories, as they write back to colonial geographies of the West during their travel.

A cartography of homelessness and errantry in the nomadic indulgences of the poetry of Nasir Kazmi is the theme of Hamza Iqbal's article. The unknown space is as much his home, as the new town across the border, which is becoming home through the transformative processes of memory. The article unravels the notions of homelessness through Harney and Moten and Edouard Glissant, as it leads them to join hands and converse with Nasir Kazmi.

Ruth Prakasam's article maps how, in an attempt to impress visiting travelers, a performance of colonial housekeeping was staged to showcase colonial standards of complete control of the domestic space. She examines the chinks in the authority of a Victorian housekeeping manual. Intending to evoke awe at domesticated compliance in the colonial home, the manual, instead, became the reason why many travelers left unimpressed by the domestic space. The article looks behind the veil of scripted performance to reveal the ways in which it diverged along rhizomatic lines under the gaze of adventurous women travelers.

Sushmita Sihwag reads Tsewang Yishey Pemba's novel, *White Crane, Lend Me Your Wings*, to dwell on the theme of exile both as a historical and real-life experience. Tibetan and Nyarong-Khampa identities in the face of a real or imaginary foreign remain a bone of contention for the self-critical mode of diasporic subjectivity. The article is continuously in conversation with Gilles Deleuze, Edward Said, and Dibyesh Anand on nomadic epistemologies, exile, and identity. This cartography of exile, diaspora, history, fiction, and identity negotiates with a deeply layered and complex model of self-critical subjectivity.

After dwelling on "Nomadic Assemblages" and "Maps in Non-Oedipal Cartographies," the third section takes stock of another kind of entanglement: a montage of narratives of journalism, tabloid, social media, television shows, and cinema. The concept of the montage is borrowed from the Deleuzean understanding of cinema, where he discusses the spacing of time and timing space, asserting that every image in space-time is interconnected to themselves as well as to the entire exteriority.

Significantly, the first article by Debra Castillo is about slow cinema where time is stretched through uneventful and trivial longshots. The article contends with the view that slow cinema only allows contemplation of beautiful shots to enable viewers to indulge in some quiet aesthetic pleasure. It argues, instead, that the slow cinema of Natalia Almada purposefully takes us back to the violence of killing time for boredom. The article deals with two filmic texts: a documentary, *El velador* (2011), and a feature film, *Todo lo demás* (2017). In both, long-drawn silences and slowness actually articulate characterizations of insignificant peoples whose stories otherwise, would not merit any attention.

Leigh McKagen interprets the television series of *Star Trek: Voyager* (1995-2001) as a reproductive tracing of the American imperial ideology. Hence the crew of the Voyager space refuses to "become" refugees and continue to call themselves castaways/ adventurers/ travelers/ explorers, only to colonize new territory and thereafter have the single agenda of going back home. The article holds that this pattern of storytelling has normalized the expansive ideologies of post-World War II American imperialism that presumes the superiority of the West.

The next article reads three texts alongside one another: a cover page of the travel magazine *Conde Nast*, an episode on black French footballers in a Trevor Noah television show, and a satirical cartoon by Pikaso on Indian migrants walking hundreds of kilometers back home after the lockdown due to the pandemic. Antara Mukherjee uses these three texts to take on cosmopolitanism as problematic and hypocritical. She dissects the use of selective codewords of universalism, charity, and political correctness by hegemonic forces for migrants and refugees or any other nomad to reveal the false empathy of elite cosmopolitanism.

The article by Nicole Crevar shows how the Chicana poet and activist Odilia Galván Rodríguez's poem, "Poem 25 ~ Giving Voice" montages Gloria Anzaldúa's conception of the politically charged mestiza consciousness on Facebook. Galván Rodríguez as a co-founder and contributor of marginalized groups such as "Poets Responding to SB 1070," takes on the police enactment of Arizona Senate Bill 1070, which legitimizes discrimination against Mexican-Americans and immigrants living along the borderland. She uses the digital space to argue for solidarity and education through art as the solutions to combat these human rights violations.

Sanghita Sen and Indrani Mukherjee explore Tarun Bhaduri's *The Cursed Chambal*, a journalistic narrative from 1960, Eduardo Galeano's "Phoolan," a vignette in *Mirrors* (2009), and Shekhar Kapur's *Bandit Queen* (1995), a Bollywood film, in order to dwell on the deep ecology of the spatiality of the Chambal occupied by women dacoits, Putli and Phoolan. Deleuze and Guattari's theorization of nomadism and Walter Mignolo's agendas of location of enunciation serve to expose the terror of the women-dacoit-infested Chambal as a War Machine performing its own nomadic maneuverings.

Visions of posthumanist nomadisms, which have emerged from this book, we hope, will serve as an exciting saddle-breaking experience for anyone who might want to ride (through) this wild nomadic terrain of the chaos of our times. Deep ecology, bioethics, technology studies, earth studies, and animal studies comprise the newer additions to the old disciplines of social sciences, the general sciences, and humanities of this machine-like assemblage of the war machine. Matters of literary aesthetics, fine arts, pure and applied sciences, critical theory, and even cultural studies have become wet with this Non-Oedipal spatiality of the global oceans and astronomical spaces, of local deltas, mountains, deserts, river valleys, and savannas, of nostalgic memories amidst a diasporic or exiled presence across continents, of ongoing nomadisms in media, in social media and in real territories, across unfathomable limits of borders, layers, and depths. The risk-taking agenda is, therefore, of paramount importance and implicates a dispensing with all old baggage of habits of language-based ideas and semiotic normals. Significantly, the outbreak of the pandemic has been an unexpected surprise attack from nomad space, so, as we cope with this new normal imposed upon us, we hope that most potential readers will be geared up to mount this war machine and dare to (un)learn the new.

Bibliography

Braidotti, Rosi. *The Nomadic Subject*. New York: Columbia University Press, 2002.

Deleuze, Gilles, and Félix Guatarri. *A Thousand Plateaus*. London and Minneapolis: University of Minnesota Press, 1987.

Glissant, Edouard. *Poetics by Relation*. University of Michigan Press, 1997.

Mignolo, Walter. *Local Histories/Global Designs: Coloniality, Subaltern Knowledges, and Border Thinking*. Durham: Duke University Press, 2000.

Mignolo, Walter, and Catherine E. Walsh. On Decoloniality: Concepts, Analytics, Praxis. Durham: Duke University Press, 2018.

Nomadic Assemblages

Chapter 1

Ambiguous mobilities:
Nomadism, interpretation and action

Didier Coste

Université Bordeaux-Montaigne, France

Abstract

The article attempts to clarify the notion of nomadism, which is often taken as synonymous with wandering (even with a loss of bearings and bonds, or aimlessness) while, anthropologically, many actual nomadic groups always follow the same regular routes determined by local resources, the cycle of seasons, and/or trade activities; in such traditional societies, roles are strictly distributed and practices highly ritualized. There is a rather obvious difference between "errant" and "itinerant." Hence, the conceptual ambiguity of "nomadism." Before we can decide whether "nomadism" can still be used as an enlightening simile or metaphor to explore contemporary modes of occupation of or transience through (physical, social, emotional, epistemological) spacetime and whether it would betray opportunism or dissidence, community breaking, community construction or tribalism, tradition, rupture or regression, it is necessary to examine some influential and representative samples of the very abundant contemporary literature on or rather around nomadism.

I will first focus critically on a generation of senior writers/thinkers who still operate in France: Kenneth White, Michel Maffesoli, and Jacques Attali. Secondly, I discuss the practice of fiction and essay-fiction by J.M.G. Le Clézio. Thirdly, I will concentrate on one particular case study: the Russian expatriate to North Africa and Francophone writer Isabelle Eberhardt whose transvestism and other transgressions have been heatedly debated by many biographers and critics. This way, rather than dealing with present issues of forced migrations and identity trouble, I aim to contribute a historical/theoretical background to contemporary revivals of the nomadic concept.

Keywords: Transvestism, essay-fiction, Algeria, infra-nomad, hyper-nomad

***

In the last half-century or so, the multifaceted notion of nomadism, thanks to a certain primitivist, exotic aura, has often been transferred from anthropology and ethnography where it initially belonged and from the Romantic vision of the natural law and equalitarianism of the good savage that established it in the literature and lives of many, to the realm of cultural theory and critique. There, on the edge of Philosophy and Psychoanalysis, on the margins of Sociology, Ecology, Border Studies and Gender Studies, in the no man's land between Narrative Theory, Fiction and Translation Theory, conceptual nomadism has prospered and come to encompass almost any form of mobility, whether intellectual or physical, globalized or localized, commuting or with no return, tribal or anarchistic, traditional or revolutionary, technological or toolless.

It would be fastidious to retrace in great detail how a simply descriptive characterization of the way of life of certain human communities in relation to geographical space and its resources could be figuratively manipulated in ways that increased its extension almost without bonds, correspondingly reducing its intension, which constitutes a very paradoxical evolution when such a notion is turned by some into an operational concept or quasi-concept. John K. Noyes, while allowing for the "changing popular imagination," still considers that "the knowledge of nomadic social orders on the fringes of empire has provided a challenge to Western philosophy from the age of antiquity up to the present day."[1] But the border between actual knowledge and imagination is very porous in this case. It is surprising to see how people of rather different political persuasions have exalted "nomadism", explicitly in their essays or more implicitly in their works of fiction or self-fiction, sometimes to the level of a panacea against social evils, a communion with diversity, a mystique, a "way," unless it is felt and represented as a desperate protest against the "system" or all constraints of conventional sociability. In the course of these confusing expansions and fantasies, the notion may have gained some heuristic aptitudes, almost like a reverie (if it is critically analyzed), but it has lost much of its descriptive and hermeneutic power. It is therefore advisable to discriminate between widely different forms of mobility that are unduly subsumed under the term "nomad," whose original meaning—a member of a herder group in a collective quest for grazing—is derived from the Greek word νομάς, pasture. In the remote past, the root word was sometimes metaphorized as spread or growth, and there is no reason not to metaphorize "nomad," like its usual antonyms "civil," "urban" and "sedentary" or "settled," but the fundamental features of the vehicle of the metaphor should not be disfigured: the mobility of the nomads, whether they are hunters-gatherers, pastoralists,

---

[1]. John K. Noyes, "Nomadism, Nomadology, Postcolonialism. By Way of Introduction," *Interventions* Vol. 6(2), (2004): 161.

tinkers or entertainers, is functional, not arbitrary, collective, not individual, and it is not a migration with no return.

Before we can decide whether "nomadism" can still be used as an enlightening simile or metaphor to explore contemporary modes of occupation of or transience through (physical, social, emotional, epistemological) spacetime and whether it would betray opportunism or dissidence, community breaking, community construction or tribalism, tradition, rupture or regression, it is necessary to examine some influential and representative samples of the very abundant contemporary literature on or rather around nomadism. Since it is impossible to do justice to its richness—and its aberrations—I will first focus critically on a generation of senior writers/thinkers who still operate in France and are younger than Deleuze (1925-1995) and Guattari (1930-1992). Secondly, I discuss the practice of fiction and essay-fiction by J.M.G. Le Clézio from the 1960s to the 80s and beyond. Oscillating as it does between reverie, utopia, dystopia and *roman à thèse*, this practice is also revealing, in its more talented way, of the floating, confusing uses to which "nomadism" has been put not so long ago in rather sentimental terms: it signifies by turns tradition and dissidence, despair and hope beyond despair, gendered roles and affects and resilience beyond gender. Thirdly, I will concentrate on one particular case study: the Russian expatriate to North Africa and Francophone writer Isabelle Eberhardt whose transvestism and other transgressions have been heatedly debated by many biographers and critics, especially in the framework of postcolonial and feminist studies. Compared with the exoticist travel writer and novelist Pierre Loti, an older, gay contemporary whom she much admired and who has also inevitably been reminisced, much later, in Le Clézio's *Désert*, and to the famous Naturalist Maupassant, what lessons, if any, can we draw from her crossing religious, cultural, linguistic and gender borders repeatedly?

Three post-romantic, confusing essays

I say "post-romantic" because the following representations and symbolizations of "nomadism", whatever distortions and falsifications they may practice, suggest or allow, are indebted to the early Romantic postulate of the "noble savage", to philosophies, poetics and aesthetics of nature developed in the West between the mid-18th and the mid-19th century, with Rousseau, Diderot, and the American transcendentalists Emerson and Thoreau among the philosophical protagonists.

Wishing to provide more evidence of a diffuse zeitgeist regarding "nomadism" around the end of the second millennium, I have selected three essays in French by well-known authors who belong to separate intellectual circles: *L'Esprit nomade* (*The Nomad Spirit*), 1987, by Kenneth White, *Du nomadisme : Vagabondages initiatiques* (*About Nomadism: Initiatory Wanderings*), 1997, by Michel Maffesoli, and *L'Homme nomade* (Nomadic Man), 2003, by Jacques

Attali. White is a Scottish bilingual writer born in 1936, established many years ago in France but also a great traveler who has tried to found a trans-discipline and movement called "geopoetics"—not to be confused with geopolitics or "geocriticism."[2] Maffesoli, born in 1944, is a Professor of Sociology at Paris Descartes University; close to the esoteric Jungian philosopher/anthropologist Gilbert Durand, and a highly public personality, he has been involved in a number of scandals, for his self-promotion to the highest rank of full professorship and as adviser and promoter of an astrologer who defended a Ph.D. thesis without any scientific credentials. Jacques Attali, born in 1943, is an economist, former high-ranking public servant, former adviser to President François Mitterrand, who has turned lobbyist and an editorialist for the major French capitalist economic daily; he has written all sorts of essays and several novels.

What these three books share is an almost unlimited extension of the "nomadic" concept. Maffesoli, from the prologue to the last chapter, breaks records in this respect. First of all, "nomadisme" and "errance" (wandering, roaming or errancy) are named together, linked by the coordinator "et" in such a way that it is impossible to know whether they are two different things, or one and the same: "wandering and nomadism, in their various modulations, are becoming a more and more obvious fact."[3] On the next page, it is "errance" that is supposed to be an eternally recurrent structure, manifesting "the plurality of the person, the duplicity of existence," as well as it expresses a revolt against the established order. "Errance" prevails until the remote historical origins of the domestication against which it rebels are evoked: it was a "sliding of nomadism towards sedentariness."[4] Sedentariness is equated with politics and police, with a quasi-totalitarian rationalization strangely seen as a legacy of the Enlightenment (strangely, if one considers Rousseau and Diderot as eminent representatives of this critical philosophy, and Sterne or Lesage as two of its most representative writers). According to Maffesoli, rational sedentariness crushes and chokes the obscure, deeper, original components of individuals and communities, but these forces reappear as a return of the repressed in the form of uncontrolled, or even controlled mobilities of all sorts (intellectual, cultural, social, sexual, touristic and leisurely), subsumed under the general category of "nomadism." Thus, hippies, homeless migrants, plurilingual writers, business

[2]. See, among other many publications, Bertrand Westphal, *Geocriticism. Real and Fictional Spaces*, trans. Robert T. Tally Jr. (New York: Palgrave Macmillan, 2011) and Robert T. Tally Jr., *Spatiality* (London and New York: Routledge, 2013).
[3]. Michel Maffesoli, *Du nomadisme: vagabondages initiatiques* (Paris: "Inédit" Le Livre de Poche, 1997), 12; all translations mine unless otherwise specified in the bibliography.
[4]. Ibid., 22.

commuters, international pop singers and philosophical travelers around their rooms would all take part—most of them unwittingly—in an initiatory upheaval against sedentary modernity.

Chronic chronological disorder is a common disease among reactionary pseudo-philosophers and cultural theorists who, under the guise of liberation, advocate an impossible return to feudal or tribal enclosures, presenting them as actual democracies. In Europe, the Crusades had nothing of a liberation movement, but, from the Renaissance to the middle of the 19th century, and even later, traveling for knowledge, by accident, for war or for survival, was the sine qua non condition of the emergence of a unified notion of humanity— opposed by racialist colonial settlers and exploiters. The enslavement of alien populations has not been the privilege of sedentary moderns: Arab nomads greatly contributed to the enslavement of Africans for centuries. Historical nomads (other than the "pre-historical" hunters-gatherers) have always been partly dependent on their exchanges with sedentary people, and on plundering forays, raids or razzias carried against them. The idealization of ancient nomadic modes of living combined with the amalgamation of all kinds of contemporary mobilities paves the way for a mystique of emancipation from a supposedly repressive modernity through "spiritual" adventures that would lead us back to the authentic sources of our existence. Maffesoli rather perversely uses the rhetorical tools of postmodernity—oxymoron and paradox—to promote pilgrimages as another kind of orgiastic excess, and he calls this impulse "dynamic rootedness,"[5] whatever it means (certainly not the same as Appiah's "rooted cosmopolitanism").[6]

Jacques Attali doesn't manage much better to avoid self-contradiction as his sweeping, overarching, panoptic "theory" ranges from the origins of humankind to a utopian global networked governance. Like all self-appointed prophets, he justifies his improbable and conditional predictions by the authority of supposed origins: "Sedentariness is only a brief parenthesis in human history."[7] The nomads have invented everything, including sedentariness—logical, if they came first—and globalisation is making humankind nomadic again.[8] "The great conflicts of tomorrow will not oppose civilisations between them, but the last sedentary empire, the American Empire, to three nomadic, off-ground empires, competing with America and fighting each other to govern the world for their

---

5. Ibid., 121.
6. Kwame Anthony Appiah, "Rooted Cosmopolitanism," in *The Ethics of Identity* (Princeton: Princeton University Press, 2005), 213-272.
7. Jacques Attali, *L'Homme nómade* (Paris: Le Livre de Poche, 2005), 13.
8. Ibid., 97.

own benefit: the market, Islam and democracy."[9] How sedentary is the American Empire, when its armies, its warships, its major companies and its Mormon or Evangelist preachers constantly roam the world? This is not explained when executives have no fixed office and their promotion depends on their mobility.[10] Also, if you call the market an empire, does it not include its chief actor to date, the US economy? Although Attali, contrary to Maffesoli, has the apparent merit of differentiating "infra-nomads" (poor, uprooted people, who cannot have a stable home, or are homeless) from other varieties, such as the "hyper-nomads" (business people, highly qualified engineers, etc. who do not need a stable home), incomparable situations are still all collapsed together in the last chapters of his book. What do impoverished migrants from rural areas to the slums of the next city have to do with Bengaluru computer wizards who settle in California, or with those backpackers who have taken a year off college to roam South East Asia? The (rhetorically) predictable outcome of the mess-up of all the descriptive and analytical categories that have to do with mobility, change and exchange, is that, in the not very remote future, *we* should all learn to become nomadic and sedentary at the same time. The fall of the American Empire will be a repeat of the fall of the Roman Empire, and, "there will remain only a huge disorder, a formidable diversity, a joyful miscegenation, a jubilant transgression [...]. Will only remain lively the nomadism of ideas, the aspiration to difference and the increasing interdependence of people, wherever they be and whatever their situation."[11] Francisco Rüdiger, in his critique of Maffesoli, remarks that, for this author, the postmodern era is one of nomadism without nomads.[12] Similarly, in Attali's epic essay, nothing remains of the specificity of a nomadic existence; even in the domain of ideas, the notion becomes an empty shell.

Let us see whether a poet, translator, traveler and linguistic migrant like Kenneth White (not mentioned by Attali who uses some of his lexicon, any more than by Maffesoli) fares better. His book, which collects and bonds several previously published essays as well as a synthesis of "geopoetics" at an early stage, opens on an avowedly metaphorical "sketch of the intellectual nomad" to end on a "poetics of the world" after evoking in the middle part a number of significant "figures, places and trajectories," especially those of Thoreau, MacDiarmid, John Cowper Powys, and Segalen. White's approach is more rooted in a serious philosophical and literary tradition from Heraclites to the

---

9. Ibid., 14.

10. Ibid., 398.

11. Ibid., 461.

12. Francisco Ricardo Rüdiger, *Civilização e barbárie na crítica da cultura contemporânea: leitura de Michel Maffesoli* (Porto Alegre: EDIPUCRS, 2007), 80.

20th century with the corresponding benefits and shortcomings: while he evokes Deleuze's "nomadic thought," he hardly names Kerouac or gives any credit to Beat itinerancies. Just like most other popular books on the topic I have been able to consult or the authors he quotes, White makes nothing of feminist or queer thought, he cares for "nature" and the last traditional societies like Thoreau or Élisée Reclus, but this cosmic sense of the world leaves no visible room for a critique of gendered and/or religious, cultural and linguistic effects of domination that could and can exist in traditional as well as in modern societies. If the image of the modern, or rather the future intellectual nomads is certainly not that of a western anarchist, they are nevertheless unlike people who go by the rules of the herd, even wandering ones. These "anarchists of dawn," somehow detached from customs, social bonds and earthly ties, tend to commune with the World as nature, that is also the nothingness of the World, like the sannyasin, but, contrary to "converts to the Orient" they will be and meditate within the World (as it is).[13] The proximity, in the bibliography, of Alexandra David-Neel with Gilles Deleuze translates a persistent hesitation between a theoretical and an experiential, personal approach to something that belongs to the symbolic order, not to actual cultural models that could inform a social way of life. Anyway, pure nomadism in the sense of a deterritorialized errancy has never existed as a collective way of life. The figures that prevail in most of this literature are eremitic or ascetic, figures of separation and lone wandering, those of castaways, outcasts, exiles or self-exiles.

One's way or out of it

Moving from essays that purport to recapitulate past thoughts and manners and provide predictions and guidance to fictions, travelogues and partly autobiographical narrative sketches, we generally find a fascinated attitude towards nomadism, mainly in hot desert settings, associated with various forms of mystery and transcendence. It seems that, at least in western literatures, a biblical background prevails even when the Judeo-Christian tradition is superficially displaced by Islam or other religious beliefs. Fictional nomadism is hardly ever secular. However, both the viewpoints from which nomadism is considered, and the proportions of descriptive, empirical realism, on the one hand, and imaginary constructs (fancy, reverie, mysticism, symbolism, myth), in the aesthetic and interpretative proposals or requisites of the texts, can be totally different. Affective, descriptive and narrative viewpoints can range from distant contemplation to identification with the

---

[13]. Kenneth White, *L'Esprit nomade* (Paris: Grasset, 1987), 75-76.

nomads and tentative adoption into their societies. In the first case (Buzzati), they can be a pure threat, an external projection of the enemy inside, or, on the contrary, an elusive object of desire, nostalgic or futuristic.[14] In the second case (Coetzee), participation and integration of the subject of fiction can prove rewarding and redeeming, or painful, difficult, eventually failed or destructive.[15] In this sense, as it has been often noted, the nomad is an emblematic other, if not the other par excellence, as perceived, represented, or projected from the a priori oneness and continuity of narrative. But the encounter with this other often has destabilizing, disruptive effects on the genres that thematize nomadism as well as on the initial ideology of the text: nomadism becomes a tool to produce forked paths, doubt, conversions, metamorphoses at every level. An unstoppable elsewhere is the name of the game.

This is why it is not that surprising that major contemporary novelists who do not belong ideologically to an Orientalist lineage nevertheless continue this tradition, probably unconsciously, as soon as their narratives have a desert setting and are concerned with nomads. The Nobel Prize winner J.M.G. Le Clézio is one of them. From the very first pages of his characteristic fiction of 1980 titled Désert, the nomads are surrounded by a dreamlike haze of unreality, they are going always forward as if lost in space and in time after such a long journey, an infinite wandering:

> They appeared as if in a dream at the top of the dune, half-hidden in the cloud of sand rising from their steps. Slowly, they made their way down into the valley, following the almost invisible trail.
> [...]
> They were the men and the women of the sand, of the wind, of the light, of the night. They had appeared as if in a dream at the top of a dune, as if they were born of the cloudless sky and carried the harshness of space in their limbs.
> [...]
> They'd been walking like that for months, years maybe. They'd followed the routes of the sky between the waves of sand, [...] or else the endless route that penetrates into the heart of the desert [...][16]

The point of view, remote and aerial, is very different from that of Pierre Loti in his travelogue Le Désert, the character-narrator having arranged for himself a

---

[14]. Dino Buzzati, *The Tartare Steppe* (Manchester: Carcanet, [1940] 1985).

[15]. J.M. Coetzee, *Waiting for the Barbarians* (London: Penguin, 1982).

[16]. J.M.G. Le Clézio, *Desert*, trans. C. Dickson (Boston: Verba Mundi Books, 2009), 6-8.

caravan expedition to take him on camelback from Egypt to Jerusalem. However, Loti already insisted, this time from inside, on a feeling of loss along the longest and wildest possible route, through the Sinai and the Petra desert: "We stop there for the night, at this anonymous point of infinite solitude."[17] Later on, the sedentary realizes his insufficiency with regards to the grandiose harshness of nomadic life: "Then we clearly feel that we are not really people of the tent despite the charm of nomadic life during bright sunny days. The stone house man that has coalesced deep in us through so long atavisms, becomes vaguely anxious for lack of a roof, of walls, and knowing that there aren't any around in this shadowy desert whose extension is frightening." [18] It is no surprise then that, whether Le Clézio reminisced Loti or not, the latter had written about a family of nomads crossed in the desert: "They are coming from very far maybe, and they don't know very well where they are heading to, to find something better."[19] Conversely, although Loti doesn't make any special profession of faith to Christianity, he is happy to find traces of the Crusaders on his way to Palestine and his one-way caravan successfully terminates its course in Gaza: "Tomorrow at sunrise, we'll ascend towards Jerusalem."[20]

With Loti, the first-person narrative of a wealthy Westerner travelling with others through the desert severely limits identification with either the land or the nomads who roam it without peopling it. On the contrary, in Le Clézio's Desert and other fictional narratives of "nomadism," wandering and escape, third-person narrative creates the paradox of a participative distance, a quasi-fusion with the elected, fascinating character, an "other" by definition—other to the ordinary world of sedentariness and centrality—whose elusive, precarious but miraculous existence is surrounded by a strange aura while it lasts, at some indefinite point in eternity. Truth resides in a kind of elementary presence in and to a limitless world, alien to humankind, not disfigured by them:

> The sky was boundless, of such a harsh blue that it burnt the face. Still farther out, men walked through the maze of dunes, in a foreign world. But it was their true world. The sand, the stones, the sky, the sun, the silence, the suffering, not the metal and cement towns with the sounds of fountains and human voices. It was here—in the barren order of the desert—where everything was possible, where one walked shadowless

---

[17]. Pierre Loti, *Le Désert* (Paris: Calmann-Lévy, 1895), 11.
[18]. Ibid., 39-40.
[19]. Ibid., 112.
[20]. Ibid., 288.

on the edge of his own death. The blue men moved along the invisible
trail toward Smara, freer than any creature in the world could be.[21]

Le Clézio's inspired and inspiring young characters—such as Nour and Lalla in
Desert—possess an almost innate knowledge of the earth, in its purest and
therefore most barren condition, they "know all the paths," they are intimate
with the elements.[22] Able to name the wind by its true, natural name, they reach
a form of happiness with a lack of demands that is not even a renunciation,
rather a letting-go: "Perhaps he was no longer waiting for anything, no longer
knew anything, and now he resembled the desert—silence, stillness,
absence."[23] The inner wildness of these people, their radical "otherness" to the
cities, the institutions, the written word, anything fixed, makes them able to
become one with the natural landscape, its plants, if any, and its animals: "He
too is watching the hawk. But it's as if the bird were his brother and nothing
separated them. They both have the same look in their eyes, the same courage;
they share the same interminable silence of the sky, the wind, and the desert."[24]
The embrace of human beings is the same as being one with the primeval cave:
"As if their bodies were now one with the inside of the cave or were prisoners in
the entrails of a giant."[25] Escaping into the natural world is belonging, and vice
versa. So that when Lalla cannot finish crossing the desert and is eventually reunited with her aunt in Marseille—the "land of the slaves"— she goes on
walking across the whole city, wandering through its immense labyrinth as if
the city were another desert: "Lalla keeps walking, aimlessly, following the
roads."[26] Needless to say, there is no happy outcome for any of the four different
young nomadic characters who proceed to their destinies in two different
historical periods, 1910-1912 for Nour during the colonial conquest of Morocco
and the 1960s for Lalla Hawa, the orphan brought up in a slum and later a
migrant in Marseille, the Hartani, the wild shepherd boy with whom Lalla had
a passionate friendship, and finally, Radicz, the Rom boy trained to steal from
cars. The Hartani disappears in the South, Nour closes the eyes of the defeated
old warrior he revered, Radicz is run over by a bus. The only sign of survival of
a nomadic culture is a repetition of Lalla's own story when, returning to where
she roamed the dunes of the Moroccan coast, she gives birth like her mother
had done, clinging to a fig tree.

---

[21]. Le Clézio, *Desert*, 16.
[22]. Ibid., 51.
[23]. Ibid., 55, 22.
[24]. Ibid., 98.
[25]. Ibid., 108.
[26]. Ibid., 218.

It is only in dreamlike, surreal or psychedelic evocations that a kind of modern errancy somehow akin to traditional nomadism—except that it is individual instead of tribal, and this is a capital difference—can bring the satisfaction supposedly inherent in spiritual "freedom," detachment from mundane bonds. Variations on this symbolic plot can be found in a number of short stories and several novels and mixed genre books by Le Clézio, beginning with his first published work, The Interrogation, War, The Book of Flights, L'Inconnu sur la terre, Voyages de l'autre côté.. Mobility in Le Clézio is at the same time absolutely necessary and impossible, determined and the only escape from determinacy[27]. Just as the practice of language is the only possible escape from the silence of death, but it leads to silence, walking on and on is the only escape from the stillness of death, although death is always somehow at bay at the end of the path, in the ordinary form of a last breath or in that of ecstasy, access or return to presence, sharing the materiality of what is (anywhere). Simply wanting to disappear, like Naja Naja in the Voyages is a valid motivation to "go away all the time, in everything [one] does," travelling in the trees, or transforming oneself into a speck in the cloud of smoke ascending from one's cigarette.[28] Transposed into the lyrical first-person subject of L'Inconnu's prose poetry, the narrative becomes a Rimbaldian discourse of transcendence, prompted by aesthetic idealization:

> They are beautiful, of a strange and boundless beauty, the nomadic people. Nations without masters, without monuments, without roads: they have not imagined an end to their voyage, for nothing must stop them.[29]
> Then I let desire grow, and I leave, with those who can fly. They carry me away on their wind, they go fast on the roads of light. Where are they going? They are restless travellers who don't know the names of the countries.[30]

Once again, whether in bliss or in distress, the Romantic "nomads" are depicted as ignorant of territories, without bearings in unlimited space. The "solitude of movement" [31] however ascetic it may purport to be, remains as possessive and panoptic as it was in the early colonial voyages of discovery, in Orientalist visits

---

[27]. Didier Coste, "Nomad's Land (on J.-M. Le Clézio's persona as "Great Wanderer"), Guest Lecture at the University of Rajasthan, 2003, https://www.academia.edu/8897685/NOMAD_S_LAND_on_J.-M._Le_Cl%C3%A9zio_s_persona_as_Great_Wanderer_.

[28]. J.M.G. Le Clézio, *Voyages de l'autre côté* (Paris: Gallimard, [1975] 1995), 46, 101, 40.

[29]. J.M.G. Le Clézio, *L'Inconnu sur la terre* (Paris: Gallimard, 2006).

[30]. Ibid., 197.

[31]. J.M.G. Le Clézio, *The Book of Flights. An Adventure Story*, trans. Simon Watson Taylor (London: Vintage Books, 2010), 76.

to new possessions, or as it is in Olivier Rolin's global simultaneist fresco L'Invention du monde (1993).

Exotic women, unreachable passers-by, naive, frail and at the same time resilient women may be autonomous, but they are still turned into textual objects of male desire by their very (primeval or recovered) autonomy. Are then all these metaphorical discourses of nomadism marred by the persistence of a phallic or patriarchal vision? Can a female "nomadism," or, more generally "gender mobility" reverse, upset or liberate a construction of the world in which the other is, if not a prey, an appropriatable symmetric image of the self? This is what we are going to investigate now, examining the figure of Isabelle Eberhardt and various responses to her personality, in life and words.

Imitation nomadism, and gender mobility

Isabelle Eberhardt (1877-1904) was an illegitimate child born of Russian parents in Geneva. Her mother had been married to a much older dignitary, a widower with whom she had several children. The mother had moved to Geneva with the tutor of poor origin, married, but separated, and all the children but the two eldest girls. When her noble husband died, her liaison with the tutor resulted in Isabelle's birth, barring everyone in the Swiss household from being accepted by "good society" in Russia if they ever returned there. Isabelle was born a banned exile whose passport was that of a nation that rejected her and whose country of birth and residence was reluctant to accept her and also placed her under surveillance. This fact, combined with the original education provided at home by Trophimovitch, her father/tutor who knew or studied many languages, is certainly not enough to explain her cross-dressing, her attraction to the Maghreb, her conversion to Islam, her incipient career as a journalist and writer, and the rest of her tragic and passionate destiny. The involvement of her father in anarchist movements, whose role in Isabelle's upbringing is considered as decisive by Annette Kobak's sensationalist biography, is probably less important than the contradictions of a former pope and jack-of-all-trades who had become a passionate botanist and tried to make a living out of his tropical greenhouse near Geneva.[32] But these influences may contribute to understanding why the word "nomad" has stuck to her from one of the earliest literary articles to the latest academic research on her, and from one biography or anthology to the next.[33]

---

[32]. Annette Kobak, *Isabelle, the Life of Isabelle Eberhart* (London: Virago Press, 1998), 3-10.

[33]. See, among others, Eberhardt, 1987; Rice, 1990; Abdel-Jaouad, 1993; Charles-Roux, 1995; Belenky, 2011.

Instead of documenting directly the literal or implicit presence and possible meanings of "nomadism" in Isabelle's writings, I shall begin with a critical examination of a 1911 review article by Norman Douglas. It contains all the symptoms that can let us diagnose the birth and the lasting impact of the "nomadic" metaphor, noting that a displacement occurs from the ideal of the "noble savage" or "nature's gentleman," primarily a social being, to a dominant figure of solitude—from Las Casas and Montaigne to Chateaubriand through Dryden. Douglas's article, titled "Intellectual Nomadism," begins with evoking Isabelle's death, crushed in a flash flood by the fall of the dilapidated house she shared in a semi-desertic region of Algeria with her Arab husband, and how her manuscript notes, although much damaged, buried in the mud, were miraculously saved, reconstructed, edited and published by a journalist friend. The value of these writings is announced: they were well worth savings as "fragments of Sahara life," and because "a critic has called Isabelle 'the most virile and sincere writer of the Algerian country'."[34] In other words, Isabelle is authentic (she possesses a "fundamental simplicity") and she shows strength in her portrayal of a rough and exotic culture or way of life, combining three elements: "her impressions of scenery interspersed with tales of native life and her own reflections."[35] Douglas, without taking into account that Isabelle wrote in French and was brought up in French-speaking Switzerland, explains her affinity with the Algerian South ethnically: "her nature being essentially Russian, she can sympathize to an exceptional degree with the nomadic Arabs."[36] Curiously, the "freedom" that naturally nomadic Russians seek abroad in the middle of other nomads, is contradicted by the assertion that the Russian "autocratic system [...] merely represents the nomadic family principle of which every household in the land is a replica."[37] Moreover, "nomadism" is redefined as a disposition of the mind and the senses rather than constant physical mobility: "Isabelle Eberhardt [was not] gadding across country all day long with a portmanteau slung over her shoulders. But [...] the nomad's definite but indefinable states of yearning and exaltation, the nostalgic note, are prominent in these volumes."[38] Although "Russians must have a measureless horizon, and as their bodies roam, so do their minds," Isabelle's writing remains, like herself, simple, efficient, to the point, while being more evocative, impressionistic, than photographic. She is an artist, "like all artists," there is

---

34. Norman Douglas, "Intellectual Nomadism," in *The North American Review*, vol. 193, n°665, April (1911): 523, https://www.jstor.org/stable/25106908, accessed February 1, 2020.
35. Ibid., 524.
36. Ibid.
37. Ibid., 525
38. Ibid.

"mirage hanging about [her pictures]," "almost in the sense of Turner's landscapes," but she is not a "creative artist."[39] How are so many complexities and contradictions possible in someone who is so "naturally" dictated by her "race"? If these exciting singularities cannot be exclusively ethnic, it must be some other fact that blurs contours and makes interpretation (not evaluation) difficult. As we have already seen it, Isabelle is "virile," leaving many Arab words untranslated an unexplained in her texts is even "an ultra-virile method of introducing local color," but she has a feminine sensitivity, this young woman riding a white stallion, her gender ambiguity complements, or is perhaps at the root of a totalizing ambivalence[40]: "It is difficult, indeed, to conceive another writer emerging on the scene with the very unusual equipment she possessed: to be both man and woman, a scholar and a savage of the waste, a visionary hashish devotee and fin-de-siècle journalist; a Mohammedan, christian and agnostic."[41]

Clichés about femininity abound—almost inevitably under a male pen, one would say, in 1911. A woman, to gain insight into "a race like the Arabs," has the advantage of being "less disposed to theorize, to read wrong meanings into what she sees, less prone to err in interpreting primordial tracts of feeling," "a man can rarely immerse himself in the strange life of a savage race with the *naif* abandonment of a woman."[42] There is something childlike in women, they are "arrested" at an early "emotional stage" when the lure of imaginary adventure lets us identify with raw, primitive, barbarian people. How is naiveté compatible and how does it profitably combine with much learning, training and "a refined intelligence?"[43] Douglas does not solve the riddle himself, but, for various reasons, including his own lifestyle, his exile in Capri and his bisexuality, plus the prevalent symbolism and myths in turn-of-the-century British and continental literature and artistry in general, we can safely assume that Isabelle is seen and presented by Douglas as an exemplary and exotic androgynous figure, nostalgic and representative of a primordial completeness, unity and purity. "Nomadism" across cultures, "races," genders and languages was, for Isabelle as for Douglas— he insists on it, a provider of "jouissances fortes." Douglas could have subscribed to Flaubert's exclamation: "Madame Bovary, c'est moi!"

Now, if we turn to Isabelle's writings and a more political, less projective interpretation of her narrative plots, her philosophical reflections and her style,

---

39. Ibid, 528, 529, 538.
40. Ibid., 533.
41. Ibid., 532.
42. Ibid., 534.
43. Ibid., 527.

what will remain of the impact of a certain "nomadism"? And what can it tell us about its relation to a possible liberation from colonial, capitalist and patriarchal domination? Let us examine one of her best-known short stories, "Yasmina."[44] Yasmina is a teenage shepherdess who lives in a douar of Timgad, in the district of Batna, not far from the Aurès Mountains. She is supposed to get married to a much older, one-eyed, ugly grocer in the city, Batna. On leave for the day, a Sunday, Jacques, a young French officer riding his horse to hunt near the Roman ruins, in the scorching heat, is looking for some slightly cooler place to rest and finds Yasmina with her sheep in a ravine, the riverbed of a wadi. What follows is entirely expected: the *rumi* is attracted to the pretty wild girl, goes as far as learning dialectal Arabic to communicate with her, seduces her, makes promises to her, pretends to convert to Islam, and is desperate when he is notified a prompt transfer to a post many miles away, south of Oran. The girl feels betrayed, but sadly accepts her destiny. Jacques sends news once only, forgets her. She is married to a spahi, an indigenous soldier of the French army who beats her and is sentenced to ten years forced labour for a fight with a higher-ranking officer. Yasmin becomes a prostitute in the "Black Village," the sinister brothel area on the outskirts of Batna and contracts tuberculosis. Five years after their short-lived love story, Jacques, now married to an elegant French girl, returns to Batna. Yasmina calls him on the street, blames and curses him for his lies. He throws her some money. Jacques has become "another man." The same night, she dies on the bench near the door of the hovel.

There are many ways of reading this short story. First of all, it is obvious that its sentimental plot line belongs to a popular European genre, the melodrama, that emerged on stage and in novelistic form in the late 18th century and, with or without music, remained highly successful all along the 19th century and even later. Melodramas combine in varying proportions Romantic exaltation and Realist mimesis. You need to have burning passion, dark treason and streams of tears, but you also need a recognizable social, cultural, historical and geographic setting. Wilkie Collins, Eugène Sue, Luis de Val fulfill all these criteria in their major, complex or complicated novels. But strong strains or more delicate traces of melodrama can be found in historical novels, in Naturalist narratives, or even in so-called Symbolist and Decadent works. In the case of "Yasmina" as well as several other short stories by Isabelle, we have a little of all this in spite of the simplification of the plot demanded by the format. How then does "Yasmina" differ from a simple transposition to an exotic setting of a rather standard European melodrama? One part of the answer lies in the apparent empathetic adoption, at times, of the point of view of the supposedly

---

44. Isabelle Eberhardt, "Yasmina," in *Œuvres complètes, Écrits sur le sable* (Paris: Grasset, 1990), 94-118.

unsophisticated mind of the illiterate tribal girl and, in fine, the Muslim RIP attributed to the spahi who finds Yasmina dead near the door of the brothel. However, the third-person narrator always possesses much knowledge in excess of the female protagonist who is not very clearly aware of the colonial situation, cannot imagine French social conventions and has little access to Jacques' mind. The narrator, without condoning Jacques' behavior, can explain and understand it, which will make the reader's identification with Yasmina more difficult: Jacques did all he could to avoid his transfer, but Yasmina found it hard to believe; he considered eloping with her, going native, but, for him, it would have been a huge step out of his established way. Yasmina's mind was too elementary not to cede to desire and, eventually, to gullibility. In fact, it is only Yasmina's most *feminine* psychological aspects (feminine according to the gendered clichés of male prejudice), her deep intuitions and distrust, that will prove right. In what sense can Isabelle Eberhardt, the author, still be labeled a feminist icon? And how far her *nomadism* can be held determinant in the fabrication of this image?

Whether or not Isabelle had read many Naturalists beside Zola, her narratives are often reminiscent of Maupassant, who himself was indebted to Balzac and others—with less irony and some more sentimentalism. Maupassant visited Algeria as a reporter for the daily Le Gaulois in 1888. If he was somewhat critical of the colonial development model applied there, he nevertheless called Algeria "a piece of France." One of his lesser-known short stories, "Allouma," is set there, interestingly not far from Cherchell (homophone, in French, of "look for her"). The framed story of Allouma, a nomadic girl from the South, is told by a colonist settler, M. Auballe, who owns a farm and a bordj, a fortresslike house, to the first person framing narrator, an old Parisian acquaintance of Auballe who had been wandering on foot on a tour of Algeria and had got lost one night in a hilly part of the country. When asked about his life in Algeria after leaving Paris, Auballe focuses exclusively on his relationship with beautiful and wild Allouma, first found under the tent of the faithful servant Mohammed. Allouma, when she becomes Auballe's "slave mistress," Orientalist style, he believes, is moved to the house and given a mirrored wardrobe, but she cannot stand immobility, life inside. She flees a first time, and a second time, not returning till the day of the storytelling. Although Auballe describes her in animal terms, as an unknowable creature, although he feels humiliated that she preferred poverty with a barbarian shepherd to luxury in his company, and was even tempted to kill her, he eventually states that he would "take her back" if she returned: "With women, you always have to forgive...Or ignore."[45] Maupassant's apparently misogynous views are innumerable in his work,

---

[45]. Guy de Maupassant, "Allouma" in *La Main gauche* (Paris: Paul Ollendorff, 1889), 64.

including his travelogues, but women are equally often depicted, quite objectively, as victims of men and the patriarchal society, in situations of exploitation, abandonment, negligence, scorn, etc. As some critics have noted, Maupassant should not be read as a standard Saidian Orientalist.[46] His own "wandering life" episodes, particularly in North Africa, as he called them in *La Vie errante* (1890, one of his very last publications) take place in the disgust of "modern," industrial and consumerist life and the remaining nomads (like the Touareg people) are emblems of nostalgia for the supposed "simplicity," closeness to nature, of deprived, isolated, tribal groups, accustomed to scarcity—a deep nostalgia, because one can never become a tribal nomad, it is always too late. Isabelle Eberhardt, both the character and the author, is not very different from Maupassant and his male characters in relation to Algeria, and especially the interior. In his preface to Isabelle's unfinished novel, *Trimardeur* ("Hobo") Victor Barrucand, her devoted friend and admirer, wrote: "Isabelle Eberhardt cannot in any way be confused with the women of the South that she wanted to depict. She had very different goals, she wore another costume. What was mainly important to her was to be poor enough of care, simple enough of heart to be able to possess the land in passing."[47] "Possession in passing" accurately describes the relationship of the nomads to the territories they roam as well as sexual/sentimental intercourse not governed by the law of property. Contrary to the rule of the settler-colonist and the reproductive continuity of the name of the father in patriarchal societies, it is concerned with using and exchanging, with open space and unmeasurable temporality.

Where there is a clear evolution, if not a revolution or reversal of perspective and manner between Isabelle and earlier "realist" literature is well exemplified by how her writing contrasts with Balzac's short story "Une passion au désert" ("A Passion in the desert") of 1832. This "episode of an epic that we could call 'The French in Egypt" retells the story, told by an old soldier, of his passionate adventure in a cave with a panther when he was lost in the desert and waiting to be rescued during Napoleon Bonaparte's expedition in Egypt. From fear to tender familiarity, a quasi-erotic relationship develops between the Western

---

[46]. Didier Coste, "Allouma, ou ce que la main gauche n'a pas dit à la main droite," *French Forum*, vol. XIII n°2, (1988): 229-242.

Mary Poteau-Tralie, "Reframing Guy de Maupassant's 'Allouma' through the lens of Assia Djebar: Postcolonial Algeria Confronts Colonial France," *Dalhousie French Studies*, vol. 94 (Spring 2011): 146-147.

[47]. Isabelle Eberhardt, *Trimardeur,* preface by Victor Barrucand (Paris: Bibliothèque numérique romande, [1922] 2012), 13, https://ebooks-bnr.com/eberhardt-isabelle-trimardeur/.

man and the big Arab cat (always presented as a lascivious female), until the latter one day plants her teeth, although not deeply, in the former's thigh. He stabs "her" in the neck and "she" dies looking at him "without anger."[48] The soldier feels guilty like a murderer who has killed "a real person" and cries. Many years later, after traveling and fighting—"walking his corpse"—in many more places, he still feels the same about it sometimes, "only when he is sad." When asked about his fascination for the desert, he answers: "In the desert, there is nothing and there is everything. [...] It is God without the humans."[49] The structural and stylistic similarity with "Allouma" is striking, but Balzac's panther has become a gazelle, she does not live in a cave but in open space, the land may have been conquered, but not her freedom.

With Isabelle's "Yasmina," another turn is taken again which increases ambiguity and precludes early foreclosure. First, like Le Clézio's Lalla much later, Yasmina is no longer a proper, traditional nomad, she lives in a hut made of solid materials in a fixed place, not far from the city. She is even less of a nomad than Lalla in her head, and her whole life is contained within a very narrow radius. Secondly, in contrast to Auballe, the farming settler, with his house of stone for the rest of his life, Jacques moves from garrison to garrison, returns to France on leave and meets his future wife in Nice, the fashionable cosmopolitan resort, he is a "modern nomad" who abandons the settled Arab girl because he falls short, by far, of going native, not because he is not tempted to do it. Going native may result from a fetishization, of the mysterious other, as per Sara Ahmed's theory, but, although fetishization can be linked to commodification and consumption it can reveal other dimensions, including a re-creation of oneself as other, a conversion, a mystic loss of oneself into the very strangeness of the stranger which resembles a potentially self-destructive gnosis.[50] Viewed from the cold external eyes of the modern State's standards, this risky transformative step of the self, a metamorphosis, is commonly diagnosed as alienation: Isabelle was considered as dangerous and crazy by many authoritarian authorities (the Russian czarist regime, the police of the Swiss bourgeoisie, the French colonial control system). That, remaining halfway in life, she could not become one with her fetishized other (the tribal Muslim nomad) but in death, is a tragic, inevitable outcome, but does tragedy indict the tragic hero? Thirdly, Isabelle's style, while trying to retain the brutal (male?) efficiency of the earlier realists' short sentences, abounds in adjectives that confess to a subjective, sensitive narration; it is probably a feature of

---

48. Honoré de Balzac, *Une passion dans le désert* (Paris: eBalzac, [1832] 2018), 36.
49. Ibid.
50. Sara Ahmed, *Strange Encounters. Embodied Others in Post-Coloniality* (Oxford: Routledge, 2000), 114.

symbolist/post-symbolist writing shared with authors of sentimental novels of her time writing under masculine pen names, but, in terms of the reader's perception at the beginning of the 20th century, this style could amount to a feminisation of realism as much as a masculinisation of the sentimental. The double in-betweenness of the style and the characters' uncertain localization is an indication that the "decolonial" indictment of Isabelle as a false nomad and a real colonialist is an a-historical, insensitive distortion of the political impact of "thinking nomad" in a bourgeois, nationalist and harshly patriarchal society. On these grounds, I would firmly defend Leila Sebbar's title Isabelle l'Algérien against the attacks of Lynda Chouiten who accuses Isabelle of "re-writing her subversive gestures so as to conform with the transgressed codes."[51] Ignoring how transgressions are (historically) coded, overlooking the convergence of modes of dissidence and escapism in different cultures across wide spaces and various social classes, cannot but lead to this kind of retrospective, irrelevant condemnation. We should not neglect the similarities of Isabelle, the (auto-)biographical character, alternating masculine and feminine first persons, with Proust's Albertine (The Sweet Cheat Gone), or Colette (The Vagabond).

Thanks to the ambiguity of nomadism (of all kinds) maintained by Eberhardt and others who must not be reduced to Orientalist appropriation, let us hope that the metaphor can be revived once more after Deleuze and Guattari. It might be productive and perhaps necessary if we want to understand how, at times, "even violets resist domestication," as the feminist playwright Timberlake Wertenbaker puts it in New Anatomies, her reconstruction of Isabelle's personality.[52] However, there are many obstacles on the track of giving a second life to "nomadology." We shall see whether they can be overcome in the "Afterword" of this volume.

Bibliography

Abdel-Jaouad, Hédi. "Isabelle Eberhardt: Portrait of the Artist as a Young Nomad." Yale French Studies, 83, 1993: 93-117.

Ahmed, Sara. *Strange Encounters. Embodied Others in Post-Coloniality. Oxford*: Routledge, 2000.

Appiah, Kwame Anthony. "Afterword." In *Cosmopolitanisms*, edited by Bruce Robbins and Paulo Lemos Horta, 271-274. New York: New York University Press, 2007.

---

[51]. Lynda Chouiten, *A Carnivalesque Mirage: the Orient in Isabelle Eberhardt's Writings*. Ph.D. thesis (U. of Galway, 2012), 14, http.//hdl.handle.net/10379/3600.

[52]. Timerlake Wertenbaker, "New Anatomies," in *Plays 1* (London: Faber and Faber, 1996), Act I, scene 1.

Attali, Jacques. *L'Homme nomade*. Paris: Le Livre de Poche, 2005.

Balzac, Honoré de. *Une passion dans le désert*. Text established by Tania Duclos et Maxime Perret. Paris: eBalzac [1832] 2018.

Belenky, Masha. "Nomadic Encounters: Leila Sebbar writes Isabelle Eberhardt." Dalhousie French Studies, vol. 96, Fall 2011: 93-105.

Buzzati, Dino. *The Tartare Steppe*. Manchester: Carcanet, [1940] 1985.

Charles-Roux, Edmonde. *Nomade j'étais: les années africaines d'Isabelle Eberhart 1899-1904*. Paris: Grasset, 1995.

Chouiten, Lynda. *A Carnivalesque Mirage: the Orient in Isabelle Eberhardt's Writings*. Ph.D. thesis, U. of Galway, 2012. http://hdl.handle.net/10379/3600

Coetzee, J.M. *Waiting for the Barbarians*. London: Penguin, 1982.

Coste, Didier. "Allouma, ou ce que la main gauche n'a pas dit à la main droite." French Forum, vol. XIII n°2, 1988: 229-242.

Coste, Didier. "Nomad's Land (on J.M. Le Clézio's persona as "Great Wanderer"). Guest Lecture at the University of Rajasthan, 2003. https://www.academia.edu/8897685/NOMAD_S_LAND_on_J.-M._Le_Cl%C3%A9zio_s_persona_as_Great_Wanderer_

Deleuze, Gilles, and Guattari, Félix. *A Thousand Plateaus*, translated by Brian Massumi. Minneapolis: University of Minnesota Press, 1987.

Diamond, Jared. *The World until Yesterday: What Can We Learn From Traditional Societies?* New York: Viking, 2012.

Douglas, Norman. "Intellectual Nomadism." The North American Review, vol. 193, n°665, April (1911): 523-538. https://www.jstor.org/stable/25106908. Accessed: February 1, 2020.

Eberhardt, Isabelle. *Œuvres complètes 1. Écrits sur le sable (récits, notes et journaliers)*, edited by Marie-Odile Delacour and Jean-René Huleu. Paris: Grasset, 1988.

Eberhardt, Isabelle. *Œuvres complètes 2. Écrits sur le sable (nouvelles et roman)*, edited by Marie-Odile Delacour and Jean-René Huleu. Paris: Grasset, 1990.

Eberhardt, Isabelle. *The Passionate Nomad. The Diary of Isabelle Eberhardt*, translated by Nina de Voogd. Introduction by Rana Kabbani. London: Virago, 1987.

Eberhardt, Isabelle. 2nd ed. as *The Nomad. The Diaries of Isabelle Eberhardt*, introduction by Annette Kobak, edited by Elizabeth Kershaw. Chichester: Summersdale Travel, 2001.

Eberhardt, Isabelle. *Trimardeur*. Preface by Victor Barrucand. Bibliothèque numérique romande. [1922] 2012. https://ebooks-bnr.com/eberhardt-isabelle-trimardeur/.

Kerouac, Jack. *On the Road*. London: Penguin classics, [1957] 2000.

Kobak, Annette. *Isabelle, the Life of Isabelle Eberhart*. London: Virago Press, 1998.

Le Clézio, J.M.G. "Entretiens avec Jean-Louis Ézine." *Ailleurs*. Paris: Arléa, 1995.

Le Clézio, J.M.G. *Desert*, translated from the French by C. Dickson. Boston: Verba Mundi Books, 2009.

Le Clézio, J.M.G. *L'Inconnu sur la terre*. Paris: Gallimard, [1978] 2006.

Le Clézio, J.M.G. *The Book of Flights. An Adventure Story*, translated by Simon Watson Taylor. London: Vintage Books, 2010.

Le Clézio, J.M.G. *Voyages de l'autre côté*. Paris: Gallimard, [1975] 1995.

Lorraine, Tamsin. *Deleuze and Guattari's Immanent Ethics*. Albany: Suny Press, 2011.

Loti, Pierre. *Le Désert*. Paris: Calmann-Lévy, 1895.

Maffesoli, Michel. *Du nomadisme: vagabondages initiatiques*. Paris: "Inédit" Le Livre de Poche, 1997.

Maupassant, Guy de. "Allouma." In *La Main gauche*, 1-64. Paris: Paul Ollendorff, 1889. https://gallica.bnf.fr/ark:/12148/bpt6k69064m/f7.image.r=Maupassant%20La%20main%20gauche

Noyes, John K. "Nomadism, Nomadology, Postcolonialism. By Way of Introduction." Interventions Vol. 6(2), 2004: 159-168.

Poteau-Tralie, Mary. "Reframing Guy de Maupassant's 'Allouma' through the lens of Assia Djebar: Postcolonial Algeria Confronts Colonial France." Dalhousie French Studies, vol. 94, Spring (2011): 141-148.

Rice, Laura. "Nomad Thought": Isabelle Eberhardt and the Colonial Project." Cultural Critique, Nº17. Winter (1990-1991): 151-176.

Rolin, Olivier. *L'Invention du monde*. Paris: "Fiction et Cie" Seuil, 1993.

Rüdiger, Francisco Ricardo. *Civilização e barbárie na crítica da cultura contemporânea: leitura de Michel Maffesoli*. Porto Alegre: EDIPUCRS, 2007.

Sebbar, Leila. *Isabelle l'Algérien*. Neuilly: Al Manar, 2005.

Wertenbaker, Timberlake. "New Anatomies." In *Plays* 1, 1-57. London: Faber and Faber, 1996.

White, Kenneth. *L'Esprit nomade*. Paris: Grasset, 1987.

Chapter 2

The little grain that could: Nomadic incursions of amaranth in hegemonic territories

Java Singh

Doon University, India

Abstract

Amaranth was a protagonist in major religious rituals of the Nahua people of central Mexico, and miniature figurines of deities made from amaranth paste were sacred offerings during festivals. As a part of the ceremonies, worshipers broke and ate the grain statuettes. The colonizers banned amaranth cultivation because Christian priests thought that the act of symbolic theophagy crudely mimicked the Eucharist tradition of communion. They burnt amaranth fields and punished cultivators. Maize did not suffer the same fate despite being the divine source of all human life in myths of creation in Mesoamerican mythology, because it was already a staple of the colonial diet by the time the empire expanded westwards towards amaranth growing regions. Maize flourished under colonial rule and continues to be the dominant Mexican crop. However, it is amaranth that carries the banner of decoloniality in present-day Mexico, where chefs, farmers, activists, and government agencies are pushing for an expansion of amaranth cultivation. In parallel, the nutrition industry, agricultural research establishments, philanthropists, and multilateral development apparatus in the Global North project amaranth as a miracle food. This article visualizes elements of nomadic transgression in amaranth's survival in the face of both destructive violence of colonization and mercantile violence of coloniality/modernity. It reads the nomadic incursions of amaranth from several perspectives, including Walter Mignolo's "reconstitution," Rosi Braidotti's "bio-centered egalitarianism," Nahua philosophy's "teotl" and "neltiliztli" and some semiotic mutations in literary representations. Through these, this article presents how amaranth has crossed many borders of sacred-profane, ideological-commercial, cultural-scientific, and personal-political.

Keywords: Reconstitution, Mesoamerican philosophy, modernity, bioethics, bio-centered egalitarianism

***

Transcultural survival under colonial assault

At the time of the colonial conquest of Mexico, Mesoamerica, and the Andean regions had been home to amaranth for five millennia, since 3400 BCE.[1] Called huauhtli by the Mesoamerican people and kiwicha in the Andean regions, it was part of the staple diet, along with maize, beans, squash and chia. Instead of using its existing name, Friar Bernardino de Sahagún refers to huauhtli, pejoratively, as bledo and cenizo, words that mean worthless and ashen.[2] The magazine Arqueología Mexicana, co-published by the Mexican culture ministry, reports that "it was considered inferior and worthless, it was even declared a weed in the fields [...] and its cultivation was discouraged."[3] Colonial priests objected to the cultivation of the crop because huauhtli was used in Aztec community rituals. Sahagún records that it was used during panquetzalizli, the festival dedicated to the Huitzilopotchli, the warrior sun god. Friar Diego Durán informs us of a similar use during tepeítlhuil, celebrated to appease the volcano Popocatépetl and atemoztli, to seek blessings of the rain god, Tlaloc. Náhuatl speaking people ground amaranth seeds into a paste called tzoalli to make idols of their deities.[4] During festival rituals, the figurines were broken up and eaten by the faithful in the act of symbolic theophagy. These ritual practices were unacceptable to the colonial clergy because they resembled the Eucharist tradition of the Christian communion where, in a similar act of symbolic theophagy, "the priest sacrifices a God to himself and distributes his flesh to be eaten by his worshippers and his holy body and blood become the food of the faithful."[5] A 1992 report on the marginalized crops of Latin America by the United Nations notes that "its cultivation was persecuted and its consumption was prohibited."[6] The report adds that colonial chroniclers, especially religious ones, make constant "references to the diabolical nature of amaranth," and there are

---

[1]. Eduardo Espitia Rangel et. al, *Conservación y uso de los recursos genéticos de Amaranto en México* (Celaya: INIFAP, Centro de Investigación Regional Centro, 2010), 11.

[2]. Bernardino de Sahagún, *Historia General de las Cosas de Nueva España Tomo Primero* (Mexico: Alejandro Valdés,1829), 21.

[3]. Ana María L. Velasco Lozano, "Los cuerpos divinos. El amaranto: comida ritual y cotidiana", *Arqueología Mexicana* núm. 138, Marzo-abril (2016), n.p., digital edition.

[4]. Fray Diego Durán, *Historia de las Indias de Nueva España E islas de Tierra Firme, tomo II* (México: Editora Nacional, [1880] 1951), 204; quoted in Gabriela Uruñuela Ladrón de Guevera and Patricia Plunket Nagoda, "Las maquetas de montes-deidades de amaranto de Posclásico," *Arqueología*, núm. 138, Marzo-abril (2016), digital edition.

[5]. Preserved Smith, "Christian Theophagy: An Historical Sketch," The Monist Vol. 28, No. 2 April (1918): 161.

[6]. J.E. Hernández Bermejo and J. León, eds., *Cultivos Marginados, Otra Perspectiva de 1492* (Rome: FAO de la ONU, 1992), 91.

"two direct mentions to the prohibition of its cultivation by Fray Bernardino de Sahagún in 1570 and by Ruiz de Alarcón, in 1626."[7] Alarcón's 1626 invective against tzoalli, the amaranth paste, shows that even after a century of colonization, the practice was as extant as the religious persecution against it. Furthermore, a survey conducted by the Mexican Government in 1890, indicates that at the close of the nineteenth century, the cultivation of amaranth had disappeared almost entirely in independent Mexico.[8]

The eradication of amaranth was typical of the cultural war waged by the colonizers against indigenous practices and artforms. Along with the intangible heritage of languages, religions, and oral literatures, material culture embodied in monuments, codices, and crops was destroyed to enervate the spirit of resurgence. The aesthetic violence of melting down "fine cast gold artifacts" into ingots for convenient transportation to imperial shores was as devastating as the ignoble transfer of wealth contained in gold.[9] Despite the sustained efforts to annihilate indigenous civilizations, spiritually and materially, the targeted practices and objects survived. In a classic case of transculturation, the paste made from amaranth seeds, maize, and maguey honey that had been banned by colonial Catholic priests, came to be widely used in Catholic celebrations within a few decades of the crop's disappearance from Mexican fields.[10] Writing in 1950, Carl O. Sauer observes, "the cakes of huautli or tzoal are still seen in markets of many towns and villages now celebrating Catholic feast days."[11] Describing the flourishing trade in tobacco, despite opposition from the colonial Church, Fernando Ortiz writes that tobacco, successfully "passed from the cultures of the New World to those of the Old" through an

---

[7]. Ibid., 92.

Jules Whicker, ed., *The Plays of Juan Ruiz de Alarcón* (Woodbridge: Tamesis, 2003), 29. Juan Ruiz de Alarcón was a permanent appointee to the Royal Council of Indies, the principal body of the Spanish court for administering the colonies. He was also a noted dramatist of the Spanish Golden Age.

[8]. Emma Cristina Mapes Sánchez, "El Amaranto (Amaranthus spp.) planta originaria de México," *Academia, Ciencia y Cultura AAPAUNAM,* (4), (2010): 219, https://www.medigraphic. com/pdfs/aapaunam/pa-2010/pa104e.pdf.

[9]. Colin McEwan, Andrew Middleton, Caroline Cartwright, and Rebecca Stacey. *Turquoise Mosaics from Mexico* (Durham and London: Duke University Press, 2006), 86.

[10]. Though some accounts allege the use of human blood in the preparation of tzoalli, the amaranth paste, Mapes Sánchez clarifies that it contained only honey and toasted seeds.

[11]. Carl O. Sauer, "Cultivated Plants of South and Central America," in *Handbook of South American Indians,* edited by J.H. Steward (Washington D.C.: United States Government Printing Office, 1950), 497.

"extraordinary process of transculturation."[12] Even though amaranth's survival was not as robust as Cuban tobacco, it managed to mark out a path of nomadic incursion into hegemonic territories. Like a nomad seeking survival, it relied upon an "inventory of traces" of where it had already been to inhabit a bridge between Nahua and Catholic rituals.[13]

Reclaiming a lost (bio)ethics towards decoloniality

This article visualizes an inviolable relationship of safekeeping between habitat and ethical habit. The indigenous Mesoamerican and Andean cultivation of amaranth, quinoa, and numerous other crops was carried out in a habitat of safekeeping sustained by ethical habits of minimum ambient damage, judicious use of natural resources, and sufficient ground healing. These ecological practices represented the praxis of a complex Nahua cosmovision. A glimpse of this cosmovision is visible in the conversations between Nahua *tlamatinimes*, or philosophers, and Spanish friars that took place in 1524 after the Aztec empire had been annihilated. According to Miguel León Portilla, these conversations were probably the "last and most dramatic public performance" of protest against the cultural violence of colonization.[14] In extremely "respectful and cautious words," the Nahua philosophers tell their colonizer-interlocutors that "the Nahuatl mode of thinking about divinity can be and should be respected," because it is based on "a rich and elevated concept of the Giver of Life."[15] They explain that the gods made sacrifices to provide everything that "conserves" human life; therefore, human beings must honor the gods by "bleeding" and sacrificial offerings.[16] It is this cyclical order which made agriculture and consumption patterns sustainable; the Giver of Life also needs to live; therefore, there is a need to nurture the nurturing soil, and protect the sustaining biodiversity. The cosmovision of the Aztecs was non-oedipal, self-sustaining in their everyday banality. The world view where all objects, animals, plants, and humans were moving and rooted at the same time was both lair-laden and also morally marked. There was a discernible entanglement of nature, gods, and human beings. Sacrifice was a necessary expression of reciprocal responsibility and a reinforcement of the "habit" to give back to the habitat some measure of what it had given.

---

[12]. Fernando Ortiz, trans. Harriet de Onis, *Cuban Counterpoint: Tobacco and Sugar* (Durham and London: Duke University Press, 1995), 183.

[13]. Rosi Braidotti, *Nomadic Subjects* (New York: Columbia University Press), 14.

[14]. Miguel León Portilla, *La Filosofía Náhuatl* (Mexico: UNAM, 1993), 129, original in Spanish, translation mine.

[15]. Ibid., 130.

[16]. Ibid., 131.

The amaranth's nomadic ethics and that of the thirty-six other crops that became marginalized after colonization were enabled by these indigenous cultivation practices, which were guided by soil rotation and intercropping, as in the milpa system.[17] The scale of agriculture in the complex pre-Hispanic civilizations was well beyond the sustenance level. The Mendoza Codex, created around twenty years after the Spanish conquest, informs us that the "seventeen conquered provinces paid eighteen trojes of huauhtli, equivalent to four-thousand tons of amaranth seeds," as a tribute to the Aztecs.[18]

Figure 2.1: An illustrated catalog of the annual tribute paid by the towns of the Aztec empire

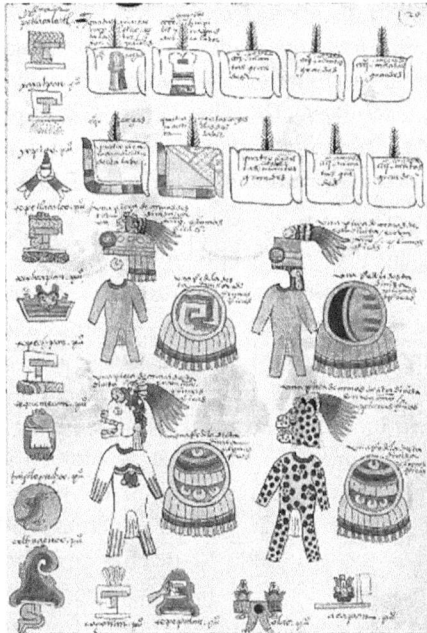

Source: Bodleian Library digital archives[19]

---

[17]. Hernández Bernejo and J. León, eds., *Cultivos Marginados*, vii-ix.
The above mentioned FAO report recognized 17 species of edible crops from pre-Hispanic Mesoamerica, 15 from the Andean region, and 9 from the Amazon area and the Caribbean, as marginalized and meriting revival. Three species of Amaranth and two of quinoa were included in the report.
[18]. Velasco Lozano, "Los cuerpos divinos," n.p.
[19]. Codex Mendoza, Bodleian Library, accessed March 25, 2020, https://iiif.bodleian.ox.ac.uk/iiif/viewer/2fea788e-2aa2-4f08-b6d9-648c00486220#?c=0&m=0&s=0&cv=49&r=0&xywh=-615%2C1187%2C7960%2C3670.

Though the scale of cultivation was significant, it did not exceed the limits of sustainability. The ethical orientation of indigenous cultivation practices confirmed the pre-philosophical, Homeric connotation of the word "eethos," which denoted the animal's lair, its habitat, where it is safe from the inclemency of weather and attacks of predators.[20] Thus, in describing these practices as "bioethical," this article is conscious of the earlier spatial connotation of ethics.

Paulina Rivero Weber, a professor of Philosophy at UNAM in Mexico City and a leading voice in bioethics, and Ruy Pérez Tamayo understand bioethics as a science of survival in which "the survival of the total ecosystem" is implicit.[21] Therefore, according to them, "[what] very often has negative consequences for nature and damaging implications for ourselves is what we still do not know (and often think that we do) about reality, as much of the world in which we live as of our own biology."[22] The stress on knowing ourselves echoes a similar refrain in Nahua philosophy where "[t]he role of a Nahua philosopher was that she or he 'puts a mirror before others.' The philosophers should make people 'cautious,' to cause 'a face (a personality) to appear in them.' Because we are on earth only in passing: 'Here, we only come to know ourselves.'"[23]

This article locates Rosi Braidotti's bio-centered egalitarianism at the core of an ethics traced by the habitat-habit relationship. Zoe or "bare life" of the marginalized human being or earth others—"animal, vegetable, viral" is the actant in this egalitarian relationship. Once more, a transversal connection emerges between contemporary and Nahua ethics in which "teotl" is a "dynamic, self-generating power or energy [...] Teotl is both metaphysically immanent and transcendent."[24] An ethics of bio-centered egalitarianism affirms the "radical immanence" or the "teotl" of the zoe, that is, a life force that is independent of discursive recognition. Such an ethics accepts "the impossibility of mutual recognition [...] replacing it with mutual specification and mutual co-dependence."[25] Thus, the nomadic multiplicity of sacred, political, and staple uses of amaranth stemmed from relations of mutual

[20]. Paulina Rivero Weber and Ruy Pérez Tamayo, "Ética y Bioética," *nexos*, July 2006: 23.
[21]. Van Rensselaer Potter, "Bioethics, the Science of Survival," *Perspectives in Biology and Medicine*, Volume 14, Number 1, Autumn (1970): 127.
Rivero Weber and Pérez Tamayo build upon Rensselaer's understanding of "survival."
[22]. Rivero Weber and Pérez Tamayo: 25, original in Spanish, translation mine.
[23]. Dag Hebjørnsrud, "The Mesoamerican Philosophy Renaissance," *Blog of the APA*, January 9, 2020, accessed July 7, 2020, emphasis mine, https://blog.apaonline.org/2020/01/09/the-mesoamerican-philosophy-renaissance/.
[24]. Hebjørnsrud, "The Mesoamerican Philosophy Renaissance," emphasis mine.
[25]. Rosi Braidotti, *Transpositions* (Cambridge and Malden: Polity, 2006), 111.

specification with the indigenous populations. Amaranth was put to numerous uses because it was abundantly available. It is an undemanding crop, which multiplies quickly and is resistant to drought and heat. For an equivalent area of land, amaranth would give a higher yield than maize. Yet, the indigenous people did not focus on only one staple, as they, through myths of a cyclical, inter-relational cosmology and organic-scientific knowledge, were committed to a diversified food platter. In the absence of androcentric determination, amaranth moved nomadically from one soil tract to another.[26] The focus on wheat, maize, and rice, the top three grains in present-day global consumption, represents a controlling Oedipal relationship because it is not based on mutual specification between the environment and androcentric thinking. This Oedipal space is the striated zone that the war machine of the marginalized crop can smoothen, even in the face of many nefarious adversarial strategies.

Reconstitution and the techno-managerial gaze of globalization

Nomadic routes are fraught with danger, and the nomad frequently encounters inhospitable terrain. The nomadism of amaranth is under threat from the discursivities of the "Miracle Foods Narrative (MFN)."[27] The MFN traces hunger alleviation and malnutrition reduction programs of multilateral, bureaucratic behemoths like the FAO, IFAP, and WFP to unveil the underlying colonial imperiousness in the claims of "benign humanitarianism" for these projects.[28] Since the beginning, their common tactical element has been the identification, projection, and eventual deification of a single crop as a panacea for nutritional challenges. Their efforts are bolstered by the participation of profit-seeking corporations and non-profit organizations, usually from the Global North. In the 1960s, the miracle food was O2 corn, a protein-enriched variety that, despite extensive promotional measures by the agencies, failed to become a staple food and ended up being used as fodder for animals as it was found to

---

[26]. This article posits the notion of organic-scientific knowledge as opposed to techno-scientific knowledge. The former works through slow healing, gradual adaptation and dialogic interventions. Techno-scientific knowledge privileges quick results, rapid transformations by imposing solutions from above.

[27]. Emma McDonnel, "Miracle Foods: Quinoa, Curative Metaphors, and the Depoliticization of Global Hunger Politics," *Gastronomica*, Vol. 15, No. 4 (Winter 2015): 70. https://www.jstor.org/stable/10.2307/26362298.

[28]. Ibid., 70.

FAO is the Food and Agricultural Organization, IFAP is the Information for All Program, and WFP is the World Food Program. All three work under the aegis of the United Nations Organization.

be unsuitable for human consumption. In the 1990s, the MFN spun the tale of Golden Rice. The vitamin-enriched rice hybrid was announced with a conspicuous campaign. Still, it could not make the journey from the laboratory and test sites to farmers' fields because of the lack of evidence of its vitamin absorption capacity. Despite previous failures, the MFN relaunched itself with a third protagonist: quinoa.

In its most recent adaptation, the MFN chose a different script for its protagonist. Whereas the promotion of the new hybrids of maize and rice as "curative metaphors" invoked the inventive potency of scientists and technical finesse of researchers, quinoa was contrived as a repository of traditional practices and ancient knowledge.[29] Moreover, the other two miracle foods possessed the star power of a single "charismatic nutrient": O2 corn was lysine enriched, and Golden Rice had beta-carotene.[30] In contrast, quinoa was a medley of high protein, amino acids, vitamins, and minerals; thus, no lab work was needed to improve it. In its proclamation, the United Nations General Assembly declared the year 2013 the "International Year of Quinoa," "in recognition of ancestral practices of the Andean people, who have managed to preserve quinoa in its natural state as food for present and future generations, through ancestral practices of living in harmony with nature."[31] In the declaration, the erstwhile grammar of inventive techniques of science ceded ground to a newfound dialect of preservative practices that sustain an inherited legacy.

Quinoa's projection as a catch-all metaphor for the shortcomings of commercial agriculture is a failed attempt at the synchronization of the expectations of globalization with the ethics of bio-centered egalitarianism manifest in pre-Hispanic food habits and cultivation habitats. Braidotti explains that synchronization is "not about the confirmation of steady identities, or the claim to counter-identities, but [...] about co-synchronicity: shared time zones shared memories and shareable time-lines of projects."[32] The U.N. declaration does not attempt activating "shared time zones, shared memories," and it does not acknowledge the impossibility of "shareable time-lines." The program that accompanied the declaration set out to accomplish in a decade what was acquired over centuries. It fossilizes the Andean cultivators

---

29. Ibid., 70.
30. Ibid., 72.
31. "Quinoa 2013 International Year," FAO, accessed March 29, 2020, http://www.fao.org/quinoa-2013/mobile/home/en/, emphasis mine.
32. Braidotti, *Transpositions*, 95.

as mere preservers whereas, it is well established that "domesticated plants are not naturally occurring or accidentally domesticated but result from the hard work of seed selection and adaptation."[33] It exoticizes the crop temporally by deeming it the preserve of the ancients and fetishizes it as a reification of harmony with nature. The most significant impediment to synchronization is the silence on the historical reasons that pushed numerous indigenous crops into oblivion.

As activists, government agencies, philanthropists, and nutritionists try to expand amaranth production in Mexico, its future trajectory will likely get entwined with the Macro Food Narrative that has enmeshed quinoa. Under colonial rule, quinoa cultivation and consumption were also declared unlawful, and like amaranth, cultivators continued to grow it in highland areas. Quinoa was extracted from its mountain lair for large-scale production when the Bolivian and Peruvian governments began to see it as a profitable export crop. Their efforts were successful; by the late 1980s, quinoa was widely available in U.S. health food stores, and the "Quinoa Boom" exploded at the turn of the millennium. The price of quinoa increased fourfold, making it too expensive for the urban poor in Peru.[34] The U.N. proclamation further inflated prices, worsening the situation. In a striking similarity with colonization, globalization had, once again, put the indigenous crop out of reach of the indigenous consumer. The Quinoa Boom also resulted in pressures on indigenous producers to make the quinoa's germplasm freely available to international researchers for breeding trials. The mismatch of time zones is a crucial factor in the revival project's failure. The multinational operators ask for free access to traditionally preserved germplasm but deny participation in profits generated by expanded market size. This demand implies that TEK, "traditional ecological knowledge" should be free so that managerial tech alone appropriates financial returns.

Examining decolonial aspects of bio-centered egalitarianism seems counter-intuitive because of the apparently contradictory, tension-generating vectors that pull a consummately humanist ideology away from posthumanist articulations. Yet, such an attempt constitutes precisely the kind of transversal connection that the nomadic perspective seeks to trace. Walter Mignolo has observed that "decoloniality emerged as an option to the rhetoric of modernity

---

33. McDonnel, "Miracle Foods," 80.

34. "Peru Retail Price: Cereal and Related: Quinoa: Complete," CEIC, accessed March 28, 2020, https://www.ceicdata.com/en/peru/retail-price/retail-price-cereal-and-related-quinoa-complete.

and to the combined rhetoric of 'development and modernization.'"[35] The "rhetoric of salvation and newness" that accompanied was framed on "the dispensability (or expendability) of human life and of life in general from the Industrial Revolution into the twenty-first century."[36] Braidotti also interrogates the ethics of modernity because "[m]odernity reached an aporetic moral condition by marching under the twin banners of universality and firm foundations."[37] Braidotti relies on Zygmunt Bauman's ideas of postmodern ethics, but Mignolo finds postmodern thought antithetical to decoloniality because postmodernity, while critiquing Western modernity, remains silent on its "darker side," that was and continues to be coloniality.[38] Though these thinkers are on opposite sides of the postmodern imperative, both thinkers are in search of pluriversal, transversal options to the universalizing logic of modernity.

A typical example of abortive modernity projects is found in the efforts of Puente a la salud comunitaria (Puente), a well-intentioned organization that is trying to revive large-scale amaranth cultivation and consumption in Oaxaca, in southern Mexico.[39] Puente was founded in 2003 by two North American women and aims to reduce the "high rate of birth defects," obesity, and alleviate the problem of child malnutrition.[40] Giving a "universal thumbs up" to Puente's efforts, Nancy Matsumoto writes, "The next steps [...] will be for the group to figure out costs, pricing, and profit margins. Once they've developed their packaging and logo, they can sell their alegrías at local markets and restaurants, or at the two amaranth specialty shops that Puente operates."[41] To increase the market for amaranth, both as a sweet treat such as alegría and as a staple food in dishes like *tlayuda*, the organization is seeking to incorporate traditional knowledge systems into the kit of modern managerial tactics. The asynchronous nature of their aspiration is manifest in a photograph of a publicity event that featured a massive tlayuda.

---

35. Walter D. Mignolo, *The Darker Side of Western Modernity* (Durham and London: Duke University Press, 2010), xxviii.

36. Ibid., 6.

37. Braidotti, *Transpositions*, 23.

38. Mignolo, *The Darker Side*, 85.

39. "Nuestra Historía: Impacto a través de Amaranto y Agroecología," Puente Mexico, accessed March 28, 2020, https://www.puentemexico.org/historia/

40. Nancy Matsumoto, "Why Mexican Chefs, Farmers and Activists are Reviving the Ancient Amaranth," *npr*, May 1, 2017, accessed March 24, 2020, https://www.npr.org/sections/thesalt/2017/05/01/526033083/why-mexican-chefs-farmers-and-activists-are-reviving-the-ancient-grain-amaranth.

41. Ibid.

Figure 2.2: A promotional event organized by Puente

Source: npr[42]

The tlayuda is a popular, traditional Oaxacan dish with many variations. On this particular occasion, it was made from amaranth flour, maize seeds, leaves, toasted grasshopper, avocado, radish, and salsa. The photograph shows volunteers carrying certificates of participation and staffers dressed in clean white aprons, smart chef jackets, masks, hairnets, and gloves. This article argues that the cheery image captures the core of the problem with organizations like Puente that do not rid themselves of the techno-managerial gaze, and is a visual representation of their failure as ethical projects of "reconstitución epistémica."[43] Laura Macdonald, writing in the mid-1990s, which she identifies as the period of an "NGO Boom" in Latin America, points out that the paternalistic attitude of the "northern NGOs" combined with "the wrong-headed assumption that modern technology could solve 'Third World' problems" and a failure to account for unjust socio-economic-political hierarchies at the national and international levels are vital factors in defeating

---

[42]. "A 12-meter-square *tlayuda*, incorporating amaranth flour," *npr*, accessed March 25, 2020, https://www.npr.org/sections/thesalt/2017/05/01/526033083/why-mexican-chefs-farmers-and-activists-are-reviving-the-ancient-grain-amaranth

[43]. Walter D. Mignolo, "Reconstitución epistémica/estética: la aesthesis decolonial una década después," *Calle 14: revista de investigación en el campo del arte* 14 (25) (2019): 19, https://doi.org/10.14483/21450706.14132.

philanthropic objectives.[44] The failure of commercial grammar and managerial rhetoric—comprised of logos, packaging, promotional events, specialty shops, and hierarchical organization structures with a clear division between management and staffers—to solve local issues is not atypical.

Like many members of civil society in the Global North, Puente may have responded to a genuine realization of injustice, but the public image of its co-founders gives some pause in discounting their self-promotional agenda. Their career trajectories suggest that founding Puente was a necessary step in the professional ladder, securing legitimacy for their larger ambitions in the Global North.[45] Though they continue to serve on the Puente board, their partial involvement cannot offer a functional substitute for leadership that is rooted or at least transplanted in the community. Though Puente is located in Oaxaca, which is a Zapoteca and not a Nahua region, common strands in the cosmologies of pre-Hispanic cultures permit one to examine the issue of rootedness through Nahua ethics. Rootedness or *neltiliztli* is a foundational precept of Nahua ethics, which should not be confused with fixity or immobility. Lynn Purcell explains that "for the Nahuas, one's life appears to take root at four related levels: in one's body, in one's psyche, in one's community by social rites and role, and in teotl."[46] Thus roots can move; they can be transplanted when the body, psyche community, and teotl all move together. A contrast to the modus operandi of Puente is visible in the "eethos" of the community that participated in the locally organized fair in Puebla. The fair was called "Huauhtlicalco," which means the house of huauhtli in Nahuatl. One speaker pointed out that the first step towards revaluing agrarian life is to start calling amaranth by its original name huautli, to accord the historical value owed to this grain.[47] Another speaker cautioned that some people from foreign

---

[44]. Laura Macdonald, "A Mixed Blessing The NGO Boom in Latin America, NACLA Report on the Americas," *NACLA Report on the Americas*, 28:5 (1995): 30, doi: 10.1080/10714839.1995.11 725795.

[45]. "Katherine Lorenz President," The Cynthia and George Mitchell Foundation, accessed March 27, 2020, https://cgmf.org/p/katherine-lorenz.html.
"Kate Seely, Senior Director," North California Grantmakers, accessed March 29, 2020, https://ncg.org/staff.

[46]. Lynn Sebastian Purcell, "Eudaimonia and Neltiliztli: Aristotle and the Aztecs on the Good Life," *Newsletter The American Philosophical Association*, Volume 16 No. 2, Spring (2017): 16.

[47]. Patricia Gutiérrez Rodríguez, "Recuperación del Cultivo de Amaranto va por buen camino," *La jornada de oriente*, October 12, 2018, accessed March 24, 2020, https://www.lajornadade oriente.com.mx/puebla/recuperacion-del-cultivo-del-amaranto-va-por-buen-camino-colegio-de-posgraduados/

countries were bringing new varieties, which was not a bad thing, but it should be done in an orderly manner.[48] Such remarks manifest a far greater understanding of the communitarian scope and historical depth of the challenge of *recuperación* or revival of traditions than the glib pseudo-technical grammar adopted by Puentes: to cure malnutrition and obesity by growing and selling more amaranth. Any revivalist project that aims to draw communitarian cultures into the modern economy of transactional relations, which necessarily implies shifting "to a salary system that breaks the links between family life and work," replicates the colonial matrix of power.[49] It will, sooner or later, generate resistance, and fail in its revivalist mission.

A commitment to the ethos of reconstitution determines the genuineness of a project aimed at *recuperación*. Mignolo explains that reconstitution "demands a complete turnaround in the geography of the argument and a disobedient conceptualization of the hegemonic vocabulary of epistemology and aesthetics."[50] The spatio-linguistic aspect of reconstitution is directly relevant for amaranth revival, even if the aesthetics are not. A functional *recuperación* strategy should find a way out of hegemonically dictated conversations. A decolonial vocabulary creates "differentiated spaces of enunciation anchored in the land and the bodies that inhabit and enunciate/ are enunciated in the border."[51] Thinking of the human-nature relationship as Pachamama, an Aymara and Quechua word, illustrates the reconstituting capacity of a disobedient vocabulary. Pachamama may be translated to Mother Nature or Mother Earth. When Bolivia and Ecuador constitutionalized the environment as a legal personality in 2008 and 2010, respectively, the enacted laws granted rights to "Madre Tierra," or Mother Earth.[52] By not thinking of the rights merely in terms of *nature*, which evokes a nature-culture binary, and by making it clear that the constitutions understand that the stipulated beneficiary of the laws is Madre Tierra or Pacha Mama, the terms of the conversation change. The vocabulary moves away from the idea of nature as a "destructive and dominating masculine entity who 'separates' herself from those she supports [...]," nor does it project Mother Earth as a "weak and subjugated female"; instead, she "is celebrated as a sacred and powerful maternal entity" as

---

48. Ibid.
49. Néstor García Canclini, "Cultura transnacional y culturas populares en México," *Cuadernos Hispanoamericanos*, núm. 431 (mayo 1986): 9.
50. Mignolo, "Reconstitutción epistémica/ etética," 31.
51. Mignolo, "Reconstitutción epistémica/ etética," 31.
52. Pablo Sólon, "The Rights of Mother Earth," in *The Climate Crisis*, ed. Vishwas Satgar (Johannesberg: Wits University Press, 2018), 108.

the Bolivian constitution refers to the strength of Pachamama.[53] These laws may also be seen to evoke a reciprocal relationship with the "mothers" in the Nahua myth of the five "primordial women who had sacrificed their lives to set the fifth sun in motion."[54] They revive the onus that pre-Hispanic mythology placed on human beings to acknowledge the bequest of the mothers and deities by imitating their sacrificial act.

A rhetoric of modernity that focuses on salvation rather than reconstitution is a mercantilizing mission, no different from the colonial civilizing mission. Criticizing capitalist appropriations of "counter-cultures" as "objects of commodified consumption," Braidotti states that, "[t]he ethics of sustainability combines a flair for and commitment to change with a critique of excess for its own sake."[55] Globalization's colonial gaze, Puente being a case in point, appropriates traditional practices to tackle problems created by coloniality such as malnutrition and obesity without criticizing the excesses of coloniality. The link between increasing amaranth consumption and nutritional imbalance is presented as a simple input-output relationship, notwithstanding numerous missing catalysts that are necessary to produce the desired cause-effect sequence. The problem is intentionally simplified to avoid addressing the more significant issues of poverty in the Global South and the concentration of wealth in the Global North. The mercantilizing mission suffers from all the ills of a colonial project precisely because it is conceived as a mission: a project "of conversion of achieving an[d] end programmed in the blueprint (sic)."[56] Therefore, there can be no decolonial "missions," only decolonial options.[57] The idea of options has been espoused in renaming the Bolivian state as "plurinational" and the notion of a "plural economy."[58] Whereas northern philanthropists, salvation activists, innovation scientists, and modernity enthusiasts remain caught up in a colonial conversation.

---

[53]. Paola Villavicencio Calzadilla and Louij J. Kotzé, "Living in Harmony with Nature?," *Transnational Environmental Law,* 7:3 (2018): 408.

[54]. Cecilia F. Klein, "A New Interpretation of the Aztec Statue Called Coatlicue, 'Snakes-Her-Skirt'," *Ethnology,* April (2008): 240.

[55]. Braidotti, *Transpositions,* 219.

[56]. Mignolo, *The Darker Side,* xxviii.

[57]. Ibid., xxviii

[58]. "Ley Nº 300 Ley De 15 De Octubre de 2012," FAO, accessed March 22, 2020, http://www.fao.org/fileadmin/user_upload/FAO-countries/Bolivia/docs/Ley_300.pdf

Amaranthine semiotics in literature

So far, the article has discussed some discursivities of huauhtli that have framed its consumption and production. It now takes up amaranth semiotics in literature to show how, in another instance of nomadic incursion, the grain has gradually moved into a non-Oedipal, decolonial literary space. We know that the name Amaranth "had been in use in Europe for two thousand years since antiquity; the ancient Greek word came from the temple of Amaryntia or Artemis, the virgin huntress worshipped as the goddess of childbirth."[59] Derived from its Greek etymon amarantos (αμάραντος), the Latin amarantus also means immortal or everlasting.[60] In Greek mythology, flowering stalks of the immortal amarantos were given as offerings to Venus by those wishing for eternal love. At this time, Amaranth denoted the yellow flowering stalks of Helichrysum Arenarium.[61] By the 15th and 16th century, the name Amaranth was used for three distinct species: the European amaranth, the huautli grown by ancient American cultures, and the amaranths native to Asia.[62] Thus, the name amaranth traveled from plant to plant. The association of amaranth with undying love, established in antiquity, has been a continual source of imagery in European poetry. Discussing the "disemic" valence of amaranth in the pastoral semiotics of sixteenth-century Golden Age Spanish poetry, Solez Pérez Abadín Barro explains that amaranth as the everlasting, death-defying flower was linked to both love and death; it signified not only perpetuity but also bitterness.[63] The critic points to an epitomic use of this disemia in a famous Italian eclogue in which a character named Amaranta can "sweeten every poison"; because of this quality, her lover's "existencia áspera y amarga," harsh and bitter existence becomes "dulce y querida," sweet and desirable.[64] Perhaps, Gabriel García Márquez considered these twin qualities of funerary bitterness and amorous perpetuity when he chose the name Amaranta for a female character in *Cien Años de Soledad* who, first rejects her suitor; then, after he commits suicide, burns her hands on a stove and keeps them wrapped in a

---

[59]. Mihai Costea and Francois J. Tardiff, "The Name of the Amaranth: Histories of Meaning," *SIDA, Contributions to Botany*, 29 July 2003, Vol. 20, No. 3 (2003): 1073-1074.

[60]. "amaranthine," merriam-webster, accessed March 28, 2020, https://www.merriam-webster.com/ dictionary/amaranthine.

[61]. Ibid., 1075.

[62]. Ibid., 1076.

[63]. Soledad Pérez-Abadín Barro, *Resonare silvas: la tradición bucólica en la poesía del siglo XVI* (Santiago de Compostela: University Press, 2004), 147.

[64]. Ibid., 147, 19.
Quotes "Eclogue III" of *Arcadia* by Jacobo Sannazaro written between 1484 and 1486.

black gauze as a sign of mourning for the rest of her life.[65] The amaranth has been part of the postcolonial Latin American poetic imaginary as well from the very start. Andres Bello and Pablo Neruda insert it in their beatus ille; César Vallejo describes moments of passionate recollections as "una tarde amaranto," an amaranth evening; Neruda also sees the wine-stained mouth of the beloved as amaranth-coloured in his Cien Sonetos de Amor.[66] The poets were struck by the fuchsia, pink, purple, red, abundant efflorescence of amaranth, and García Márquez by its abstract qualities, leaving the grain itself unnoticed. The grain finds a place in the literary imaginary in the twenty-first century when the Mexican writer Laia Jufresa gives it a significant role in *Umami*.[67] This novel presents not only a postcolonial but also a decolonial portrait of the seed-grain.[68] Amaranth is brought into the narrative as the life work of an anthropologist, Dr. Alfonso Semitiel, who studies pre-Hispanic diets. Jufresa sees the irony in the geopolitics of cultural appreciation and appropriation, and through Alfonso's musings, shows that the mindset of the modern knowledge industries is as tarnished with coloniality as that of openly profit-seeking globalized corporations. Alfonso finds himself in a "rotten mood after reading an article" that falsely claims that only maize was "grown on the manmade chinampa islands of Lake Xochimilco," when in fact, it used to be an amaranth cultivating region.[69] His anger leads him to mull on the historical fate of the crop. He recalls the violent destruction of amaranth fields during colonial times then reflects on the continued epistemic violence of modernity/coloniality against traditional knowledges. He narrates the amaranth story in a stream of consciousness:

> It winds me up, even now, that so many of our discoveries are systematically ignored at the hands of ignoramus machistus pharaonicus. Sometimes I honestly think that we're only working in the institute for the benefit of gringo academics: we're the manufacturers of juicy details [...] It'll go like this: one day some overeducated little gringo who hasn't eaten a

---

[65]. Gabriel García Márquez, *Cien Años de Soledad* (Barcelona: Debolsillo, [1967] 2010), 138.
[66]. Pablo Neruda, "Alturas de Macchu Pichu IX," in Canto General (Ayacucho: Fundación Biblioteca, 1981), 27;
César Vallejo, "Capitulación," The Complete Poetry a Bilingual Edition (Berkeley, Los Angeles, and London: University of California Press, 2007), n.p. ebook;
Pablo Neruda, "Soneto XCVIII," *Cien Sonetos de Amor*, UNAM, accessed July 6, 2020, https://www.ingenieria.unam.mx/dcsyhfi/material_didactico/Literatura_Hispanoamer icana_Contemporanea/Autores_N/NERUDA/Cien.pdf
[67]. Laia Jufresa, *Umami*, trans. Sophie Hughes (London: Oneworld, 2016), n.p. Kindle.
[68]. Ibid.
[69]. Ibid.

single crumb of amaranth in his life is going to write a book called Amaranthus, and in that book, he'll include all the stuff I've been saying for years. Or maybe he'll use the Náhuatl word, to give it an autochthonous edge: Huautli for Dummies, on sale in all good retailers and airports. They'll offer the gringo tenure in Berkeley, and then the Chinese, who already plant more amaranth than anyone, will have themselves a whole new market: middle-class America (so lost in questions of diet, so lacking in tradition, so at the mercy of the latest food-group elimination fad). Tell Me What to Eat could be the description in five words of the average, educated gringo. They'll put that processed Chinese amaranth in shiny packaging, advertise it on T.V., and export it like plastic toys. In Mexico, we'll buy it at crazy prices [...].[70]

Jufresa gives a concise summary of the failures of revivalist projects that follow the script of the Macro Foods Narrative. Availing itself of the "autochthonous edge," this narrative negates the complexities of relationships that supported traditional cultivation. These mercantilizing missions use "shiny packaging," T.V. advertisements, "good retailers, and airports" to sell the product. Their techno-managerial gaze distorts the very culture they sell—"in Mexico, we'll buy it at crazy prices." The evangelism of northern activists and philanthropists is as dangerous as the epistemic appropriation of the "gringo" who writes an entire book titled Amaranthus without having "eaten a single grain of amaranth in his life, " or the mistaken belief of consumers "at the mercy of the latest food-group elimination fad," who think that their perfunctory purchase makes a meaningful contribution to the revival of forgotten traditions.[71]

At another place in the novel, Alfonso gives a much shorter, pithy, perspective of the issue, "[...] amaranth is the food of the future. And of the past. Above all, the past."[72] The temporal affirmation was as true when the colonizers "razed kilometers of plantations, and came up with severe punishments for whoever planted it" as it is in the twenty-first century when it is snared in the narrative of modernity and the logic of coloniality.[73] The colonizers tried to erase its "future" and modernity its "past;" neither succeeded.

---

[70]. Ibid.
[71]. Ibid.
[72]. Ibid.
[73]. Ibid.

Conclusion

As it draws to a close, the article points to the vital force that fuels the nomadic incursions of the Mesoamerican and Andean amaranth, ensuring its survival despite centuries of sustained efforts towards its destruction, first by colonizers then by colonial modernity. The amaranth has acted as a "the zoe-centered embodied subject [...] shot through with relational linkages of the symbiotic, contaminating/viral kind that interconnect it to a variety of others, starting from the environmental or eco-others," wherein the human society is one of the eco-others to the amaranth.[74] The seed-grain possesses the "immanent force of zoe, that is life in its non-human aspects," it has stayed in a vital relationship with its growers, due to its nutritional content, drought resistance, and abundant yield as well as its ability to recreate gods in the form of tzoalli.[75] It possesses zoe or teotl because it has escaped "the control of the supervisory agency of the Self—built on the twin pillars of narcissism and paranoia."[76] If "zoe stands for the mindless vitality of Life carrying on independently of and regardless of rational control" and "is the dubious privilege attributed to the non-humans and to all the 'others' of Man, whereas bios refers to the specific social nexus of humans," then amaranth collapses the zoe-bios frontier, sustaining both forms of life simultaneously.[77] A researcher has posited a "cosmopolitan amaranth" because, among other reasons, it goes by "a hundred different names in innumerable local languages" in Indonesia, India, China, the Caribbean, and of course, in Latin America.[78] This article, following suit, has posited a nomadic amaranth that has repeatedly refused to occupy the time and space allocated to it, striking up new relationships, making new conversations with the changing habits and habitats around it. Recognizing the teotl and the zoe of amaranth enables one to visualize the relations it has tried to make with its earth-others, including human beings. Attempts at its techno-scientific transplanting have failed because transplanting is not a mere act of uprooting and re-rooting the plant but also the soil, air, water, and the economy of sustainable relations that allowed the plant to flourish in the first place. A superimposed bios blueprint imbued with the economy of transactions,

---

74. Rosi Braidotti, *After Cosmopolitanism* (Abingdon: Routledge, 2013), 23.

75. Rosi Braidotti, *The Posthuman* (Cambridge: Polity, 2013), 66.

76. Rosi Braidotti, *Metamorphoses* (Cambridge: Polity, 2002), 132.

77. Braidotti, *Transpositions*, 37.

78. Christopher De Shield, "The Cosmopolitan Amaranth: a Postcolonial Ecology," *Postcolonial Text*, Vol 10, No 1 (2015): 1-22, https://www.postcolonial.org/index.php/pct/article/view/187 8/1784.

Amaranthus spp., an edible genus of the species is called *bayam* in Bahasa Melayu; *cheera* in Malayalam; *yin choi* in Mandarin; *callaloo* in the Anglophone Caribbean; *cararu* in Brazilian Portuguese.

enforced assimilation, and homogenizing integration is not sustainable, a radically immanent zoe is.

Bibliography

Braidotti, Rosi. *After Cosmopolitanism.* Abingdon: Routledge, 2013.

Braidotti, Rosi. *Metamorphoses.* Cambridge and Malden: Polity, 2002.

Braidotti, Rosi. *Nomadic Subjects.* New York: Columbia University Press, 2002.

Braidotti, Rosi. *The Posthuman.* Cambridge and Malden: Polity, 2013.

Braidotti, Rosi. *Transpositions.* Cambridge and Malden: Polity, 2006.

Costea, Mihai, and Francois J. Tardiff, "The Name of the Amaranth: Histories of Meaning," SIDA, Contributions to Botany, 29 July 2003, Vol. 20, No. 3 (2003): 1073-1083.

De Shield, Christopher. "The Cosmopolitan Amaranth: a Postcolonial Ecology," Postcolonial Text, Vol 10, No 1 (2015): 1-22. https://www.postcolonial.org/index.php/pct/article/view/1878/1784.

Durán, fray Diego. *Historia de las Indias de Nueva España E islas de Tierra Firme, tomo II.* México: Editora Nacional, [1880] 1951.

Espitia Rangel, Eduardo, C. Mapes Sánchez, D. Escobedo López., M. De la O Olán, P. Rivas Valencia, G. Martínez Trejo, L. Cortés Espinoza, J.M. Hernández Casillas. *Conservación y uso de los recursos genéticos de Amaranto en México.* Celaya: INIFAP, Centro de Investigación Regional Centro, 2010.

García Canclini, Néstor. "Cultura transnacional y culturas populares en México," *Cuadernos* Hispanoamericanos, núm. 431 (mayo 1986): 5-18.

García Márquez, Gabriel. *Cien Años de Soledad,* Barcelona: Debolsillo, [1967] 2010.

Gutiérrez Rodríguez, Patricia. "Recuperación del Cultivo de Amaranto va por buen camino." La jornada de oriente, October 12, 2020. Accessed March 24, 2020. https://www.lajornadadeoriente.com.mx/puebla/recuperacion-del-cultivo-del-amaranto-va-por-buen-camino-colegio-de-posgraduados/.

Hebjørnsrud, Dag. "The Mesoamerican Philosophy Renaissance." Blog of the APA, January 9, (2020). Accessed July 7, 2020. https://blog.apaonline.org/2020/01/09/the-mesoamerican-philosophy-renaissance/.

Hernández Bermejo, J.E., and J. León, eds. *Cultivos Marginados, Otra Perspectiva de 1492.* Rome: FAO de la ONU, 1992.

Jufresa, Laia. *Umami,* translated by Sophie Hughes. London: Oneworld, 2016. Kindle ed.

Klein, Cecilia F. "A New Interpretation of the Aztec Statue Called Coatlicue, 'Snakes-Her-Skirt,'" *Ethnology,* April (2008): 229-250.

León Portilla, Miguel. *La Filosofía Náhuatl.* Mexico: UNAM, 1993.

Macdonald, Laura. "A Mixed Blessing: The NGO Boom in Latin America, NACLA Report on the Americas." In *NACLA Report on the Americas,* 28:5 (1995): 30-35. doi: 10.1080/10714839.1995.11725795.

Mapes Sánchez, Cristina. "El Amaranto (Amaranthus spp.) planta originaria de México." *Academia, Ciencia y Cultura AAPAUNAM,* (4) (2010): 217-222. https://www.medigraphic.com/pdfs/aapaunam/pa-2010/pa104e.pdf.

Matsumoto, Nancy. "Why Mexican Chefs, Farmers, and Activists are Reviving the Ancient Amaranth," *npr*, May 1, 2017. Accessed March 24, 2020. https://www. npr.org/sections/thesalt/2017/05/01/526033083/why-mexican-chefs-farmers-and-activists-are-reviving-the-ancient-grain-amaranth

McDonnel, Emma. "Miracle Foods: Quinoa, Curative Metaphors, and the Depoliticization of Global Hunger Politics." *Gastronomica*, Vol. 15, No. 4 (Winter 2015): 70-85. https://www.jstor.org/stable/10.2307/26362298.

McEwan, Colin, Andrew Middleton, Caroline Cartwright, and Rebecca Stacey. *Turquoise Mosaics from Mexico*. Durham and London: Duke University Press, 2006.

Mignolo, Walter D. "Reconstitución epistémica/estética: la aesthesis decolonial una década después," *Calle 14: revista de investigación en el campo del arte* 14 (25) (2019): 14-32, https://doi.org/10.14483/21450706.14132.

Mignolo, Walter D. *The Darker Side of Western Modernity*. Durham and London: Duke University Press, 2010,

Neruda, Pablo. "Alturas de Macchu Pichu IX," In *Canto General*. Ayacucho: Fundación Biblioteca, 1981.

Neruda, Pablo. "Soneto XCVIII." In *Cien Sonetos de Amor*. UNAM, n.p. Accessed July 6, 2020, https://www.ingenieria.unam.mx/dcsyhfi/material_didactico/Literatura_Hispanoamericana_Contemporanea/Autores_N/NERUDA/Cien.pdf

Ortiz, Fernando. *Cuban Counterpoint: Tobacco and Sugar*, translated by Harriet de Onis. Durham and London: Duke University Press, 1995. https://archive.org/details/cubancounterpoin02orti/page/n7/mode/2up

Pérez-Abadín Barro, Soledad. *Resonare silvas: la tradición bucólica en la poesía del siglo XVI*. Santiago de Compostela: Santiago de Compostela University Press, 2004.

Potter, Van Rensselaer, "Bioethics, the Science of Survival." *Perspectives in Biology and Medicine*, Volume 14, Number 1, Autumn (1970): 127-153.

Purcell, Lynn Sebastian. "Eudaimonia and Neltiliztli: Aristotle and the Aztecs on the Good Life." *Newsletter: The American Philosophical Association*, Volume 16 No. 2, Spring (2017): 10-21.

Rivero Weber, Paulina, and Ruy Pérez Tamayo, "Ética y Bioética." *nexos*, July (2006): 23-27.

Sahagún, fray Bernardino de. *Historia General de las Cosas de Nueva España Tomo Primero*, México: Alejandro Valdés, 1829.

Sauer, Carl O. "Cultivated Plants of South and Central America." In *Handbook of South American Indians*, edited by J.H. Steward., 487-583. Washington, D.C.: United States Government Printing Office, 1950.

Smith, Preserved. "Christian Theophagy: An Historical Sketch." *The Monist* Vol. 28, No. 2 April (1918): 161-208. https://www.jstor.org/stable/27900680.

Sólon, Pablo. "The Rights of Mother Earth." In *The Climate Crisis*, edited by Vishwas Satgar, 107-130. Johannesburg: Wits University Press, 2018.

Uruñuela Ladrón de Guevera, Gabriela, and Patricia Plunket Nagoda, "Las maquetas de montes-deidades de amaranto de Posclásico." *Arqueología*, núm. 138, Marzo-abril (2016): n.p. Digital edition.

Vallejo, César. "Capitulación." In *The Complete Poetry*, a Bilingual Edition, n.p. ebook. Berkeley, Los Angeles, and London: University of California Press, 2007.

Velasco Lozano, Ana María, "Los cuerpos divinos. El amaranto: comida ritual y cotidiana." *Arqueología Mexicana* núm. 138, Marzo-abril (2016): n.p. Digital edition.

Villavicencio Calzadilla, Paola and Louij J. Kotzé. "Living in Harmony with Nature?" Transnational *Environmental Law*, 7:3 (2018): 397—424.

Whicker, Jules, ed. *The Plays of Juan Ruiz de Alarcón.* Woodbridge: Tamesis, 2003.

Chapter 3

The Serengeti-Mara ecosystem: Interactions between human and non-human species

Olivia A. Kurajian

Michigan State University

Abstract

Lions, wildebeest, hyenas, and giraffes dominate the imagination when one thinks of African savannas. The Serengeti-Mara is an ecosystem that is poorly understood by many despite being one of the most studied ecosystems in the world. The region comprising today's artificially constructed bordered countries of Tanzania and Kenya is home to millions of animals and humans. Although this ecosystem is referred to as the Serengeti in Tanzania and the Mara in Kenya, the Serengeti-Mara is an interconnected system. Its health and sustainability rely on the interactions between human and non-human species of animals and fauna. Since the world has lost one-fourth of all large grazers in the last couple of centuries, preservation of the migration of wildebeest, zebras, gazelles, and other species is absolutely essential to maintaining the rich diversity of this vast ecosystem. One such method of preservation, pastoralism, is a vital example of savanna wildlife-human interaction. While cast as a backward, uncivilized, or primitive when seen through the Western, colonial lens, pastoralism has served human and non-human species in a variety of ways. The complexity and history of the Serengeti-Mara are laced with environmental narratives, numerous conservation efforts, and Indigenous resistance and agency while facing colonial land dispossession and climatic changes. This paper discusses how the survival and sustainability of pastoralism in the Serengeti-Mara are challenged by competing colonial powers, inequalities in power, environmental destruction, and both human actions and inaction.

Keywords: Pastoralism, Serengeti-Mara, ecosystem, sustainability, Indigenous studies, colonialism

***

While the Serengeti-Mara's ecosystem has been extensively studied by ecologists, there remains a dearth of study on the agency of pastoralist Indigenous communities.[1] This area of African savanna is geographically situated within the internationally recognized national borders of Tanzania and Kenya. The physical space encapsulates a diverse socio-ecologic structure. The region is a receptacle for incalculable interaction between human and non-human species. The ecosystem carries two names—the "Serengeti" in Tanzania and the "Mara" in Kenya. Restructuring the Serengeti-Mara system of environmental management from a bottom-up approach would be beneficial to the preservation of the region. While the world has lost one-fourth of all large grazers in the last couple of centuries, the Serengeti-Mara ecological landscape has been similarly threatened. Preservation projects for animals like wildebeest, zebras, gazelles, are urgently required as tourism, government, and grassroots efforts towards sustainable development, and hunting, directly and indirectly, diminish their populations.[2] Pastoralism is one vital example of savanna wildlife-human interaction. Pastoralists are often the subject of Western romanticization. Bruce Chatwin's *It's a Nomad Nomad World,* and Raymond Williams' *The Country and the City* illuminate a simplistic and romantic view of nomadism and pastoralism.[3] However, pastoralists' relationship with the region's ecology is complicated. Their actions are vital to the maintenance of biodiversity in the Serengeti-Mara. The object of this current study is to reimagine pastoralists as people who positively impact their environment and support diverse ecosystems while dispelling the discriminatory and harmful Western notions of primitiveness and simplicity. Rather, the relationship between humans and wildlife in the savanna landscape is, in the absence of disruptive interventions, symbiotic, mutually beneficial, and complex. Champions of the environmental conservatism movement clash with indigenous activists and local pastoralists.[4]

Environmental and Ecological Understanding

The Serengeti-Mara ecosystem is commonly conceived along manmade lines—physical fences, imaginary national borders, and distinct human communities. One of the ways in which this natural landscape has been divided

---

[1]. Robin Spencer Reid, *Savannas of Our Birth: People, Wildlife, and Change in East Africa* (Berkeley: University of California Press, 2012), 22.

[2]. Ibid, 42-45.

[3]. John Ure, In Search of Nomads : An Anglo-American Obsession from Hester Stanhope to Bruce Chatwin, Carroll and Graf. New York: 2003 and Raymond Williams and Tristram Hunt, The Country and the City, Vintage Classics. London: Vintage, 2016.

[4]. Reid, *Savannas of Our Birth,* 160.

was through the creation of protected spaces. To maintain the area's biodiversity and preserve resources for future use, both the Tanzanian and Kenyan governments have each created national parks. Disruptions to the region's biodiversity compromise the balancing forces of its ecosystem.[5] As such, the Serengeti National Park in Tanzania and the Maasai Mara National Reserve in Kenya serve as a haven for both human and non-human species of animals. While the national reserves only encompass a small fraction of the Serengeti-Mara's ecosystem that spans some 25,000 km squared, they are important to the maintenance of biodiversity in the area. As three-quarters of the ecosystem lies in Tanzania and one-quarter lies in Kenya, both countries have an obligation to protect the ecosystem within their national borders.[6]

During dry seasons and droughts, the Serengeti-Mara serves as a haven. Its higher preponderance of water attracts vast migrations. Two notable migrations of wildebeest, the Serengeti migration and the Loita migration, present a unique aspect of this ecosystem. Threats to the biodiversity and health of the ecosystem continue to grow as humans populate the area, and their collective actions propagate pollution. However, "At low human population densities, people can extract sufficient resources and receive additional benefits from PAs (protected areas) without compromising them, and conversely, PAs can profit from the presence of people."[7] Climate change will worsen and suffocate communities of human and non-human species as competition for resources is augmented.[8] Drought and other variable meteorological phenomena will force more competition for resources. The preponderance of infectious diseases has also wreaked havoc on wildlife populations as weather conditions and space limitations continue to manipulate the environment. Temporal trends and variation in rainfall can predict the availability of potable or usable water and the health of vegetation in a given place.[9] Destruction of natural habitats and climate change can lead to outbreaks of infectious animal diseases. The unavailability of quality vegetation for herbivores prompts irregular migrations.[10] These diseases and conditions displace animals and people

---

[5]. Jeffrey Sachs and Ban Ki-moon, *The Age of Sustainable Development* (New York: Columbia University Press, 2015), 24-28.

[6]. Reid, 102.

[7]. Michiel P Veldhuis et al, "Cross-Boundary Human Impacts Compromise the Serengeti-Mara Ecosystem." *Science* 363, no. 6434 (2019): 1.

[8]. Ibid, 1.

[9]. Gundula S Bartzke et. al, "Rainfall Trends and Variation in the Maasai Mara Ecosystem and their Implications for Animal Population and Biodiversity Dynamics," *Plos One* 13, no. 9 (2018): 2.

[10]. Ibid, 2.

already caught in the interwoven narratives of colonialism and environments. There is a cap on the number of people that can coexist alongside the wildlife and environment of the Serengeti-Mara without compromising its health and while contributing to it. Unfortunately, the human populations surrounding the parks have already surpassed a sort of "tipping point."[11] Wildlife populations have reduced outside of the parks. In fact, "population growth and urbanization have occurred in parallel with land tenure changes in," the Serengeti-Mara as, "rapid population increase has led to more settlements which in turn has led to the fabrication of fences being built, blocking the traditional wildlife migration routes."[12] By rerouting wildlife and challenging the environment with increased human populations, conversations about privatized property and land rights are increasingly important.[13]

Property and Land Rights

Dispossession, disparity, and the politics surrounding land use are issues in today's African pastoralist communities. In the Serengeti-Mara, these issues are exacerbated by the regional divides between the two bordering countries: Tanzania and Kenya. Most recently, two specific transformations have changed the savanna landscape. Humans exert increasing pressure on the land through the growing population. They have "modif[ied] the open nature of savanna landscapes by erecting fences, clearing farms, constructing towns, and the like."[14] Colonial and postcolonial governments and agencies are attracted to the biodiversity and riches of the Serengeti-Mara yet, have been consistently dismissive of the welfare of Indigenous inhabitants—both human and non-human.[15] The second transformative change is the closing of land for conservation purposes. Protective isolation can be damaging to Indigenous populations. Governmental measures of land control too often result in the dispossession or annexation of land traditionally managed and cultivated by pastoralists. With a majority (more than 85%) of households in Kitengela engaged in some sort of economic activity off their land, there is room to

---

[11]. Reid, 172-180.

[12]. Katherine Homewood, Patricia Kristjanson and Pippa Trench, *Staying Maasai?: Livelihoods, Conservation, and Development in East African Rangelands* (Studies in Human Ecology and Adaptation, New York, NY: Springer, 2009), 120.

[13]. Richard H Lamprey and Robin S Reid, "Special Paper: Expansion of Human Settlement in Kenya's Maasai Mara: What Future for Pastoralism and Wildlife?" *Journal of Biogeography* 31, no. 6 (2004): 998.

[14]. Reid, 169.

[15]. Jeffrey Sachs and Ban Ki-moon, *The Age of Sustainable Development.* (New York: Columbia University Press, 2015), 55-68.

consider that the fenced parcels that peoples like the Maasai are increasingly inhabiting do not provide enough resources for survival.[16] It is worth noting that:

> [...] many local Maasai realize how difficult it can be to keep large herds within a fast-shrinking grazing space, with multiple landowners and increasing mobility restrictions. More and more are investing in plots in the shopping centers, whether developed or undeveloped, with the hope of earning a regular income that is less susceptible to droughts and other periodic shocks.[17]

As grazing areas are threatened, and a capitalist cash economy threatens to uproot the social order of the human activities in the savanna, the delicate balance between human and wildlife is disrupted. The collapse of the wildlife-human relationship in the Serengeti-Mara would be disastrous as "the long-term viability of both the hunted and hunter livelihoods are contingent upon the presence of shared mutual ecologies, within which the dynamics of wildlife populations directly influence both the coproduction of niches and the renegotiation of hunters' nature-culture."[18] Unsurprisingly, the Indigenous peoples like the "Maasai have very little influence over decisions made regarding their resources" despite their proximity and knowledge of the needs in their families and communities.[19] In this colonial and paternalistic worldview, Indigenous peoples are cast not as vulnerable, but incapable of enacting change in their communities as far away others 'know best'. Seen as actors with little to no agency and in need of salvation from external forces, Indigenous peoples are subjected to the disastrous white savior complex. In The Will to Improve, Tania Li asserts that "the need to protect culturally distinct and especially vulnerable others has been a repetitive theme among trustees from colonial officials of the old school reacting to native dispossession in the late nineteenth century continuing through present times."[20] Currently, however, Indigenous agency is starting to become more prevalent in response

---

[16]. Katherine Homewood, Patricia Kristjanson and Pippa Trench, *Staying Maasai?: Livelihoods, Conservation, and Development in East African Rangelands* (Studies in Human Ecology and Adaptation, New York, NY: Springer, 2009), 120-144.

[17]. Ibid.

[18]. Carolyn A Jost Robinson Melissa J Remis, "Entangled Realms: Hunters and Hunted in the Dzanga-Sangha Dense Forest Reserve (Apds), Central African Republic," *Anthropological Quarterly* 87, no. 3 (2014): 623.

[19]. Homewood, Kristjanson and Trench, *Staying Maasai*, 125.

[20]. Tania Murray Li, *The Will to Improve: Governmentality, Development, and the Practice of Politics* (Durham: Duke University Press, 2017), 34.

to continued inequalities and disputes over land rights. Maasai, in particular, are resisting parks aimed to protect capitalist interests and contain species of animals threatened by human action and inaction. In some ways, the creation of parks propagates capitalist interests as natural reserve borders serve as a hub for local commerce and tourism activities. All human activity in the parks has resulted in ecosystem engineering, which is defined as "an innovative concept that recognizes that organisms impact their environment and that these changes can be detected over time."[21] Indigenous peoples, who have worked as ecosystem engineers and have served an increasingly understood role in maintaining the health and biodiversity of the ecosystems now enclosed within protected areas, are now criminalized.[22] Through committing small acts of disobedience in order to maintain autonomy like continuing to use parkland for their animals, pastoralists are making their agency apparent.[23] With millions of people living on the fringe of these parks, herders and their livestock enter the reserve frequently when grass or other resources are exhausted in designated pastoral lands outside the reserve. These small actions often create a considerable impact as sometimes large-scale disruptions can lead to chaos instead of progress.[24] Restricting hunting and firearm possession is often to the detriment of the local people. Hardened borders and restrictions of activities endanger their livelihoods. Although there are serious implications with overcrowding and resource management, the enactment of hard boundaries designating parkland inaccessible to surrounding settlements has allowed Indigenous groups to unsustainably reap the benefits of ecotourism or wildlife payments. Consequently, previously pastoral households are un-knowingly participating in the phenomenon Reid calls "The Honey Pot Effect," wherein they benefit from this model.[25] As more and more tourists come to the park, local people are enticed by settlement near a reliable cash source. However, the wildlife contained within the parks and the humans positioned at the margins of the parks simultaneously encounter problems. Pastoralists bear witness to wild predators, predominantly hyenas, threatening their livestock. Often, pastoralists resort to poisoning predators with cheap insecticide, killing predators and scavengers who eat the now toxic carcasses of the predators.

21. Ventresca Miller et al, "Ecosystem Engineering among Ancient Pastoralists in Northern Central Asia," *Frontiers in Earth Science* (2020): 1.

22. Johan Colding and Carl Folke, "Social Taboos: 'Invisible' Systems of Local Resource Management and Biological Conservation" *Ecological Applications* 11, no. 2 (2001): 584.

23. James C. Scott, *Two Cheers for Anarchism: Six Easy Pieces on Autonomy, Dignity, and Meaningful Work and Play* (Princeton: Princeton University Press, 2014), 43-44.

24. Ibid, 468-472.

25. Reid, 158-170.

Thus, the local population's attempt to protect its livestock impacts the entire system by the state impacts the entire system.[26] In an attempt to curb the damage to livestock or to fulfill subsistence needs, some Indigenous groups also hunt these predators. The animal killings serve to substantiate claims made by the government that indigenous people are destroying the biodiversity and upsetting the ecological health of the savanna. These examples should not overshadow the experience and expertise that pastoralists have shown in managing the lands in traditional and locally-oriented ways. Nonetheless, in 2010, the Kenyan government adopted a new constitution in which local peoples have a stronger voice in the decisions regarding land use.[27] Maasai and other Indigenous peoples are ejected off their lands to make room for conservancies and at the will and service of central and local government bodies. As Tania Li explains, the poorest sections of society are the easiest to manipulate and displace.[28] Moringe Ole Parkipuny, the former Tanzanian minister of Parliament, stated regarding the Maasai resistance to the parks, "The eviction of Indigenous people from their land is a barbaric alienation of those people who have been the vanguards of conservation."[29]

Conservation

Pastoralists, like the Maasai, are inextricably linked to the landscape of the Serengeti-Mara. For centuries, the rich biodiversity of this region relied upon complex relationships between animals and humans to control the population and enhance the land. However, the Western conceptualization of 'conservation' has historically conceived solutions to animal extinction and environmental destruction as those absent from human intervention or involvement in the landscape. According to Muhumuza, too often, "conservation of biodiversity in National Parks is done through the...preservation approach, which aims at setting aside National Parks to exclude human activities except for tourism."[30] The preservation approach excludes pastoralists, who previously have the land for their daily activities. In light of this knowledge, conservation measures for wildlife are consequently exclusionary and unsustainable. The idea of the

26. Ibid.
27. Ibid.
28. Li, *The Will to Improve*, 88.
29. Reid, 179.
30. Moses Muhumuza Kevin Balkwill, "Factors Affecting the Success of Conserving Biodiversity in National Parks: A Review of Case Studies from Africa," *International Journal of Biodiversity* 2013, 1.

landscape, as an area devoid of human activity, coalesced in colonial times.[31] This characterization is disseminated in Western popular media. Conservation efforts must seek to restore this utopian balance.[32] Although the beloved Western childhood Disney film, The Lion King (1994), perpetrates these harmonious images, the 'circle of life' does not exclude human beings.[33] Nor does it mean that the pastoralists who have coevolved and coexisted in the savannas are the fundamental source of environmental destruction. Humans have had and continue to have indisputable impacts on the ecosystem engineering of the Serengeti-Mara as hunters, pastoralists, farmers, and active participants. Thus:

> [...] it is possible that humans—hunter-gatherers and herders—actually created this open Serengeti-Mara landscape. If people created the Serengeti-Mara ecosystem in the first place, it could suggest that the best way to sustain the ecosystem is for people to continue to use and maintain it in a similar, traditional way.[34]

Capitalists and colonial forces tend to view large-scale farming as a productive, profitable, and preferred method of land use. In a short 35-year-span, three-quarters of the water from the Mara River during the dry season has been pumped into irrigation fields, and more than one-third of the trees in the Mau Forest was destroyed to fuel the drive towards capitalism and human population growth.[35] While "livestock sales are a particularly important aspect of life in pastoral communities as these sales provide the mechanism and opportunity for pastoralists to integrate into the cash economy, allowing access to a variety of non-traditional products (e.g., tea, sugar, maize meal)," these small-scale financial exchanges are not damaging to wildlife populations, and environmental hazards like farming can be.[36] In fact, farming is "wildlife-incompatible" and traditional uses of the land practiced by pastoralists is

---

[31]. Melissa Leach and Robin Mearns, *The Lie of the Land: Challenging Received Wisdom on the African Environment* (African Issues. Oxford: International African Institute in association with James Currey, 1996), 89-103.

[32]. Li, 77.

[33]. Megan S. Lloyd, *To Be or Not to Be The Lion King Existentialism in Disney and Shakespeare* in Richard Brian Davis, ed. *Disney and Philosophy: Truth, Trust, and a Little Bit of Pixie Dust*, The Blackwell Philosophy and Pop Culture Series, Hoboken, NJ: Wiley-Blackwell, 2020, 148.

[34]. Reid, 176.

[35]. Reid, 104-20.

[36]. Katherine Homewood, Patricia Kristjanson and Pippa Trench, *Staying Maasai?: Livelihoods, Conservation, and Development in East African Rangelands* (Studies in Human Ecology and Adaptation, New York, NY: Springer, 2009), 144.

infinitely better in terms of sustaining biodiversity and ecological conservation.[37] Even so, today, the majority of pastoralists engage in some form of land cultivation. This cultivation can be for personal or economic advancement.[38] The fencing off of the land for farming and certain conservation goals obstruct wildlife migration and is particularly problematic in terms of access to essential resources like water for both humans and animals. The Tanzanian government has considered the construction of a highway that would irrevocably reduce the wildebeest population in the ecosystem.[39] As water accessibility is one of the most controversial components in this narrative, it is often at the forefront of conversations regarding conservation.[40] Unfortunately, the "Serengeti-Mara ecosystem is governed by a variety of models of conservation, principally differing by who has the power to decide who uses the land and how who bears the cost of conservation and who garners the benefits (profits) from wildlife."[41] What is apparent is that the benefits are often split between governments and tourism businesses.[42] As parks were created as a form of conservation, "The Asi, Ishenya, Ngorme, Ikoma, Sukuma, Kuria, Tautog, Sikazi, and Maasai peoples lost a great deal of their land when the colonial and postcolonial governments created the Tanzanian and Kenyan parks and reserves, which was done sometimes with and sometimes without consultation."[43] Without local knowledge and consultation, conservation groups are doing a great disservice to the cause they are trying to further. As seen in various ecosystems around the world, many conservation plans are enacted and managed by those who have no direct connection with the land, often international corporate actors and faraway governments.[44] These governments often misunderstand the positive impacts that pastoralism has on the savanna, and thus they problematize and forbid traditional activities. In fact, as ecosystem engineers, pastoralists have practiced environmental conservation through their activities without explicit intent.[45] However, this type of conservation is often downplayed

---

[37]. Reid, 104-20.

[38]. Katherine Homewood, Patricia Kristjanson and Pippa Trench, *Staying Maasai?: Livelihoods, Conservation, and Development in East African Rangelands* (Studies in Human Ecology and Adaptation, New York, NY: Springer, 2009), 148.

[39]. Ibid.

[40]. D. J Campbell, H. Gichohi, A. Mwangi and L. Chege, "Land use conflict in Kajiado District, Kenya," in *Land Use Policy*, 17, 4, October 1, (2000): 337-348.

[41]. Reid, 174.

[42]. Ibid.

[43]. Ibid.

[44]. Dan Egan, *The Death and Life of the Great Lakes* (First ed. New York: W.W. Norton & Company, 2017), 56.

[45]. Reid, 174.

as ecotourism, and the creation of parks can take center stage. This values nature in financial terms instead of as something inherently worthy of conservation.[46] Yet, a place with such impressive biodiversity is still one of the poorest regions in the world. Even though Tanzania has experienced economic growth in the last decade, the beneficiaries of this growth are often urban dwellers, not those on the outskirts of nature reserves.[47]

Humans and wildlife have interacted in the Serengeti-Mara savanna for thousands of years. This ecosystem has been home to billions of inhabitants; human and non-human. Fauna, animals, and humans have all participated in the formation and maintenance of this ever-changing environment. Infectious diseases like rinderpest, tsetse flies, and smallpox, explosions in human populations, colonial and postcolonial governments, climate change, human land dispossession, and illegal poaching have contributed to the problems facing the Serengeti-Mara today. However, pastoralists have contributed to its survival "by using it only moderately, they sustained it, intentionally or unintentionally, over millennia, and that is why the ecosystem is as rich as it is today."[48] Pastoralists, although incredibly powerful as ecosystem engineers, have had a difficult time unifying their interests and causes in a political arena. Yet, pastoralists have coexisted and coevolved with wildlife for centuries and continue to be influential in conservation efforts, whether or not it is intentional. The misunderstanding on the part of faraway governments that pastoralists are detrimental to the Serengeti-Mara runs contrary to the way in which these groups have been ecosystem engineers and have promoted wildlife migrations. Today, the Mara is primarily managed by local peoples, whereas the Serengeti is managed by governments located far from the source of issues.[49] Just as wildebeest continue to migrate in search of water in the dry season, the poorest households in the savanna tend to seek employment as wage laborers in the towns and cities. Those who have remained pastoralists tend to be in constant contact with wildlife and in touch with ecological patterns.[50]

Moving forward, it is important that conservation efforts are compatible with social goals. The best way to ensure that the wildlife-human interactions in the

46. Ibid, 168-179.

47. Ibid.

48. Ibid.

49. Ibid.

50. Katherine Homewood, Patricia Kristjanson and Pippa Trench, *Staying Maasai?: Livelihoods, Conservation, and Development in East African Rangelands* (Studies in Human Ecology and Adaptation, New York, NY: Springer, 2009), 56-78.

Serengeti-Mara stay healthy is to "provide information to help [local peoples] understand, adapt and cope as it is the communities themselves that must negotiate the new and more evidence-based land, agricultural, wildlife conservation and other policies that will improve their levels of wellbeing sustainably over the long run."[51] Both Indigenous peoples and wildlife have been subjected to land dispossession and hardened borders, making access to resources less reliable. The destruction of forests and diversions of rivers to irrigate farmlands create insurmountable barriers to vast migrations of large mammalian species and threaten human livelihoods. The Serengeti-Mara is a landscape dominated not only by elephants and lions but by human-wildlife interactions and relationships. The solution is restructuring community-based conservation efforts that reimagine pastoralists as a source of local and ecological knowledge whose lives and livelihoods depend on the relationship between themselves and their environment.

Bibliography

Bartzke, Gundula S, Joseph O Ogutu, Sabyasachi Mukhopadhyay, Devolent Mtui, Holly T Dublin, Hans-Peter Piepho, and Suzannah Rutherford. "Rainfall Trends and Variation in the Maasai Mara Ecosystem and their Implications for Animal Population and Biodiversity Dynamics." *Plos One* 13, no. 9 (2018). https://doi.org/10.1371/journal.pone.0202814.

Campbell D. J, H. Gichohi, A. Mwangi and L. Chege, "Land use conflict in Kajiado District, Kenya," in *Land Use Policy*, 17, 4, October 1, (2000): 337-348.

Colding, Johan, and Carl Folke. "Social Taboos: 'Invisible' Systems of Local Resource Management and Biological Conservation." *Ecological Applications* 11, no. 2 (2001): 584—600.

Davis, Richard Brian, ed. *Disney and Philosophy: Truth, Trust, and a Little Bit of Pixie Dust*. The Blackwell Philosophy and Pop Culture Series. Hoboken, NJ: Wiley-Blackwell, 2020.

Egan, Dan. *The Death and Life of the Great Lakes*. New York: W.W. Norton & Company, 2017.

Homewood, Katherine, Patricia Kristjanson, and Pippa Trench. *Staying Maasai?: Livelihoods, Conservation, and Development in East African Rangelands*. Studies in Human Ecology and Adaptation, New York, NY: Springer, 2009.

Lamprey, Richard H, and Robin S Reid. "Special Paper: Expansion of Human Settlement in Kenya's Maasai Mara: What Future for Pastoralism and Wildlife?" Journal of Biogeography 31, no. 6 (2004): 997—1032.

Leach, Melissa, and Robin Mearns.*The Lie of the Land: Challenging Received Wisdom on the African Environment. African Issues*. Oxford: International African Institute in association with James Currey, 1996.

Li, Tania Murray. *The Will to Improve: Governmentality, Development, and the Practice of Politics*. Durham: Duke University Press, 2017.

---

51. Ibid.

Muhumuza, Moses, and Kevin Balkwill. "Factors Affecting the Success of Conserving Biodiversity in National Parks: A Review of Case Studies from Africa." *International Journal of Biodiversity* (2013): 1-20.

Reid, Robin Spencer. *Savannas of Our Birth: People, Wildlife, and Change in East Africa.* Berkeley: University of California Press, 2012.

Robinson, Carolyn A. Jost, and Melissa J Remis. "Entangled Realms: Hunters and Hunted in the Dzanga-Sangha Dense Forest Reserve (Apds), Central Africa Republic." *Anthropological Quarterly* 87, no. 3 (2014): 613-36.

Sachs, Jeffrey, and Ban Ki-moon. *The Age of Sustainable Development.* New York: Columbia University Press, 2015.

Scott, James C. *Two Cheers for Anarchism: Six Easy Pieces on Autonomy, Dignity, and Meaningful Work and Play.* Princeton: Princeton University Press, 2014.

Ure, John. *In Search of Nomads: An Anglo-American Obsession from Hester Stanhope to Bruce Chatwin.* New York: Carroll and Graf, 2003.

Veldhuis, Michiel P, Mark E Ritchie, Joseph O Ogutu, Thomas A Morrison et al. "Cross-Boundary Human Impacts Compromise the Serengeti-Mara *Ecosystem.*" Science 363, no. 6434 (2019): 1424-1428.

Ventresca Miller, Alicia R., Robert Spengler, Ashleigh Haruda, Bryan Miller, Shevan Wilkin, Sarah Robinson, Patrick Roberts, and Nicole Boivin. "Ecosystem Engineering among Ancient Pastoralists in Northern Central Asia." *Frontiers in Earth Science* (2020). https://doi.org/10.3389/feart.2020.00168.

Williams, Raymond, and Tristram Hunt. *The Country and the City.* London: Vintage, 2016.

Chapter 4

Adda as a cultural discourse of the Bengali Bhadralok's provincial cosmopolitanism

Prantik Banerjee

Hislop College, Nagpur, India

Abstract

Adda became very popular in nineteenth-century Bengal when the British ruled India. Its popularity was both enabled by westernization and a reaction to it. Europe, world politics, and especially England were always tied to adda. Historically, adda has been a cultural marker that has defined Bengali urban, middle-class, male identity. It is a kind of informal social talk in Bengali, among friends and colleagues, but its content is always of intellectual significance, addressing issues such as local/global politics, art, literature, and music. The article will analyze the manner in which adda as a verbal performative act created two seemingly contradictory narratives: one, which helped instill among Bengali men from the urban, educated middle-class, a provinciality that gave their subjugated status as a colonial subject a certain degree of pride bordering on subversion; second, a contradictory narrative of the Bengali as a cosmopolitan citizen of the world; one who could, with others, generate a collective and participatory discourse where Baudelaire and Bankim, communism and communalism, football and cricket, Che Guevara and Chairman Mao, and jatra and opera were all mingled in a celebratory mode. The article argues that the oppositional attributes of adda are held in fine balance as it tracks the ways in which the provenance of adda in Bengali cultural identity moved from nineteenth-century rural meeting spaces to today's worldwide web chat rooms.

Keywords: Male identity, colonial subject, provincial cosmopolitanism, performative, collective identity

***

Adda is a part of Bengali modernity and has historically been a cultural marker that has defined the identity of the Bengali urban middle-class male. It is a kind of informal social talk in Bengali among friends and colleagues, but its content is always intellectual, addressing issues such as local/global politics, art, literature, and music. Also notable is the urban setting of adda situated in padas (phonetically /pa:[a/) or localities. As a word, it means both a form of talk and a place associated with it. In Kolkata, for instance, young men cluster on "rawks" (narrow platforms outside a dwelling house), parks, bus-terminals, and canteens too. Adda became very popular in Bengal in the nineteenth and twentieth centuries, when the British ruled India. Its popularity was both enabled by westernization and a reaction to it because the cultural horizons of Europe, England, and world politics always provided the intellectual lens for articulation in adda. Today in the popular imagination, adda has become synonymous with Bengaliness, a cultural marker as prominent as the Bengali's craze for rosogollas and football.

My paper investigates the role adda played in the formation of Bengali identity, giving it a singular attribute that I call provincial cosmopolitanism. Dipesh Chakrabarty, in his seminal book *Provincializing Europe: Postcolonial Thought and Historical Difference*, terms this peculiar speech act of the Bengali community as "national," but I extend its scope to signify a worldliness that was rooted simultaneously at home—home not just as a country to which one belongs or even a "national imaginary," but also home as localized as one's street, road and pada (locality).[1] This worldliness indicated a Weltanschauung, a certain intellectual orientation that made the Bengali's love of adda a lifestyle and a cultural mode often reflecting the contestatory pulls of cosmopolitanism and nationalism. In my paper, I have also termed this unique cultural and social phenomenon as bhadralok cosmopolitanism to signify a form of cosmopolitanism that was prevalent among a particular class in the Bengali community—the middle-class. My paper aims to show that in its normative, privileged, and exclusionary traits, this was a cosmopolitanism from above and not below, and was partly responsible for the failure of Bengal's modernity project.

I will attempt to demonstrate that the adda as a verbal performative act created two seemingly oppositional narratives for the Bengali bhadralok of the late nineteenth and early twentieth centuries. On the one hand, it helped instill a claim to provinciality in the Bengali urban educated man from the middle-class, which gave a certain degree of pride and exclusivity, bordering on resistance and subversion, to his subjugated status as a colonial subject. On the other hand, embedded in the formation of this adda identity was another narrative of the Bengali as a cosmopolitan citizen of the world. It generated a transnational, collective and participatory discourse where Baudelaire and Bankim Chandra Chatterjee, communism and communalism, football and

---

[1]. Dipesh Chakrabarty, *Provincializing Europe: Postcolonial Thought and Historical Difference* (Princeton: Princeton University Press, 2000).

cricket, Che Guevara and Chairman Mao, jatra and opera, could mingle in a sort of carnivalesque celebratory mode.

As a supplementary to my main argument, I will also show that with reference to the Bengali's adda, the cultural and social tropes of ghare-baire (home and the world), local/global, provincial/cosmopolitan, may not be seen as limiting binaries signifying only geographical and cultural distinctions.[2] Instead, I will demonstrate that the adda for the "permanently interstitial Bengali middleclass" got traction because, in its practice, both were held in fine balance.[3] My essay uses the theoretical framework of the revisionist writing of Bengal's social history that Dipesh Chakrabarty, Partha Chatterjee, and Ashish Nandy have constructed in the last thirty years.

The word adda is translated, by the Bengali linguist Suniti Kumar Chattopadhyay, as a place for conversation. According to the online edition of the Oxford Dictionary, adda (pronounced, ud-dah) is "a place where people gather for conversation" or an act of informal conversations among a group of like-minded people.[4] The word adda denotes both a place and the action itself. To give adda, or adda deya in Bengali, actually means the situated activity and the participation in the activity itself. Adda is thus both a mediated speech genre and a discursive practice through, and in which (hi)stories are told and contested. Satyajit Ray, the famous Indian film-maker, in his film Agantuk, showed the adda as originating in ancient Greece where rhetoric was practiced in the pursuance of truth.[5] The central character in the film is a globe-trotting uncle who, on a visit to India, strikes a friendship with a young boy, the son of his only relative. In one of his many tales of traveling abroad, the uncle regales his young listener about the origin of adda and its unique place in Bengali culture.

In 1991, on the occasion of the tercentenary celebrations of the founding of the city of Calcutta, an anthology titled *Kolkatar Adda* was released during the annual book fair. The historian Shamrendra Das noted in his preface to the book that adda was a perennial practice of enriching the principle of life through discussions, collaborations, and deep engagement in various debated topics. It is worth mentioning here that Kolkata's boi mela (festival of books) is one of the city's annual signature events that draws thousands of footfalls from

---

[2]. *Ghare Baire, At Home and Outside* is a novel by Rabindranath Tagore published in 1916. The novel is read as a metonymic expression of the conflict in Tagore's mind between his love for Western culture (*baire*) and his patriotism for his country (*ghare*).

[3]. Amit Chaudhuri, *Clearing a Space* (New Delhi: Penguin India, 2008).

[4]. "adda," *Lexico.com* (Oxford: Oxford University Press, 2019).

[5]. *Angantuk*, directed by Satyajit Ray (India: NFDC and DD Production, 1991), DVD.

people who come to the venue not only to browse and buy books but also to witness special adda spaces to mark the occasion.

Scholars have examined historical documents to study what adda looked like in the Kolkata of the nineteenth and twentieth century.[6] In the nineteenth century, the adda in the baithakkhanas (visiting parlor) was the epicenter of ideas about reformation, revolution, and nationalism. The birth of a modern Bengali intelligentsia or the Bengali bhadralok happened with the production and presentation of political and cultural ideas on freedom, nation, and national culture among members who belonged to the same socioeconomic strata. Many addas were started by Bengali zamindars, who often acted as patrons by providing their living rooms (baithakhana) as the venue for the gatherings. By the late nineteenth century, adda got disassociated from the wealthy patron and his baithak. It moved out to public spaces of gathering, thereby becoming more egalitarian. The change happened on account of the growth of the Bengali educated middle-class (sikkhito madhyabitto sreni).

Adda in the twentieth century took on a hybrid form, combining elements of gatherings in baithakhana with that of a coffeehouse conversation. The venues ranged from tea stalls, office cafeterias, bus stops, or at times the rawk where young men of the neighborhood assembled to have their daily chitchat over a cup of tea or coffee. The chief difference between the older adda in the *baithakhana* of a rich patron and the newer form held in public places was the latter's affiliation to a democratic membership and its performative speech register. Adda was at a juncture where three movements characterized it: moving out of domestic spaces to public venues, moving away from an exclusively male domain to allow (a few) women to participate, and finally, from upper-class patrons to membership from different socioeconomic classes.

The changes mentioned earlier in the constituency of adda blurred the boundaries between ghare and baire, reconfiguring Kolkata's urban space. Whereas the adda in the living room disrupted the domesticity of ghare, turning the private into a public space, baire, the adda on the rawk or in the pada club house relocated these places neither completely inside the home nor exactly on the street. The rawk, usually a sit-out right outside a house or by the lane, and the pada clubhouse are fluid spaces blurring the fixed boundaries that

---

[6]. Chakrabarty, *Provincializing Europe.*

Sunitikumar Chattopadhyay, "Hostel Life in Calcutta," in *Jiban Katha* (Calcutta: Jijnasha, [1913] 1979), 210.

Nishithranjan Ray, "Preface," in *Kolkatar Adda*, ed. Samendra Das (Calcutta: Mahajati Prakashan, 1990).

separate inside-outside. Social historians have interpreted this phenomenon in different ways. Partha Chatterjee, for instance, has attributed this peculiar sociability of Bengalis to the hegemonic demarcation of colonial spaces, to the denial of civic roles for colonial subjects by the British administration.[7] In The Nation and its Fragments: Colonial and Postcolonial Histories, he has argued that the Indian middle-classes, being marginalized from the public sphere of colonial life by the British, sought refuge in the private sphere where individuality and communality could be asserted through culture, language and the familial. This private space was a contesting space of potential decoloniality. It was in this reconstituted domain of the private that the nation was "brought into being."[8]

Tithi Bhattacharya, on the other hand, takes a different view. In her book, The Sentinels of Culture: Class, Education and the Colonial Intellectual in Bengal, she asserts that the binding control of the colonial political economy forced Bengalis from diverse and, often, contradictory locations, to unite under the rallying cry of Bande Mataram.[9] According to her, "the nation was brought into being, not in the private world of the 'elite' as Chatterjee has argued, but in the ideological dissolution of class conflicts."[10] A new social middle-class called the bhadralok emerged comprising members from a landed rentier class and the petite-bourgeoisie. The altered social composition resulted in the breakdown of traditional hierarchies that had stratified Bengali samaj, making it easier for the nationalist movement to gather momentum. Notwithstanding these different viewpoints, what is clear is that the adda provided to the bhadrasamaj a fecund context of production in the realm of high culture at a time when colonial modernity and the nationalist project came together in conflict, contradiction, as well as co-option. In my paper, I present three theses to demonstrate the complex relationship that the bhadralok's adda had with the dominant competitive narratives of nationalism, provincialism, and cosmopolitanism.

The Emergence of Bhadralok Cosmopolitanism

The first thesis of my paper is that the popularity of the adda coincided with the growth of a new social class towards the late nineteenth century. This bhadralok middle-class was also a colonized other. The emergence of the bhadralok samaj as a social category with its unique political and cultural provenance is an

---

7. Partha Chatterjee, *The Nation and its Fragments: Colonial and Post-Colonial Histories* (Princeton: Princeton University Press, 1993).

8. Ibid.

9. Tithi Bhattacharya, *The Sentinels of Culture: Class, Education and the Colonial Intellectual in Bengal* (New Delhi: OUP, 2005).

10. Ibid., 21.

extraordinary phenomenon in Bengal's history. In its double location in the national and the political on the one hand, and in the universal and human on the other, it was at once oppositional and closed, receptive, and open-ended. It provided the basis for resistance to the colonizer and also a welcoming receptivity to assimilate many things from the master's culture. The site of the adda became a transformative space that brought colonial modernity along with nationalist aspirations to shape the bhadralok sensibility. It gave to the bhadralok's notion of modernity a dislocating, distinctive note of confidence and a magpie-like instinct toward intellectual entitlement. Indeed, the modern, educated, Bengali middle-class has been characterized by the historian Nitish Sengupta as "the first Asian social group of any size whose mental world was transformed through its interactions with the West."[11]A long series of illustrious members of this social group—from Raja Rammohun Roy, sometimes called the father of modern India, toManabendranath Roy, who argued with Lenin in the Comintern—warmly embraced the themes of science, rationalism, equality, and human rights that the European Enlightenment promulgated. It is this special, historical breed of gentlemen—humanist, rational, secular, seeking international affiliations but at the same time deeply immersed in local and national politics, that Amartya Sen calls the "argumentative Indian."[12] As practitioners of a loquacious culture, addabajis made discourse and argument a quintessentially important aspect of the Bengali community.

By the late nineteenth century, Bengal had become the site of India's first modern middle-class culture, a culture neither feudal nor entrepreneurial. The bhadralok as a social class occupied a political and cultural space where they could engage with the provincial and the cosmopolitan simultaneously through the discourse of colonial modernity. Infused with the liberal spirit and knowledge of the European Renaissance, the new emergent class started envisioning the project of nation-building. Rabindranath Tagore was the epitome of this manifestation—embracing the world at home and exhibiting a home-grown cosmopolitan worldview in his writings and travels abroad. Growing up in the great house in Jorasanko, Tagore would have experienced the stirrings of the new urban cosmopolitanism around him, and also sensed in his own family's changing lifestyle a gradual distancing from his grandfather, Dwarkanath's world of business activity to his world of cultured or *bhadrasamaj*. According to the Amit Chaudhuri, it was Tagore who brought "nationalism into the domain of aesthetics, and create(d) crucial reciprocity

[11]. Nitish Sengupta, *History of the Bengali-speaking People* (New Delhi: UBS publishers, 2001).
[12]. Amartya Sen, *The Argumentative Indian* (London: Penguin, 2005).

between the two: to not only involve the beginnings of secular 'culture' in a nationalist project but make the nation, once and for all, a cultural one."[13]

My second thesis is that in the practice of adda, the Bengali bhadrasamaj negotiated alternative modernity that I call bhadralok cosmopolitanism. The idea of modernity as a plural condition has led several theorists to establish more explicit links between cosmopolitanism and modernity.[14] Many cosmopolitan movements cannot be subsumed in an overarching notion of modernity. Furthermore, theorists like Gaonkar and Chakrabarty have suggested that the pluralization of cosmopolitanism can be linked to modernity as a dialogic process, as opposed to a strictly universalistic one. Cosmopolitanism is now seen as plural and post-universalistic notion by scholars like Gaonkar and Chakrabarty. Thus, in contrast to the dominant Enlightenment notion of cosmopolitanism as a transnational republican order, I suggest that the bhadralok in his pada adda constructed a post-universalistic cosmopolitanism that took, as its point of departure, different kinds of modernity and processes of societal transformation. The pada adda did not presuppose the separation of the social and the cultural from the political or postulate a single world culture. It thrived in its provincial singularity as well as the many rhizomic connections it established with the world outside (ghare-baire).

During the period of colonial modernity, for bhadralok sociality, English education, a cosmopolitan outlook, and the ability to access the civil service became markers of culture and power. It was out of his desire to enter into modernity's narrative that the bhadralok reinvented the peculiar content and discrete style of adda. However, notwithstanding the somewhat cultivated posture of an intellectual savant, the bhadralok with his penchant for adda unwittingly lent credence to the colonial stereotype of Bengalis as a lazy, even effeminate community. Nirad Chaudhuri, the last true Englishman, has this to say about the "gregariousness" of the Bengali:

> What the native of the city [Calcutta] lacked in sociability he made up in gregariousness. No better connoisseur of company was to be found anywhere in the world, and no one else was more dependent on the contiguity of his fellows with the same incomprehension of his obligation towards them. The man of Calcutta found the company he needed so badly and continuously readily assembles, without any effort on his part, in his office, or in his bar-library, or in his college, which were no less places for endless gossip than for work.

---

13. Chaudhari, *Clearing a Space*, 24.
14. Dilip Parameshwar Gaonkar, *Alternative Modernities* (Durham: Duke University Press, 2001).

[...] Every able-bodied person after his return home from office and a hurried wash and tea rushed out of his house with the intention of meeting his friends [at]...fixed rendezvous or, as they were called in Bengali, addas.[15]

The colonial prejudices lurking behind Chaudhuri's disapproval of adda are not hard to discern. In *The Intimate Enemy*, Ashish Nandy has demonstrated that in imperial Bengal, the colonizers deliberately constructed a racist dichotomy—the English as masculine masters and the Bengalis as effeminate servants.[16] The "cultural and psychological pathologies" of colonialism produced a progressive emasculation of the Bengali male by the British regime, causing a split in his personality.[17] In a reactionary moment, Swami Vivekananda is reported to have said that the salvation of the Hindus, in general, and Bengalis, in particular, lay in three Bs: beef, biceps and the Bhagavad-Gita. The way to restore pride and infuse patriotic fervor among religious-minded Hindus was to take part in physic—al activities that required vigor and strength. Further, in order to build strong bodies to fight the physically superior Englishman, it was important for Hindus to change their dietary habits and take to meat-eating. Unfortunately, the addabaji bhadralok did not dispel the colonial stereotype of the lazy Bengali by preferring the cultivation of mind over the body.

Of course, Dipesh Chakrabarty has shown that the adda was not a utopian activity: it was a bourgeois space predicated on the separation of the sexes and an escape, largely for men, from domestic responsibility; its leisurely conversations were "opposed to the idea of achieving any definite outcome."[18] In Chakrabarty's account, adda was an activity that involved using the material of Anglo-Irish and U.S. literary modernism to create new mannerisms. It was, Chakrabarty writes, "an arena where one could develop new techniques of presenting oneself as a character—from Wilde or Shaw or Joyce or Faulkner— through the development of certain mannerisms (meant for the enjoyment of others), habits of speech, and gestures."[19]

It was not until the twentieth century that the word adda gained respectability when its spaces became associated with the production of a modern intellectual Bengali community. The so-called respectability was associated primarily with the cultivation of literary and artistic tastes. The essential

---

[15]. Nirad C. Chauduri, *The Autobiography of an Unknown Indian* (New Delhi: Jaico, 1996), 42.
[16]. Ashish Nandy, "The Intimate Enemy," in *The Intimate Enemy: Loss and Recovery of Self Under Colonialism* (New York: Oxford University Press, 1983).
[17]. Ibid., 30.
[18]. Chakrabarty, "Adda, Calcutta," 141.
[19]. Ibid., 146.

qualification to be a member of an adda group was to be literary. Debates in addas required a certain level of sophisticated reading, cultivation of superior aesthetic tastes, a gift for rhetoric, and the demonstration of a certain style—all in a manner that gave to the local performance an international breadth and its provincial participants a cosmopolitan air. To be an addabaj, or better still, to be conferred the title of "adda raja" (king of adda) or "adda chakravarty" (Emperor of adda) as some of the illustrious Bengali writers, artists and thinkers were, was to cast oneself in the role of a citizen of a global literary cosmopolis and to enact a "performative cosmopolitanism."[20] The extract given below, from Jibendra Singha Ray's *Kalloler Kal* (The Age of Kallol), reports a snatch of an adda conversation between two friends:

> Gokul asked me one day, "What's going on in your mind? I feel as though I am also thinking the same thought as you are but cannot quite tell what the thought is." I said, "I imagine a [kind of] resting-house [an inn]—where people tired by the burden of their lives can come and rest, where nationality, sex, and position will not be any barriers, [where]men will make their work joyful and by freely mixing with others will find themselves fulfilled in the easy working out of their desires." Gokul put his hand over mine, clapped, and cried out in joy, "That is the dream of my life too, but I could not figure out its exact shape until now!"[21]

This reported anecdote shows the kind of world view to which the educated Bengali youth of the early twentieth century was attracted—a sense of universal humanity transcending national identity. With his head full of radical notions inspired by their reading of Tom Paine and European thinkers, the addabaj infused the nationalist project with a cosmopolitan, secular culture.

What I hope to have demonstrated is that the utopian idea of a cosmopolitan community that the bhadralok envisioned by stepping out of his house to meet others at a common resting-house (adda in a pada) often conflicted with his search for a habitus where local and national identities could be forged. The Bengali's adda was a place of enunciation where the cosmopolitanism of modernity's discourse and the provincialism of nation and nationality intersected. As a unique marker of Bengali cultural identity, adda—its locations, beliefs, and practices—became a site where the different forms of cosmopolitanism, nationalism, and provincialism could be contested, negotiated, but not always, resolved.

---

[20]. Craig Jeffery and Colin McFarlane, "Performing Cosmopolitanism," *Environment and Planning D: Society and Space* (2008): 420-27.

[21]. Jibendra Singh Ray, *Kalloler Kal* (Calcutta: Deys, 1973), 5.

From the Bengal Renaissance to Coffee-house Performative Cosmopolitanism

As pointed out by several historians, the popularity of adda as a social and cultural practice coincided with the advent of the so-called Bengal renaissance in the nineteenth century, signaling the emergence of humanism and modernity. The Bengal renaissance, a period of great social and intellectual ferment, in many ways became the precursor to the national movement. The term renaissance was probably first applied to the development of a literary and cultural awakening of Bengali language and literature by the eminent Brahmo Samaj leader Shibnath Shastri; it was later employed by Marxist historians such as Susobhan Sarkar. In *Notes on the Bengal Renaissance*, he writes:

> The impact of British rule, bourgeoisie economy, and modern Western culture was felt first in Bengal and produced an awakening known usually as the Bengal Renaissance. For about a century, Bengal's conscious awareness of the changing modern world was more developed than and ahead of the rest of India. The role played by Bengal in the modern awakening of India is thus comparable to the position occupied by Italy in the story of the European Renaissance.[22]

The Bengal renaissance is supposed to have originated from the adda that took place in the house of the famous teacher and poet Henri Derozio.[23] Later on, the addas held in the office premises of newspapers and periodicals like Probasi, Porichay, ShanibarerChithi, Kalloland Desh contributed hugely to the evolution of Bengali culture and tradition. Europe, as the source, paradigm, and catalyst of progress and history, was installed in the narratives of the nation in Bengal. The intellectual and artistic movements of Europe were often the indexical markers framing these addas. The influence is evident from the honorific titles given to the leading writers of Bengal: Bankimchandra Chatterjee, India's first major novelist, was called the Walter Scott of Bengal, and Michael Madhusudhan Dutta, the Byron of Bengal. Tagore himself was "at once the product, spokesman, and inquisitor of the Bengal Renaissance."[24] His house at Jorasanko was the seat of many addas; apart from literary and philosophical debates, its open spaces witnessed the regular performance of

---

[22]. Susobhan Sarkar, *On the Bengal Renaissance* (Calcutta: Papyrus, 1979), 353.

[23]. Sandipan Deb and Ashish K. Biswas, "Much Adda about Nothing," *Outlook*, June 19, 1996, accessed June 25, 2020, https://www.outlookindia.com/magazine/story/much-adda-about-nothing/201561.

[24]. Chaudhuri, *Clearing a Space*, 74.

plays, poetry recitals, and songs in which his large but extremely talented family took part. Unquestionably, Tagore may be regarded as the archetypal bhadralok who advocated cosmopolitan sensibilities in the high noon of nationalism in India, while remaining unwilling to repudiate nationalism completely. In an essay on nationalism, he declared that "neither the colorless vagueness of cosmopolitanism nor the fierce self-idolatry of nation-worship, is the goal of human history."[25]

My paper with regard to its first thesis, therefore, has tried to show that, despite being a highly localized cultural habit, the adda for the Bengali intelligentsia was the site of a vigorous engagement with European ideas of modernity and progress. Its source and inspiration may have been European modernity, but its practice was provincial and nationalistic. Adda then was a unique linguistic and cultural experiment carried out by the bhadralok samaj with utmost self-reflexivity. Through endless debates and discussions on politics, arts, and literature, its avid practitioners were trying to construct a postcolonial identity that could give them a sense of place in the world at large.

Any account of the social history of adda mentioned above will be incomplete without bringing up the role played in the twentieth century by the Indian Coffee House, formerly called Albert Hall, at College Street in Kolkata. The Coffee House is not just another landmark like the Victoria Memorial that maps Kolkata's colonial history. It is an institution in itself, similar to the Parisian cafe. It has been the favorite hangout of famous writers, artists, filmmakers, and left-leaning radicals. It has often borne witness to the start of major political and cultural movements and trends in Bengal's history. Built-in 1944, this cafeteria is located within a stone's throw from the University of Calcutta and Presidency College. In the past, some significant projects originated in conversations within the walls of the College Street Coffee House. Two important literary journals—Ekshan and Krittibas—were conceived here. In the late 1940s and 1950s, Signet Press, an innovative Bengali publisher, used to bring its authors to this place for signing deals over coffee and adda. Soumitra Chatterjee, the stage and film actor, best known for his work with Satyajit Ray, used to hold court in the Coffee House in the early 1960s before he became a sought-after star. Around the same time, Kamal Kumar Majumdar (1914-79), a major fiction writer and a superb raconteur, would pull a crowd around his table with jokes and anecdotes in three languages—Bengali, English, and French. Indeed, the Coffee House as the most popular site of adda is venerated as an immutable symbol of Bengal's social and cultural imaginary.

---

25. Ibid., 65.

The adda is now perceived to be a dying practice. Modernity's development project and the transformation of Kolkata's urban scape pockmarked by huge apartment buildings and shopping malls, has left the city and its citizens less spaces, little time, and lesser inclination to indulge in adda. Today, the adda survives only in a few pockets in North Kolkata, while for the diasporic Bengali community, it exists in different guises like the internet adda.

The Death of the Bhadralok and the Decline of the Adda

In the paper's final section, I engage with one of the central questions of cosmopolitanism's discourse: whether cosmopolitanism is the exclusive domain of high culture, or is it embodied in acts of everyday life? My contention, which is my third thesis, is that in the case of adda, it appropriated and subsumed both. From the nineteenth to the first half of the twentieth century, the bhadralok's adda was synonymous with the notion of high culture, thereby alienating its upper and middle-class participants from the popular masses. While its operating principle was ostensibly one of democratic inclusion, in reality, it produced a privileged, exclusive community. Entry to this space, as mentioned earlier, required a certain degree of cultural capital that only the upper/middle-class, to which educated male Bengalis had access. For example, to be well-versed in Bengali, European, and British literatures and/or in western/Indian classical philosophy was considered a sine qua non for realizing the adda's purpose of engaging in discourse, well-informed and wide-ranging in scope. Something that is historically claimed to be quintessentially Bengali, an indispensable part of the Bengali identity. The adda was an integral source of living since it provided "life" and "vitality" to the colonial babus and the bhadraloks of Kolkata. It allowed this exclusive class to transcend the provinciality of a local habit of socialization with the help of a shared exchange of modern and global concerns.

I designate adda then as the singular marker of bhadralok cosmopolitanism, a cosmopolitanism from above, rather than from below. Acquiring a degree of influence far in excess of their strength, the bhadralok constructed "new forms of public discourse, laid down new criteria of social respectability, set new aesthetic and moral standards of judgment and [...] fashioned the new forms of political mobilization."[26] They became the principal agents of nationalism in colonial Bengal and, along with the middle-classes elsewhere in India, constituted colonial India's nationalist elite. One may conclude that the construction of cultural identity that gave the bhadralok agency, power, and

---

26. Chakrabarty, "Adda, Calcutta," 112.

articulation was made possible by the dynamic performance of adda despite its many inherent ambiguities and contradictions.

It may also be surmised that the death of the bhadralok and the decline of the adda occurred almost concurrently. By the mid-1980s, as the first wave of neoliberal capitalism was opening up India's economy, the power of adda to pull people together began to wane. Today the adda as a unique experiment of sociability is barely recognizable in the diluted form in which it survives. The Bengali bhadralok, too, once regarded in high esteem as the repository of cultural values, is today "stuck in stagnant provincialism and sterile despair."[27] A feature article in the *Outlook* magazine, tellingly titled "Death of the Bhadralok," certifies that "Bengal today is a volatile wasteland dotted with closed factories [...] peopled by a smug and parochial bhadralokdom."[28]

The writer almost crafts an epitaph for the fall of this historic class: "the fabled slothful bhadralok is hoist on his own petard, out of sync with modern-day realities."[29] His article draws out the inexorable cultural logic of late capitalism by trying to establish connections between the perceived decline of a community, its culture of adda, and the supposed un-modern orientation of its genteel practitioners. Ironically, the article issues the same colonial certificate of "sloth" to the bhadralok and alleges that the ideals of bhadralok society are opposed to the vectors of development.[30]

Conclusion

The adda may be considered as a social practice of the bhadralok that developed out of a specific encounter of the colonial, the global, the cosmopolitan with the national, local, and the provincial in Bengal's history. It was an attempt made by the Bengali bhadralok from colonial times to situate and move in a kind of "liquid modernity" characterized by transience, ambiguity, and uncertainty.[31] A small minority of Hindu male reformers, thinkers, and writers pioneered political and cultural modernity in Bengal, steeped in pada cosmopolitanism, whose articulation was defined by an indigenous communicative model of world openness, even though the openness was closed off by class and gender boundaries. Using the cultural strategies of posture, sensibility, and refinement, the bhadralok who were denied public space and civic roles by the colonial machinery, made adda a discrete tool of compliance, acculturation, and subversion. The adda was a

---

27. Souvik Biswas, "Death of the Bhadralok," *Outlook India*, September 4, 2000.
28. Ibid., 47.
29. Ibid.
30. Ibid., 47.
31. Zygmunt Bauman, *Liquid Modernity* (Cambridge: Polity Press, 2000).

cultural site constructed by the bhadralok samaj to cultivate a cosmopolitan imagination driven by the changing relations between the self, other, and world at a time of great social and political change. The adda will forever be associated as a provincial marker of the cosmopolitan bhadralok as an ever-changing cultural and social space.

Bibliography

Bauman, Zygmunt. *Liquid Modernity* (Cambridge: Polity Press, 2000).

Bhattacharya, Tithi. *The Sentinels of Culture: Class, Education, and the Colonial Intellectual in Bengal.* New Delhi: Oxford University Press, 2005.

Chakrabarty, Dipesh. *Provincializing Europe: Postcolonial Thought and Historical Difference.* Princeton: Princeton University Press, 2000.

Chakrabarty, Dipesh. "Adda, Calcutta: Dwelling in Modernity." In *Alternative Modernities*, edited by Dilip Parameshwar Gaonkar, 123-164. Durham, London: Duke University Press, 2001.

Chatterjee, Partha. *The Nation and its Fragments: Colonial and Postcolonial Histories.* Princeton: Princeton University Press, 1993.

Chattopadhyay, Sunitikumar, "Hostel Life in Calcutta." In Jiban Katha. Calcutta: Jijnasha, [1913] 1979.

Chaudhuri, Amit. *Clearing a Space.* New Delhi: Penguin India, 2008.

Chaudhuri, Nirad C. *The Autobiography of an Unknown Indian.* New Delhi: Jaico, 1996.

Deb, Sandipan, and Ashish K. Biswas, "Much Adda about Nothing." *Outlook India,* June 19, 1996, accessed June 25, 2020. https://www.outlookindia.com/magazine/story/much-adda-about-nothing/201561.

Gaonkar, Dilip Parameshwar. *Alternative Modernities.* Durham: Duke University Press, 2001.

Jeffrey, C. and C. McFarlane. "Performing cosmopolitanism," *Environment and Planning D: Society and Space*, 26 (2008): 420-427.

Ray, Jibendra Singh. *Kolloler Kal.* Calcutta: Deys, 1973.

Ray, Nishithranjan. "Preface." In *Kolkatar Adda*, edited by Samendra Das. Calcutta: Mahajati Prakashan, 1990.

Ray, Satyajit, director. *Angantuk.* NFDC and DD Production, 1991. DVD.

Sarkar, Susobhan. *On the Bengal Renaissance.* Calcutta: Papyrus, 1979.

Sen, Amartya. *The Argumentative Indian.* London: Penguin, 2005.

Sengupta, Nitish. *History of the Bengali-speaking People.* New Delhi: UBS publishers, 2001.

Chapter 5

Language (E)scapes: Linguistic diversity and integration of South Asian migrant women in Barcelona, Spain

Swagata Basu

Doon University, India

Abstract

To physically live in a space but to remain invisible and inaudible to its surrounding is a peculiar reality for many South Asian women in Spain who usually join their working migrant spouse or other family members after a reunification process as they get transplanted from their usual socio-cultural and linguistic environment to a completely new one. This paper is an attempt to closely understand the complex spaces that they inhabit after their migration. We call those spaces language (e)scapes: places of flow, hybridity, and interaction of languages and cultures drawing on Arjun Appadurai's theory of scapes. The paper is based on eight in-depth interviews, one focussed group discussion and participant observation carried out as part of the doctoral research in Barcelona in 2018 by the author, a Spanish-speaking South Asian woman herself. The study shows that there is a broad spectrum that the subjects experience, which is shaped by various factors. It finds that the inability to communicate in (and thus interact with) the already diverse, host society languages along with the traditionally limiting role inside the home, trap some of the subjects into alienating bubbles where they can remain for days, months or years. However, the pre-existing language repertoire and their ability to learn new languages or to translanguage, i.e., using the repertoire in new ways to communicate, determine their migration experience to a large extent. While previous research establishes that the knowledge of local languages helps in the social integration of adult migrants, this paper fills the gap of an in-depth study of the chosen group: South Asian women in Barcelona.

Keywords: Migration, South Asian women diaspora, linguistic superdiversity, identity, integration

***

Migration and movement have always been part of human life. It has become a subject of systematic academic inquiry giving rise to the research field called migration studies only in the last few decades (the 1980s onwards).[1] No doubt, the academic interest has been propelled by the enormous growth of migration during these decades. The total number of people living outside their country of birth has increased from about 100 million in 1960 to 155 million in 2000 and 214 million in 2010.[2] As per the 2020 World Migration Report, 3.5% of the world population are international migrants.[3] However, the report states that "international migrant population globally has increased in size but remained relatively stable as a proportion of the world's population."[4] Stephen Castles et al. state that while growth in migration is relatively stable, what has increased over the past half a century is "the political salience of migration."[5] Women migrate almost as much as men. 52% of international migrants are male and 48% female.[6] However, their migratory experiences are different than those of men. "Migration is very much a gendered phenomenon; gender norms and expectations, power relations, and unequal rights shape the migration choices and experiences of women and girls as they do men and boys (sic)."[7] While in many situations, women migrate as independent agents in search of better work opportunities just like their male counterparts, often they migrate along with or to join their male spouses or other male family members. Migration for family reasons is especially true of South Asian women.[8]

Luis Eduardo Guarnizo states that there are various aspects to migration worth exploring such as the economic, social, and psychological changes produced by transnational movement, mobility, and transnational living of

---

[1]. Asya Pisarevskaya, Nathan Levy, Peter Scholten, and Joost Jansen, "Mapping migration studies: An empirical analysis of the coming of age of a research field," in *Migration Studies* (Oxford: Oxford University Press, 2019), 1, https://doi.org/10.1093/migration/mnz031.

[2]. Stephen Castles, Hein de Haas and Mark J. Miller, *The Age of Migration: International Population Movements in the Modern World* (New York: Palgrave Macmillan, 2014), 7.

[3]. Marie McAuliffe and Vinod Khadria, *World Migration Report, 2020* (Geneva: International Organization for Migration, 2019), 21.

[4]. Ibid., 22.

[5]. Castles et al., *The Age of Migration*, 1.

[6]. McAuliffe and Khadria, *World Migration Report*, 22.

[7]. Tam O'Neil, Anjali Fleury, and Marta Foresti, "Women on the move Migration, gender equality and the 2030 Agenda for Sustainable Development", *ODI Briefing Papers*, July (2016): 4, https://www.odi.org/publications/10476-women-move-migration-gender-equality-and-2030-agenda-sustainable-development.

[8]. Rashmi Sharma, "Gender and International Migration: The Profile of Female Migrants from India in *Social Scientist*, Vol. 39, no. 3/4 March-April (2011): 41, accessed: March 15, 2020. https://www.jstor.org/stable/41633793.

people: "Transnational living refers to a wide panoply of social, cultural, political, and economic cross-border relations that emerge, both wittingly and unwittingly, from migrants' drive to maintain and reproduce their social milieu or origin from afar."[9]

Studies have explored how migration and integration are closely interconnected to the sending countries and the impact of migration on those left behind.[10] Within the field of migration studies, integration understood as the process of inclusion of immigrants in the receiving or host society has been of significant interest to researchers and policymakers. Adrian Favell was one of the first to systematically study and propose 'integration' as a way of accommodating immigrants in British society in the 1990s.[11] In an article from 2013, he observes how the changing realities of migration and mobility problematize the concept of integration. He criticizes the double standards present in European societies where immigrants are expected to integrate into the concept of a nation.

In contrast, for the non-immigrant population, increasingly, the expectation is that they should feel part of a collective supra-national identity beyond the nation (European identity).[12] Integration, which is closely associated with identity and sense of belonging are complex concepts that are shaped by several factors. In the present paper, I will be looking at the role of knowledge of local languages in the integration of immigrants in the host society. The Council of Europe has recognized the importance of language in the integration of migrants and has issued several guidelines and reports on this theme.[13]

---

[9]. Luis Eduardo Guarnizo, "The Economic of Transnational Living," *The International Migration Review,* vol. 37, no. 3, Transnational Migration: International Perspectives, Fall, (2003): 666-699. https://www.jstor.org/stable/30037753.

[10]. A. Di Bartolomeo et al., eds., *Migrant Integration between Homeland and Host Society Volume 2* (Cham: Springer, 2017), 2. https://doi.org/10.1007/978-3-319-56370-1_1.
Artjoms Ivlevs, Milena Nikolova and Carol Graham, "Emigration, remittances, and the subjective well-being of those staying behind," *Journal of Population Economics,* (2019): 113-151. https://doi.org/10.1007/s00148-018-0718-8.

[11]. Adrian Favell, *Philosophies of Integration: Immigration and the Idea of Citizenship in France and Britain* (London: Palgrave Macmillan, 2001), 100.

[12]. Adrian Favell. "The Changing Face of 'Integration' in a Mobile Europe" *Council For European Studies Newsletter,* June (2013): 3, http://www.adrianfavell.com/CESweb.pdf.

[13]. Jean-Claude Beacco, David Little and Chris Hedges, *Linguistic integration of adult migrants Guide to policy development and implementation* (Council of Europe, Language Policy Unit). https://rm.coe.int/16802fc1cd.

South Asian Women Migrants in a superdiverse and complex space:
Barcelona

The present article deals with female migrants from India, Pakistan, and Bangladesh[14] (henceforth referred to as South Asian Women) in Barcelona, Spain, by focussing on their experience with the local languages of their receiving society in order to understand the relationship between language and integration of immigrants. The paper is based on the ethnographic fieldwork I did in Barcelona as part of my doctoral research in 2018. Through this article, I would attempt to highlight the role that the ability to learn new languages and translanguaging plays in the social integration of migrant women from South Asia in Barcelona. [15] This article is based on eight semi-structured in-depth interviews that included both open-ended and closed-ended questions, one Focus Group Discussion (FGD), and participant observation. Below is the table of the eight respondents that form the primary sample.

Table 5.1: Demographic Composition of the focus group

Sr. N	Name (Changed)	Age	Country of Origin	Status in Spain	No. of years in Barcelona	Profession	Independent user of Spanish or Catalan
1	Tripti	53	India	Resident	11	Homemaker	No
2	Jhumoor	23	Bangladesh	Resident	5	Homemaker	No
3	Manu	26	India	Resident	2	Jointly runs Grocery Shop	No
4	Sunita	36	India	Resident	12	Proprietor of a Beauty Salon	Yes
5	Laila	17	Pakistan	Citizen	17	Student	Yes
6	Naaz	25	Pakistan	Resident	12	Voluntary worker, Teacher, and NGO coordinator	Yes
7	Saadifa	27	Pakistan	Resident	2	Homemaker	No
8	Hina	18	Pakistan	Citizen	12	Student	Yes

---

[14]. The number of women from other countries such as Nepal, Afghanistan and Sri Lanka is negligible thus not included in this study.

[15]. Ofelia García, "Problematizing Linguistic Integration of migrants: the role of translanguaging and language teachers", in *The Linguistic Integration of Adult Migrants Some Lessons from Research*, eds., Jean-Claude Beacco, Hans-Jürgen Krumm, David Little, Philia Thalgott. (Berlin and Boston: De Gruyter, 2017), 17.

Roughly *translanguaging* means communicating with multiple language and non-linguistic resources studied as a phenomenon of superdiverse space discussed later in the paper.

The FGD was with a group of 12 women of different ages from South Asian backgrounds who together attended a Spanish language class for adults. The participant observation method was used whenever possible during the course of four months in a variety of contexts.[16]

Arjun Appadurai's theory of scapes inspired the term Language (E)scapes used in this paper.[17] In his well-known theory, he argues that in the globalized world, cultures are in constant flow and influence each other. My term also resonates with Steven Vertovec's concept of superdiversity to talk about the contemporary social reality of Europe, which is "distinguished by a dynamic interplay of variables among an increased number of new, small and scattered, multiple-origin, transnationally connected, socio-economically differentiated and legally stratified immigrants."[18] Sociolinguists have observed a linguistic superdiversity in the various European cities like Barcelona, where people with over a hundred nationalities or ethnic origins live together, as migrants, tourists, refugees, and member state workers.[19]

Appadurai's ethnoscape is the result of the unprecedented global flow and movement of people. In the same way, a language (e)scape would be the result of the diversity of languages spoken by such people, which is in continuous flux. Further, in these linguistically superdiverse spaces, I will argue that we can observe the use of what Jan Blommaert calls 'repertoire' rather than 'languages' by the migrant subjects in their day to day life.[20] He argues that while languages are ideologically constructed as a unified, homogenous entity, in complex contemporary superdiverse spaces, people use any resource available to them to communicate: "The collective resources available to anyone at any point in time are a repertoire; repertoires are biographically emerging complexes of indexically ordered, and therefore functionally organized, resources. Repertoires include

---

[16]. Barbara B. Kawulich, "Participant Observation as a Data Collection Method" *Forum: Qualitative Social Research* Vol. 6 No. 2 Art 43 May, Online (2005), https://www.qualitative-research.net/index.php/fqs/article/view/466/996.

[17]. Arjun Appadurai, *Modernity at Large-Cultural Dimensions of Globalization* (Minneapolis and London: University of Minnesota Press, 1996), 33.

[18]. Steven Vertovec, "Super-diversity and its implications," *Ethnic and Racial Studies* Vol. 30 No. 6 November (2007): 1024.

[19]. K Arnaut, Jan Blommaert, B. Rampton and M. Spotti, *Language and Superdiversity* (New Yourk: Rotledge, 2016), 22.

[20]. Jan Blommaert, "Langauge- The great diversifier" in Routledge International Handbook of Diversity Studies, ed. Steven Vertovec (London and New York: Routledge, 2015), 85.

every resource used in communication—linguistic ones, semiotic ones, socio-cultural ones." [21]

Barcelona is the capital city of Catalonia, which is a multilingual and devolved but not federal state.[22] The two local languages: Spanish and Catalan, exist in a competitive framework.[23] It is precisely the kind of superdiverse and complex context that needs new metaphors and a close ethnographic study to understand the challenges of immigrants who live there. [24] The percentage of the foreign population in Catalonia and Barcelona is 15.11 % and 20.2% respectively.[25] Among Asians, immigrants from Pakistan are the largest South-Asian community, followed by China and the Philippines. Although the total numbers of South Asians are small compared to immigrants from the Latin American countries or Morocco, the phenomenon is worth studying because of the sudden increase in numbers: the total population of South Asian people multiplied more than ten times within the first decade of the twenty-first century.[26] It is important to clarify that this article focuses on low-skilled labor migration. There is a trend of highly skilled workers who move to Spain to work in multinational companies, especially the IT sector, but my present study does not include them.[27]

The current migration pattern is male-dominated. The typical immigrant profile from South Asia is that of single young males who come to work as laborers in sectors such as construction, mining, and agriculture. South Asian women almost always come to Spain through family reunification.[28] Most of the women interviewed for this article are first-generation migrants who joined

---

[21]. Ibid.

[22]. Ferran Requejo, "Is Spain a Federal Country," in *50 Shades of Federalism*, n.p., http://50shadesoffederalism.com/case-studies/spain-federal-country/.

[23]. Elvira Riera Gil, W*hy Languages matter to people. Communication, identity and justice in Western democracies. The case of mixed societies* (Barcelona: Generalitat de Catalunya - Institut d'Estudis de l'Autogovern. EA.2, 2016), 225.

[24]. Jan Blommaert, *Ethnography, Superdiversity and Linguistic Landscape, Chronicles of complexity* (Buffalo, Toronto and Bristol: Multilingual Matters, 2013), 14-16.

[25]. "Evolución de la población total y extranjera" *Idescat*, accessed April 25, 2020. https://www.idescat.cat/poblacioestrangera/?b=0&lang=es.

[26]. Nachatter Singh Garha, Juan Galeano and Andreu Domingo Valls, "South Asian Immigration to Spain: Socio-demographic Profile and Territorial Distribution, 2000-2014," *Asian and Pacific Migration Journal*, vol.25, Issue 2. March (2016): 196, https://doi.org/10.1177/0117196816639166.

[27]. German Gómez Ventura, "Highly skilled Indian migrant population in Spain," in *CARIM-India RR* (Migration Policy Centre: European University Institute, 2013), 5.

[28]. Garha et al., "South Asian Immigration," 196.

their husbands after they acquired permanent residency in Spain and applied for family reunification. Since this is only possible after several years of residence in Spain for the male member of the family, by the time the woman comes to Spain, the man will have already established a circle of friends, acquaintances, and neighbors. He will also have at least some knowledge of the local languages. As is typical in /their societies back home, these women generally do not seek employment and are financially dependent on their husbands. A report in *El País* paints a grim picture of women who traveled from Pakistan to Barcelona, but sin salir de casa, that is, without leaving home.[29] The ethnographic study I conducted provides a nuanced understanding of the reasons why most of the migrant women do not "leave home" and also highlights the exceptions to this pattern.

Bubbles in the language (e)scapes

Tripti, a middle-aged Bengali woman, has been living in Barcelona for 11 years. Tripti is the only member of her family who is yet not a Spanish national. When asked if she hopes to get citizenship, she expresses that due to her lack of Spanish skills, she has no hope of getting it.[30] Every Sunday, she comes to a small closed space that has the structure of a small shop but acts as the temple for a small community of Bengali vaishnavs[31] in the Raval neighborhood, home to the maximum number of South Asian immigrants in Barcelona. It would be challenging for anyone outside the community to reach the temple on their own unless they know an insider. The temple was being run without the necessary official permission. The women who came one by one to the temple started contributing to the kitchen work. They peeled and chopped fruits and vegetables. An older woman was cooking in a small makeshift kitchen. All the women were wearing South Asian traditional clothes, either sarees or salwar kameez.

At about 6 pm, a South Asian man about 30-years-old arrived, who acted as the priest. Jhumoor, one of the women present there, started to arrange the things required for the ceremony. A little later, she was encouraged by other women of the group to have a more significant role in the rituals as they joked about her being the priest, while she seemed to shy away. She sang a prayer

---

29. Charo Nogueira, "De Pakistan a Barcelona sin salir de casa," *El País*. August 17, 2002, accessed April 26, 2020, https://elpais.com/diario/2002/08/17/opinion/1029535209_850215.html.
30. Respondent number 1 in discussion with the author on May 9, 2018.
31. Vaishnavs are followers of *Vaishnavism* which is one of the three main denomination within Hinduism. Vaishnav traditions are centred around Vishnu as the primary deity.

song when the priest asked her. Slowly others joined in the kirtan.[32] After the rituals were over, the evening ended with a community Bengali dinner, which was cooked and served by the women. The men were served before the women, and everybody sat on the floor to eat the food in the manner typical of community religious festivals among Bengalis in India.

Even though Bengali is my mother tongue, the accent in which many of the women spoke, and the songs they sang were unfamiliar to me. As time passed, the audience started to increase, with men joining later. As is usual in South Asia, the space was segregated by gender. The few children present there spoke in Spanish among themselves. Some of the mothers of children who were at the age of learning to speak were using their broken and accented Spanish with them. One of the mothers informed me that she wanted to make sure that her child does not face any problems in school.[33] In my next visits, I found out that the priest, whom I later interviewed, worked as a waiter in a restaurant. He was parallelly studying religion and training to be a priest or a preacher.

The group dynamics in the temple show that the rules and norms of a society, its customs and habits, and especially the patriarchal aspects remain intact even in a new geographical space. The situation of these migrants and especially women can be described using bubbles as a metaphor. There is an invisible border that every woman carries around her in the new geographical space. Unless she breaks out of this bubble, her migration is partial. She has physically moved from a location in India or Pakistan, or Bangladesh. Still, she continues to inhabit the same psychological and social spaces that she belonged to in her origin country. I am using the term language (e)scapes to denote this bubbled reality of South Asian migrant women in Barcelona.

Breaking out of the bubble or stepping out

Most South Asian women migrants in Barcelona come from rural societies where it is widely accepted that the woman's primary role is taking care of a household. They mostly stay within the domestic space, spending their days cooking, cleaning, feeding the children, and on other household chores. They continue with the same role after migrating. They do step out, for example, to pick and drop the children from school, but it is an extension of their domestic caregiving responsibility. Within the research sample, Tripti, Jhumoor, and Saadifa represent this typical profile. They hardly know the city in which they

---

[32]. A *kirtan* is a typical religious ritual where devotees sing songs in chorus, in praise of Krishna.

[33]. Consent forms and audio-recordings were used for in-depth interviews only. Several conversations were natural and not recorded.

live. None of them has joined the labor market. They also are the least proficient in the local languages.

In an informal discussion, Jhumoor explained why she thinks women like her do not work. She said that it is because there are not many jobs in Spain as there are no small factories or sweatshops like in Canada or the US. She added that some women do find work in other people's houses or as janitors in hotels or old-age homes. Those who have no other option have to do that kind of work, but most would not like to.[34] Many Latin American women join the care and hospitality sector in Spain. Cultural notions about respectable work influence the choices women make. Working outside the home is not the only indicator of women's empowerment or autonomy. What matters is whether they can access the public space. These women feel alienated, more than anything, due to their lack of interaction with the local people, which they attributed to their lack of knowledge of local languages. Even though they had spent a few months in a language school, they could not speak the local languages confidently. They identify the lack of interaction with Spanish or Catalan-speaking people as the main reason for this. All of them want more interaction with the local people. Thus, they are trapped in a vicious cycle of needing the word to interact with the local population but lacking language proficiency due to the lack of such interaction.[35] They want to learn local languages because they want to be independent. Without knowledge of local languages, they feel infantilized. They do not like feeling vulnerable. Their mobility and capacity to be on their own, be it to go to the doctor or to do the grocery shopping, is drastically restricted unless they speak the local languages. Economic independence is not the main factor here. The feeling of autonomy in day to day social life is.

Since their husbands arrived in Barcelona several years before them, naturally, they have more knowledge of local languages. These men tend to be busy in their work like any other migrant worker. They have little social life outside work. Generally, they build a social circle with their own countrymen within the work setting. However, South Asian women, especially when they are newly arrived, desire to establish relations with local people, and enter into the existing social circles of neighbors, school teachers, nearby shopkeepers and quickly realize that language is essential for it.

When women can go to their children's school and interact with their teachers or visit the doctor or bank on their own, they feel empowered. The respondents

---

[34]. I met Jhumoor every Sunday and also a few times a week as she showed interest in learning Spanish from me. Only one structured interview was recorded. Respondent no. 2 in discussion with author, May, 2018, Barcelona.

[35]. Data collected in the questionnaire by the author as part of doctoral research. Thesis to be submitted.

stated that they would prefer not to have to wait or depend on their husbands to visit the doctor or child's school. Saadifa, 27, from Pakistan who lives in Poblenou, a mixed neighborhood with more local population than San Antoni, (where Tripti and Jhumoor live), talks about her experience with Spanish, "I feel like it that someone should talk to me, and if I don't understand, then I wish that they explain what they had said, I feel then I will learn the language. Someone should talk in Spanish with me."[36] Her main concern is how her knowledge of Spanish impacts her interaction with her son's school. She reports that sometimes she feels that the teachers and other school functionaries simply ignore them, but she does not view it as a racist or anti-immigrant feeling. She says, "they ignore us sometimes, they act as that when they don't understand us, then what is the use."[37] One of the women during the focus group discussion held in a Spanish language school expressed her gratitude to the local people, especially other women in the host society, for treating her with respect and giving her confidence. She said, "I go to the hospital and say poco hablo español, so she says, no pasa nada. Even if I speak a little, she says 'muy bien'."[38]

The 12 respondents who were part of the FGD are all women who are consciously trying to make efforts to learn Spanish and Catalan but talked about the difficulty of acquiring the languages. Responding to these difficulties, South Asian women have come up with their own ingenious and alternatives ways of learning the language. Saadifa explains, "I write on paper, I look up words from mobile, then learn them as, and when I can, that is why I am learning also. But I am unable to devote time because I just don't have time."[39] She added that she tries to use Catalan and Spanish terms at home with her children, although primarily they use Urdu or Punjabi at home. So even though the mothers do not know the language, they have the responsibility to teach it to their children. Then again, ensuring that the child knows their mother tongue, origin culture, and religious teachings all fall on the mother's shoulder as well. But ironically, as reported by respondents of the Focus Group Discussion, as children start growing up, they acquire the local languages, and may use it at home among siblings or cousins, and even with the fathers, but not with mothers. That creates a new complex among women.

---

36. Respondent no 7 in conversation with author on May 18, 2018. Original response in Hindustani, translation mine.
37. Ibid.
38. One of the respondents of the Focus Group Discussion, held author on May 11, 2018.
39. Respondent no 7 in conversation with author on May 18, 2018.

Carving out their Own Space

Despite all the contradictory forces at work, there are enterprising South Asian women who have devised ways and carved out a unique space for themselves in the diaspora. Sunita is an example of an enterprising woman. She speaks Spanish fluently. She is the sole proprietor of a beauty and esthetic center in the city of Sabadell, 20 kilometers from Barcelona. She is also a mother and wife. She reported that her clients were people from all nationalities, including Spain, Catalonia, Bolivia, and India. She has acquired not just language skills, but the gestures and behaviors typical of a beauty salon in an economically developed country. She speaks Spanish with a local accent.[40] The name of her aesthetic center reflects her Indian ethnicity, but she asserts that her skills are based on rigorous training in Catalonia. She handles her client's communication, receives calls to give appointments, checking her diary, taking a pause from her ongoing sessions, thus multitasking through the structured interview.

Manu, 26-years-old from Punjab, India, has not yet picked up the language thoroughly. She expressed that she did not find the language very appealing. Therefore, she does not enjoy learning it. But she runs a grocery shop along with her husband in Poblenou. She has picked up the words and phrases required to interact with clients when her husband is not at the shop. She has also devised mechanisms to manage difficult situations. She does not let it show when she does not understand her clients. She is full of confidence, and although her Spanish is accented, her gestures are like that of the local people. There are many women like Manu who interact with their clients from the host society. In Spain, these small supermarkets, tienda de alimentación, are colloquially called Paquis, because Pakistani nationals run many of them. However, quite a few of these shops are managed by migrants from India and Bangladesh, where one finds women at the caja, the cashier. The proprietor on paper is generally the man who keeps the accounts and goes to get the stock. If a woman within the family, be it the wife, the daughter, or the mother, is at the caja, she is not paid for her service. The participation of many family members allows these shops to stay open for longer hours in comparison to when the local people ran them.[41]

Both Sunita and Manu's day to day interactions have the elements of Jan Blommaert's translanguaging mentioned in this article earlier. When Sunita was pregnant during her early months in Spain, she used to go to a park, sit

---

[40]. Based on observation of during multiple visits by the author during May, 2018, Sabad.
[41]. Solé Montserrat Aubia and Josep Rodríguez Roca, "Pakistaníes en España: un estudio basado en el colectivo de la ciudad de Barcelona," *Revista CIDOB d'Afers Internacionals*, No. 68 (2004): 111-112.

there and listen to the conversations of old Spanish/Catalan women. They tried to talk, but with no knowledge of each other's language, through gestures and expressions. She also said that now, although she knows Spanish, once in a while, she has interactions with people in Catalan. The interlocutor speaks in Catalan, she understands and responds in Spanish, and this goes on without any issues. When asked to respond to the question "Who are you?" her response reveals a sense of identity that is highly layered and complex:

> I cannot say much about this, but I can only say that I try to learn something, every day, as much as I can, I help someone, this is my routine, apart from my business, meeting nice people, looking for nice people, being with them, learning from them, there should be a friends circle but a good one, and then my family, my kids, my family, my husband, these are more important [...] I want to learn more, but the problem is I don't have time now. I return home at 9:30, my children have exams, I pay attention to them, but it is pending for me, I have to do an English speaking course and of Catalan.

When asked what her response is when she is asked de dónde eres, "Where are you from?" Sunita said, "I like it a lot that I am Indian. I like it. Honestly, I am speaking from my heart. I feel very proud that I am from India."[42] When told that she seems to be equally comfortable with her origin identity and her integration with her present place of residence and the local society, she added, "I always try that wherever you live, wherever you go, you should adopt the things of that place, the benefit of this is that the people there would also adopt you (sic.) if we think, our culture is not like this, and I am fine the way I am, then you cannot expect from anyone that."[43] We may deduce from the above conversation that for Sunita being a businesswoman, a mother, a wife, and someone who likes to learn something is her identity. She did not associate the usual markers of identification such as origin country (India), religion (Sikhism), mother tongue (Punjabi), gender (female), or sexuality (heterosexual) to define her identity. Her work, her passion for learning and her role as a wife and mother, is what she claims is most important to her. Languages are tools for her that have helped in her integration, which has enabled her to be successful, but she did not have to discard her origin country/culture/language for that. A woman like Sunita is not trapped in the bubbles of in-communication. Knowledge of local languages allows her to interact and thus understand and also be understood by the local population. In her case, the integration is a mutual process of understanding and acceptance, and language is at the heart of it.

---

42. Respondent No. 4 in conversation with the author on May 15, 2018, Sabadell.
43. Ibid.

Flowing between two worlds

Three of the respondents, Laila, Naaz, and Hina, came to Barcelona as children when their family was reunited and therefore received at least a part of their school education in Catalonia. They represent the second generation of South Asian women in Spain. They have some knowledge of their home languages or mother tongues as well, be it Hindi/Urdu, Hindko, or Punjabi, but Spanish and/or Catalan are their first languages—the languages that they use the most, and in which they are most fluent. Compared to their mothers, they all seem more empowered, independent, and well-integrated in the host society. They are ambitious; they have either already joined or plan to enter the labor market. They seek additional educational qualifications to expand their work opportunities. They have only faint memories of the initial challenges with the language they had, if any. Unlike their mothers, language skills are not an issue for them at all.

The language (e)scapes for these three subjects are more complex than the ones discussed so far because these subjects are continually flowing between at least three languages and cultures, their origin or home language/s, and the two local languages: Spanish and Catalan. Apart from the language and culture of their parents, these younger subjects are impacted by the dynamics between the two local languages. [44] The presence of a strong Catalan nationalist movement escalated to a major constitutional crisis in October 2017. [45] The Spanish State and the Government of Catalonia have remained in conflict ever since. It is a fact that most of the immigrants—such as the parents of our respondents—primarily speak Spanish and either already have Spanish citizenship or aspire to it. As children of immigrant parents in a superdiverse city, they have also interacted and grown up with children from various nationalities who also speak multiple languages in their respective homes.

When asked how they define their identity and how integrated they feel to the host society, most of them had a complex response. None of them feels that they are Catalan or Spanish despite having lived there their whole lives. They tended to identify with their culture of origin through its customs and habits even though the languages they are most fluent in are different from the ones that their origin culture speaks. They did not feel discriminated against or differentiated by the host society.

---

[44]. Kathryn Woolard, *Singular and Plural Ideologies of Linguistic Authority in 21st Century Catalonia* (Oxford University Press, 2016), 301.

[45]. Kathryn Woolard, "Catalan Language, identity and independence," *OUPblog*, January 18, 2018, accessed January 28, 2018, https://blog.oup.com/2018/01/catalan-language-identity-independence/.

An example that illustrates the existing tension between Spanish and Catalan among the respondents and how each of them has a different relationship with the languages is this: Naaz and Hina are sisters but have different views on Catalan independence movement as well as the notion of a common language for people in Barcelona. While Naaz expressed the view that Catalan is the elite language and Spanish is the language of the street, Hina completely disagreed and said Catalan is the language of the pueblo [the ordinary people] and Spanish the historically imposed language.[46] Out of the three, Hina was the most emotionally attached to the Catalan language. She said Catalan is for her lengua de emoción, the language of emotion, the language in which she likes to hear, or say poetry. Hina is a student of Law and Politics, and her interview expressed a lot of the ideas of Catalan intellectuals. Naaz, on the other hand, acts as a mediator or a bridge between South Asian women and the host society. She runs an NGO that provides short-term assignments to South Asian women who earn by using their traditional skills such as mehendi application, decoration, cooking South Asian cuisine, and traditional embroidery. [47] Both Laila and Naaz also work as teachers of Spanish or Catalan to South Asian women under a program sponsored by an organization that promotes intercultural understanding.[48]

Conclusion

It is through language that human beings communicate, which enables them to form groups, record knowledge, and pass it on to the next generation. Cultures and civilizations are therefore embedded into languages, and they play a significant role in the formation of group identities. This article has shown that knowledge of local languages is an essential tool for migrant women from South Asia in the diasporic condition. It helps in bringing them out of the limited domestic space and fixed gender roles. It is what opens the doors of opportunities and breaks out of bubbles of confinement and incommunication.[49] The socio-economic condition and cultural background of the woman in the country of origin play some role, but what she makes of the new opportunities afforded by migration depends primarily on her capability to learn the local languages. The host society members' willingness to interact with the migrant

---

[46]. Respondent number 6 and 8 in discussion with author on July 6, 2018, Barcelona.

[47]. *Mehendi* is a herb based paste used by many communities to make patterns of temporary nature on the palms or feet.

[48]. The author cannot reveal the name of the organization and the project as she is obliged to conceal the identity of the respondents and due to the uniqueness of the project mentioning it may make it easy to identify them.

[49]. A term used in Spanish law where one is denied the right to communicate

is a significant determinant of this capability. Many of the conversations during this study revealed a pang of guilt, a feeling of being a burden—on the immediate earning family member as well as the new country they have come to work to—,and a sense of gratitude for being 'tolerated.' Their position of being migrants and financially dependent merge to give them that feeling. Any progressive society should provide channels for replacing the sense of gratitude for being tolerated with a sense of belonging and solidarity among women, the mothers of the future generations of a diverse Catalonia, Spain, Europe, and the world.

Bibliography

Appadurai, Arjun. *Modernity at Large- Cultural Dimensions of Globalization.* Minneapolis and London: University of Minnesota Press, 1996.

Arnaut, Karel, Jan Blommaert, Ben Rampton, and Massimiliano Spotti. *Language and Superdiversity.* New York: Routledge, 2016.

Aubia, Solé Montserrat and Josep Rodríguez Roca. "Pakistaníes en España: un estudio basado en el colectivo de la ciudad de Barcelona." *Revista CIDOB d'Afers Internacionals,* no. 68. (2004): 97-118.

Bartolomeo, Anna Di, Sona Kalantaryan, Justyna Salamońska, and Philippe Fargues. *Migrant Integration between Homeland and Host Society. Volume. 2. Global Migration Issues.* Cham: Springer, 2017. DOI 10.1007/978-3-319-56370-1_1.

Beacco, Jean-Claude, David Little, and Chris Hedges. *Linguistic Integration of Adult Migrants Guide to Policy Development and Implementation.* Council of Europe, Language Policy Unit, 2014. https://rm.coe.int/16802fc1cd.

Blommaert, Jan. "Langauge- The great diversifier." In *Routledge International Handbook of Diversity Studies,* edited by Steven Vertovec, 83-90. London and New York: Routledge, 2015.

Blommaert, Jan. *Ethnography, Superdiversity, and Linguistic Landscape, Chronicles of Complexity.* Buffalo, Toronto, and Bristol: Multilingual Matters, 2013.

Castles, Stephen, Hein de Haas, and Mark J. Miller. *The Age of Migration: International Population Movements in the Modern World.* New York: Palgrave Macmillan, 2014.

Eduardo Guarnizo, Luis. "The Economic of Transnational Living." The International Migration Review 37, no. 3. *Transnational Migration: International Perspectives.* (Fall, 2003): 666-699. https://www.jstor.org/stable/30037753.

"Evolución de la población total y Extranjera." *Idescat.* Accessed April 25, 2020. https://www.idescat.cat/poblacioestrangera/?b=0&lang=es.

Favell, Adrian. "The Changing Face of 'Integration' in a Mobile Europe." *Council For European Studies Newsletter* (June 2013). http://www.adrianfavell.com/CESweb.pdf

Favell, Adrian. *Philosophies of Integration: Immigration and the Idea of Citizenship in France and Britain.* London: Palgrave Macmillan, 2001.

García, Ofelia. "Problematizing Linguistic Integration of migrants: the role of translanguaging and language teachers." In *The Linguistic Integration of*

Adult Migrants Some Lessons from Research, edited by Jean-Claude Beacco, Hans-Jürgen Krumm, David Little, Philia Thalgott, 11- 26. Berlin and Boston: De Gruyter, 2017.

Garha, Nachatter Singh, Juan Galeano, and Andreu Domingo Valls. "South Asian Immigration to Spain: Socio-demographic Profile and Territorial Distribution, 2000-2014." *Asian and Pacific Migration Journal*, vol.25, Issue 2. (March 2016): 195-205. https://doi.org/10.1177/0117196816639166.

Gil, Elvira Riera. *Why Languages matter to people. Communication, identity, and justice in Western democracies. The case of mixed societies.* Barcelona: Generalitat de Catalunya. Institut d'Estudis de l'Autogovern, 2016.

Gómez Ventura, German. "Highly skilled Indian migrant population in Spain." In *CARIM-India RR 2013*, San Domenico di Fiesole: Migration Policy Centre European University Institute, 2013.

Ivlevs, Artjoms, Milena Nikolova, and Carol Graham. "Emigration, remittances, and the subjective well-being of those staying behind." *Journal of Population Economics* no. 32 (2019): 113-151. https://doi.org/10.1007/s00148-018-0718-8.

Kawulich, Barbara B. "Participant Observation as a Data Collection Method." In *Forum: Qualitative Social Research* Vol. 6 No. 2 Art 43 May, Online, (2005): n.p.. https://www.qualitative-research.net/index.php/fqs/article/view/466/996

López-Sala, Ana. "From Traders to Workers: Indian Immigration in Spain." In *CARIM-India RR 2013*. San Domenico di Fiesole (FI): European University Institute, 2013.

McAuliffe, Marie, and Vinod Khadria. *World Migration Report, 2020.* Geneva: International Organization for Migration, 2019.

Nogueira, Charo. "De Pakistan a Barcelona sin salir de casa." *El Pais*. August 17, 2002. https://elpais.com/diario/2002/08/17/opinion/1029535209_850215.html.

O'Neil, Tam, Anjali Fleury, and Marta Foresti. "Women on the move Migration, gender equality, and the 2030 Agenda for Sustainable Development." *ODI Briefing Papers* (July 2016): n.p. https://www.odi.org/publications/10476-women-move-migration-gender-equality-and-2030-agenda-sustainable-development.

"Part I: Perfil de la població estrangera a Barcelona." Ajuntament de Barcelona. Departament d'Estadística i Difusió de Dades. January (2019). Accessed April 25, 2020.https://www.bcn.cat/estadistica/catala/dades/inf/pobest/pobest19/part/nt110.htm

Pisarevskaya, Asya, Nathan Levy, Peter Scholten, and Joost Jansen. "Mapping migration studies: An empirical analysis of the coming of age of a research field." In *Migration Studies*. Oxford University Press, 2019. https://doi.org/10.1093/migration/mnz031

"Població estrangera per països." *Idescat.* Accessed April 25, 2020. https://www.idescat.cat/poblacioestrangera/?b=12.

Requejo, Ferran. "Is Spain a Federal Country." Shades of Federalism. Accessed March 3, 2020. http://50shadesoffederalism.com/case-studies/spain-federal-country.

Sharma, Rashmi. "Gender and International Migration: The Profile of Female Migrants from India." Social Scientist 39, no. 3/4 (March-April 2011): 37-63. https://www.jstor.org/stable/41633793.

Vertovec, Steven. "Super-diversity and its implications." Ethnic and Racial Studies 30 no.6. (November 2007): 1024-1054.

Woolard, Kathryn. "Catalan Language, identity and independence" in OUPblog, January 18, 2018. Accessed January 28, 2018. https://blog.oup.com/2018/01/catalan-language-identity-independence/.

Woolard, Kathryn. *Singular and Plural Ideologies of Linguistic Authority in 21st Century Catalonia.* London: Oxford University Press, 2016.

Maps in Non-Oedipal Cartographies

Chapter 6

Becoming a phantom people: Non-Oedipal spatialities, the Sunderbans and the bhadralok gaze

Tonisha Guin

Forum on Contemporary Theory, India

Abstract

The Bengali mainstream is closely associated with the demographic category of the bhadralok (loosely translated as Bengali gentleman). It is a loaded word and a heterogeneous category. Simply put, it stands for the part of Bengal's population that is middle-class in its sensibility, literate, (largely) Hindu, urban-oriented (if not always physically urban-located), caste-Kayastha or Brahmin, mostly service-sector, mostly identifying as modern, secular or humanist. Within the Bengali mainstream social imaginary, the Sunderbans have persistently occupied a liminal space. A sustained practice of othering persists in mainstream representations of its peoples, lived practices, and mutable geographies both within juridico-political institutions and, more crucially, in the domain of what may be loosely termed culture. The Sundarbans can be discursively accessed predominantly only through texts that locate themselves within the Bengali Bhadralok identity project. When one is confronted with the epistemic violence of all Sunderbans representation being Bhadralok representations, with the Bhadralok gaze implicit in them, instead of countering it with an as yet unavailable or inaccessible counter-hegemonic stance, it is more productive to look at the liminal spaces where these neat polarizations are destabilized. This paper argues that Atin Bandopadhyay's Bengali short story for children, "Atapurer Bagh" ("Atapur's Tiger"), provides one such stance insofar as it is located in the Sunderbans but is simultaneously evocative of the Bhadralok. It creates a space that manages to take the Bhadralok identity project vis-a-vis the Sunderbans and turns it into fluid indeterminacies.

Keywords: Opacity, oedipal, liminal, epistemic violence, counter-hegemonic

***

How can space be Oedipal or its opposite? There are two ways of imagining a response: First, space, especially land or territory, has been frequently anthropomorphized like nature is, most commonly as a goddess and/or a mother figure.[1] So, one way in which space can be Oedipal is in terms of the patriarchal trope that imagines men as agentive carriers of civilization who harvest and make land (and other natural elements) fecund and reproductive: men across generations may harvest—or otherwise use—the same tract of land, and call it by the same name of a mother, thus making the relationship Oedipal.[2] The other way of trying to explore this notion links space to the notion of anxiety. The word Oedipal is overwhelmingly coined as a crisis, after all. It refers to either the anxiety of breaking a taboo unknowingly, or, perhaps more devastatingly, the awareness of something familial being also a taboo, and being incapable of resisting it, nonetheless. Either way, the common denominator of both explanations has the figure of an agentive man (whether as an act of omission or generalization) as the anxious position. Spaces are cultural concepts, and not purely physical, literal ones. They are imagined and represented within the cultural frameworks of meaning-making. Symbolic values can alter the way they are perceived. They can therefore act as cultural constructs as any other entity. Postmodern political geographer and urban theorist Edward Soja argues that an understanding of space is essential to an understanding of society since spaces are socially constructed and intertwined with social relations over time.[3]

As one sees, therefore, the word bhadralok is bandied a lot within Indian postcolonial academia. Across the extraordinary moments of mainstream History writing, the Bengali bhadralok has been discussed at length because Kolkata, then Calcutta, was the nerve center of colonial trade and administration. The peculiarity of the bhadralok identity lies in its overwhelming emphasis on the code of conduct of bhadrata, which is as ambiguous as it is invasive, blurring and overshadowing all other quantifiable parameters like class, caste, religion, language, and gender.

The word bhadralok is gender-inflected, and by default, masculine. It relates implicitly to fluency in a certain dialect of (Calcuttan) Bengali, and explicitly to habitation and education in or around, or oriented towards Kolkata. It is common enough to say, "Speak or act like a bhadralok!" the moment a conversation turns heated, assuming that that is the only 'proper' way to behave.

---

[1]. David Leeming and Christopher Fee, *The Goddess: Myths of the Great Mother* (Islington: Reaktion Books, 2016), 48.

[2]. Knut A. Jacobsen, *Encyclopedia of Religion and Nature* (New York: Bloomsbury Academic, 2008), 1299-1300.

[3]. Edward W Soja, *Thirdspace* (Malden: Blackwell, 1996), 57.

Unless one addresses this normalization, one cannot adequately account for how caste, class, regional or linguistic discrimination function within mainstream Bengal. Thus, Bengali migrants from neighboring Bangladesh, who live in small towns and villages within Bengal, and itinerant laboring communities from other Indian states are either treated as static stereotypes or occluded within mainstream Bengali representations and representations of Bengal within India.

The Sundarban area, because of its proximity to Kolkata and location in Bengal, is presumed to be a familiar, accessible space for the bhadralok. The communities living in the Sundarbans speak various dialects of Bengali, prepare and consume similar food, worship gods who are familiar to if not worshipped by the bhadralok. There are certainly points of cultural difference: the label of being folk, the lack of civic amenities and infrastructure, and the economic, cultural, and social capital normalized by the bhadralok, the presence of migrant and refugee communities. However, these distinctions are usually read in the mainstream imaginary as points of inferiority, as are the difficult terrain and the necessary cohabitation with the wilderness.[4] These hierarchized differences make the Sundarbans a liminal space from the perspective of the bhadralok, insofar as it is Bengali but not quite so. The story at hand takes matters further, progressing from a liminal to a non-Oedipal space.

Non-Oedipal spatialities create in their wake an anxiety of ownership that may be articulated in terms of territorial boundaries, access to resources, legal right to call a place home, or inferior or superior to one's milieu, but mostly, overwhelmingly, in terms of the overarching sense of belonging, identity and identifying practices. The systems of knowledge that legitimize grand narratives around identity projects extend themselves to these anxieties around space. Thus, for instance, Kolkata's prestige as the commonly lauded cultural capital of India is deeply intertwined with how the Bengali Bhadralok identity project assumes high cultural associations and identifies Kolkata as its ideal "habitus," a set of embodied predispositions that influence an individual or community's ways of perceiving their lived environment and responding to it.[5]

---

4. Numerous prose and fictional pieces from the Bengali literary canon perpetuate this stance in what may appear as a timeless exercise. Within young adult fiction, as far back as Bibhutibhushan Bandopadhyay's *Sunderbane Saat Botsor (Seven Years in the Sunderbans)* written in 1949-50 to the opinion pieces published in *Anandamela Patrika* in July 2019, little has changed.

5. Pierre Bourdieu, "Physical Space, Social Space and Habitus" (Oslo: Rapaport, University of Oslo, 1996), 16-17, 21-22, https://archives.library.illinois.edu/erec/University%20Archives/24

I

A sustained practice of otherizing persists in mainstream representations of the Sundarban communities, lived practices, mutable geographies both within juridico-political institutions and, more crucially, in the domain of what may be loosely termed 'culture'. Precarious, liminal spaces like the Sundarbans can be discursively accessed predominantly only through texts that locate themselves within the Bengali bhadralok identity project. Now, while the binaries, in this case, that of the Bengali bhadralok and the individual living in the Sundarbans, are essential to our understanding of the politics of representation and occlusion that are played out along their matrices, they are hardly sufficient. If one is confronted with the epistemic violence of all Sundarbans representation being bhadralok representations, with the bhadralok gaze implicit in them, instead of countering it with an as yet unavailable or inaccessible counter-hegemonic stance, it is more productive to look at the liminal spaces where these neat polarisations are destabilized.

No identity, including the bhadralok one, is watertight. Being a construct, it contains within itself the possibilities of its own deconstruction. Atin Bandopadhyay's fiction, which one may call liminal insofar as it is located in the Sundarbans but is simultaneously evocative of the bhadralok, creates a space that manages to take the Bhadralok identity project vis-a-vis the Sundarbans and turns it into fluid indeterminacies. The Kolkata/Sundarbans binary dissolves to create performativities that subsume and invert each other, and above all, problematize and baffle the bhadralok gaze. This paper takes up a Bengali, a supernatural short story by Bandopadhyay penned for young adults, "Atapurer Bagh" (Atapur's Tiger), to examine the question of the Bhadralok gaze in the alienated spaces of Sundarbans and the disruptions in its wake.

"Atapurer Bagh" is told from the perspective of Bengali bhadralok Radhamohon Babu, a retiree plagued with many troubles at home: negligent sons and daughters-in-law, missing domestic staff, and loneliness. Radhamohon Babu feels humiliated at having to run errands and perform what may be called emasculating and demeaning domestic labor like cooking, shopping, and serving food that is typically not assigned to a Hindu, Bengali paterfamilias. [6] His sufferings are exacerbated by the sudden, unplanned absence of their most

---

01001/Production_website/pages/StewardingExcellence/Physical%20Space,%20Social%20S pace%20and%20Habitus.pdf#:~:text=PHYSICAL%20SPACE%2C%20SOCIAL%20SPACE%20 AND%20HABITUS%20by%20Pierre,Distinction%20into%20norvegian.%20Thanks%20to%2 0the%20publishing%20house, accessed February 9, 2017.

[6]. *Babu* is a genteel Bengali form of address to a man, can be translated as both "mister" and "master."

dependable domestic help, an unnamed woman from the Sundarbans area whom he employed, in part, as an act of charity. Peripatetic and voluble, this woman becomes Radhamohon Babu's only conversational companion and comrade in aide, spooling out stories of her life in the Sundarbans and her son, Bagharu. In these stories, Bagharu attains slightly mythic proportions, at once a half-starved teenager and a young man whose very name can be used to scare away tigers. While he does not explicitly say as much, Radhamohon Babu's disbelief at the tigers' fear of Bagharu is implicit in the narrative.

Troubled by her absence, and increasingly dissatisfied at home, Radhamohon Babu sets out to find Bagharu's mother and coax her back into service. The unfamiliar territory of the Sundarbans discomfits and disorients him once he leaves home and is gradually stripped from familiar, civic amenities. Arriving at dusk at the ghat closest to Bagharu's village, he is relieved when Bagharu chances upon him. This relief is short-lived, since a tiger joins their walk, slinking close to Radhamohon Babu as they walk to Bagharu's home. When he reaches there, he discovers that he has been pacing with a tiger and a ghost who can master it. The story ends with him fainting, overwhelmed.

The narrative is primarily structured around the conversations between two apparently polarized characters: Radharomon, an old, retired, white-collar Bengali Bhadralok residing in Kolkata, and Bagharu's Mother (the only identifier for the character, who does not receive a name in "Atapurer Bagh"). The absence of her given name gains narrative importance in due time because of the role Bagharu plays in the story's climax but also hints at her abjection.[7] Insofar as her name goes, the descriptor of being Bagharu's mother is all we have in the place of a proper noun and are compelled to treat as such. Abjection, as one of the most extreme iterations of otherizing, may not imply simply powerlessness, or dehumanization, but can also stand for a subject position that actively disturbs conventional identities or practices. She is a younger, impoverished woman from one of the villages of the Sundarbans area, described as skeletal and malnourished. The power equation between the two shows itself in her deeply polite, often obsequious conversation and his occasional, open disbelief or ridicule. The story provides a detailed physical description of her physical being ("skeletal creature," "hollowed deep sunk eyes," "no flesh on bones") while the narrator, Radharomon, is described primarily in terms of his social relations: with his family, his past job, and his neighbors. Given the lack of physical description, one may assume that readers are expected to imagine a figure that for them best embodies a 'typical' Bengali, city-bred, white-collar, elderly man. Primarily, however, the reader witnesses a friendship/companionship that is

---

7. Julia Kristeva, *Powers of Horror: An Essay on Abjection* (New York: Columbia University Press, 1982), 7-8.

evidently interdependent: nobody else in the household seems likely to entertain Bagharu's Mother and her need for conversation, to cope with the way she must be homesick. Similarly, Radharomon, despite being the paterfamilias of what looks like an urban middle-class household, is peculiarly victimized, undermined despite age and familial position, by being made into an errand-boy and man-of-all-work. Significantly, these tasks devolve even more onto Radharomon following the unplanned absence of Bagharu's Mother, perhaps indicating a certain process of identification and commonality between these characters, despite their polarized positionalities.

The story itself is narrated like one long rambling conversation full of disconnected anecdotes, flashbacks, and non-chronologically embedded events and recollections. It is effectively structured to resemble one of Bagharu's Mother's roundabout rambles, with several subplots and asides. Despite this, significantly for us, the narrative expects the reader's gaze to emanate from Radharomon's stated location: he is the suturing figure in the story. His responses—ridicule, awe, justifications, wonder and unease in the latter part of the story—are the emotional interpellative signposts for the reader, even as Bagharu's Mother is relied on to provide the descriptions to which these responses are made. Bagharu's mother's and Radharomon's power relation embodies the Kolkata-Sundarbans power relation.

II

Identity projects, in both practice and theorization, are and have been preoccupied with the act of mystifying and demystifying the Other because of their preoccupation with the Self.[8] In practice, however, this watertight binary is disrupted; praxis itself is necessarily contingent and disruptive, even as it is reiterative. The process and location of liminality emerge instead as a fecund and accessible site of locating selfhood and alienation in their complex interactions. In the mainstream Bengali social imaginary, the Sundarbans serves as an appropriate site to trace out this oscillation between liminality and binaries, because of both its physical geography hemming the state (and country) and the cultural associations attributed to the space and its inhabitants. The identity and social location of the speaking subject, therefore, becomes especially important in trying to read these tensions in any discourse

---

8. Though modern identities are treated as hybrid, fractured cultural constructs in Cultural Studies, in the works of Stuart Hall, Raymond Williams et. al, identities are imagined in terms of neat, coherent grand narratives, with a distinct beginning, middle and end. Whether mainstream or marginal, these narratives or identity projects anchor discussions around how an identity is conformed to and represented.

of the Sundarbans. There is a lot of emphasis on the visibility of alternative lives and norms in identity-centric politics, as a reaction to the mainstream, to foreground adequate, non-mediated, non-distorted representations of peripheral identities. One may see this in the work of the Subaltern Studies Initiative's deliberations to represent the epistemic violence meted out to minority, so-called non-modern, communities, and practices.[9] The norm of visibility has formed the backbone of identity projects: it is what one is constantly in conversation with, whether through conformity or opposition.

The selected story renders in its narrative a different trajectory, beginning with two deeply polarized characters, their conversations, and, following what appears to be commonsensical responses from the perspectival character, who serves as a site for suturing, about the incongruencies in those conversations. Thus, early on, one reads:

> "Bagharu's Mother! What kind of a name is that!" Radharomon Babu was very surprised.
> "Bagharu is my eldest son."
> "What does he do?"
> "Please, Sir, he beats tigers."[10]
> "Tigers? What are you saying! It is illegal to kill tigers. If the government finds out, he will end up in jail."
> "Please, Baba, he beats and chases away tigers like cattle to the other side of the river. Even poor peasant folk like us understand that it is a sin to kill tigers."[11]

However, the structure of the story refuses a clear resolution. The incongruencies are allowed to persist. The neat polarizing of modern/backward, urban/rural power relations are irrevocably disrupted in Radharomon's journey to the Sundarbans, and further when he is rescued by proximity to Bagharu. This, even more than the subsequent discovery that his savior Bagharu is already dead, is the primary point of disruption, which overcomes the tricks and tropes of suspension of disbelief, plausible deniability, and assorted explanations Radharomon was using to accommodate Bagharu's Mother's stories till that point.

Intriguingly, however, this disruption, though crucial, doesn't form the focal point of the story. The narrative instead foregrounds a gradual rise of unease and

---

9. The Subaltern Studies Initiative was spearheaded by Ranajit Guha, with contributions from numerous Indian scholars, with commentaries on Bengal especially by scholars like Partha Chatterjee, Sudipta Kaviraj and Dipesh Chakrabarti.

10. The text uses "mara", a Bengali word which means both "to beat" and "to kill."

11. Atin Bandopadhyay, "Atapurer Bagh," in *Kishore Rachana Samagra* (Kolkata: Ananda Publishers, 1990), 33-34, translation from Bengali mine.

alienation that Radharomon feels in the face of Bagharu's Mother's accounts, and later, in his journey towards her home. This unease and alienation climax with him losing consciousness on realizing that he was not only walking through the forest next to a curious tiger. The latter did not kill him because of a defenseless young boy, but further that the circle of domestic light is no guarantee of familiarity. Instead, his savior is, in fact, a ghost who is as alienating and altruistic in death as he was in life. The discovery that the logic of Bagharu's Mother's stories is sound, inarguably rooted in lived experiences, fractures Radharomon's worldview: his own experience now proves that her perspective and knowledge system cannot be dismissed or trivialized.

Following this, it would be reductive to return to the polarizations one faced in the story's outset about Radharomon and Bagharu's Mother in terms of modern/backward, urban/rural, educated/illiterate, etc. It scarcely matters whether one needs to objectively evaluate whether Bagharu's Mother is right or wrong, it would even be reductive to do so if done as a part of evaluating the story itself. The focus of this article, and arguably the narrative at hand, is Radharomon's growing unease and sense of alienation, both from the world he inhabits and the space into which he ventures, despite its physical proximity, his relatively superior subject position, and, by the very structure of the story. Radharomon's disbelief and ridicule about Bagharu's Mother's accounts are only matched by his curiosity about and wonder at her home, which is only a few hours away from the urban hub of Kolkata.

One may turn to the concept of opacity to examine this sense of unease despite its innate familiarity, even interiorization. Edouard Glissant's promulgation of opacity responds to, and vehemently opposes the call for transparency in— particularly peripheral—identities and norms to make them discursively comprehensible. Opacity resists structuration and neat ordering, in favor of advocating for the marginalized and vulnerable to retain the right of refusal to be understood entirely, in absolutist terms. Transparency, Glissant suggests, would open them up to epistemic violence by calling them inferior, through normalized acts of erasure or hegemonic indifference. Glissant argues, "[t]he imaginary does not bear with it the coercive requirements of idea. It prefigures reality, without determining it a priori [...] The thought of opacity distracts me from absolute truths whose guardian I might believe myself to be."[12]

Accommodating a "different" identity, cultural beliefs, and normative practices within an idealized hierarchy of civilizational parameters reduces the different to the inferior. Whereas Walter D. Mignolo's work on decoloniality

---

[12]. Edouard Glissant, *Poetics of Relation* (Ann Arbor: University of Michigan Press, 1997), 192.

suggests that knowledge systems across the globe are hierarchized with a marked normalization of the understanding that Western, Global North ones— or those derived from the Global North rationalizations such as the Bhadralok identity project—are superior to that of the Global South.[13] Glissant's foregrounding of the term opacity and its relevance when talking about difference delves in the practices of otherizing, inferiorizing that get hegemonically normalized.

Glissant suggests that transparency and clarity, though they might lead to better categorization and comprehension, also lead to the newly understood norm or identity or experience being reduced in the process because of the inevitability of hierarchized taxonomies produced by hegemonic knowledge systems. He emphasizes that "[t]he opaque is not the obscure, though it is possible for it to be accepted as such. It is that which cannot be reduced, which is the most perennial guarantee of participation and confluence."[14] One may turn for an example to Partha Chatterjee's discussion of the ways in which colonial (and often postcolonial) anthropology dehumanizes tribal subjects or indigenous populations that don't appear to be equal participants in the project of modernity.[15] Thus, a book about the identity and norms of a tribe, written by someone from the Global North, will gain more prestige and value than a book written by someone from that tribe, whether written in English or the local language. One may also look at the ways in which the Bhadralok relies on Global North-centric science and technology for his knowledge on Sundarbans and sidesteps local norms and conventions as objectively inferior or valuable only as anthropological-historical 'folk' curiosities.

Attempts to create a counter-hegemonic stance by flipping the North-South binary do not help in the long run; while they create useful points of meaning, they remain dependent on a binary structure. Mignolo suggests that coloniality/modernity ought to be conceptually clubbed together rather than treated as sequential, whether coloniality is thought of as preceding or preceded by modernity. In so doing, he uses Anibal Quijano's conceptualization of the Colonial Matrix of Power (CMP), articulating it in the context of internal colonialism.[16] The knowledge systems and epistemic hierarchies created

---

[13]. Walter D. Mignolo, "Epistemic Reconstitution(s), Colonial/Imperial Differences and Border Thinking," in *Balvant Parekh Memorial Lecture Series* (Baroda: Balvant Parekh Centre, 2019), 68.

[14]. Ibid., 193.

[15]. Partha Chatterjee, "Itihaser Uttaradhikar," in *Nimnabarger Itihas*, eds. Gautam Bhadra and Partha Chatterjee (Kolkata: Ananda Publishers, 1998), 121.

[16]. Walter D Mignolo and Catherine E Walsh, *On Decoloniality: Concepts, Analytics, Praxis* (New York: Duke University Press, 2018), xiii-xv.

through colonial intervention, whereby knowledge produced in and/or by the Global North takes precedence over that created in the Global South, have persisted and proliferated through colonial modernity.

How, then, may one escape this colonial matrix of power that is integrated into postcolonial modernities, or the hierarchized binary of Global North/Global South in favor of Mignolo's decoloniality? One may turn to Glissant's conceptualization of opacity for an answer. Within critical discourses of identity politics in India, a lot of emphasis has been given to rendering the lived experience/s and cultural productions of disenfranchised communities visible, especially in the last few decades. In this vein, Dalit scholars like Gopal Guru call for not just making lived experiences visible but also theorizing on them by Dalit academics and intellectuals. Guru calls attention to the reiteration of caste hierarchies in mainstream intellectual exercises, where the archives of Dalit narratives may be treated as primary sources of theorizing by academics from the most privileged sections of the society.[17] The transparency Glissant resists is arguably comparable to the way scholars like Guru resist the unilateral relation between the proliferation of Dalit and other subaltern narratives of lived experience by Dalit authors, and the apparent monopoly of theorizing about them by academics who typically come from more privileged positions in caste hierarchies.

In the story at hand, Radharomon Babu, with his Bhadralok gaze, identification, and location, wields that power. Regardless of how companionable their conversation is, or the kinds of loneliness he faces, this understanding frames Radharomon's interactions with Bagharu's Mother. He can ask questions, expect answers, judge the truthfulness of the responses, discard them, and name her convictions "backward" or "superstitious" or "illiterate" if he so chooses. The reader's interpellation or suturing is de facto expected to follow his gaze and agree with his stances. In a binary model, the right to question and to normalize the act of questioning belongs to the powerful, and in turn, cements their power. However, opacity undercuts power in the narrative in the way in which Radharomon cannot comprehend Bagharu and his milieu as more than phantasmagoria and in the way in which the Sundarbans are half-familiar but irreducibly alien to his Bhadralok gaze. Though the story never mentions the term, its success as a horror story that evokes unease and fear relies heavily on the way the fact of Radharomon being a Bhadralok, and the reader's interpellation with what may only be called the Bhadralok gaze haunts it.

---

[17]. Gopal Guru, "How Egalitarian Are the Social Sciences in India?" *The Economic and Political Weekly*, December (2002): 5003-5009.

III

The Sundarbans is an extremely sensitive and endangered mangrove swampland to the south of Bengal, rich in biodiversity, especially endangered species, poor in resources and governmental aid because of the informal refugee colonies and economically disenfranchised communities living there. It falls within the taxonomies of high cultural, standardized identities and systemic cultural violence in peculiar ways. Direct, devastating state violence, including incidents of sexual violence as well as beatings or property damage, is part of a bigger cultural institution of otherization-occlusion that plays out in ordinary, everyday life problematics.[18] There is very little visibility of the cultural discourse and genealogies of everyday, ordinary politics of representation, exclusion, and epistemic violence around this strip of land and its peoples. Academic work has predominantly centered around its ecological vulnerability or the acts of direct violence—often in the hands of the government—experienced by its disenfranchised communities[19]. The normalized acts of exclusion, otherizing and objectification within the Bengali mainstream that frame these extraordinary moments of assault have not gained as much academic attention and critical commentary as is, perhaps, called for.

There is a need to trace the genealogy of the bhadralok differently, decolonially. Overwhelmingly, postcolonial mainstream History writing in India creates similar grand narratives. Regardless of whether the histories are in the "modern, progressive" mold of Nehruvian social imaginaries, or follow subaltern studies, which coined expressions like the "subaltern elite," or even the so-called "traditional," histories, which are considered pre-modern or proto-modern in terms of caste-religious clusters.[20] While these narratives may

---

[18]. Deep Halder, "'We Were Attacked Thrice' A Survivor's Story of the Left Front Government's Siege of Marichjhapi," *Scroll,* May 17, 2019, accessed April 15, 2020, https://scroll.in/article/923325/we-were-attacked-thrice-a-survivors-story-of-the-left-front-governments-siege-of-marichjhapi.

[19]. Many of these eyewitness accounts and scholarly texts examine the Marichjhnapi massacre, like Deep Halder's *Blood Island: An Oral History of the Marichjhapi Massacre* and Ross Mullick's "Refugee Resettlement in Forest Reserves: West Bengal Policy Reversal and the Marichjhapi Massacre," or Sukharanjan Sengupta's *Marichjhapi Beyond & Within.* Other texts, like Prafulla Kumar Chakrabarty's *The marginal men: The refugees and the left political syndrome in West Bengal,* touch upon the Sundarbans while discussing larger issues; of this ilk is Kavita Punjabi's work on Tebhaga, which discusses the Kakdwip area in detail. There is also a great deal of environmental work about the Sundarbans by scholars like Pranabesh Sanyal, which necessarily discuss the human aspect.

[20]. Ranajit Guha, "On Some Aspects of the Historiography of Colonial India," in *Selected Subaltern Studies,* ed. Ranajit Guha (Oxford: Oxford University Press, 1988), 35-44.

not be factually false, there is a politics of representation that normalizes and standardizes, and, simultaneously, occludes the processes of normalization and standardization, in the guise of respectability. For a general audience to read the inflections of behavior coded in the text, this is the context that has produced the story, and one must be attuned to it in order to explore the ways in which the story represents the Sunderbans in a non-oedipal way.

The mainstream hegemony of the bhadralok faces a curious contradiction in both the author and the content of "Atapurer Bagh." Atin Bandopadhyay hailed from a Bengali Brahmin family from Dhaka, was educated in Dhaka and Kolkata, and worked in white-collar jobs all his life in and oriented towards Kolkata. He spent the latter part of his life in the city, and premier Kolkata Bengali publishing houses published his works: he may, therefore, be treated as the very embodiment of the Kolkata bhadralok male sensibility. But simultaneously, he was also a refugee from Bangladesh, crossing over to India after the Partition, and spent much of his life in the Sunderbans region in both Bangladesh and West Bengal. One may see in Bandopadhyay's stories that the characters, practices, and worldviews depicted. At the same time, part of the larger Bengali-speaking community, are distinctly different from those of the typical Kolkata bhadralok, who is so often used as a shorthand for that community.

Lived experiences and performative acts around the grand narrative of an identity project cannot afford its neat, cohesive watertight boundaries (in this case, of delimiting the ideal, therefore only bhadralok-Bengali). The story follows suit, locating itself in a liminal space, most evidently in its narrative movement to and from between the Kolkata middle-class household and the impoverished Sunderbans village. One may see this liminality also in the way in which, despite Radharomon being the sutured/interpellated person, he is constantly confronted by experiences that disprove his assumptions and people and places. His oft-displayed ridicule and patronizing of Bagharu's Mother is implicitly debunked in the latter half of the story. However, this does not alter the largely sympathetic portrayal of Radharomon into someone the reader is expected to dislike. The reader continues to empathize with him, as both he and the person reading are proved wrong in what, at first look, appears as a fairly straightforward narrative.

Unaccountable, supernatural things happening beyond the civilized populated spaces is a familiar trope. But, even as the story reiterates it, it cannot offer any easy resolutions. In participating in life in the forest, and being protected by Bagharu from the tiger, Radharomon is no longer a pure outsider. He occupies the hybrid, plural subject position that perhaps reflects the author's, just as Bagharu's Mother is neither a bhadramahila nor entirely from the Sunderbans anymore, despite months of living in Kolkata and her friendship with Radharomon. The Kolkata, white-collar sensibilities of scientific rationality with which he identifies are never rejected. Still, they are neither sufficient nor foolproof in the face of his experience in his walk from the ghat. Conversely, in terms of the knowledge offered to him, one could argue that Bagharu's Mother, if not Bagharu himself, maintains a disarming amount of transparency. The opacity continues. The Sunderbans, Bagharu, and his family, all draw from and partially reject Radharomon's attitudes and resources, making the space non-oedipal for Radharomon.

Cultural productions from the Sundarbans are rarely a part of the mainstream or accepted as much, and when accepted, are mediated by city-based bhadralok groups as niche folk productions. The government's attitudes are reflected and further proliferated in cultural productions and vice versa. One may track this epistemic violence in the first place by tracing the disruptions bhadralok fiction performs. Additionally, one can treat fiction as theory, following N'Gugi wa Thiong'o, who looks to fiction as a way of ordering history, and believes that it can be seen "as a theory of felt experience" especially in relation to colonization.[21] Here, if biopolitics is understood as an individual's life gaining political, social value, one may look at how the story treats what life is preservable and what isn't. Bagharu, younger—therefore more vulnerable but also arguably, more deserving to live—dies while the elderly city man lives, and lives by being saved by him.

Bagharu's ghost becomes the abject figure who, even after his death, continues to haunt the living, and in them, focuses on saving the bhadralok exception who has entered the domains that, ipso facto, endanger him. In dying, Bagharu doesn't escape the biopolitical paradigms of what life is preservable and what is not. He becomes the liminal-abject figure about whom the mainstream's guilt is now absolved. The mainstream can now continue to put him to service: from saving other residents of his village who the Kolkata state and social machinery cannot spare resources to provide safe passage, to a Kolkata man who needs saving—his life falling in the preservable part of the dichotomy—when he especially endangers himself to chase the physical and emotional labor provided by Bagharu's Mother. The abject is no more a monolith or homogeneous, closed group. Bagharu before and after death and Bagharu's Mother occupy different parts of it. In this, the story not only reflects extant biopolitical norms that are not openly stated but presumed but arguably constitutes conditions of abjection within the liminal spaces and positionalities it opens up.

---

[21]. N'gugi wa Thiong'o, *Globalectics: Theory and the Politics of Knowing* (New York: Columbia University Press, 2012), 45-49.

"Atapurer Bagh," while published in a children's anthology of ghost stories, and certainly qualifying for inclusion, does not devote much narrative space to either the ghost or the jump-scare—the two usual ways in which stories of this sort operate. Instead, this story devotes only a fifth of its narrative length to what is supposed to be the climactic crux: the encounter with not just a spirit, but also a tiger, two elements of preternatural and supernatural terror that might be expected to interest young adults. One may speculate that what really makes it a scary and uneasy experience for Radharomon, and therefore a scary and uneasy horror story for the intended reader is its play with the uncanny. Freud speaks of the uncanny as the psychological experience, not of the absolutely mysterious, but instead of the strangely familiar.[22] The Sundarbans, while a part of Bengal, has to emerge as a site of exception, irrefutably contradicting the bhadralok Identity Project, even as a bhadralok ventures into it and finds it familiar enough to reinforce the assumptions of the identity project. In this way, for Radharomon, and, in this case, only Radharomon, the Sunderbans become a non-oedipal space.

IV

Precarious spaces like the Sundarbans make for a curious site of inquiry because they are neither considered entirely outside the imagined habitus of the Bengali bhadralok nor can they be entirely reconciled to them. If one locates modern identities in terms of their identity projects—an imagined grand narrative of the past, present, and hoped for future—examining the way the Sundarbans continue to be a liminal presence within the bhadralok identity project itself can act as an act of intervention. Located on the fringes of India and Bangladesh, the deltaic Sundarbans have survived as an endangered ecosphere with its rich flora, fauna amidst the natural disasters besetting it, most recently the super-cyclone Amphan in May 2020.[23] The space has provided refuge to innumerable disenfranchised migrant communities seeking political asylum and escaping natural disasters along the Indo-Bangladesh borders. Civic, state-sanctioned neglect and occasional acts of police brutality are normalized within a larger framework of alienation and occlusion of the people of Sundarbans as not quite citizen-subjects, but not entirely out of the domain of the imagined community of the state and its mainstream stakeholders.

---

[22]. Sigmund Freud. *The Uncanny*, trans. David McClintock (London: Penguin Books, [1919] 2003), 124.

[23]. Shoaib Danyal, "'Sundarbans is finished': Super cyclone Amphan leaves a trail of misery in Bengal," *Scroll*, May 26, 2020, accessed June 13, 2020, https://scroll.in/article/962916/sundarbans-is-finished-super-cyclone-amphan-leaves-a-trail-of-misery-in-bengal.

Despite a thriving print industry in Kolkata, there are more publications about the ecology of the Sundarbans in English rather than Bengali commentaries on the social ecologies of its people and their lived environments. Bengali mainstream representations of the Sundarbans in fiction, whether in English or Bengali, tend to be penned about the Sundarbans rather than emerging from it. While Bengali is a shared language, and cultural ethos have distinct overlaps, own-voices local narratives are rarely published and even more rarely publicized. The Sundarbans presents itself as something of an anomaly in the narratives of the Bengali bhadralok identity project with its caste, class, and city-centric affiliations, perhaps because of its perceived wildness, suspension of religion-caste sanctions, or deep impoverishment. Atin Bandopadhyay's account of this everyday marginalization escapes the established mainstream discourses distancing and exoticizing the Sunderbans, perhaps by virtue of its inclusion in a ghost story aimed at children. Supernatural fiction and fiction for children, while policed for "immoral" elements, are also allowed a certain disruption of the status quo, even without a subsequent stabilization, a return to normalcy. Since it is not intended to be an adult, formal treatise, or account, a resolution or conclusion can be sidestepped, bringing to the fore only the opacity that Radharomon experiences. This is what Bandopadhyay makes the most of in making the Sundarbans a setting for a ghost story for children and adolescents. He escapes mainstream expectations of a distinct resolution or conclusion expected from an adult, formal treatise, or auto/biographical account. It shifts the focus to the bigger cultural institution of otherization-occlusion that plays out in everyday problematics by foregrounding the different subject positions occupied by Radharomon, his family, and Bagharu's Mother and hers, without polarising them to the point of incomprehension.

In doing this, this story becomes pivotal in its treatment of knowledge systems, and a niggling awareness of how reductive it would be to call Radharomon modern. At the same time, Bagharu's Mother is dubbed superstitious and backward, and how easily it would deprive her of agency. It is also fascinating to note the treatment of truth and truth-effects, information, and facticity in the story. It begs the question of how one may engage with the notions of knowledge systems and power relations vis-a-vis Radharomon's overwhelming experience of dissonance. This story draws attention to how one knowledge system cannot be entirely subsumed or written off by another, without forcing the reader to choose one unequivocally in favor of the other: while the suturing with Radharomon as the story's protagonist-narrator and mainstream spokesperson holds throughout the story, the disruptions, contradictions, and dissonances experienced by Radharomon don't allow for an easy discrediting of him, nor of Bagharu's Mother.

V

This article has examined the ways in which power relations not only between the Global North and Global South but also between privileged and marginalized regions in the Global South influence the hierarchization of knowledge systems. The narrative studied echoes and draws on normative practices in Bengal, particularly among the Bhadralok of Kolkata, in relation to the Sundarbans and an implicit cultural polarization of spaces. If a space becomes Oedipal because of a sense of familiarity and ownership, due to patriarchal inheritance laws and the symbolization of the land as female, then Radharomon's inability to claim the Sundarbans through inherited or entitled familiarity, inferiorizing or ridicule render it non-Oedipal. This dissonance, and the anxiety to which it gives rise, is not one that affects Bagharu's Mother or her son. The Oedipal crisis enacted in the narrative about their space leaves them untouched, secure as they are in the sense of reciprocally belonging to the land, such that the space, tigers and ghosts and all, is their milieu. In fact, this understanding is attuned to Bagharu's deeply opaque resistance to sharing it with those he perceives as outsiders. They are both at home, with the natural, preternatural, and supernatural aspects of the Sundarbans; it is only Radharomon's hegemonic, mainstream gaze which is unable to accommodate and indeed truly perceive it without debilitating dissonance.

Bibliography

Bandopadhyay, Atin. "Atapurer Bagh." In *Kishore Rachana Samagra*. Calcutta: Ananda Publishers, 1990.

Bourdieu, Pierre. "Physical Space, Social Space, and Habitus:" University of Oslo, 1996. https://archives.library.illinois.edu/erec/University%20Archives/2401001/Production_website/pages/StewardingExcellence/Physical%20Space,%20Social%20Space%20and%20Habitus.pdf#:~:text=PHYSICAL%20SPACE%2C%20SOCIAL%20SPACE%20AND%20HABITUS%20by%20Pierre,Distinction%20into%20norvegian.%20Thanks%20to%20the%20publishing%20house. Accessed February 19, 2018.

Chatterjee, Partha. "Itihaser Uttaradhikar." In *Nimnabarger Itihas*, edited by Gautam Bhadra and Partha Chatterjee. Kolkata: Ananda Publishers, 1998.

Danyal, Shoaib. "'Sundarbans is finished': Super cyclone Amphan leaves a trail of misery in Bengal," *Scroll*, May 26, 2020. Accessed June 13, 2020. https://scroll.in/article/962916/sundarbans-is-finished-super-cyclone-amphan-leaves-a-trail-of-misery-in-bengal.

Freud, Sigmund. "The 'Uncanny'." https://web.mit.edu/allanmc/www/freud1.pdf. Accessed February 2, 2020.

Halder, Deep. "'We Were Attacked Thrice' A Survivor's Story of the Left Front Government's Siege of Marichjhapi." *Scroll*, May 17, 2019. Accessed April 15, 2020, https://scroll.in/article/923325/we-were-attacked-thrice-a-survivors-story-of-the-left-front-governments-siege-of-marichjhapi.

Glissant, Edouard. *Poetics of Relation*. Ann Arbor: University of Michigan Press, 1997.

Guha, Ranajit. "On Some Aspects of the Historiography of Colonial India." In *Selected Subaltern Studies*.Oxford: Oxford University Press. 1988.

Guru, Gopal. "How Egalitarian Are the Social Sciences in India?" *The Economic and Political Weekly*, December (2002): 5003-5009.

Jacobsen, Knut A. *Encyclopedia of Religion and Nature. New York*. Bloomsbury Academic, 2008.

Leeming, David and Christopher Fee. *The Goddess: Myths of the Great Mother. Islington*. Reaktion Books, 2016.

Kristeva, Julia. "Powers of Horror: An Essay on Abjection." In *Powers of Horror*, n.p. http://users.clas.ufl.edu/burt/touchyfeelingsmaliciousobjects/Kristevapowerso fhorrorabjection.pdf. Accessed November 30, 2019.

Mignolo, Walter D. "Epistemic Reconstitution(s), Colonial/Imperial Differences, and Border Thinking." In *Balvant Parekh Memorial Lecture Series*, Baroda: Balvant Parekh Centre, 2019.

Mignolo, Walter D. and Walsh, Catherine E. *On Decoloniality: Concepts, Analytics, Praxis*. New York: Duke University Press, 2018.

Soja, Edward W. *Thirdspace*. Malden: Blackwell, 1996.

Sturken, Marita and Lisa Cartwright. *Practices of Looking: An Introduction to Visual Culture*. Oxford: Oxford University Press, 2009.

Thiong'o, N'gugi wa. *Globalectics: Theory and the Politics of Knowing*. New York: Columbia University Press, 2012

Chapter 7

Postcolonial "Geography Lessons" from Sri Lanka: Travel, globalization, and diaspora

Shelby E. Ward

Virginia Tech; Tusculum University

Abstract

Following the work of scholars like Debbie Lisle that is critical of the sustained coloniality of travel narratives and the resulting implications on global politics, this article offers a close reading of selected verses of two Sri Lankan poets: Jean Arasanayagam and Ramya Chamalie Jirasinghe. Both women are conscious of the interconnections between globalization, colonialism, and international travel. Therefore, their work provides examples of the transformative potential of travel writing.[1] This transformative potential is revealed by reading these poems through Gilles Deleuze and Félix Guattari's conceptualization of "mapping" versus "tracing." While traditional narratives can be described as "traces," or reproductions of Empire and past colonial legacies, Arasanayagam and Jirasinghe provide a map that connects nomadically through systems such as colonialism and globalization as they travel and write back to geographies of the West in processes of becoming. The article suggests that such a map provides postcolonial geography lessons that implicate two primary elements: the relationship between self/identity and home/displacement. These geography lessons offer a way to explore rather than mask the anxieties of globalization and colonialism. The article further argues that these writers provide a methodology for addressing the hegemonic power relations that have historically constituted the political practice of both writing and mapping as a western discursive project that continues to manage the world.

---

[1]. Debbie Lisle, *The Global Politics of Contemporary Travel Writing* (Cambridge University Press, 2006).

Jean Arasanayagam, *The Almsgiving* (Colombo: Social Scientists' Association, 2014).

Ramya Chamelie Jirasinghe, *There's an Island in the Bone* (Battaramulla: Yara Press, 2010).

Keywords: Mapping, tracing, Sri Lanka, Empire, diaspora

***

In the preface to her book, The Global Politics of Contemporary Travel Writing, Debbie Lisle tells the story of a trip to Saigon, while traveling solo through Asia and Africa. During the trip, she exchanged her copy of Milan Kundera's *The Joke* for Paul Theroux's *The Happy Isles of Oceania*, with an American traveler.[2] This moment mattered because while reading Theroux, she realized that there was something wrong, as she emphasizes, not just with this book in particular but with travel writing more generally. Connecting the historical trajectory of globalization and the continued thread of imperial power relations, she states:

> [t]here may be good travelogues and bad travelogues, but as a whole, the genre encourages a particularly conservative political outlook that extends to its vision of global politics. This is frustrating because travel writing has the potential to re-imagine the world in ways that do not simply regurgitate the status quo or repeat a nostalgic longing for Empire. To be sure, a small part of me remains hopeful that travel writing might take hold of its transformative potential, but I have to admit that it is a very small part indeed.[3]

This issue of travel writing, and what ultimately implicates the concerns of contemporary travel writing with the historical condition of colonialism is that "travel writing participated in the international realm by disseminating the goals of Empire: stories of 'faraway lands' were crucial in establishing the unequal, unjust and exploitative relations of colonial rule."[4]

It is not only that travel writing implicates the imaginaries and politics of Empire, and continued power relations within contemporary global politics, but the claiming and marking of place: mapping and geography, is directly connected with the narrative of place. Tariq Jazeel indicates how postcolonial thought has helped and continues to help "interrogate privilege, power, and inequality in our world." [5] It also brings "into view both the spatial interconnectedness of our common world and its irreducible mixed-up-ness— what postcolonial theorists call 'hybridity'," as he "emphasizes throughout [...]

---

2. Lisle, *The Global Politics*, xi.

3. Ibid.

4. Ibid., 1.

5. Tariq Jazeel, "Postcolonialism: Orientalism and the Geographical Imagination," *Geography* 97, no. 1 (2012): 4.

on the potential that postcolonialism offers for a critical and inquisitive undoing of our received geographical knowledge; what [he] refer[s] to as geographical unlearning."[6] While engaging with this ongoing conversation between postcolonial thought and geography, I mean to highlight the relationship between place, geography, and writing, as processes of becoming.

Further, this article suggests that if travel writing does possess such a transformative potential, as Lisle suggests, then it will not be found by looking in narratives that geographically continue to traverse from West to East, but instead by examining, for example, the ways in which power, place, and language are negotiated when the postcolonial writes back. While we may be able to talk generally of hegemonic imperial power relations, the postcolonial experience was and is not universal. This paper specifically explores the historical and contemporary politics of Sri Lanka, seen through two Sri Lankan poets.

The first is Jean Arasanayagam, who is perhaps best known for her poetry investigating identity politics within Sri Lanka, which often includes personal reflections on her own identity or the relationship with her husband's family, who is Tamil. Arguably her most well-known collection of poems is Apocalypse '83, which follows the start of the ethnic civil war in Sri Lanka and her own family's forced displacement into a relocation camp. However, Arasanayagam does not only explore issues of identity as implicated in political and ethnic conflict but within international travel, as well. For example, the collections *The Alms Giving and Destinies, Destinations* include travel poems to places like India, Australia, and the U.S. Instead of investigating one of her more autobiographical travel poems, this article suggests that the poem, "Geography Lessons" provides a kind of ontological study for how we might examine the relationship between travel and geography. Playing off of the title of the poem, this section suggests that Arasanayagam provides a kind of 'postcolonial' geography lesson when it comes to the politics of global travel narratives.

The second Sri Lanka poet is Ramya Chamalie Jirasinghe. Jirasinghe is a diverse writer, and her work includes academic scholarship, food writing, newspaper articles, advertising, and books of poetry, as well. The poem included in this article is from *There's an Island in the Bone*, which was published in 2011 and has received international recognition. This collection also includes several travel poems, particularly to places of the Global North,' including the U.K., Holland. The U.S. The poem examined here, "Sri Lankan nights in L.A." follows the poet's travel to California and her attendance at a dinner party, which aptly demonstrates her ability as a poet and her interest in

---

6. Ibid.: 4

food as she investigates themes surrounding identity, travel, the civil war, and the Sri Lankan diaspora. Together, the poets provide analysis on postcolonialism, global politics, and diaspora through their travel writing.

Sri Lanka's colonial past included the presence of the Portuguese, Dutch, and British, with the British taking full and sole control of the island in 1815 after the collapse of the Kandyan Kingdom, until independence in 1948. However, the ethnic antagonisms that developed during the colonial period only became exacerbated in the independent state, which would eventually lead to a nearly 30-year-long civil war from 1983 to 2009. The civil war was primarily fought against the majoritarian Sinhala-Buddhist government and the armed insurgency mounted by the Liberation Tigers of Tamil Eelam (LTTE). The Sri Lankan diasporic population numbers approximately 3 million worldwide, and most members of this group migrated directly or indirectly as a result of the civil war.[7] While travel often invokes a sense of 'privileged' displacement, diaspora includes a continuum of travel from forcibly displaced to chosen opportunity. While both of the poets here are traveling from Sri Lanka to elsewhere, Jirasinghe's travel poem particularly will also explore the identity politics of diaspora, bringing together travel and migration as contemporary issues of global politics. But both Arasanayagam and Jirsinghe's work includes literary representations of the underlying conditions and consequences of the Sri Lankan civil war.

The close reading of this article, including Arasanayagam's "Geography Lessons," and Jirasinghe's "Sri Lankan Nights in L.A.," indicates the transformative potential of travel writing, or rather travel poetry. The paper considers what develops from a close reading of these poems as 'postcolonial geography lessons.' Postcolonial geography does not attempt to mask the anxieties of globalization and colonialism but examines these anxieties as spaces of departure and exploration. This paper argues that these writers provide a methodology for contesting such hegemonic power relations, which have historically constituted the political practices of writing, and mapping as a western discursive project that continues to manage the world, as well as its implication in contemporary global politics.

---

[7]. Peter Reeves, Rajesh Rai, and Hema Kiruppalini, eds., *The Encyclopedia of the Sri Lankan Diaspora* (Editions Didier Millet, 2013).
Dhananjayan Sriskandarajah, "Tamil Diaspora Politics," in *Encyclopedia of Diasporas: Immigrant and Refugee Cultures Around the World*, eds. Melvin Ember, Carol R. Ember, and Ian Skoggard (Boston: Springer US, 2005), 492, https://doi.org/10.1007/978-0-387-29904-4_50.

The methodology that I employ in these close readings, which emphasizes movement or mapping, follows Gilles Deleuze and Félix Guattari's concept of "Nomad Art."[8] What Deleuze and Guattari refer to as the "nomad line" does not seek to avoid anxiety or contradiction, but instead, it "traces" between these as points of smooth space.[9] That is,

> the nomad line is abstract in an entirely different sense, precisely because it has a multiple orientation and passes between points, figures and contours: it finds a positive motivation in the smooth space it traces, not in any striation performed in order to ward off anxiety and subordinate the smooth. The abstract line is an affect of smooth space, not a feeling of anxiety that calls forth striation.[10]

In contrast to traditional travel writing wherein affects is a consequence of the anxieties and contradictions that play between colonialism and globalization, the tracings that are made by these Sri Lankan poets do not seek to smoothen striated or anxious spaces; instead they emphasize the intimate connections between systems like colonialism, nationalism, and globalism. But as Deleuze and Guattari suggest, "traces" should always be put back on the map.[11] Deleuze and Guattari's distinction between tracing and mapping is "a question of method" for what they refer to as a "rhizomatic assemblage."[12] The map is the rhizome, the rhizome is the map, "ceaselessly establish[ing] connections between semiotic chains, organizations of power, and circumstances relative to the arts, sciences, and social struggles."[13] Tracings can be found within maps, but if the map is the laboratory itself, then tracings are experiments of interactions.[14] Deleuze and Guattari implore, "[m]ake a map, not a tracing."[15] They explain that:

> [t]he tracing has already translated the map into an image; it has already transformed the rhizome into roots and radicles. It has organized, stabilized, neutralized the multiplicities according to the axes of significance and subjectification belonging to it. It has generated,

---

[8]. Gilles Deleuze, and Félix Guattari, "Nomad Art," *Art & Text* 19 (October 1, 1985): 16—24.

[9]. Ibid., 16.

[10]. Deleuze and Guattari, "Nomad Art," 20.

[11]. Gilles Deleuze and Félix Guattari, *A Thousand Plateaus: Capitalism and Schizophrenia*, trans. Brian Massumi (London: Continuum, 2003), 13.

[12]. Deleuze and Guattari, *A Thousand Plateaus*, 13.

[13]. Ibid., 7.

[14]. Félix Guattari, *The Machinic Unconscious: Essays in Schizoanalysis* (Los Angeles, CA: Semiotext(e), 2011): 172.

[15]. Ibid., 12.

structuralized the rhizome, and when it thinks it is reproducing something else, it is, in fact, only reproducing itself. That is why the tracing is so dangerous.[16]

For example, "[t]he orchid does not reproduce the tracing of the wasp; it forms a map with the wasp, in a rhizome."[17] This paper suggests that traditional travel narratives make "traces," that is, in their attempt to celebrate and move past the legacy and history of Empire, they end up reproducing it.

Both poets use what Heather Yeung terms the poetic "I/ eye" to find the political spaces home continually and identity in displacement.[18] However, even as Arasanayagam and Jirasinghe's respective writings still provide moments of isolated traces, these are always a part of a greater rhizomatic whole. Many western travel writers, as Lisle remarks, are dealing with the embarrassment of a colonial past, while "also recognizing that there are no undiscovered places left to explore [.]"[19] What Arasanayagam and Jirasinghe provide is an alternative way to think about and explore the process of mapping and traveling. Instead of "smoothing over" the anxieties of colonialism and/ or globalization, these unsettling or anxious moments become travel opportunities, for displacement. Mario Vrbančić's describes the potential in Deleuze and Guattari as "[t]he flexible, nomadic thought constantly forms connections between different systems of discursive practices: it is a cartography of living, the new version of a map, the guild of cartographers experimenting with the multiplicity of equations between a map and a territory."[20]

Finding the nomad line gives a mode of operation that helps us relate the emergence of contradictions and collisions of spaces. Therefore, what emerges from these poems are not reproductions or traces, but maps.

For example, a couple of geography lessons emerge from these alternative approaches to travel writing. The first is, what is always left to explore is identity itself. Given the complicated relationships of colonialism in our contemporary world, this should indicate the need to continually re-explore and retrace our different subject and geographic positions. For example, Arasanayagam, as a Sri Lanka Burgher, with both colonial and indigenous ancestry, often uses

---

[16]. Ibid., 13.

[17]. Ibid., 12.

[18]. Heather Yeung, "Affective Mapping in Lyric Poetry," in *Geocritical Explorations: Space, Place, and Mapping in Literary and Cultural Studies*, ed. Robert T. Tally (New York: Palgrave Macmillan, 2011), 209.

[19]. Lisle, 3.

[20]. Mario Vrban i ,"Burroughs's Phantasmic Maps," *New Literary History* 36, no. 2 (2005): 11.

themes of hybrid identity and home in her writing. Melanie A. Murray observes that "Arasanayagam maps the land in her writing as a way of finding her identity/ home," and that the "the dichotomy of her hybrid ancestry is reflected in her rendering of a divided landscape."[21] For Arasanayagam, writing about identity is a way to map, simultaneously, the anxieties and contradictions of her own contested identity, and the broader traces of colonial histories within contemporary spaces and politics.

Therefore, the second geography lesson is that in addition to identity and self, mapping implicates notions of home and not only displacement. This is, perhaps, nowhere more so than with the diasporic body. Trinh T. Minh-ha writes that "[t]oday, when I'm asked where home is for me, I am struck by how far away it is; and yet, home is nowhere else but right here, at the edge of this body of mine."[22] Spatial knowledge is not only produced visually but bodily as well. What is the feel of place, the taste, the sound, and what does it mean to map not only from a multi-perspective but a multi-sensory experience of place? Doing so would also implicate Deleuze and Guattari's understanding of "mapping," one that does not follow a single trace or mode, but finds the intersections of systems, whether that is between colonialism and globalization, or home and away. Home is, therefore, also located in the mappings of the body itself. As Minh-ha observes, home is:

> [n]ot only in the eye, the tongue, and the nose, but it is also, as in my case, actually in the ear. It is said, for example, that writers or the diverse Diasporas around the world live in a double exile: away from their native land and away from their mother tongue. Displacement takes on many faces and is our very everyday dwelling.[23]

Jirasinghe takes on a very sensory-oriented mapping of home and elsewhere, by examining diasporic identities through food, language, clothing, and dancing, as she relates a story of visiting some friends from Sri Lanka while in L.A.

In what follows, this paper first explores Arasanyagam's "Geography Lessons" as its own theoretical lens through which to read the relationships between language, geography, colonialism, and ethnic and political violence. Next, the process of identity formation for the Sri Lankan diaspora, as seen in Jirasinghe's "Sri Lankan Nights in L.A." Jirasinghe's poem also implicates notions of geography, nationalism, and authentic Sri Lankaness. Each of these larger

---

21. Melanie A. Murray, *Island Paradise-The Myth: an Examination of Contemporary Caribbean and Sri Lankan Writing* (Amsterdam: Rodopi, 2009), 144.
22. Trinh T. Minh-Ha, *Elsewhere, within Here: Immigration, Refugeeism and the Boundary Event* (London: Routledge, 2011), 12.
23. Ibid.

systems is read through two very different travel narratives: the first imaginative and abstract, the second, biographical. Beyond just questioning the process of mapping and the politics of place, these postcolonial geography lessons indicate the ways in which such concepts such as self and home can become entry points to examine larger systems, including postcolonialism and global politics, as well as spaces of becoming.

Jean Arasanayagam's "Geography Lessons" serves as a theoretical lens through which one may understand the connections of geography, mapping, and language as performed by the poet. Although the island state's population is around 80% Buddhist, there are also a number of practicing Christians, as a result of the historical interactions of colonialism. As a Sri Lankan Christian, Arasanayagam sets her own introduction of geography and travel paradoxically against, and parallel to, that of the creation myth of Genesis.

She begins the poem by linking geography and God: "Maps were alien to me, I had no knowledge / of a greater world, all I had in my mind were / the words of the Great Creator, God and the / Word that was made flesh embodied in mankind, everything stemmed from the Biblical Genesis."[24] Juxtaposing ignorance and knowledge, the poem opens with a comparison of, on the one hand, the Word of God, the Bible, and on the other, the spatial texts of "Maps." While Arasanyagam situates the poem in Biblical Genesis, she does not introduce the concept of knowledge with the tree of the knowledge of good and evil.[25] Instead, knowledge is aligned with maps, as these are the keys to a "greater world." Placing the context of knowledge production in this way, also allows her to claim and position herself as the producer of knowledge, as she continues, "so how was I to know, how was I to name/islands and continents I was still to step on, / oceans that I would traverse in voyages of my own discovery."[26] The world, including islands and continents, emerge in the moment of her own discovery. More precisely, she claims the position of both the cartographer and creationist. The world emerges in front of her as she names it; it does not appear initially to exist before the ability to both name it and write it. In these moments, she works not only as a writer but also as a cartographer, implicating the direct meaning of cartography: earth writing.

---

[24]. Arasanayagam, *The Almsgiving*, 79.

[25]. From the Abrahamic tradition, the tree of knowledge of good and evil was one of two important trees in the Garden of Eden (the other was the tree of life). God forbid Adam and Eve from consuming the fruit of the tree of knowledge of good and evil. When Eve convinces Adam to taste the fruit after being tempted by the serpent, the two were cast out of the garden by God, in what is known as the *fall of man.*

[26]. Ibid., 79.

Aranasanyagam laments that she longs to be one of the great adventurers and that in her solitary wanderings in the garden that she "searched / for magic talismans, golden rings and sparkling gems / but all I often found were fragments of broken crockery / with colors and patterns," which she "gathered / to create a mosaic with flowers, coronets, willow patterns, / strange Chinese symbols over which [she] uttered spells and incantations of [her] own making."[27] Within this world, she creates a map of her own making, producing articulations from found pieces. Nothing is 'new'; everything comes together as a disjointed whole, as she makes it. Arasanayagam appears to present contradictory claims first to indicate that the world does not exist before the ability to name it, and then to find that nothing is new. One way to address this contradiction is through Deleuze and Guattari's conceptualization of maps, which have no origins. In Arasaynamgam's poem, when these moments are isolated, her creations appear new, but as she continues writing, we get a larger understanding or view of the map itself. Therefore, what appears to be original is actually a part of a much larger system or systems, as various stories, images, and associations begin to emerge. Finding the nomad line, these are moments, spaces of becoming as disjointed pieces become one: making as she writes, or even what we might refer to as poetic mapping.

Therefore, for Arasanayagam things, images, worlds emerge or gather presence in a field of play, creating them through her own magic. Maps and language merge together as she marks them with incantations and spells. As noted above, affects are able to pull together connections between systems. These incantations and spells might also be thought of as experimentations of interactions, in the terms that Guattari specifically explains of tracing.[28] But as implored in *A Thousand Plateaus*, these traces are not left alone. They are continually placed back on the map.[29] She confesses that the "world of / deceptive enchantment fed my imagination from those beginning/tales with furtive hints of dangers always lurking / monsters, witchcraft and wizardry, bandits, brigands, pirates." [30] She also states that they did not know, was unaware of the darkness and violence that grew in the act of map-making. There is also a noticeable shift in perspective and voice, moving from a singular confession to a collective "we." Cartography is no longer an act that just belongs to her, but it becomes collective guilt. This confession develops as she writes:

> [...] but then we did not know, were unaware
> of clouds of evil, black and ominous, hovering over us,

---

27. Ibid., 80.
28. Guattari, *The Machinic Unconscious*, 172.
29. Deleuze and Guattari, *A Thousand Plateaus*, 1.
30. Ibid., 80.

we had to unroll those maps to trace our future
routes over land or sea, we had to spin the globe,
we did not know the histories of those oceans and
islands, atolls, and peninsulas, we had to study,
read the names of continents, never dreaming that
one day we would be familiar with each valley,
mountain, city or village, there was yet no necessity
to explore ancestral voyages, strange destinies had
named us, we were undisturbed, unperplexed, all
unknowing of the bloodlines that engendered us.[31]

The collective "we" appears to be the found objects and bits that she gathered in her nomadic wanderings. This collection begins to take on a dark presence in the processes of mapping and naming. Making these found things an extension of the self, of her own identity does not smooth over or erase her collection or theft but becomes a tool to help her further explore the anxieties and contradictions between knowledge and ignorance, between discovering and colonizing. Placing herself and her found things as colonizers, they remained undisturbed, un-perplexed as they rolled the world out, mapping and naming as they went. "We had to," Arasanayagam attempts to explain, but they did not know "the histories" of the islands, places, and oceans that they traveled. The point is that there is unquestioned violence in the act of map-making in the process of carving up and claiming/ naming places.

Arasanayagam is purposeful in this change from a singular self to a collective. She does not deny the seduction of naming and writing the world; instead, this allows her to emphasize that these acts go beyond a singular, individual act; mapping the world is a collective and conscious effort that has ties to imperial and colonial histories. These histories are not past but are the genealogies of our current world maps. Arasanayagam alludes to the current political turmoil stating, "[t]he new maps show warfare raging in the streets, / houses blasted, the artifacts of daily life exposed / to the voyeur's eyes, rooms with gaping holes."[32] In the final stanza, she further connects the history of geography and colonialism as developing across time, languages, and politics:

[...]
the old maps long changed will be the death of ancient
civilizations and conquests, recognizable now
only through the archaeologists ferreting out
secrets of buried centuries, pillaging the

---

[31]. Ibid., 80.
[32]. Ibid., 80.

treasures of that past, measuring craniums
and bone fragments, pottery shards and precious,
priceless jewels, studying the murals of daily
life in the tombs of the Pharaohs, deciphering
the hieroglyphs of the Rosetta Stone, unfolding
its meaning where exactly was it located for
that French soldier to stumble on it [...].[33]

Arasanayagam's geography lessons indicate nothing remains the same when we displace ourselves and travel. To cross the boundary, to mark the edge and then move against it, to play between these positions of knowledge and ignorance is in of itself a violent act. But she extends the discussion of boundary-crossing from just the opening of individual lifeworlds to the violent history of crossings embedded in imperialism and colonialism. There is a dark history of subjugation and death, which is reflected in the very text of the world map. I suggest that this poem serves as a lens for reading the ways in which geography is still implicated in the power and traces of global politics and our contemporary conditions. As the poem indicates, Arasanayagam connects the histories of geography and imperialism to contemporary events and violences. Given her and her family's personal experience during the Sri Lankan civil war, it is hard to imagine that she does not have this in mind. But by not naming the civil war outright, she provides the poem with a "map" instead of just a "trace," choosing to indicate a more universal or globalized condition of violence and conflict. However, it is the space between, or in movement that histories of violence can also be named and identified. It is within this last point that the transformative potential in travel writing is really seen. Geographies, as spaces of becoming, also trace around questions of identity and the self. While maps are made for the outsider, the self, the internal is always already complicit in the violations. The places that are explored within these traces, therefore, do not just show what the traveling body finds, but what it remembers. Departures are always already mapping home, as well. Thus, the following poem will look at the traveling body as she traces the circumferences between home and away, as both spaces of becoming and displacement.

Jirasinghe's collection, *There's an Island in the Bone*, includes several travel poems, including to the U.S. and Europe. Here, home is a real and imagined space that shifts and changes as the traveling body traces it, un-traces, re-traces it. By her very presence, the traveling body performs and is also a performance of the home, of what she remembers, imagines, recalls, retraces each time. This is particularly true for those who are forced to leave home, including those who

---

33. Ibid., 81.

are displaced due to political conflict. As noted above, many Sri Lankans left the country during the tumultuous years of the 26-year-long civil war, while others remained, either by choice or against their will. Traveling to California, in "Sri Lankan Nights in L.A.," Jirasinghe writes of an evening when all of these different continuums of Sri Lankan travel and displacement came together, as they perform and trace, laying claims to what "Sri Lankan-ness" might be. As is not uncommon, there is a strong connection between identity and food, particularly for diasporic populations. For example, Maureen Chinyere Duru writes that "[t]he combination of diaspora and food, in turn, brings to the fore the question of identity and how diaspora food habits are relevant or reflected in the identification process of the diaspora communities."[34] Similar issues are brought to the forefront in this poem as Jirasinghe describes how cooking dinner and entertaining becomes a performance of Sri Lankan-ness.

Jirasinghe opens the poem with this scene: "[c]rushed curry leaves, pounded cinnamon, dashed lime / And hand-carried spices; Colombo to Narita to L.A.; burst into va-/ pour and swim with flaked tuna into the centrally heated room."[35] She describes how the hot cutlets and wattalappan gently wobble in the tray, as it becomes clear that these dishes also offer a test of authenticity, of "Sri Lankan-ness." The tables begin to hold more than just food, and culinary reputations become signifiers for more than just recipes:

> Tables bear the weight of food,
> authentic recipes, recreated for the pot-luck party.
> Each morsel will soon pass or fail
> the dinners' acid test of nostalgia,
> judged by palate-memories
> cleansed by historical amnesia and geographical dislocation.
> Soon Mala's or Sumana's culinary reputation will be made or shat-
> tered in one gulp.[36]

There is a growing tension for Jirasinghe as different forms of privilege emerge: of those that have the ability to travel, to leave the country, and those that remain. Tariq Jazeel, specifically looking at Sri Lankan women's groups in Britain, observes that "[r]esearch on privileged diasporic communities has unsurprisingly been superseded by the study of working-class South Asian

---

34. Maureen Chinyere Duru, *Diaspora, Food and Identity: Nigerian Migrants in Belgium* (New York: Peter Lang, 2017),15.
35. Jirasinghe, *There's an Island in the Bone*, 6.
36. Ibid., 6-7.

diaspora politics often rooted in social marginalization."[37] In "Sri Lankan Nights in L.A.," Jirasinghe offers an investigation of privilege among the Sri Lankan diaspora by examining the complex relationship of privilege, geography, and social structures. But the idea of "'[p]rivilege' in a postcolonial geographical context is shown not as a disenabling term, implying passivity, assimilation, or de-politicized subject position."[38] As Jirasinghe also observes, "[s]o solutions are/found to be broken boundaries in Sri Lanka. / Assistance given to those keeping illusions alive about myths in / written texts and / the purity of our beginnings, / and the importance of preserving the / 'nation-ness' of the nation."[39] In the poem, these observations are placed adjacent to statements like "It's great to meet like this / We must do something" by Mr. Sumanapala and "We might go there this summer..., but only if the war situation is not too bad, you know," by Mr. Perera.[40] While the reader is not provided much information about who the different characters are that are introduced in the poem, the placement of observations and dialogue together help to emphasize a certain privilege of geography. That is, the different group members can discuss the war passively (i.e., "we must do something," "we might go") without actually being in direct danger or politically involved. The poem does not provide any implication that these professed longings to "do something" have any direct plans or intent. There is perhaps an underlying tension here between those living in L.A., and the author herself, who is only traveling and will return to Sri Lanka. While physically and geographically distant, the speakers also indicate the need or desire to be close to Sri Lanka, as well. This discussion implicates one's authentic "Sri Lankan-ness," the authenticity and legitimacy of a geo-cultural assemblage of a place called "Sri Lanka" and the "nation-ness" of the nation. The title that Jirasinghe gives to this poem also appears to indicate that it is not just the people, the Sri Lankans that are dis/placed to L.A., but that it is the geo-spatially defined island itself which is displaced. Sri Lanka exists as it is performed, it emerges in its point of play between the guests, in the preparing, serving, and eating of food. Even in the complaining of losing Sri Lankan traditions, and in the suggestions that something must be done about it.

---

[37]. Tariq Jazeel, "Postcolonial Geographies of Privilege: Diaspora Space, the Politics of Personhood and the 'Sri Lankan Women's Association in the UK,'" *Transactions of the Institute of British Geographers* 31, no. 1 (2006): 20, https://doi.org/10.1111/j.1475-5661.2006.00192.x.

[38]. Jazeel, "Postcolonial Geographies of Privilege," 20.

[39]. Jirasinghe, 7.

[40]. Ibid., 7.

This need to confirm and perform "Sri Lanka" is a call back to a remembered home, and it is not just for themselves that they must do this. Still, they also perform for it to be remembered for the next generation, who already have other images, sounds, tastes of what home means. They dance, saris falling, because "the kids must see / how we lived-it-up during our Ceylon days."[41] Jirasinghe observes that Sri Lanka is not just conflicted by the civil war that ravaged the country, but it is also here, in this room that home and away, here and there are conflicted in the poem. In contrast to Lisle's critique of travel narratives that fall into the trap of nostalgia, Jirasinghe holds the evening's interactions accountable as more than just "the dinners' acid test of nostalgia." She explains:

> But there's conflict on these shores too.
> Picket fences are pushing aside the cinnamon stakes. Jayasekera's
> youngest son had refused to attend. In some families,
> daughters are dancing to different tunes.
>
> The cooks are losing control; new ingredients are falling in. There's
> a dish of heartbreak simmering on the stove
> for those who refuse to stomach Rosemary with Ambulthial.[42]

The identity performance surrounding food comes back in this final stanza, but here the performance becomes unstable, seemingly reflecting these new politics of the diaspora. As identities are judged and emerge, they also unravel in relation to food. Instead, she examines, very much like Arasanayagam's nomadic lines, all the found objects that they have gathered: dishes, memories, dances, clothes, etc., and shows how it makes a very political map of Sri Lanka. Home and away involve constant renegotiated mappings, and as Jirasinghe indicates, these maps of identities and nations are, therefore, also precarious.

There is no singular experience that can comprehensively indicate Sri Lankan "island-ness" or "nation-ness;" Sri Lanka is always in excess of its own definition. Remarking on the development of Sri Lanka's own "island-ness," Tariq Jazeel has stated that "[e]ach time knowledge is produced about Sri Lanka, the place itself is reiterated, reproduced slightly differently. As well as a geopolitical object, then, Sri Lanka is also [a] subject existent in language, in knowledge, in our representations."[43] These poets are examples of such

---

41. Ibid., 8.
42. Ibid.
43. Tariq Jazeel, "Reading the Geography of Sri Lankan Island-Ness: Colonial Repetitions, Postcolonial Possibilities," *Contemporary South Asia* 17, no. 4 (2009): 412, https://doi.org/10.1080/09584930903324138.

oscillations and re-mappings, as they, too, reproduce their own geographical object called Sri Lanka.

The travel narrative or poem captures not only the mapping of difference between alternative spaces but the formations of identity within difference and displacement. For example, Robertson et al. relate that several of their contributors in *Travellers' Tales* "argue that identity is founded on imaginary trajectories of here and there, I and not-I."[44] And, if we begin to layer this palimpsest of movement within the travel narrative, between language and the physical movement of the body, here and there, I and not-I, and we connect to these traces as they follow real geographical places, with their own temporalities, histories, cultures, and socio-political networks then this literary analysis of Sri Lankan travel poetry also provides "a map" to the larger systems at work between colonialism and globalization. Subsequently, this kind of map also provides a methodological approach for understanding the relationships of identity in global politics. Furthermore, Doreen Massey writes that:

> [g]eographers have long been exercised by the problem of defining regions, and this question of 'definition' has almost always been reduced to the issue of drawing lines around a place [...] But that kind of boundary around an area precisely distinguishes between an inside and an outside. It can so easily by yet another way of constructing a counterposition between 'us' and 'them.'[45]

If we apply Massey's analysis to these poets and their own movements between and out of Sri Lankan, then the body becomes a borderland, and as the poet moves, so do the lines that previously defined the geosocial formations of Sri Lanka.

As language invokes displacement, and as the writer continually performs the self in writing, we begin to complicate and problematize what it means to travel, extending not only the historically developed boundary lines of Sri Lanka but also extending the reach and knowledge produced from the homed body. And what can this imaginary tell us about, not only how we understand the process of knowledge production, but also the fluidness of identities, bodies, and geographies. The power of the Sri Lankan body is not in its singularity but its excess. A body that is always, already finding alternative boundary lines, re-creating the maps of the region through story and myth and memory.

---

44. Robertson, et al., *Travellers' Tales*, 2.
45. Doreen B. Massey, *Space, Place, and Gender* (Minneapolis: University of Minnesota Press, 1994), 152.

Bibliography

Arasanayagam, Jean. *The Almsgiving.* Colombo: Social Scientists' Association, 2014.

Deleuze, Gilles, and Félix Guattari. *A Thousand Plateaus: Capitalism and Schizophrenia,* translated by Brian Massumi. London: Continuum, 2003.

Deleuze, Gilles, and Félix Guattari. "Nomad Art." *Art & Text,* 16-24 (October 1, 1985): 16-24.

Duru, Maureen Chinyere. *Diaspora, Food and Identity: Nigerian Migrants in Belgium. L'Europe Alimentaire, Vol. 9.* Bruxelles and New York: Peter Lang, 2017.

Guattari, Félix. *The Machinic Unconscious: Essays in Schizoanalysis. Foreign Agents Series.* Los Angeles: Semiotext(e), 2011.

Jazeel, Tariq. "Postcolonial Geographies of Privilege: Diaspora Space, the Politics of Personhood and the 'Sri Lankan Women's Association in the UK.'" *Transactions of the Institute of British Geographers* 31, no. 1 (2006): 19-33. https://doi.org/10.1111/j.1475-5661.2006.00192.x.

Jazeel, Tariq. "Postcolonialism: Orientalism and the Geographical Imagination." *Geography* 97, no. 1 (2012): 4-11.

Jazeel, Tariq. "Reading the Geography of Sri Lankan Island-Ness: Colonial Repetitions, Postcolonial Possibilities." *Contemporary South Asia* 17, no. 4 (2009): 399—414. https://doi.org/10.1080/09584930903324138.

Jirasinghe, Ramya Chamelie. *There's an Island in the Bone.* Battaramulla: Yara Press, 2010.

Lisle, Debbie. *The Global Politics of Contemporary Travel Writing.* Cambridge University Press, 2006.

Massey, Doreen B. *Space, Place, and Gender.* Minneapolis: University of Minnesota Press, 1994.

Minh-Ha, Trinh T. *Elsewhere, within Here: Immigration, Refugeeism, and the Boundary Event.* London: Routledge, 2011.

Murray, Melanie A. *Island Paradise-The Myth; an Examination of Contemporary Caribbean and Sri Lankan Writing.* Amsterdam: Rodopi, 2009.

Reeves, Peter, Rajesh Rai, and Hema Kiruppalini, eds. *The Encyclopedia of the Sri Lankan Diaspora.* Kuala Lumpur: Editions Didier Millet, 2013.

Robertson, George, Melinda Mash, Lisa Tickner, Jon Bird, Barry Curtis, and Tim Putman, eds. "As the World Turns: Introduction." In *Travellers' Tales: Narratives of Home and Displacement. Futures, New Perspectives for Cultural Analysis.* London ; New York: Routledge, 1994.

Sriskandarajah, Dhananjayan. "Tamil Diaspora Politics." In *Encyclopedia of Diasporas: Immigrant and Refugee Cultures Around the World,* edited by Melvin Ember, Carol R. Ember, and Ian Skoggard, 492-500. Boston, MA: Springer US, 2005. https://doi.org/10.1007/978-0-387-29904-4_50.

Vrbančić, Mario. "Burroughs's Phantasmic Maps." *New Literary History* 36, no. 2 (2005): 313-26. https://www.jstor.org/stable/20057894.

Yeung, Heather. "Affective Mapping in Lyric Poetry." In *Geocritical Explorations: Space, Place, and Mapping in Literary and Cultural Studies,* edited by Robert T. Tally, 209—22. New York: Palgrave Macmillan, 2011.

Chapter 8

The remnant of the journey's anguish: Homelessness and errantry in the poetry of Nasir Kazmi

Hamza Iqbal

University of Texas at Austin

Abstract

Nasir Kazmi (1925-1972) remains one of the most celebrated Urdu poets of the ġhazal genre from the previous century. In his brief life of forty-six years, he wrote enough poetry. He produced a formidable kulīyāt (collection), which sufficed to create his place in the Urdu poetic tradition and allowed him to be counted amongst the most canonical of the ġhazal poets of Urdu. The present article shall locate and then analyze the topoi of "homelessness"—as Harney and Motenn have discussed it in *The Undercommons*—and "errantry"—as Glissant articulates it in *Poetics of Relation*—in ġhazals of Nasir Kazmi. The related concept of hijrat (exile) will also be touched upon as all these themes feature rather prominently in Nasir's works (as we shall see). To achieve the aforementioned aims, however, this article, for methodological purposes, shall take the Fanonian approach of being "derelict" from "its methodological point of view." As Fanon in *Black Skin White Masks* says of such formal requirements, "I leave methods to the botanists and the mathematicians. There is a point at which methods devour themselves."[1] Therefore, for us to not be devoured by them, we leave methods aside—if only momentarily—and instead begin with introducing here the ideas or maẓāmīn (topoi) of homelessness and errantry before we turn to our poet.

Keywords: Exile, errantry, homelessness, Urdu poetry, topos

***

---

1. Frantz Fanon, *Black Skin White Masks* (New York: Grove Press, 2008), 5.

"Homelessness" in Harney and Moten

N'Jobu: I gave you a key hoping that you might see it someday. Yes, the sunsets there are the most beautiful in the world, but I fear that you may still not be welcome.

Erik "Killmonger" Stevens: Why?

N'Jobu: They will say you are lost.

Erik "Killmonger" Stevens: But I am right here.

N'Jobu: No tears for me.

Erik "Killmonger" Stevens: Everybody dies. It's just life around here.

N'Jobu: Look at what I have done. I should have taken you back long ago. Instead, we are both abandoned here.

Erik "Killmonger" Stevens: Maybe your home is the one that's lost. That's why they can't find us.

Black Panther, 2018

In their trailblazing collection of essays, also known as *The Undercommons*, Stefano Harney and Fred Moten set out to identify a group (or groups) who, in their view, can, and perhaps already are, challenging the "orders" or the "biopower of the enlightenment."[2] These are the "minorities who refuse, the tribe of moles will not come back from beyond, as if they will not be subjects, as if they want to think as objects, as minority."[3] These are "maroon communities of composition teachers, mentorless graduate students, adjunct Marxist historians, our or queer management professors, state college ethnic studies departments, closed-down film programs, visa-expired Yemeni student newspaper editors, historically black college sociologists, and feminist engineers."[4] These, amongst others, are those that constitute the "Undercommons." And that "biopower of the enlightenment" or in the face of which the "Undercommons" operate is the University.[5]

Today it is the "Undercommons" who play the part of the subversive intellectuals in order to get to the "beyond of teaching" where one has, as Harney and Moten, quoting Kant, affirm, "the determination and courage to

---

[2]. Stefano Harney and Fred Moten, *The Undercommons* (Wivenhoe; New York; Port Watson: Minor Compositions, 2013), 27.

[3]. Ibid.

[4]. Ibid., 30.

[5]. By University, we are referring to any American university or generally the American education system in the present world.

use one's intelligence without being guided by another."[6] Now, of course, all this may prima facie seem somewhat far from the topos this article is aiming to examine, however, it is imperative that we start precisely here to get a better grounding for our topic because the theme of homelessness, after all, is discussed, broadly speaking, within this very context.

The Undercommons have access to is the site or space of "blackness," which is a concept that is not unilinear and thus, which means a lot of things. Still, according to Harney and Moten's one iteration, it means, "to render unanswerable the question of how to govern the thing that loses and finds itself to be what it is not."[7] The notion of homelessness, which is referred to in quite a few ways in The Undercommons is related to the notion of blackness' and this particular meaning will be propitious in discussing Nasir's poetry.

Be that as it may, the direct manner in which homelessness is invoked again in relation to blackness where blackness is "the standpoint, the home territory, chez lui, Markman's off the mark, blind but insightful, mistranslation is illuminative, among his own, signifying a relationality that displaces the already displaced impossibility of home."[8] There was a home that was impossible. That impossibility of having a home is displaced; blackness even displaces that displacement. Home, therefore, is not all that important. Still, homelessness is, for they ask, rhetorically it seems, that

> can this being together in homelessness, this interplay of the refusal of what has been refused, this undercommon appositionality, be a place from which emerges neither self-consciousness nor knowledge of the other but an improvisation that proceeds from somewhere on the other side of an unasked question? Not simply to be among his own, but to be among his own in dispossession, to be among the ones who cannot own, the ones who have nothing and who, in having nothing, have everything.[9]

---

6. Ibid., 27.
Clearly, Harney and Moten begin with locating the Undercommons in the University, it is not at all the case that that is the only place where Undercommons can or necessarily exist. As Harney says, "the Undercommons is a kind of comportment or ongoing experiment with and as the *general antagonism*, a kind of way of being with others, it's almost impossible that it could be matched up with particular forms of institutional life. It would be cut though in different kinds of way and in different spaces and times (Ibid., 112)." In essence, what is said here is suggestive of the ontology of the Undercommons.
7. Ibid., 49.
8. Ibid., 96.
9. Ibid.

Not having a home in this way or similarly "never being on the right side of the Atlantic" is akin to feeling "at home with the homeless" and partaking in a kind of homelessness.[10]

Yet in another iteration of blackness and its intertwined homelessness, Moten says, "there's a certain way of thinking about that impossibility of being located, of that exhaustion of location, that only can be understood as deprivation."[11] The reason why this way is preferable is due "the possibilities that it bears, hard as that is, hard as they are."[12] "Homelessness is hard, no doubt about it," he continues, "but home is harder."[13] In this framework, homelessness is something that is not chosen voluntarily, but once it does come about, it is embraced wholeheartedly. In the wake of the Partition of the Indian Sub-Continent in 1947, Nasir Kazmi, too, came to realize something similar. When the Hindus of what is now Pakistan were leaving in large numbers to come to India, the young and impressionable college graduate, Nasir of the city of Ambala in present-day India, said to his father, "Father, sell this house and get a small estate or buy some house in Lahore because many Hindus and Sikhs were selling their houses and moving to Hindustan. God knows what circumstances might develop, and we may come to be coerced into moving to Lahore."[14] Thus, ensued Nasir's enduring relationship to homelessness. Be that as it may, let us now go to Glissant's deliberation over errantry in his book *Poetics of Relation*.

Glissant's Erranty

Édouard Glissant's (1928-2011) translator notes that the sense in which he uses the word is not merely "idle roaming" but "includes a sense of sacred motivation."[15] Thus, from the outset, the virtuosity of nomadism is visible as Glissant draws upon the concept of rhizome that had been coined by Deleuze and Guattari. In Glissant's words, rhizome is "an enmeshed root system, a network spreading either in the ground or in the air, with no predatory

---

[10]. Ibid., 97.

[11]. Ibid., 139.

[12]. Ibid., 140.

[13]. Ibid.

[14]. Saghra Bibi, "Bum, Kabūtar, aur Shayirī," in *Hijr kī Rāt kā Sitārā*, eds. Ahmed, Mushtaq and Basir Sultan Kazmi (Lahore: Sang-e-Meel Publications, 2013), 12.
"*Ābā jān makān farokht kardeiñ aur Lāhore meiñ kothī banwāleiñ yā koi makān kharīd leiñ kyunki bohat log Hindu Sikh makān farokht karke Hindustan jarahe haiñ. Khudā jāne kaisā waqt ājāye aur humaiñ Lāhore jānā pare.*"

[15]. Edouard Glissant, *Poetics of Relation* (Ann Arbor: University of Michigan Press, 2010), 211.

rootstock taking over permanently. The notion of rhizome maintains, therefore, the idea of rootedness but challenges that of a totalitarian root."[16]

Nomadism as such, in spite of its innocuous appearance, says Glissant, need not be one that is incapable of "overturning the order of the world."[17] The first thing to consider about this form of nomadism or errantry is that it is in direct opposition to modernity or the nation-state. Secondly, as Glissant conveys, "the errantry of a troubadour or that of Rimbaud is not yet a thorough, thick (opaque) experience of the world, but it is already an arrant, passionate desire to go against a root", suggesting that the poet and the poetry are already, in some capacity, inclined towards the kind of nomadism that is against the totalitarian rootedness that the nation-state with its "linguistic intransigence" seeks.[18] Thus, it is a nomadism that is favorable. By calling it nomadism as such here, however, we mean to call attention towards the other type of nomadism Glissant himself introduces and then elaborates upon it. This is the one that we are concerned with, and which he first cites is "circular nomadism: each time a portion of the territory is exhausted, the group moves around. Its function is to ensure the survival of the group by means of this circularity." Next is "invading nomadism [...] whose goal was to conquer lands by exterminating their occupants [...] it is an absolute forward projection: an arrowlike nomadism," and it is nothing more than a "devastating desire for settlement", and most importantly, says Glissant, "there is no pain of exile bearing down, nor is there the wanderlust of errantry growing keener."[19] In fact, modern colonization is a form of the arrowlike errantry: what is worse and unfortunate though is that even decolonial projects have "tended to form around an idea of power—the totalitarian drive of a single, unique root—rather than around a fundamental relationship with the Other."[20] This root the postcolonial states also came to take is monolingual or of linguistic intransigence. But of course, the colonized, "the conquered or visited peoples were forced into a long and painful quest after an identity whose first task was the opposition of the denaturing process by the conqueror. For more than two centuries, whole populations have had to assert their identity in opposition to the processes of identification or annihilation triggered by these invaders."[21] Conquest is temporary, but colonization is permanent. If there is an identity, there will be a crisis; in modernity, it is almost like smoke and fire. This is the gift bestowed upon the

16. Glissant, *Poetics of Relation*, 11.
17. Ibid., 12.
18. Ibid., 15.
19. Ibid., 12-13.
20. Ibid., 14.
21. Ibid., 17.

colonized in the form of inheritance by the colonizers. As an Indian born in the 1920s and who lives through the bloody Partition riots of 1947 and then is forced to leave his hometown at a young age and move into a newly formed country and assume a new identity, Nasir Kazmi undergoes more or less these very experiences of uprootedness that came about due to someone else's arrowlike nomadism. As the prominent Urdu critic, Firaq Gorakhpuri, too notes, "Nasir Kazmi's tone has such wariness and tinkling in which the citizens of both India and Pakistan will get to listen to their own hearts' beats."[22]

But the point that we are trying to make with regard to Nasir's uprooting is that: "In this context, uprooting can work toward identity, and exile can be seen as beneficial when these are experienced as a search for the Other rather than as an expansion of territory."[23] Indeed it is almost mind-boggling that in one his ġhazal's shě`r (couplet), Nasir expresses this somewhat hopeful sentiment very much in line with Glissant's; it is almost as if they both are already within a Poetics of Relation. The shě`r goes:

Mil hī jāe gā raftagān kā surāgh
Aur kuch din phiro udās udās

You are bound to find a trace of the departed
Keep up this melancholy wandering for a few more days[24]

Let us now turn to the locations of homelessness and errantry in our poet's works. But before we begin to consider Nasir's ġhazals, it is imperative that we say something briefly about the ġhazal genre.

The Ġhazals or two-line poems

Nasir was indeed a prolific poet and had left a modest number of ġhazals, a work of fiction as well as a notebook. This article considers poetry from his published dīwān (collected poetic writings), which may include many (indeed, it does include more than a hundred) but surely not all of his ġhazals. But before we get to Nasir's ġhazals, we should first clarify what a ġhazal is in itself.

---

22. Firaq Gorakhpuri, "Nasir Kazmi ke lehjay meiñ woh k̲hattak aur k̲hanak hai jis meiñ Hindustān aur Pākistān dono meiñ basne wāle apne diloñ kī dhadkaneiñ sunaiñ ge," in *Hijr kī Rāt kā Sitārā*, eds. Ahmed, Mushtaq and Basir Sultan Kazmi (Lahore: Sang-e-Meel Publications), 66.
23. Ibid., 18.
24. Nauman Naqvi, *Mourning Indo-Muslim Modernity: Moments in Post-Colonial Urdu Literary Culture* (Columbia University, 2008), 189.

Ghazal is the most prominent lyrical genre of classical Persian and Urdu poetics. The poem's form is as such that it has couplets or two-line verses. The particular order of the couplets within the whole poem does not really matter; that is, any verse could be read before or after. Similarly, neither does it matter if the speaker or reader, while reciting a ghazal leaves out a couplet or two entirely. Classically, a ghazal would have an odd number of couplets in it (say, five or seven), but again there are no rules that cannot be compromised, at least not in the contemporary tradition.[25] The pattern of the ghazal is as such that the first couplet (also called the maṭla) will have a fixed word or radīf in both lines of the couplet. The rhyme (qāfiya in Urdu) precedes the radīf, thus giving a pattern of AA. In the subsequent couplets too, the radīf remains constant in the second line of the couplet, and so the pattern just comes to be of bA, cA, dA, and so on and so forth.

Moreover, even just one couplet could be considered a whole ghazal or a poem unto itself, and arguably, even the order of that single couplet, as a poem, could be interchanged without giving rise to any qualms whatsoever. The poem has a beginning and an end, but no middle, and this precept is most fully and beautifully conspicuous in the genre of the ghazal.[26] As a case in point, we can go back to Nasir's shi'r that we encountered above, albeit in reverse order:

Aur kuch din phiro udās udās
Mil hī jāe gā raftagān kā surāgh

Keep up this melancholy wandering for a few more days
You are bound to find a trace of the departed[27]

---

[25]. The genre of the *ghazal* and its related poetic experience has transformed (perhaps it is more apt to say that it has declined) over past two centuries but what changed even more dramatically—at least in a certain historical moment—was its reception. In the colonial era, the *ghazal* came to be seen, for the first time in its history, as a feminine, decadent and *unnatural* form of poetry first by the colonizers and, under their influence then by many thinkers and critics (often of a more conservative bent) within the Urdu literary milieu itself. Their reasoning—or lack of reasoning thereof—was that the classical *ghazal* is courtly (or elitist hence thing of the past), abstract, apolitical, and charged with homosexual innuendos and hence it is decadent and should be banned. This was a time of Victorian morality and the so-called trends of realism and naturalism in poetry and one cannot help but wonder if there is a correlation between these seemingly distinct phenomena. Be that as it may, for a splendid defense of the *ghazal* genre against such myopic (in case of homosexual suggestiveness) or ill-founded (such as *ghazal*s alleged apoliticality) see Naqvi, 2008.

[26]. I am grateful to Roger Reeves for this idea about what a poem is during our in-person conversation.

[27]. Naqvi, *Mourning Indo-Muslim Modernity,* 189.

We do not even have to get to the meaning of what it could have meant in its first iteration, and what it could mean now, but we surely do not seem to lose any broader sense, coherence, or excellence of the couplet (or should we say a poem?).

The task of the ġhazal writer is also unique because, in the ġhazal world, it is not just ideas that matter but also the aesthetics, i.e., the subtlety and nuance with which a couplet is uttered.[28] No Urdu poet is trying to re-invent the wheel; they merely try to run with it in their unique ways, which is to say Urdu poets of the classical world are not necessarily concerned with trying to formulate new ideas or maẓāmīn. Instead, it is the manner in which similar ideas are conveyed by ġhazal poets across centuries that is important for the aesthetic quality of a particular shě`r. The language plays a significant role here, and a couplet may be judged simply by its ability to strike chords with the hearts of the listeners (or generate instant appreciation for itself in the form of wāh-wāhs or bravo! in poetic gatherings known as mushā'arahs in Urdu) as soon as it is uttered. The shě`rs are also evaluated for their ability to be grasped mnemonically by their listeners as the genre is primarily oral and collective. Moreover, `ishq (passion) is perhaps the most significant topic within the Urdu poetic universe, but the ġhazal genre is also almost incomplete without the motifs of wine and drunkenness, etc. which prominently feature in it.[29]

A ġhazal writer, as has already been suggested, has a unique task for he may be constricted by the genre to work around certain classical topoi (such as those of love, separation, melancholy, wine and spirituality et al.) as well as required to stick to the ground or radīf. When, in fact, there is a lot of unrestraint. Similarly, "since each couplet of a ġhazal is in effect an independent poem"[30], the task of the literary critic becomes formidable too especially if one is preconditioned to look for the meaning of a whole poem or grasp the intention of the author, search for the poet's life's details or their political ideology. It is possible that sometimes there may not even be any intention behind a couplet, and it might be thrown in by a poet only to continue to write with a particular radīf.

Finally, it can be argued that in the classical tradition, the artist's biography is mostly—but not necessarily entirely—absent from his poetic creations, the

---

[28]. Pritchett has a fabulous discussion on aesthetics in Urdu literature in *Nets of Awareness* (Berkeley: University of California Press, 1994).

[29]. The word `*ishq* is rather difficult to translate faithfully, if not outright impossible given its polysemic nature; therefore, we shall do with the translation as passion for lack of a better English term.

[30]. Naqvi, 35.

reason, again, being the requirement of poetry falling within or around certain well-defined tropes. But this is certainly not to say that the 'political unconscious,' to use Jameson's term, does not exist in the ġhazal; it is only not that forthright to be grasped so effortlessly.[31] But let us turn our gaze towards Nasir's poetry now.

Nasir: The Homeless Errant

...and when she went out, it seemed to her that she too had migrated, that everyone migrates, even if we stay in the same houses our whole lives, because we can't help it. We are all migrants through time.

Mohsin Hamid, *Exit West*

Ġhazals mostly do not have names as such, and so the first line of the first couplet just becomes the title of that ġhazal. All the shěˋrs of the ġhazals that we would be looking may not have the same themes throughout that poem, as has already been implied, however, the themes of homelessness and errantry would be conspicuous. Let us look at first of our shiˤrs from a ġhazal titled, 'Musalsal bekalī dil ko horahī hai' (The heart endures constant anxiety):

Maiñ kyuñ phirtā huñ tanhā mārā mārā
Ye bastī chain se kyuñ sorahī hai[32]

Why do I wander in loneliness purposelessly
Why is this town sleeping so peacefully

The poet here questions his own errantry, which appears to him to be purposeless or directionless. It seems as if the poet is a stranger to himself, at a distance from himself, and so removed from himself that he queries himself about "how to govern the thing that loses and finds itself to be what it is not."[33] On the contrary, the community or the town, the poet remarks, is able to sleep peacefully. Now obviously, it is fair to assume that the community that he is referring to is his own, and hence the pressing disorientation for in his mind, the community should have partaken in this peaceless 'errantry'. According to the poet, in his aimless wandering, he does not find a home with others in homelessness. Bastī, however, is quite an interesting term. The word is almost archaic now both in its usage and function since it connotes a sense of a small town or a close-knit neighborhood whereas, in the present day, these entities

---

[31]. Fredric Jameson, *The Political Unconscious: Narrative as a Socially Symbolic Act* (Ithaca: Cornell University Press, 2014).

[32]. Nasir Kazmi, *Dīwān*. (Lahore: Ilqa Publications, 2016), 10.

[33]. Harney and Moten, *The Undercommons*, 49.

do not really seem to exist anymore as much—not at least the way they used to—in the modern postcolonial nation-states of Pakistan and India. While exile in the actual sense may have somewhat came to an end after his family left India for Pakistan, it seems that our poet, in Glissant's words, is going through the "torments of internal exile."[34] Let us look at another shě`r of the same ġhazal:

> Chale dil se umīdoñ ke musāfir
> Ye nagrī āj k̲h̲ālī horahī hai[35]

> From the heart are departing the wayfarers of hope
> This city today is being abandoned

This couplet also utilizes the imagery of the departure of the travelers. In the first line (known as miṣra in Urdu) of the couplet, the poet remarks upon the fact that hope, in the shape of a traveler, is leaving the heart. It is fascinating that hope, to begin with, was always akin to a journeyer for the poet: for hope was always on foot, ready to depart and never stationary. Meanwhile, this city, as the poet refers to his heart, is emptying today. A heart that is full of hope is like a city that is full of people. Both are being evacuated, and the poet does not influence this. One cannot stop a journeyer from leaving the city as one cannot stop hope from abandoning a heart. Both are their own masters, as the poet seems to think, but as we remarked earlier, homelessness is not voluntary. Here, hope leaves the heart, but whoever's heart is being abandoned is the one who is going to end up being homeless. The poet here appears to be at the point where embracing homelessness, as Harney and Moten would suggest, is yet to come.

However, homelessness, it seems, or at least its perception, has come about in the following verse forcefully in a poem titled, Sunatā hai koi bhūlī kahānī (Someone narrates the forgotten story):

> Taṣawwur ne usse dekhā hai aksar
> K̲h̲īrad kehtī hai jisko lā-makānī[36]

> Imagination has often witnessed that
> To which the intellect calls homelessness

Here our poet has already conceived a phenomenon which his intellect, quite literally, calls homelessness. It is a place that cannot ever possess the qualities

---

34. Glissant, 19.
35. Kazmi, *Dīwān*, 10.
36. Ibid., 15.

that constitute a home. What is remarkable, though, is that the word lā-makānī, which literally means homelessness, is also attributed to the Divinity since He does not possess any particular point or home or a station. He is omnipresent and not one, but all dwellings are His, whereas homelessness or uprootedness, quite interestingly, refers to the conditions of being without a home or one root. Taking this thought further, perhaps when one completely embraces his homelessness in the world, he gets most close to the Divine. Because of this word, though, the polysemy in the couplet is enriched as, on the one hand, we have the poet anticipating homelessness in the world. Still, on the other, he is just remarking upon his encounter with the Divine. The other delightful detail is the juxtaposition of imagination with the intellect, which could be extended to the dichotomy between passion and reason. The ǧhazal lover most often rejects the calls of intellect and instead follows the trail of his beloved whom he has only been able to imagine without ever even looking. Let us now consider two verses of another ǧhazal by the name of, Sheher sunsān hai kidhar jāeñ (Where do I go for the city is abandoned):

Sheher sunsān hai kidhar jāeñ
Khāk ho kar kahīñ bikhar jāeñ[37]

Where do I go for the city is abandoned
I might as well turn to dust and scatter somewhere

The poet laments the desolation of his city, implying that he is unable to find his home and thus questioning himself about where he can go. In the second miṣra, however, the poet finds the answer to the question within the question as he, lost in a desolate city, expresses a desire of turning into dust and being dispersed somewhere. Where exactly he wishes to be dispersed, we do not know. What we can see though is how rhizomatic or in favor of anti-totalitarian rootedness our poet is with his desire of dispersal in this way. The second shě`r of this ǧhazal is:

Rāt kitnī guzar gai lekin
Itnī himmat nahiñ ke ghar jāen[38]

How much of the night is gone but
I do not have enough strength that I return home

Clearly, our poet realizes the fact that much of the night has gone by and that it is time for people, generally speaking, to return home. Night entails darkness, and the deeper the night, the darker the darkness, and in the midst of such

37. Kazmi, 34.
38. Ibid.

darkness, most of humanity seeks the warmth of the light of one's home and the solace of familiar things. But Nasir is hesitant due to his frailty to return home. Or maybe the darkness or burden of home is as such that he rather not return and again, one refers to Harney and Moten as they have so aptly observed, "Homelessness is hard, no doubt about it but home is harder."[39] The expression of the experience articulated by our poet more than fifty years ago has not become obsolete as Glissant, too, states, "Poetry is not an amusement nor a display of sentiments or beautiful things. It also imparts form to a knowledge that could never be stricken by obsolescence ."[40] While obsolescence usually signifies the passing of time, however, in terms of space too, this experience cannot be 'stricken': not for Black Americans, South Americans, and Muslims in the US, not for the denizens of the postcolonial states across the world, and not for the Undercommons. In signifying time, obsolescence signifies certain kinds of objects, too; objects which may take the forms of anachronisms, mementos, or memorabilia, objects which are out of their time and which serve as reminders of their time. Of course, errantry and homelessness with their inherent notions of passing and leaving are related to these objects. The imagery of such things is also prevalent in Nasir's poetry.

Consider the following couplets from a ġhazal of his titled: Kuch yādgār-e-sheher-e-sitamgar hī le ćhalaiñ (I should take some mementos from the city of tormentor):

Kuch yādgār-e-sheher-e-sitamgar hī le ćhalaiñ
Āye haiñ is galī meiñ toh patthar hī le ćhalaiñ[41]

I should take some mementos from the city of tormentor
Now that I have arrived in this street, I might as well take stones

The poet realizes that he is in a familiar place—perhaps even his own home—albeit one which is not his to frequent anymore; hence he tells himself that he might as well collect some souvenirs from the city of his tormentor. Now, this tyrant, in typical ġhazal fashion, may very well be his beloved; however, it is plausible that the tormentors are other people, circumstances, or incidents that came about in that city. This city or home, interestingly, gets identified only as the city of the tormentor(s). But in collecting such memorabilia after having to return to this street that he once knew, what the poet wishes to take back are only stones. This is symbolic of the possibility that the poet is not willing to—or perhaps is simply unable to—do away with the memory of what once stood

---

39. Harney and Moten, 139.
40. Glissant, 81.
41. Kazmi, 192.

in this street: most likely his own old home. Therefore, he wishes to take the stones because it is with stones that we lay the foundation in constructing our new houses from scratch. The poet wants to embark upon creating a home with the stones of homelessness as its foundations. The second shĕ`r we consider from the same ġhazal is:

Ranj-e-safar kī koi nishānī toh pās ho
Thorī si khāk-e-kuchā-dilbar hī le ćhalaiñ[42]

At least there should be some remnant of the journey's anguish
Let me take with me a little dust of the street of the beloved

Having to leave the street of the beloved, the journeyer wishes to journey possess a relic to assuage the grief of the subsequent journey. The poet contents himself with some dust of that street that will serve to rid him of the human tendency of forgetfulness. What is noticeable is the role of dust in this couplet because dust, in South Asian as well in Islamic discourses in general, is an extremely significant thing. From the contention that humans are made of dust in the Scripture to the belief that the dust of the city of Karbala where Imam Hussain was martyred possesses capabilities of spiritual healing as well as the reverence for one's homeland or miṭṭī (another word for dust)—but certainly not in the totalitarian rootedness way—dust as an entity garners much symbolic importance in this cultural milieu to which Nasir belongs. Moreover, the beloved too is often not just one's romantic interest, but even if it were, in this particular couplet, it would not be a distraction because it is the beloved who once was, who could and should have been his but is not anymore. The painful involuntary exodus that he is forced to undertake exists. Let us now get to the last shĕ`r of this ġhazal for our discussion:

Is sheher-e-be-chirāgh meiñ jāyegī tu kahāñ
Ā ae shab-e-firāq tujhe ghar hī hī le chalaiñ[43]

In this desolated city where would you go
Come O night of separation I will take you to my abode

The object that is the "night of separation" has become a subject here. The poet addresses this night, telling her that where would you roam around in this city that is already so derelict; you might as well come to my house where there is perhaps still room for the agony of separation. Or maybe the poet had been frequented so much by such nights that he is eager to invite this night of

---

42. Kazmi, 192.
43. Kazmi, 193.

separation over to his place too. Homelessness or separation could occur even within one's home or what was once believed to be one's home.

There are so many such verses of Nasir that we have only started to scratch the surface of his couplets, which are along the lines of homelessness and 'errantry'. Be that as it may, the final shĕ`r on our topoi that we consider from Nasir's dīwān goes:

> Mujhe toh khair watan ćhoṛ kar amāñ nā milī
> Watan bhī mujh se garīb-ul-watan ko tarse gā[44]

> I did not get the refuge upon leaving the country however
> This country too will long for a foreigner/countryless like me

The poet acknowledges that he was unable to attain the protection he may have sought and imagined he would get, which would have allowed him to rid himself of his despair if he left his home. Maybe the poet in this instance was going through an internal exile in which he had, in Glissant's words, "an exacerbated introduction to the thought of errantry" and thus he got consumed by the ideas of "partial, pleasurable compensations" since "internal exile tends towards material comfort, which cannot really distract from anguish."[45] But unlike the previous couplets that we see above, the poet seems to take a more assured tone as he suggests that the home that he has left—or was made to leave—maybe because of the happenings of that home will actually long for him. Here, the feeling of homelessness will begin to be felt not just by the ones who left but also by the home itself once its citizens are forced to leave. The tables seem to have turned to some extent.

Conclusion

If we are to identify the groups of people that were displaced in and by the violence of the Partition of the sub-continent as a newly created community of refugees and exiles within both Indian and Pakistani borders, Nasir Kazmi's kulīyāt of poetry could perhaps be considered their founding book for his poetry is unquestionably about "exile and often about errantry."[46] Moreover, Nasir's book of poetry also goes "beyond the pursuits and triumphs of rootedness required by the evolution of history."[47] It, as a matter of fact, is indicative of an unrootedness which is demanded by the devolution of the painful collective history.

---

44. Kazmi, 199.
45. Glissant, 20.
46. Ibid., 15.
47. Ibid., 16.

This article has relied upon Harney's and Moten's idea of homelessness as it is implied in their collection of essays in the book, *The Undercommons*, as well as the concept of errantry as articulated by Glissant to propitiously locate them in some ghazal couplets of the great Urdu poet of the twentieth century, Nasir Kazmi. Indeed, what Glissant states with regards to Saint-John Perse when he says, "The work of Saint-John Perse aims at pushing memory (of a place, of people, of the things seen in childhood) far forward [...] The poet knows that he has absolutely lost the thing he always remembers, the thing he leaves behind," can be said almost verbatim about Nasir. This is conspicuous from the very first shiʿr of Nasir that we encountered in this article:

Mil hī jāe gā raftagān kā surāgh
Aur kuch din phiro udās udās[48]

You are bound to find a trace of the departed
Keep up this melancholy wandering for a few more days

By continuing to seek them, the poet pushes forward the memory of things that have been lost because he simply cannot forget them. His seeking, however, is hopeful as he feels he is bound to find their trace and such hopefulness of finding—in the present world at least—is only possible when the thing which one is seeking has a purpose; when the errantic search for that thing is driven by a "sacred motivation" in Glissant's intended sense of errantry as we saw above."[49] Until that lost or departed object is found, the poet, like the author of this article, feels at home only in exile as the latter of these two tries to articulate this collective sentiment in his shěʿr:

Rahe khāk basar kuh-e-yār se sheher-e-aghyār talak
Jilā-watanī meiñ hī humne ākhir apnā ghar pāyā

I remained stranded everywhere between the street of the beloved and the city of strangers
And was able to find my home, at last, only in exile

This exile or homelessness is where the poet and the writer is "among his own in dispossession, to be among the ones who cannot own, the ones who have nothing and who, in having nothing, have everything."[50] We, like the esoterically inclined Sufi ascetics, "in having nothing, have everything."[51]

---

48. Naqvi, 189.
49. Glissant, 210.
50. Harney and Moten, 96.
51. Ibid.

Bibliography

Bibi, Saghra, "Bum, Kabūtar, aur Shayirī." In *Hijr kī Rāt kā Sitārā*, edited by Ahmed, Mushtaq, and Basir Sultan Kazmi, 9-14. Lahore: Sang-e-Meel Publications, 2013.

Coogler, Ryan, director. *Black Panther*. Marvel Studios, 2018.

Fanon, Frantz, *Black Skin, White Masks*. New York: Grove Press, 2008.

Glissant, Edouard. *Poetics of Relation*. Ann Arbor: University of Michigan Press, 2010.

Gorakhpuri, Firaq, "Nasir Kazmi." In *Hijr kī Rāt kā Sitārā*, edited by Ahmed, Mushtaq, and Basir Sultan Kazmi, 65-66. Lahore: Sang-e-Meel Publications, 2013.

Hamid, Mohsin. *Exit West*. London: Penguin Books, 2017.

Harney, Stefano, and Fred Moten. *The Undercommons: Fugitive Planning & Black Study*. Wivenhoe. New York: Minor Compositions, 2013.

Jameson, Fredric. *The Political Unconscious: Narrative as a Socially Symbolic Act*. Ithaca: Cornell University Press, 2014.

Kazmi, Nasir. *Dīwān*. Lahore: Ilqa Publications, 2016.

Naqvi, Nauman. *Mourning Indo-Muslim Modernity: Moments in Post-Colonial Urdu Literary Culture*. ProQuest: Columbia University, 2008.

Pritchett, Frances. *Nets of Awareness: Urdu Poetry and its Critics*. Berkeley: University of California Press, 1994.

Chapter 9

A woman's 'place': How the domestic space shaped the Victorian travelers' vision of the British Raj[1]

Ruth Prakasam

Suffolk University, Boston

Abstract

While the colonial system of governance in India was undeniably constructed and administered by white British men, the role and influence of British women were less clearly defined.[2] Yet, it would have been hard to ignore such a significant minority. Alison Blunt explains in 1872, 5000 British women lived in India, and by 1901, this number had increased to over 42,000.[3] The Empire's vision was not just driven by military and administrative initiatives, but by the need for "domesticating" the Subcontinent. As the central figures in this civilizing mission, British women bore the burden of expectations of maintaining the high standards of "home" was immense. As a result, *The Complete Indian Housekeeper and Cook* by Flora Annie Steel and Grace Gardiner, an instructive manual for the domestic arts, found a captive audience when it was originally self-published in India in 1888-1889 and thereafter, with at least a further ten printed editions.[4] Images of colonial homes crafted by such

---

[1]. A version of this paper was first presented at a panel, "Tourists, Tourism, and Transnationality in the Victorian Cultural Imagination" at the Northeast Modern Language Association Conference in Washington, D.C., March 2019.

[2]. In the paper British, Great Britain, or Britain will be used; however, the names of countries and their people will remain as stated in a direct quote.

[3]. Alison Blunt, "Imperial Geographies of Home: British Domesticity in India, 1886-1925," *Transactions of the Institute of British Geographers* 24, no. 4 (1999): 426, www.jstor.org/stable/623233.

[4]. Flora Annie Steel and Grace Gardiner, *The Complete Indian Housekeeper and Cook*, ed. Ralph Crane and Anna Johnston (Oxford: OUP, 2010), xxviii.

manuals were also directed at women travelers from Britain who comprised an important group to be convinced that British women were flourishing in their jobs of domesticating colonial India as many of them would later publish their travelogues that would possibly detail the success or failure of this endeavor. In examining how *The Complete Indian Housekeeper and Cook* functioned as both a practical and ideological guide, the article explores the extent to which it was successful in implementing the civilizing mission of the Empire in India.

Keywords: Housekeeping manual, colonial, women travelers, British Raj, imperialism

***

The first edition of *The Complete Indian Housekeeper and Cook* was published between 1888-1890.[5] Its authors, Flora Annie Steel and Grace Gardiner self-published it in India and then in 1890 by Frank Murray in Edinburgh.[6] Subsequently, William Heinemann published it consistently from 1898 until 1921, a fact that is probative of its popularity as a comprehensive and authoritative Anglo-Indian lifestyle manual.[7] According to Ralph Crane and Anna Johnston, the editors of the fourth edition, published in 1898 (and the one referred to in this essay), it was the first fully revised version which served as the template for later texts; thereafter, between the years of 1899 and 1921, at least six further editions were printed.[8] If there was any confusion for whom the book was written, it was immediately clarified by the inscription included by the authors, "To THE ENGLISH GIRLS to Whom Fate May Assign the Task of Being HOUSE-MOTHERS in Our Eastern Empire This Little Volume is Dedicated."[9] Steel and Gardiner describe these young women as "GIRLS" since many of them were newly married, young, inexperienced with the task of housekeeping, and living abroad; they explained these women were living,

---

5. Ibid., xxviii.

6. Ibid., xxviii.

7. The term "Anglo-Indian" used in this essay was found in 19th century travel writing, novels, and domestic manuals, like *The Complete Indian* referred to the English living in colonial India. In a sense it is also a metaphorical description of the hybrid existence they maintained while on the Subcontinent. Flora Annie Steel and Grace Gardiner, *The Complete Indian*, xxxviii.

8. Steel and Gardiner, *The Complete Indian Housekeeper and Cook*, xxxviii.

9. Capitalized words reflect larger fonts in original quote in Steel and Gardiner's *The Complete Indian*, 4.

"under absolutely new conditions."[10] Blunt qualifies that this "Fate"[11] was the reality of 5,000 British women in 1872 who lived in India; by 1901, this number increased to over 42,000.[12] Mary Procida informs us that *The Complete Indian Housekeeper and Cook* was one of many publications within the genre of cooking and housekeeping manuals which enjoyed a robust market during the latter years of the nineteenth century until India's independence in 1947.[13] Blunt confirms this by describing the printing of such household guides as an "unprecedented number" between the late 1880s and 1920s (422).[14] Procida explained that though such texts were available, it was the increase of British women settling in India in the latter half of the century, which elevated the demand for this genre.[15]

After 1858 engaged or newlywed British women journeying to India to settle were still greater in number than women touring the Subcontinent. Still, after 1869, when the Suez Canal opened, and more hill stations were built as resorts for tourists to enjoy, women travelers became a significant cohort.[16] With the increase in this type of travelers, the interest in recording these journeys for publication also grew in popularity. Sara Mills was amazed at the "sheer volume" of travel books written by hundreds of female travelers documenting their trip through parts of the British Empire between 1850 and 1930.[17] For most of the nineteenth century, hotels were not an option for accommodation in India; therefore, travelers would reside with relatives in their homes or would be furnished with a letter of introduction to stay with acquaintances.[18] Even if women travelers did not stay overnight in the home of a British resident in India, as they traveled within India, they most likely would have been invited

---

[10]. Steel and Gardiner, 6.

[11]. Reference Inscription in Steel and Gardiner, 4.

[12]. Blunt, "Imperial Geographies of Home," 426.

[13]. Mary Procida, "Feeding the Imperial Appetite," *Journal of Women's History*, vol. 15, no. 2, Summer (2003): 123.

[14]. In the endnotes Blunt includes examples of such household manuals, like *The Calcutta Review,* she lists others when explaining, "Household guides were published in Britain and India during this period and included Chota Mem(1909), Deighton (1912), Diver (1909), Garrett (1887), I O R (1909), James (1898), Platt (1923), Steel and Gardiner (1907) and Wilson (1904)" in Alison Blunt, "Imperial Geographies," 438.

[15]. Procida, "Feeding the Imperial Appetite," 126.

[16]. Blunt, 427.

[17]. Sara Mills, *Discourses of Difference: An Analysis of Women's Travel Writing and Colonialism* (London: Routledge, 1991), 1,2.

[18]. Indira Ghose, *Women Travellers in Colonial India: The Power of the Female Gaze* (Oxford: OUP, 1998), 132.

for tea, dinner, or some other social occasion to the residence of a civil servant or military officer. Steel and Gardiner explain that from noon until 2 pm, visitors could call upon a memsahib for a visit.[19] Jane Robinson mentions that beginning at five-thirty each evening, British hostesses or memsahibs would perform this custom again.[20] Such encounters would have given British ladies visiting India a more intimate glimpse into the colonial home.

Thus, women travelers were an important group to be convinced that British women were flourishing in their jobs of domesticating colonial India as many of them would later publish their travelogues that would possibly detail the success or failure of this endeavor. According to the editors of *The Complete Indian Housekeeper and Cook* Steel and Gardiner advocated that British women could administer the same domestic standards for a household in Britain or India.[21] The underlying philosophy that drove the domestication of India was the belief that British women could implement these three core factors, "Economy, prudence, efficiency" with few problems in India since it was important to raise the country's standards to meet the high expectations of imperial domestic practices.[22] By memsahibs insisting that their homes mimic British gardens, cuisine, and the management of servants, they were resisting the dilution of British culture. They contributed to a domesticated India through "Anglocentric virtues [...] [and] the manual's didactic regimes, in order to raise up the peoples of the Empire through domestic reform."[23] "Dirt, disorder, and different cultural practices" are the opposite of Victorian principles of domestication that Steel and Gardiner outline for memsahibs to follow.[24] The repetitive, if not ritualistic, daily life of the memsahib and her household was not easy to endure, and some British women, understandably, found it tedious.[25] But, it appears that this regular routine undertaken by the entire household that included three meals, tea, visitors, and often evening entertainment was the steady process by which British domestication was introduced and inculcated in India.[26]

---

[19]. Steel and Gardiner, 68.

[20]. Jane Robinson, *Angels of Albion: Women of the Indian Mutiny* (London: Penguin Books, 1997), 21.

[21]. Steel and Gardiner, xvi.

[22]. Ibid., xvi.

[23]. Ibid., xvi, xx-xxi.

[24]. Ibid., xxi.

[25]. Ibid., xv.

[26]. Ibid., xiv-xv.

This article examines why British women residing in India were devoted to a text like *The Complete Indian Housekeeper and Cook* that established explicit standards for achieving domestic feats and expected such women to model these practices for imperial success. British women's domestic accomplishments in India would be lent greater worth if communicated to a wider audience. Women travelers were the critical observers that needed to be impressed because their published assessment of colonial domesticity would be available to readers beyond India. Indira Ghose lends my perspective support by clarifying that women travelers "collected and disseminated" their observations about India, which reinforced colonialism's central enterprise of attaining a comprehensive insight into understanding how to subjugate "the other."[27] I believe she correctly deduces that "These travellers' [sic] texts did not merely 'depict' reality, they created it. In this way, they 'helped in the ideological reproduction of the empire'."[28] As travel literature became a popular genre from the late nineteenth century until the end of the British Raj, published journeys about India resonated with the reading public at home in Britain.[29] A positive image of imperialism needed to be conveyed through this literature, as Ghose confirms that women travelers and their texts were a means for imparting, "the colonial construction of India and reaffirm[ing] colonial ideology."[30]

By reading a domestic manual like *The Complete Indian Housekeeper and Cook* alongside travel writing narratives written by women through a feminist postcolonial analysis, these sources do document how women navigated and asserted their roles to shape and sustain the Imperial mission on the Subcontinent; however, what is also distinguishable is that both distinct groups of women—residents in India and visitors to India—seemingly confronted two separate countries. They each experienced India separately with the lady traveler believing her interaction was direct, intimate, and authentic in comparison to her counterpart, the memsahib, whose corseted body seemed to epitomize her restricted distance in her contact with India.[31] Even though her physical movements in India were largely confined to her immediate domestic space, the household should not be dismissed as an insignificant stage for the memsahib to demonstrate her dominance to those in her service.

---

27. Ghose, *Women Travelers in Colonial India*, 138.
28. Ibid., 138.
29. Ghose describes women's published travel writings about India as, "[...] widely-read texts at the time" in Ghose, *Women Travellers*, 161.
30. Ibid., 138.
31. Robinson physically described the memsahib as, "[...] whaleboned (yet strangely stout) figure [...]" in Robinson, *Angels of Albion*, xvii.

Ghose claims one example of this power dynamic was the authority the memsahibs wielded over their native servants.[32] Under the chapter entitled "The Duties of the Mistress" Steel and Gardiner unequivocally declare, "The first duty of a mistress is, of course, to be able to give intelligible orders to her servants [...] The next duty is obviously to insist on her orders being carried out."[33] They strongly recommend that British women learn to speak the native language, "Hindustani"; Steel and Gardiner rationalize that if someone lived in Italy, France, or Germany for two decades, there would be an "attempt" to acquire the language and believe the same logic should be broadened to include a residence in India.[34] By doing so, their instructions would leave little room for interpretation; their imperious tone and meaning being plainly communicated. Robinson shared a less charitable image of the memsahib's linguistic skills that extended to only issuing demands to servants in an irascible manner.[35] "[...] [British] women's lives were inextricably linked to practices and understandings of British imperial domesticity," explains Georgina Gowans.[36] Any small or large domestic achievement in a British household in India, where husbands served in the Indian Civil Service or the Military, would not have succeeded without the labor of servants.[37] The equivalent middle-class women in Britain benefited from the working-class labor of servants to assist them in managing their households.[38] Gowans confirms the necessity for this daily presence of servants in the Anglo-Indian home by describing them as part of the, "ritualization of 'everyday' activities (including instructing the servants [...])" and reminds her audience that they were paramount, "to the maintenance of imperial boundaries."[39]

Procida asserts that British women could legitimately avoid the physical labor of such daily tasks as cooking and cleaning was legitimately by allocating these chores to servants, as it was an expectation of colonial society in India for such labor not to be undertaken by white women.[40] Their prominence within this domestic sphere, according to Shampa Roy, was one that satisfied most

---

32. Ghose, 140.
33. Steel and Gardiner, 12.
34. Ibid., 12.
35. Robinson, *Angels of Albion,* xvii.
36. Georgina Gowans, "Imperial Geographies of Home: Memsahibs and Miss-Sahibs in India and Britain, 1915-1947," *Cultural Geographies* 10, no. 4 (2003): 436 www.jstor.org/stable/4425 0942.
37. Steel and Gardiner, xiv.
38. Ibid., xviii.
39. Gowans, "Imperial Geographies of Home," 436.
40. Procida, 43.

memsahibs.[41] The domestic arrangements of British women in India stood in glaring contrast to many of their counterparts at home in Great Britain.[42] In order to comprehend the disparity between households in Britain and India, Blunt estimated that in the late nineteenth century, small households in India employed ten to twelve servants while larger ones would require anywhere up to 30, and in the 1920s about a dozen servants would still be needed to run a household; whereas, three to five servants would staff a comparable household in England during this same period.[43] Against this context, Procida reasoned that the heavy dependence upon servant labor allowed British women in India to have the time, energy, and space to further their imperial agenda through the domestication of the Raj.[44] Procida examined several household manuals, including Steel's and Gardiner's, arguing that:

> Anglo-Indian cookbooks thus served many imperial purposes beyond the functions of simple didactic or prescriptive texts [...] [these] cookbooks served to reshape the domestic sphere of the Raj, to construct new ideas about gender in the Empire by freeing Anglo-Indian women from many of their traditional domestic responsibilities, and to contribute to the creation, collection, and dissemination of imperial knowledge. [45]

Procida's position provides a serious insight into the exclusive space inhabited by British women living in India.[46] Contemporary scholarship no longer deems British women guided by cookbooks and manuals as the problematic "minority." Mills' seminal feminist text made clear these historical reasons— her analysis of British travel writing texts authored by women revealed that the colonial establishment was uncomfortable with the role of white women within the Empire.[47] She says, "British women were only allowed to figure as symbols of home and purity; women as active participants [in Empire] can barely be conceived of."[48] The rules for household management found in *The Complete Indian Housekeeper and Cook* reinforced this limited function British women performed in India. Colonialism and Empire were perceived as masculine; white women who recorded their experiences in India did not easily

---

[41]. Shampa Roy, "'A Miserable Sham': Flora Annie Steel's Short Fictions and the Question of Indian Women's Reform," *Feminist Review*, no. 94 (2010): 58 www.jstor.org/stable/40664129.

[42]. Procida, 124.

[43]. Blunt, 429.

[44]. Procida, 124.

[45]. Ibid., 143.

[46]. Ibid., 124.

[47]. Mills, *Discourses of Difference*, 3.

[48]. Ibid., 3.

fit into an imperial 'dispatch box'.[49] Mills recognizes that the move towards scholarly attention given to travel writing was initially attributed to colonial and postcolonial critics such as Edward Said, Mary Louise Pratt, Homi Bhabha, and Gayatri Spivak. Still, the accessibility of nineteenth and early twentieth-century colonial travelogues written by women was helped by feminist presses like Virago, who reprinted these works and by women critics who examined them through a feminist lens.[50]

Susan Zlotnick, in her article, credits literary critics and feminist historians for challenging the image of the "unthinking memsahib."[51] Blunt reminds us of this crucial shift by explaining that some imperial commentators ultimately blamed British women for the demise of the British Raj because it was believed that they created racial tensions between the British and the Indians through the domestic and social divisions they instituted.[52] It is important to realize— as Jane Rendall explains—that white women's femininity was upheld as a high standard in comparison to the "savage" or "'Eastern' women."[53] White women were to be protected. Given these boundaries, it would appear difficult for British women to make such a significant cultural and intellectual leap to embrace the other when their duties were stringently drawn: "British homes in India were seen by the Calcutta Review to foster appropriate gender roles, national virtues, and imperial rule."[54] Procida says that historians uncritically assigned negative behavior to British women, in particular, "[…] an unwillingness to adopt Indian cultural attributes, including culinary tastes, and habits, thus fostering racial divisiveness and precluding sympathetic understanding between the two groups"; this was endorsed as the cause for the friction between the British and the Indians.[55]

A paradox not obvious to British women was their exertion of authority over their servants while being dependent upon them to demarcate the perimeter between the colonial home and India. A strange dichotomy, but a reality to

---

49. Ibid., 3.

50. Ibid., 2, 4.

51. Susan Zlotnick, "Domesticating Imperialism: Curry and Cookbooks in Victorian England," *Frontiers: A Journal of Women Studies* 16, no. 2/3 (1996): 51 doi:10.2307/3346803.

52. Blunt, 423.

53. Jane Rendall, "The Condition of Women, Women's Writing and the Empire in Nineteenth-Century Britain," in *At Home with the Empire: Metropolitan Culture and the Imperial World*, ed. Catherine Hall and Sonya O. Rose (Cambridge: CUP, 2006), 206.

54. Blunt explains the *Calcutta Review* was a periodical for British residents published twice a month and many of its articles discussed the role of women in India. Alison Blunt, "Imperial Geographies," 422, 438.

55. Procida, 138, emphasis mine.

which feminist historians and literary scholars have given serious attention through analyzing the role of Englishwomen residents and travelers against the background of imperialism. Travel provided women the opportunity not to be restricted by gender norms because the experience placed them in the public domain and released them from their regular life of domestic confinement.[56] Women tourists to India enjoyed much more freedom traveling on the Subcontinent than they experienced at home in Britain. They were able to travel alone safely and were aware that this type of rare experience was possible because of the power wielded by British colonial rule.[57] Unlike women travelers, British women residents did not enjoy the same liberties. The expectations upon them were conservative and staid. For instance, by returning to Gowans' comments, which touch upon the more mundane functions servants occupied within a British household in India, her remarks should also prompt scholars to contemplate the reality of the conflicting roles and spaces that British women inhabited within their own homes in India.[58] Their efforts to maintain a façade of domestic imperial superiority may have been pierced by female travelers, whose instinct might have been more intuitive at distinguishing that British women residents masked a fragile, disconnected, and unstable union with British India.

Yet, such disparities are unacknowledged when certainty and stability are present in the form of a domestic blueprint. The purpose of *The Complete Indian Housekeeper and Cook* was to steer women through difficulties that arose within their personal residences. By co-authoring this type of book, Steel and Gardiner essentially became 'domestic colonizers'; they firmly anchored their female audience to rules devised by British women for other British women residing in colonial India in order to preserve the high standards of the Empire. Anne McClintock argues that a central trait of Victorian middle-class culture was "rigid boundaries" and described women as "the boundary markers of imperialism."[59] Women were a section of the colonial territory on which the Victorian ideology of domesticity and home were embodied.[60] Catherine Hall describes the Empire as "part of their [the British] mapping of the globe."[61] Hall

---

56. Ghose, 133.

57. Ibid., 137.

58. Gowans, 436.

59. Anne McClintock, *Imperial Leather: Race, Gender and Sexuality in the Colonial Contest* (New York: Routledge, 1995), 24, 33.

60. Ibid., 36.

61. Catherine Hall, "Going a-Trolloping: Imperial Man Travels the Empire," in *Gender and Imperialism*, ed. Clare Midgley Rose (Manchester: Manchester UP, 1998), 180.

explains that the Empire gave Englishmen a sense of national identity and masculinity—she uses the phrase, "a way of knowing."

In contrast, women as symbols of border protection for home and Empire were construed as familiar and reliable. The fundamental defense women advanced regarding the colonial agenda is echoed by Gowans, who explains that "the female efficiency and domestic discipline required for successful housekeeping in the sub-continent was seen to be part of the imperial project. Indeed, the establishment of British homes in India meant that women could not only directly contribute to imperialism but also earn recognition for their labor."[62]

Establishing a successful home in India required feminine efficacy, control, and ingenuity; it was a practical and concrete means for British women to be acknowledged for contributing to the imperial mission.[63] It is precisely the expectations upon these women to maintain the "imperial project" that draws attention to the constant convergence of conflicting oppositions that they had to maneuver.[64] For instance, never quite feeling at ease in their homes by experiencing an unsettled existence which would have been an acceptable disposition for a nomad's or traveler's state of being was disregarded for women permanently residing in India. Or, their true knowledge of India and Indians being tied to their domestic environments, as they dispatched their servants outside of their homes to translate and negotiate for them in the bazaar when purchasing food supplies or other goods.[65] Robinson remarks, "a lady never went to the bazaar herself."[66] Identifying or diverting domestic trouble was also a servant's duties. The Bearer maintained the safekeeping of the entire property by actively observing the daily activities of the whole household. As the head servant, Steel and Gardiner explained he was expected to "report openly" to the memsahib each morning about what occurred in the compound for the last twenty-four hours.[67] Literally and symbolically, servants acted as translators and guards for the British memsahib. Yet, despite this dependence upon their servants, Steel and Gardiner remained adamant that the line between colonizer and colonized remained firm.[68] Unlike British men, who were not limited by geographical boundaries to explore India, women's rational and emotional engagement with the country in terms of its physical environment, as well as its

---

[62]. Gowans, 427.

[63]. Ibid., 427.

[64]. Ibid., 427.

[65]. Steel and Gardiner, 79.

[66]. Robinson, 21.

[67]. Steel and Gardiner, 68.

[68]. Ibid., xxiii.

people, was shaped by the restrictions imposed upon them by their homes, which ranged from physical barriers to written instructions by Steel and Gardiner.

A question must be posed, did travelers to the Subcontinent saw a composed snapshot of an Anglo-Indian world viewed through the lens of a household guide like *The Complete Indian Housekeeper and Cook?* Secondly, were travelers aware that it was, in a sense, contrived for their purposes? or would they believe it was realistic and communicate its authenticity through their published letters and diaries, all the while not quite grasping that the colonial greatness on display in British homes in India was carefully choreographed by a group of individuals whose own authority only reached to the edges of their Imperial gardens?

The advice, language, and tone presented by Steel and Gardiner is evidence that the authors understood who would have an intimate view of the civilizing mission, its successes (and failures), and, most significantly, could circulate it to those at home in Britain: travelers. Letters and diaries of their travels through the Subcontinent, which were later published into travelogues, contributed to this shared version of the British Empire. Rendall points out that the nineteenth century in Britain saw the growth of print culture and that women were both consumers and creators of it.[69] Steel and Gardiner write, "We do not wish to advocate an unholy haughtiness, but an Indian household can no more be governed peacefully, without dignity and prestige, than an Indian Empire."[70] This well-repeated quote of Steel's and Gardiner's illustrates their cognizance of not just the authority of the Anglo-Indian domestic environment within India, but the British and European external audience who would be peering in from the outside. The crucial attention needed for "keeping up appearances" within the colonial context was predicated upon British women's role and gender being malleable in order to serve best what Zlotnick described as, "the always fragile, always fictional imperial state."[71]

So, in order to exude an image of authority and control, Steel and Gardiner emphasize to their audience that it is vital that no one sees the mistress undertaking household tasks: her duty is to watch the servants complete these jobs.[72] Their insistence on such rigid rules for managing a household in India was in Steel's and Gardiner's estimation of the only way to execute the running of a home seamlessly.[73] What is significant is not merely the constant demand for control, but the more pressing need to maintain the veneer of an imperial

---

69. Rendall, "The Condition of Women," 104.
70. Steel and Gardiner, 18.
71. Zlotnick, *Domesticating Imperialism*, 52.
72. Steel and Gardiner, 19.
73. Ibid., 19.

precision and faultlessness. Procida expresses a similar observation about how a cookbook, like Steel's and Gardiner's, was, in reality, a guide for how British women could preserve their dominant power over the native Indians by explaining, "Anglo-Indian cookbooks provided their readers with a recipe for imperial control that allowed them to retain their sway over the colonized peoples without becoming bogged down in the burdensome activities of daily life."[74] The "readers" were the British women whose job it was to show their Indian male cooks how to replicate British dishes; however, it is ironic that most of these women had very little actual cooking experience.[75] Steel and Gardiner did not perceive this is as a disadvantage because their essential advice to these novice mistresses for critiquing their Indian cook's dishes was to develop the "[…] art of just appraisal and dispassionate judgment […]."[76] The cavalier quality of this counsel emphasizes the importance of maintaining the pretense of possessing culinary knowledge and provides another example of how the perception of imperial influence was sustained.

In contrast, Helen C. Ford, an English tourist, whose travelogue, *Notes of a Tour in India and Ceylon,* published in 1889 was unimpressed by what she viewed as idleness on the part of Anglo-Indian women. She remarked that even to reposition a chair for her own comfort by briefly lifting it, such a physical act was frowned upon because "English ladies in India not being apparently allowed to do anything for themselves."[77] Ford is even more plain-spoken about their sedentary lifestyle compared to her own need for exercise, as she asserts, "a walk does one good. I can't stand that sitting and lounging about all day long, which Anglo-Indian ladies seem to do."[78] Ironically, Ford is unimpressed by the exact behavior that Steel and Gardiner prescribe as the formula to follow if British women are to be successful in administering their households in India; Steel and Gardiner advise their readership to oversee that tasks are done correctly by others.[79]

Ford is further disappointed when she learns that British women have nearly non-existent interactions with native Indian women.[80] Unlike most British women residing in India, women travelers to India, like Ford, wanted to

---

[74]. Procida, 124.

[75]. Steel and Gardiner, 220

[76]. Ibid., 220.

[77]. Helen C. Ford, *Notes of a Tour in India and Ceylon* (London: Women's Printing Society, Limited, 1889), 105.

[78]. Ibid., 118.

[79]. Steel and Gardiner, 19.

[80]. Ford, *Notes of a Tour,* 174.

experience what they perceived to be the real India. This included meeting Indians. Ford, and other British women travelers, would have relied on white women, who were residents in India, to introduce them to the local Indian women. She confides, "I have spoken to a good many English ladies now, who can tell me hardly anything [about Indian women]; I really don't think they know more than I do."[81] Ford's observation is echoed by another lady traveler, Anna Harriette Leonowens, who scrutinized the matter more critically. Leonowens writes in *Life and Travel in India* published in 1884 that she has witnessed the "European influence" to be negligible upon Indians since there is such a clear division between the high-ranking officials in India and those they have colonized.[82] Initially, it is startling that Leonowens characterizes the British impact on Indians as negligible, but hardly surprising.[83] Her heightened class consciousness seems to suggest that to the eyes of a traveler in order to successfully colonialize Indians, their behavior needed to reflect those of the British ruling classes.

On a visit to the holy city of Nashik, located in the northwest part of India, she reiterates a similar observation, "there was nowhere perceptible the least trace of European influence on the people or in the city."[84] Pallavi Rastogi, in her article, reminds us that Leonowens' mention of "European Influence" was typical of the style of Victorian travel writing, as Mary Louise Pratt in her book, *Imperial Eyes* probed why Europe was the model that everything else needed to aspire.[85] Pratt asked, "How has travel and exploration writing produced 'the rest of the world' for European readerships at particular points in Europe's revisionist trajectory?."[86] Fundamentally there is only one simple answer to Pratt's question: Europe saw itself as the epicenter of the world, and amongst the hierarchy of European nations, the British Empire ruled.

While the nineteenth-century British traveler's Anglo-centric attitude is hardly surprising to a twenty-first-century readership, what is revealing about Leonowens' earlier quote and Ford's astonishment at British women's lack of

---

81. Ibid., 174.
82. Anna Harriette Leonowens, *Life and Travel in India* (Philadelphia: Porter & Coates, 1884), 321.
83. Ibid., 280.
84. Ibid., 280.
85. Pallavi Rastogi, "'The World Around and the World Afar All Seemed Compassed': Cosmopolitan Ethnicity in the Victorian Metropolis," *Women's Studies* 32, no. 6 (2003): 738, doi:10.1080/00497870390221873.
86. Mary Louise Pratt, *Imperial Eyes: Travel Writing and Transculturation* (London: Routledge, 1992), 5.

knowledge about Indian women suggests that neither one of them saw the domestic efforts of British women, dictated by a guide like, *The Complete Indian Housekeeper and Cook* as evidence of an effective civilizing mission.[87] Zlotnick confidently states,

> British women's domesticity became one of the most visible and remarked upon signs of their—and their nation'—superiority [...] early Victorian cookery books [like *The Complete Indian Housekeeper Cook*] attest to the important ideological function women performed in the construction of Victorian imperialism. At both the symbolic and the practical level, Victorian women domesticated imperialism.[88]

For the Anglo-Indian community to gaze and appraise themselves on accomplishing this achievement, I would agree with Zlotnick.[89] But to assume that travelers would also arrive at the same conclusions is problematic, in part, because their experience with India would be temporary and their expectations different. For instance, early in Ford's trip while in Bombay, she writes, "We had plenty of conversation at dinner tonight [sic] [in Bombay] about natives' manners and customs, I can't help asking questions perpetually."[90] Such a reaction would have been natural for a tourist. Even though it was not that visitors like Leonowens and Ford were unable to grasp that "this," India was a staged version of the Empire. Yet, a hint of genuine human interest about the lives of those whom they colonized and who served at the colonizer's pleasure was not the British woman's mission. Simply stated, "Englishwomen in India [...] [had] to reproduce England in India. Colonial wives and mothers functioned as the living symbols of English culture when stationed with their husbands in India."[91] Zlotnick contextualized the behavior of British women to rationalize why their interactions with India lacked the curiosity that was a natural trait exhibited by travelers as they journeyed around the Subcontinent.[92]

Thus, the tourists' anticipation of what insights and knowledge their British hostesses could share about India was not as successfully communicated as Steel and Gardiner expressed to their readers. Swati Chattopadhyay reminds us that, "The first principle of the Anglo-Indian home was to keep native India at

---

87. The quote is in reference to, Anna Harriette Leonowens, *Life and Travel*, 321; the paraphrase makes reference to Helen C. Ford, *Notes of a Tour*, 174.
88. Zlotnick, 54, 65.
89. Ibid., 54, 65.
90. Ford, 23.
91. Zlotnick, 62.
92. Ibid., 62.

bay [...] The effort to distance oneself from natives allowed British women to overwrite the nurturing model of domesticity with a model of public life drawn from the pages of the colonial bureaucracy."[93] Bureaucracy would imply a level of unknowing and distance: factors that curious visitors who were looking closely inside the Anglo-Indian household very likely felt and saw. Earlier in this article, it was suggested that women's travel accounts "created" a particular representation of India.[94] But, it appears one not shared by Steel and Gardiner. Their text provides detailed directives prescribing "a utopian domestic space" for running an efficient household in India.[95] Except for travelers to the Subcontinent did not necessarily equivocate a well-managed Anglo-Indian home to a great Empire as, Steel and Gardiner advised, "insist [to the servant] on everything being done every day in the same style. Then, if a friend comes into dinner unexpectedly [...] The dinner may be plain, even frugal, but it will be correct, even to the most minute details."[96] Though accurate, the instruction sounds trite and bears no resemblance to the adventures women travelers recorded about the country they encountered, which included interactions with Indian women, learning about customs, and religions.[97]

Like other women who traveled before and after them to India, Leonowens' and Ford's dismissal of perceiving a memsahib in the role of authority is clear but expected. To provide a context for why women travelers would have reacted in this manner, Ghose rationalizes, "Independent women wandering all over the empire proved that British women were quite capable of managing their own affairs."[98] Their exchange with India was unrestrained in terms of geography, people, and cultural participation in comparison to the rigid standards of behavior that British women who resided in India followed. When scrutinized by women travelers, the memsahib's control over her servants was not remarkable; this experience did not encourage women travelers to express that colonial rule was influential on the native populations. However, the purpose of a domestic manual like *The Complete Indian Housekeeper and Cook* was not to change or revise the appearance, behavior, or practice of the resident British woman, her servants, the food served, or the décor of the home. Similar

---

[93]. Swati Chattopadhyay, "'Goods, Chattels and Sundry Items': Constructing 19th-Century Anglo-Indian Domestic Life," *Journal of Material Culture* 7, no. 3 (2002): 245. doi:10.1177/135918350200700301.

[94]. Ghose, 138.

[95]. Steel and Gardiner, xviii.

[96]. Ibid., 81.

[97]. Rendall, 115.

[98]. Ghose, 139.

to imperialism, successful implementation of the guidelines meant the memsahib was "correct."[99]

Steel and Gardiner wrote for a niche group, Anglo-Indian women living in India, whose lives were inevitably informed and managed in small and significant ways by imperialism. The housekeeping manual's indirect audience also included women travelers whose reflections and descriptions about their journey through British homes in India were supposed to transmit a premeditated message that British women residents were effectively contributing to the imperial mission. By seeking to create identical snapshots of Anglo-Indian lifestyles in every colonial home, Steel's and Gardiner's domestic/ating manual functioned as an impediment for becoming acquainted with India during their travels, in the same way, that the servants in the colonial household acted as guards against the intrusion of India into the home. However, the pervasive and compliant presence of Indian servants, mandated by the manual, led the travelers to comment upon the incompleteness of the complete housekeeper, whose sedentary lounging about received more notice than her rigid compliance with the diktats of the manual. The British women striving to reproduce a stabilized, normalized miniature image of colonial control over the indigenous population presented instead of a fragile, disconnected, and fractured assemblage that revealed the inherent contradictions of the project empire. The woman traveler and the memsahib, both participated in the civilizing mission of the British Raj. Still, their performances were unable to shape a refined image of colonial India in the script uniformly.

Bibliography

Blunt, Alison. "Imperial Geographies of Home: British Domesticity in India, 1886-1925." *Transactions of the Institute of British Geographers*, vol. 24, no. 4, (1999): 421-40. EBSCOhost,ezproxysuf.flo.org/login?url=http://search.ebscohost.com/login.aspx?direct=true&db=edsjsr&AN=edsjsr.623233&site=eds-live.

Chattopadhyay, Swati. "'Goods, Chattels and Sundry Items': Constructing 19th-Century Anglo-Indian Domestic Life." *Journal of Material Culture*, vol. 7, no. 3, Nov. (2002): 243-71. EBSCOhost, doi:10.1177/135918350200700301.

Ford, Helen C. *Notes of a Tour in India and Ceylon.* London: Women's Printing Society, Limited, 1889.

Ghose, Indira. *Women Travellers in Colonial India: The Power of the Female Gaze.* Oxford: OUP, 1998.

Gowans, Georgina. "Imperial Geographies of Home: Memsahibs and Miss-Sahibs in India and Britain, 1915-1947." *Cultural Geographies*, vol. 10, no. 4, Oct. (2003): 424-41. EBSCOhost, doi:10.1191/1474474003eu283oa.

---

[99]. Steel and Gardiner, 81.

Hall, Catherine. "Going a-Trolloping: Imperial Man Travels the Empire." In *Gender and Imperialism*, edited by Clare Midgley, 180-199. Manchester: Manchester University Press, 1998.

Leonowens, Anna Harriette. *Life and Travel in India*. Philadelphia: Porter & Coates, 1884.

McClintock, Anne. *Imperial Leather: Race, Gender and Sexuality in the Colonial Contest*. New York: Routledge, 1995.

Mills, Sara. Discourses of Difference: *An Analysis of Women's Travel Writing and Colonialism*. London: Routledge, 1991.

Pratt, Mary Louise. *Imperial Eyes: Travel Writing and Transculturation*. London: Routledge, 1992.

Procida, Mary. "Feeding the Imperial Appetite." *Journal of Women's History*, vol. 15, no. 2, Summer (2003): 123-149. EBSCOhost, doi:10.1353/jowh.2003.0054.

Rastogi, Pallavi. "'The World Around and the World Afar All Seemed Compassed': Cosmopolitan Ethnicity in the Victorian Metropolis." *Women's Studies*, vol. 32, no. 6, Sept. (2003): 735-39. EBSCOhost, doi:10.1080/00497870390221873.

Rendall, Jane. "The Condition of Women, Women's Writing and the Empire in Nineteenth-Century Britain." In *At Home With the Empire: Metropolitan Culture and the Imperial World*, edited by Catherine Hall and Sonya O. Rose, 101-121. Cambridge: Cambridge University Press, 2006.

Robinson, Jane. Angels of Albion: *Women of the Indian Mutiny*. London: Penguin Books, 1997.

Roy, Shampa. "'A Miserable Sham': Flora Annie Steel's Short Fictions and the Question of Indian Women's Reform." *Feminist Review*, no. 94, (2010): 55-74. www.jstor.org/stable/40664129.

Steel, Flora Annie, and Grace Gardiner. *The Complete Indian Housekeeper and Cook*, edited by Ralph Crane and Anna Johnston. Oxford: OUP, 2010.

Zlotnick, Susan. "Domesticating Imperialism: Curry and Cookbooks in Victorian England." *Frontiers: A Journal of Women Studies*, vol. 16, no. 2/3, Aug. (1996): 51-68. EBSCOhost, doi:10.2307/3346803.

Chapter 10

Towards a self-critical subjectivity: Tsewang Yishey Pemba's White Crane, Lend Me Your Wings

Sushmita Sihwag

Independent scholar

Abstract

Tsewang Yishey Pemba's novel, *White Crane, Lend Me Your Wings*, published posthumously in 2017, is a work of historical fiction that follows the lives of people of the Nyarong valley in Kham province of Eastern Tibet. The novel delineates Tibetan history, culture, as well as the tragedy that forced thousands of Tibetans to flee from their homeland in search of refuge. Pemba's own experiences of exile lend to the breadth of his perception of the Tibetan issue and the notions of 'Tibetanness.' The experience of exile, and to some extent that of diaspora, is a process that marks an unsettling of one's ideas of a fixed self. It is accompanied by an epistemological shift in the understanding of the self, along with the transit of the body through space. Throughout the novel, the question regarding Tibetan and Nyarong-Khampa identities in the face of a real or imaginary 'foreign' remains a bone of contention. The narrative deliberately complicates conventional markers that determine identities, such as race and religion. This article analyses the self-critical mode of diasporic subjectivity in Dr. Pemba's novel, in conversation with the theoretical frameworks of Gilles Deleuze, Edward Said, and Dibyesh Anand on nomadic epistemologies, exile, and identity, to reflect on its implications for not only the politics of identity in exile but also the questions of self and subjectivity at large, where both the self and its subjectivity are layered and complex. The argument does not restrict itself to a discussion of diasporic subjectivity in the context of the immediate cultural and political realms; it dwells additionally on the ramifications of the psychological, societal, and ideological rhizomes in their horizontal territorizations.

Keywords: Diaspora, historical novel, Tibet, self-critical subjectivity, metaphysical exile

***

Tsewang Yishey Pemba's novel, *White Crane, Lend Me Your Wings*, is a work of historical fiction that follows the lives of people of the Nyarong valley in Kham province of Eastern Tibet. The timespan covered in the historical novel extends from the arrival of Christian missionaries in the remote Tibetan valley in 1924 till its annexation by the Chinese PLA forces starting in the early 1950s, and the subsequent rebellion by the Khampa warriors and escape of other Tibetans into exile. While delineating the consequences of these fateful encounters for the Tibetan people, the story paints a panorama of the Tibetan society spanning different generations and socio-political changes which it underwent as a result: from living by the Khampa warrior code and Tibetan Buddhism to negotiating with foreign ideologies, and finally being forced to choose between resistance, exile, and servile acceptance of Communism. The internal tensions in the Nyarong society, such as the setting up of the Christian Bethlehem Lutheran Mission (BLM) station in the valley, the resultant bloody feud between the Dragotsang and Rithangtsang clans, and Tashi Rithangtsang's return as a PLA officer to make the Nyarong valley a part of the Great Chinese Motherland, render the larger historical changes taking place in Tibet at once personal, poignant, and communitarian. Geographies of Tibetan, 'foreign,' and Chinese landscapes intertwined with thinkings of Buddhism, foreign ideologies, Communism, and Christianity become the nomadic space with which the Tibetan people have to contend.

The novel traces the journey of Pastor John Martin Stevens and his wife, Mary, from San Francisco to Nyarong Valley in the Kham Province of Eastern Tibet, and the tragic events that unfold thereafter. The reader is invited to deconstruct various stereotypes about Tibet along with the Stevens on their maiden journey to the Tibetan hinterland. The remote Nyarong valley, symbolic of Tibet's isolation, is described in myriad ways before the missionaries' arrival. From a "virgin territory" waiting to be conquered to the dangerous abode of savage and blood-thirsty "Khampa bandits," the idea of Nyarong takes on an enigmatic quality built up by foreign fantasies which transform along the journey.[1] Only when the Stevens finally reach Nyarong and start interacting with the accommodating chieftain Dragotsang's family does the mysterious, out-of-bounds valley take on human contours. The arrival of the Christian missionary couple marks the beginning of a series of life-changing events for the Nyarong people. With the final attack and takeover by the PLA forces, the revered high mountains that had protected the people of the valley for centuries are transformed into an open-air prison as the Tibetans pay the price for their isolation.

---

[1]. Tsewang Yishey Pemba, *White Crane, Lend Me Your Wings: A Tibetan Tale of Love and War* (New Delhi: Niyogi Books, 2017), 25-31.

The narrator reveals an inherently male voice to expose the dominance of male chauvinism in Tibetan society. Hence what stands out most appallingly is the stereotypical and cursory treatment meted out to the female characters. They are mainly described through the binary of promiscuous whore versus pure virgin throughout the narrative: "He [Paul] was glad that she was no Tseleg, willing to sleep with a dozen men for a wager and summoning more when the competitors were exhausted. Khadro was on a pedestal, a goddess of the valley; pure, virginal without blemish [...]." [2] While Tsomo is briefly portrayed as a courageous, warrior-like character when she leads the contingent of Nyarong women to join the Khampa men in their struggle against Communist occupation, she ultimately is shown as helpless and in need of Paul's protection in exile. Her desire to fight for Nyarong's freedom against the invading PLA forces in the former scene is disappointingly reduced to becoming pregnant with Paul's child before he goes to fight alongside the Khampa guerilla warriors towards the end. [3]

The narrator's role as the devil's advocate in numerous exchanges is reminiscent of Gilles Deleuze and Félix Guattari's concept of the nomad. He occupies an outside and an a-centered position of multiplicity.[4] In this book, he demonstrates that one can hold and stand up for their political beliefs, but at the same time be critical of their own side's flaws and appreciative of the other side's achievements. The narrative is not restricted to highlighting Tibetan political concerns and displays the moral courage to look beyond such limits. At times, however, the narrator's rhizomatic moves are confusing, yet they illuminate the various particularities of a situation. The reader may think he favors the practicality and effectiveness of Chinese Communists' ideology over the make-believe of Tibetan Buddhist religious practice. In other instances, he communicates a sense of championing the spiritual emphasis of Buddhist philosophy over the Communists' mundane concerns. In these endlessly changing voices and perspectives, the narrator manages to tease out the complexity of the ideological forces in conflict at the time and the brutal outcome of their clash.

The article argues that the novel weaves a self-critical subjectivity into the exchanges between the characters as well as the function of a nomadic narrator. Such subjectivity is informed by an awareness of the ambiguous

---

[2]. Ibid., 190.

[3]. Ibid., 464.

[4]. Gilles Deleuze and Félix Guattari, "Treaties on Nomadology: The War Machine" in *A Thousand Plateaus: Capitalism and Schizophrenia* (New York: Bloomsbury Academic, 2017), 351-423.

nature of self and identity, just as what Dibyesh Anand terms "diasporic subjectivity" is guided by an acknowledgment of the constructed and contested nature of culture.[5] The author's personal experiences in India and England additionally contribute to the nuance and perceptive capacity he displays in narrating a story about the changing world of Tibet after the arrival of the Christian missionaries and its takeover by the Chinese Communists. Not only does he avoid making it a story of good versus evil, or victims versus oppressors, as many similar narratives of dispossession are bound to turn out, but also employs irony and sarcasm to undercut any dominant accounts which risk the reductionism of a one-sided narrative. Pemba's novel uses this multilayered critical subjectivity as a reference point to delineate Tibetan history, culture, as well as the tragedy that forced thousands of Tibetans to flee their homeland in search of safety. In the historical novel, he attempts to undermine both the Chinese communist narrative about Tibet being an integral part of 'the Great Motherland, the new China,' as much as the Orientalist fantasies of the exotic Shangri-la with its 'spiritual' and 'content' people in the face of a looming foreign or West.[6] In his book, *Prisoners of Shangrila: Tibetan Buddhism and the West,* Donald S. Lopez Jr. opines on the political significance of working with this assemblage: "To recognize this play of opposites strengthens the case against the Chinese occupation and underscores the dangers of romanticizing Tibet and Tibetan Buddhism."[7] A mistrust of grand narratives underlies the novel, whether it is the Christian' savior' narrative, Communist China's claim of emancipating Tibetans, or Tibetan Buddhism's emphasis on spiritual enlightenment as the ultimate goal in life. Although the narrator is technically omniscient, he exhibits a self-reflexivity in his point of view. He is undoubtedly more sympathetic towards the Tibetan perspective than the Communist or Christian or any foreign one. At the same time, he demonstrates an understanding of the individual stories of the Communist and the Christian missionary sides as well.

In the face of rigid, territorializing ideologies and narrow nationalisms, which increasingly threaten to isolate and marginalize the vast majority of people who fall out of these straightjacket categories, a subjectivity which makes room for self-criticality and self-reflexivity can prove to be a useful antidote to keep isolation and marginalization in check. Exiled peoples have long dealt with the

---

5. Dibyesh Anand, "Diasporic Subjectivity as an Ethical Position," *South Asian Diaspora* 1, no.2 (2009): 103, doi: 10.1080/19438190903109412

6. Steven J. Venturino, "Where is Tibet in World Literature," *World Literature Today* 78, no. 1 (2004): 2-3.

7. Donald S. Lopez, Jr., *Prisoners of Shangrila: Tibetan Buddhism and the West* (Chicago: The University of Chicago Press, 1998), 10-11.

multiplicity of their fragmented identities and, as a result, realize that it is not easy to have a coherent and straightforward definition of the self. Anand exhorts us to explore this "as an ethical position."[8] It is crucial to look for alternatives to our obsolete and fixed notions of Self and the Other, which would counter not only dangerous, exclusionary forms of nationalism but also present new ways of relating to ourselves and those around us.

The experience of exile, and to some extent that of diaspora, is a process that marks an unsettling of one's ideas of a fixed self. It is accompanied by an epistemological shift in the understanding of the self, along with the transit of the body in space. One finds herself having arrived in an unfamiliar place, with the mind still clinging on to the one that has been left behind. Personal or collective memory, or "Postmemory," replaces the physical markers of one's identity in space and time. Marianne Hirsch uses this term to describe the memories passed down to second-generation exiles by their elders, as the cultural realm becomes the foundation of identity formation in a foreign space.[9] The faculty of memory exhibits volatility, uncertainty, and loss. Thus, the exiled self forever remains in the process of becoming, and never entirely 'becomes,' inhabiting what Edward Said terms "a median state,"[10] instead of one or the other identity. This process can be unsettling, devastating yet empowering. While one constantly feels torn between different time-spaces and a multiplicity of fluid identities, it provides one with the vantage point of looking at situations from the perspective of "a politics of identification (that sees identity as always already a political process) [...] and thus foregrounds agency." [11]

As one starts to continually feel a sense of being ill at ease vis-à-vis one's surroundings, this difference between a complex imagined self and the unknown foreign other reveals many layers of a diasporic identity so that one consciously becomes aware of the loose and random play of these layers. Anand defines this diasporic subjectivity as "an ethical, political positioning that can be occupied by anyone with a consciousness of the contested and constructed nature of the culture to which they are seen as belonging."[12] It consists of "an affective pull from different directions, all of which creates a

---

8. Anand, "Diasporic Subjectivity," 103.

9. Marianne Hirsch, "The Generation of Postmemory," *Poetics Today* 29, no.1 (2008): 103-128, doi: 10.1215/03335372-2007-019

10. Edward Said, "Intellectual Exile: Expatriates and Marginals," in *Representations of the Intellectual: The 1993 Reith Lectures* (New York: Vintage Books, 1996), 49.

11. Anand, 104.

12. Ibid., 110.

hyper-awareness and not a predominant sense of regret."[13] In a positive sense then, exile can be considered a constructive state of being conflicted about one's identity, which heightens one's consciousness regarding the self, and which can forge new pathways of thinking about and experiencing oneself in the world. According to Said, this is a productive, even pleasurable, exercise "if the exile is conscious of other contrapuntal juxtapositions that diminish orthodox judgment and elevate appreciative sympathy."[14]

Pemba's own experiences of exile lend to the breadth of his perception regarding the Tibetan issue and the notions of 'Tibetanness.'[15] Through the function of the omniscient narrator in the historical novel, he manages to highlight the unique traditions and customs of the Tibetans, while simultaneously resisting and challenging a unified and simplistic idea of Tibetan identity through numerous counter-examples and critique of violent practices. He criticizes Tibetans' fatalistic reliance on religion, which proved to be ineffective in protecting their land against foreign attacks. The narrator notes, in a slightly mocking tone, how the Tibetan guerrilla fighters relied as much on "tsetsung (life-protection) amulets" to protect themselves against enemy bullets, as they did on their modern and traditional weapons.[16]

Further, this article posits the argument that that self-critical subjectivity is not a lens one takes up only when analyzing culture or politics. It is a radically different way of relating to the idea of self and the multiple identities one inhabits. One avenue of looking at it is to consider Edward Said's description of the metaphysical notion of exile for an intellectual: "Exile for the intellectual in this metaphysical sense is restlessness, movement, constantly being unsettled, and unsettling others."[17] Conventionally, however, we tend to see our identities as fixed and rooted. As a result, we operate in the world and relate to others from this fundamental belief because it provides us with a sense of groundedness and stability in the world.

The metaphysical notion of exile, as Said defines it, posits a challenge since it exhorts us to forego the notion of stability altogether and suggests instead that we seek it in the fragmented sub-categories of our identities. Throughout Pemba's novel, the question regarding Tibetan and Nyarong Khampa identities

13. Ibid., 104.

14. Edward W. Said, "Reflections on Exile," in Reflections on Exile: And Other Literary And Cultural Essays (London: Granta Books, 2012), 138.

15. Shelly Bhoil, Introduction to *White Crane, Lend Me Your Wings: A Tibetan Tale of Love and War*, by Tsewang Yishey Pemba (New Delhi: Niyogi Books, 2017), 6.

16. Pemba, *White Crane*, 391.

17. Said, "Intellectual Exile: Expatriates and Marginals," 53.

with all their geophysical and sociopolitical memories remains a bone of contention. The narrative deliberately complicates conventional markers that determine identity. At one point, the revered Buddhist Lama Tharsel Rinpoche jokingly notes that the American Pastor John Martin Stevens espouses Tibetan Buddhist values of compassion and tolerance despite being a Christian missionary in the Nyarong valley: "[Y]ou are most tolerant. You remember how you used to be when you first came here? Now, you don't preach your religion, even to your own son!"[18]

The next question which follows is, how can one possibly move beyond the notion of a stable self? Self-critical subjectivity doesn't merely consist of different layers of the self, or a sort of structured hierarchy or centrality, wherein a wiser self critiques a less wise and more fundamentalist self. In this case, it is helpful to think with the concept of the rhizome, as proposed by Deleuze and Guattari, which advocates a-centered, non-hierarchical multiplicities over unity and hierarchy in a structure: "There is no unity to serve as a pivot in the object or to divide in the subject. [...] A multiplicity has neither subject, not object, only determinations, magnitudes, and dimensions that cannot increase in number without the multiplicity changing in nature."[19] Hence, such subjectivity would consist of criticality towards any one of the multiple identities becoming dominant over the rest. The dangers of singular identity or self taking over are apparent. It pushes one into oblivion towards other positions that contradict the chosen stance or challenge rigid socio-political affiliations. The tragedy that unfolds in the Nyarong valley when innocent people like Tsongpon are tortured to achieve rigid ideological aims by the communists betrays the disconnect between 'one-size-fits-all' kind of policies devised at the top of a hierarchical structure and their consequences at the ground level.[20]

On the other hand, openness towards the multiple positions and identities available at any given time engenders the possibility to operate from a holistic perspective, which takes numerous, at times contradictory, positions into consideration. In a similar vein, discussing Adorno's view of the meaning of exile for the intellectual, Said writes: "For him, life was its most false in the aggregate—the whole is always the untrue, he once said—and this, he continued, placed an even greater premium on subjectivity, on the individual's consciousness, on what could not be regimented in the totally administered

---

18. Pemba, 192-193.
19. Deleuze and Guattari, "Introduction: Rhizome," 7.
20. Pemba, 352.

society."[21] He further emphasizes that there is no real escape "since the state of in-betweenness can itself become a rigid ideological position."[22] Thus, even the hyphenated identity of an exile eventually moves towards becoming a kind of stable category in itself and forming a ground, if it is not supported by critical introspection. In "Reflections on Exile," Said underlines the unsettling force of a genuine, metaphysical state of exile: "It is nomadic, decentered, contrapuntal, but no sooner does one get accustomed to it than its unsettling force erupts anew."[23]

The narrative in Pemba's novel creates a space for contesting ideologies to interact through conversations between different characters. The narrator employs an ironic tone as a tool to critique both Tibetans' overreliance on religion to explain all phenomena as well as the brute force applied by PLA soldiers in pushing forward their Communist political agenda. The use of irony upends any attempt by the reader at favoring a singular perception of the situation. As stated earlier, he continues to play the role of devil's advocate, moving rhizomically from one perspective to another, and then beyond the ones presented by subtly pointing towards their limitations. His description of the killing of several Tibetan hermits by PLA soldiers while ridiculing them in front of a crowd of Tibetan devotees is not only marked by a critique of their renunciation of the world but also evokes sympathy for their unprovoked killing:

> They tottered out, blinking, shading their eyes from the painful glare of the outside world, not comprehending what was happening, and staring at the crowd of Tibetans and the lines of unfamiliar Chinese Communist soldiers carrying automatics and pickaxes. The universe wherein they traversed and sought to find a path was far far beyond that of Mao Tse-Tung, Makasu, and Lhining. It was inexplicable to them to be forcibly dragged back into and contaminated by the mundane world they had forsaken forever.[24]

Sarcasm and humor are also employed by the narrator to juxtapose the competing worldviews and perspectives, which have been forced into conflict with each other. Rilo, a Tibetan Khampa guerrilla, fighting for the freedom of Nyarong valley, sarcastically sings his favorite Chinese Communist song praising Mao Tse-tung while he prepares to launch an attack against PLA troops

---

[21]. Said, "Intellectual Exile: Expatriates and Marginals," 55.
[22]. Ibid., 58.
[23]. Said, "Reflections on Exile," 138.
[24]. Pemba, 385.

in the high mountains of Nyarong: "(From the East a sun rises/ This sun is our Mao Tse-tung!)"[25]

The characterization in the narrative not only lays out the perspectives of different socio-political groups involved, but also the multiplicity of perspectives within each of these groups. The character of Pastor John Martin Stevens testifies that not all missionaries in Tibet at the time wanted to extend their influence and control over the elusive "virgin territory"[26] of Shangri-la, in stark contrast to Pastor Murwell and Reverend Parkinson who desired precisely that. Similarly, even within the ranks of the Communists, the reader comes across benevolent characters such as Dr. Ling and Dr. Tsao, who genuinely wanted to serve the people in Tibet.[27] The reader also sees the role of those who wanted to suppress Tibetan traditions with brute force such as PLA commander Wang Tsao-wei who "detested all monks and monasteries, and had vowed to 'liquidate' the lot [...]."[28] Further, the narrative complicates our stereotypes of the Tibetan people as happy, mantra-chanting, prayer-wheel spinning folks by presenting a panorama of eastern Tibetan society at the time. It underscores that Nyarong-Tibetan society in the early 20th century consisted not only of genteel and wise folks such as the elder Dragotsang and the Tharsel Rinpoche, but also a violent and vindictive lot represented by the Rithangtsang clan and the Khenpo of Kunga Rinchen Monastery.

The arcs of character development in the cases of Pastor Stevens and Tashi Rithangtsang emphasize the importance of multiplicity of perspectives within individual characters as they undergo a figurative metamorphosis to adopt radically different beliefs and positions than those they espoused earlier in the narrative. After spending nearly two decades in the Nyarong valley, Pastor Stevens assimilates the Tibetan Buddhist values of tolerance and patience into his Christian beliefs, no longer trying desperately to proselytize the Tibetan' heathens'. In an interesting turn of events, he later becomes "absorbed in his studies of the Tibetan religion," and consults Tharsel Rinpoche on theological matters. On the other hand, Tashi Rithangtsang remains a manipulative and multilayered character throughout the novel. His outward courteous manner belies his darker intentions, both as a young Khampa at the beginning of the novel and as a PLA officer later. He claims to have renounced his vendetta against the Dragotsang clan for the assassination of his family. Yet, he engages in a witch-hunt against his former enemies in the name of Communism upon

---

[25]. Ibid., 407.
[26]. Ibid., 25.
[27]. Ibid., 328.
[28]. Ibid., 317.

his return to Nyarong as a PLA officer after several years.[29] As the PLA troops prepare to attack the Kunga Rinchen Monastery, he ostensibly laments to have been left with no option but to persecute the anti-revolutionaries and reactionaries in the Nyarong community, despite his benevolent intentions to avoid bloodshed.[30]

A critical question that arises is how can one still mobilize collective identities to protest against political injustices, most of all, in the case of exiles and refugees themselves if one is to adopt a self-critical subjectivity? Along with providing a nuanced analysis of the complexities and conflicts at the time, Pemba's narrator manages to get across the novel's nostalgic message of wanting to return to a place and time in Tibet which no longer exists. While not trying to hide his sympathies for the Tibetan cause, he is pushing beyond the limits of his subjective point of view. He can be supportive of the Tibetan cause as well as critical of their violent practices. The narrative presents a critique of the Communists' blind pursuit of their utopic vision of the *Great Chinese Motherland* by forcefully implementing their learned ideology, while in turn, sabotaging their values and principles to achieve their rigid aims. At the same time, the narrator commends their achievements in medicine and practical outlook towards life. Akin to the rhizome, his self-critical subjectivity is neither rooted nor limited; it is indeed a-centered and multiple.

His rhizomic subjectivity becomes apparent during the debate between Tang Yang-chen, the Chinese Communist political commissar of the PLA for the Dragotsang's valley, and Tharsel Rinpoche, the revered senior lama of the valley. Prior to the debate, he presents a critique of Tharsel Rinpoche's magnificent and luxurious residence from the communists' point of view. They scorn at such opulence and the many "silent shadows" or attendants of the senior monk who has purportedly chosen to follow the path of austerity. Along with Tang Yang-chen's comments mocking this contradictory arrangement of the holy lama's place, the narrator, too, employs irony to criticize the decadence and indulgence of senior lamas in Tibetan Buddhism. On the other hand, the Tharsel Rinpoche patiently responds to the criticism mounted by Tang and highlights that both of them share the goal of promoting equality amongst all in their different pursuits. While he questions the depth and practicality of Tang's ideological aim of *liberation* for all, the narrator shifts positions. He describes Tang's stupefaction as that of "a great musician or a composer, who suddenly hears a strange exotic, unique music when he had been quite convinced that he had heard every kind of sound in this universe."[31] This

---

[29]. Ibid., 355-356.
[30]. Ibid., 371.
[31]. Ibid., 337.

description does not belittle Tang's position or uphold the supremacy of Tibetan Buddhist tradition. Still, it does demarcate the limits of his Communist ideology in realistically fulfilling the lofty aims that it delineates. The narrator manages to underline the greater depth and expanse of Tibetan Buddhist philosophy, while at the same time presenting the debate fairly from both positions.

Said's response to the question of protesting against socio-political injustices while espousing a self-critical subjectivity is "to see things not simply as they are, but as they have come to be that way. Look at situations as contingent, not as inevitable, look at them as the result of a series of historical choices made by men and women, as facts of society made by human beings, and not as natural and thereby unchangeable, permanent, irreversible."[32] An important question that Pemba's novel raises is whether the outcome of the conflict in Tibet could have been any different. Unlike many Tibetans, he avoids ascribing it to collective las or karma (fate) and resigning to it. One may simply say that he sees it as an event potential, in the Deleuzean sense. Thus while he is critical of blaming the tragic series of events to fate based on blind faith, he nonetheless stresses another Tibetan Buddhist doctrine, which states that causality of all phenomena points towards a mechanism. Phenomena that might seem as inexplicable as fate at the time have particular human ideologies and decisions behind them. The narrator in Pemba's novel performs a difficult act of negating as he tries to portray the tragedy suffered by Tibetans while presenting a fair and non-hierarchical picture of all other ideological and political positions involved.

At the same time, he provides a rare instance of solidarity amongst the people belonging to different socio-political groups finding a moment of comfort while playing Mahjong and "as their own familiar worlds disintegrated before their eyes."[33] Thus, the model of self-critical subjectivity that forms the reference point of the novel does not undermine the possibilities of finding strength in solidarity even while being critical of hegemonic narratives at all levels. My emphasis in this paper has been that identity itself isn't inherently exclusionary if one takes its multilayered complexities into account. Herein lies the importance of rhizomatic thinking that helps explore the event-potentials of an encounter with any monolithic expression and assertion of one identity that threatens to obliterate and silence all others. An obligatory, monolithic identity can become dangerous, with extreme nationalism becoming fascism. If we could look for ways of expression of our subjectivity which do not have to take the form of a binary of a 'us' versus 'them,' as reflected in Pemba's narrative,

---

[32]. Said, "Intellectual Exile: Expatriates and Marginals," 60-61.
[33]. Pemba, 230.

we could indeed create opportunities for solidarity and ease within ourselves and in society without reinforcing hierarchies.

Bibliography

Anand, Dibyesh. "Diasporic Subjectivity as an Ethical Position." *South Asian Diaspora* 1, no.2 (2009): 103-111. doi: 10.1080/19438190903109412

Bhoil, Shelly. "Introduction." In *White Crane, Lend Me Your Wings: A Tibetan Tale of Love and War,* by Tsewang Yishey Pemba, 5-10. New Delhi: Niyogi Books, 2017.

Deleuze, Gilles, and Félix Guattari. "Introduction: Rhizome." In *A Thousand Plateaus: Capitalism and Schizophrenia,* 1-27. New York: Bloomsbury Academic, 2017.

Deleuze, Gilles, and Félix Guattari. "Treaties on Nomadology: The War Machine." In *A Thousand Plateaus: Capitalism and Schizophrenia,* 351-423. New York: Bloomsbury Academic, 2017.

Hirsch, Marianne. "The Generation of Postmemory." *Poetics Today* 29, no. 1 (2008): 103-128. doi: 10.1215/03335372-2007-019

Lopez, Donald S., Jr. *Prisoners of Shangrila: Tibetan Buddhism and the West.* Chicago: The University of Chicago Press, 1998.

Pemba, Tsewang Yishey. *White Crane, Lend Me Your Wings: A Tibetan Tale of Love and War.* New Delhi: Niyogi Books, 2017.

Said, Edward. "Intellectual Exile: Expatriates and Marginals." In *Representations of the Intellectual: The 1993 Reith Lectures,* 46-64. New York: Vintage Books, 1996.

Said, Edward. "Reflections on Exile." In *Reflections on Exile: And Other Literary and Cultural Essays,* 130-138. London: Granta Books, 2012.

Venturino, Steven J. "Where is Tibet in World Literature." *World Literature Today* 78, no. 1 (2004): 51-56.

Chapter 11

Killing time: Boredom and violence in Natalia Almada's cinema[1]

Debra A. Castillo

Cornell University

Abstract

A signature element of slow cinema may be time-stretched through uneventful and trivial longshots—beautiful shots, excruciatingly long takes of nothing much happening during long train or boat trips, or people doing repetitive tasks like knitting or peeling potatoes. The article contends with the view that slow cinema allows the contemplation of beautiful shots to enable viewers to indulge in some quiet aesthetic pleasure. It argues, instead, that the slow cinema of Natalia Almada purposefully takes us back to the violence of a killing time for boredom. It deals with two texts of the Mexican-American filmmaker: a documentary *El velador* (2011) and a feature film *Todo lo demás* (2017). Agreeing with the critical position that Almada's characters slowly embody, then equally slowly empty out stereotypes: about men in dead-end jobs, about cat ladies and bureaucrats, about women in general, the paper argues that this slow accumulation of meaning around characters is what differentiates Almada's work from other works in the slow cinema genre, where we would find any minor deviation from impenetrable placidity terribly shocking.

Keywords: Mexican-American, feminist cinema, slow cinema, stuplimicity, affect

***

"It's so boring!" complained one of the spectators at the screening. "Why did she make the film so boring? Is she trying to kill us with boredom?" I had been invited by the organizers of the Spring 2018 Fingerlakes Environmental Film Festival to facilitate a discussion on Natalia Almada's recent feature film, Todo lo demás. The complaint was received with some nodding heads among other

---

[1]. This short study was conceived as a talk and was presented at the Mexican Literature and Film across Borders conference in Boston, Massachusetts, USA, October 2018.

audience members, and quite a few rebuttals, sparking a lively conversation among the people who stayed for the conversation after the screening. But I don't think we answered the question.

This response to the film, however, is not in the least anomalous: variations on the word aburrimiento came up six times in Jaime Fa de Lucas' review of the film.[2] Some other reviewers reposition the same effect by describing Almada's work in the context of the slow cinema movement, which (if you are not familiar with the genre) is generally characterized by beautiful shots, excruciatingly long takes of nothing much happening during long train or boat trips, or people doing repetitive tasks like knitting or peeling potatoes. The Norwegians are particularly into it: they even have a channel, Sakte-TV, the Norwegian term for Slow TV. One of their shows, *Reinflytting*, is a week-long, real-time, live broadcast which takes us on a journey with reindeer from their winter to their summer pastures.

The idea is that lengthy duration leads to a contemplative experience for the audience and provides a salutary break from the hectic pace of contemporary life. Slow cinema has its fans, and even (if we can use such a word in this context), its enthusiasts—witness, for example, the contemplative beauties of a website on the art(s) of slow cinema, with its engaging discussions of films you really don't want to watch, even if there are no more Marvel comics films on Netflix that you haven't seen six times.[3] That site, by the way, is the brainchild of Nadin Mai, a student-turned-distributor for Slow Cinema. Years ago, she started a blog titled *The Art of Slow Cinema*, which was initially used for her doctoral thesis on Philippine filmmaker Lav Diaz.

Carolyn Fornoff, in her analysis of the film, makes a case for Almada's *Todo lo demás* as slow cinema, asking us, is it boring?[4] And responding: that yes, it is, and that's not a bad thing: "perhaps in an age dominated by multitasking and productivity, being forced to slow down is precisely the point."[5] A night watchman in a cemetery in Culiacán, Sinaloa, slowly watering a dirt road over a continuous five minute take, an aging cat lady in a dead-end bureaucratic job working for the Instituto Mexicano Electoral; these are the focal characters in Natalia Almada's most recent films: the documentary *El velador* (2011) and her

2. Jaime Fa de Lucas, "Todo lo demás (2016) de Natalia Almada," May 11, 2017, https://www.culturamas.es/2017/05/11/todo-lo-demas-2016-de-natalia-almada/.
3. Nadin Mai, *The Art(s) of Slow Cinema*, https://theartsofslowcinema.com/.
4. Carolyn Fornoff, "The Case for Slow Cinema: Natalia Almada's *Todo lo demás*," *Mediatico*, November 7, 2016, https://reframe.sussex.ac.uk/mediatico/2016/11/07/the-case-for-slow-cinema-natalia-almadas-todo-lo-demas/
5. Ibid.

first feature-length fiction film, *Todo lo demás* (2017). Almada's takes are long (not as long as slow cinema's Norwegian masterpieces, but still), the actions repetitive. Each of these films centers on the tedium and predictability of everyday tasks, repeated mechanically, leading to minor exhaustion (an exhaustion shared by the viewer, as when the student asked, "is she trying to kill us with boredom?").

I would like to argue that Almada's leisurely exploration of these real and fictional lives have a different rhythm than watching a Norwegian woman knit—in this, I agree with Fornoff that Almada's characters slowly embody, then equally slowly empty out stereotypes: about men in dead-end jobs, about cat ladies and bureaucrats, about women in general. This slow accumulation of meaning around characters is for me precisely what differentiates Almada's work from the Norwegian knitter, or the migrating reindeer for that matter, where we would find any minor deviation from impenetrable placidity terribly shocking. This unfolding of character is one of the qualities that distinguish Almada's cinematic work.

I also want to argue that my student's perception—dying of boredom—is a stronger and more accurate response to Almada's work than the aesthetic / philosophical affect associated with contemplation that is the typical imagined goal of slow cinema. In both of the recent films I've alluded to, Almada specifically addresses the violence in contemporary Mexico by pushing the tedium of the ordinary to the foreground, where inescapability does not lead to transcendence for her focal characters and for us, the viewing public, but rather to something akin to what Sianne Ngai calls "stuplimity," an affect holding in tension the astonishing and the boring.[6] For Ngai, it is the tension between two incompatible aesthetic responses: the sublime and the stupid (or banal) that characterizes this affect, and that makes it particularly modern. I love this quote from Ngai since practically every word begs for closer attention:

> The becoming ordinary of the experience of feeling overwhelmed gets condensed in the paradoxical structure of feeling I call stuplimity, in which we find the classically sublime feeling of awe almost comically coupled to the feeling of boredom or exhaustion. Stuplimity thus offers an exaggerated version of the affective incongruity at the heart of capitalist sublimity, while at the same time gesturing at its normalization or banalization. It is somehow an intensification and domestication of it at once.[7]

---

6. Sianne Ngai, *Ugly Feelings* (Boston: Harvard University Press), 2007.
7. Sianne Ngai, Interiview, *Politicsslashletters*, February 27, 2017, http://quarterly.politics slashletters.org/critiques-persistence/

In Almada's work, this tension also encodes a kind of creeping, insidious violence. (Isn't potential for violence inherent in all tension?) Killing time is almost unbearable. It is the opposite of contemplation. And it is a phenomenon of modernity, since in earlier times only the very rich had the means to afford a claim to either the sublime, or to boredom, or indeed, to feel they had the right to complain about the violence exercised against them by the insufficiently overwhelming chunks of life.

But before I go any further, who is Natalia Almada? Born in Mexico City she is, by her own terms, the 100% Mexican, 100% American daughter of a Mexican father and a US mother. On her father's side, she is the great-granddaughter of Plutarco Elias Calles (the subject of one of her films). In total, to date, she has filmed four feature-length films since her short 2001 MA thesis film, "All water has a perfect memory" (focusing on the family trauma resulting from the drowning death of her sister). These films are: *Al otro lado* (The Other Side, a 2005 documentary about a fishing village in the narco corridor), *El general* (The General, a 2009 film about Calles, grounded in audio recordings of her grandmother speaking about her infamous father), *El velador* (The Night Watchman, a 2011 documentary about a drug lord mausoleum), and *Todo lo demás* (Everthing Else, from 2017, an intellectually freighted fiction film about a cog in the machine of Mexican bureaucracy).

A graduate of the Rhode Island School of Design, where she focused on photography, Almada is known for her impeccable eye. She is a true auteur cinematographer: producing, directing, writing, editing all her films, which have been described as minimalist, lyrical, intimate. She lingers on her images and is not afraid of silence; she says in an interview that she learned very young to rely more on images than words; images are concrete, and as a bilingual, bicultural person, she always found language to be unreliable and incomplete. She is also quite aware of her privilege as a dual citizen of two nations—her films connect her to her Mexican heritage, and her US citizenship allows her to be an independent filmmaker through her eligibility for grants. It was her MacArthur genius award, for example, that allowed her to finance Todo lo demás.

If we look at Almada following Ngai, we might want to note that she works in a particular register in Velador and Todo lo demás, one that focuses on the tedium of the ordinary pushed to the filmic extreme by a duration that is just a bit too long, and without any transcendence (though the markers that might hopefully point in that direction are waved in front of us like temptations: the violence outside the cemetery referenced on news the velador listens to at night, something also referenced in the nightly news Doña Flor does not listen to at home; or the all-too apparent symbolism of the swimming pool for Doña

Flor). What we get instead of transcendence is a bone-deep fatigue that no competing affect can neutralize. We could say we are stupefied, a word that has the double meaning of astonishing or shocking, and having the capacity to make someone unable to think or feel properly. The offscreen violence is overwhelming and banal; it creeps into the domestic space, where it is ignored.

Both these main characters inhabit the affective ruins of the goal economy that declares their work is not very interesting, a tedium reflected in the slowed downtime of the lingering camera, reminding us how they are stuck in place, hostage to predictable, inescapable, confining jobs. We are educated to their plight by duration, by repetition. And just like the velador, who waters the road every day, so too the young narco widows come to wash the floors and replace the flowers of their husbands' mausoleums as their children play outside, so too Flor crosses paths with the janitor, who cleans up after the clerks like her in a darkening office.

Unlike rich people's existential boredom, reflected in other high toned art cinema, this is the form of filmmaking that points to a deep and deafened violence encoded in the stigmatized situation of people marked and indelibly defined by gender and by class, doing tasks that many of us might see as valueless, visible only when impatient clients find them downright obstructionist. Everyday life in late capitalism is given a very different orientation, as we are told, through the mechanisms of a feature-length film and gorgeous photography, that we should be enjoying a rich filmic experience. At the same time, the working-class characters, the long takes, the impoverished dialogue, and almost complete refusal of extra-diegetic sound tell us something quite different. Eventually, we viewers too are overwhelmed by banality and by the trailing fragments of what might once have been sublime metaphors. Interesting, we p.c. academics say, when we mean the opposite because the structure of the film disallows it. The stories of invisible working-class men and women should be told, we say to each other. They are important and interesting. Besides, Almada has told us so.

In this article, I will focus on her most recent, and only fiction film, a project she started from a concept, without a script, working in close collaboration with Adriana Barraza, the veteran actor who plays Flor in the film. She says, about Todo lo demás:

> [...] esta es la pelicula de una mujer que tiene 60 años, no es esposa, ni mamá de nadie, no tiene sexo, no es violada, no tiene esos papeles de los que 'tiene que ser una mujer' si va a salir en pantalla, es muy dificil, si pensamos que venimos de una cultura que valora la vision de cine hecho por hombres, decir que estas historias tambien cuentan y son interesantes.

[…] this is a movie about a woman who is 60 years old, is not a wife, nor the mother of anyone. She doesn't have sex, isn't raped, does not play the roles of those who "must be a woman" if she is going to appear on screen. It's very difficult if we think that, if we come from a culture that valorizes the vision of cinema made by men, to say that these stories also count and are interesting.[8]

It's an overtly feminist project, the kind of story we ironically call "fascinating" when we mean the opposite; when we yawn and say the film was stunning, sublime.

Nothing much happens in this film, which straddles an increasingly familiar line in independent cinema between documentary and fiction (I have my suspicions about this increasingly banal celebration of the use of non-actors in independent cinema, which also aligns with a kind of stuplime analysis: our mainstream actors work so hard with diet, exercise, and plastic surgery to fit our ideal mold that they become clone-like, no longer interesting on-screen). Almada describes this as a minimalist film, an observational narrative characterized by long silences; *una apuesta femenista*. Naief Yehya says that the film "ofrece una vision spectral de la vida femenina en México, rodeada de amenazas y violencia, condenada a la dictadura misogina y la discriminacion de la edad" ("offers a spectral vision of feminine life in Mexico, surrounded by threats of violence, condemned to misogynist dictatorship and age discrimination").[9]

Doña Flor gets up in the morning and dresses in one of her almost identical beige outfits. She takes the subway to work, where she quietly makes life miserable for the sequence of people trying to get their voter IDs. She feeds her cat, washes her dishes. After her meager dinner, she writes down the names of all the people she saw that day in a ledger, with a red dot next to a few of them. She goes to bed and stares at the ceiling. We know her cat is Manuelito, but don't even know her name until halfway through the film. One day her cat dies. Another day in the pool, a woman washes her back.

Let's look a bit more closely at a few stills from the film. The first set of three images shows Flor's daily routine, which consists of a scarcely varying repetition of work/subway/bed:

---

8. Eduardo Gutiérrez Segura, "Adriana Barraza agradece trabajar con no actores," *Milenio*, January 18, 2018, https://www.pressreader.com/mexico/milenio/20180118/282209421268452.

9. Naief Yehya, "Todo lo demás de Natalia Almada," *Suplemento semanal de La Jornada* October 30, 2016, https://issuu.com/lajornadaonline/docs/semanal30102016.

Figure 11.1: Boredom at Work

Source: Press release of Altamura films

Figure 11.2: Boredom at the subway station

Source: Press release of Altamura films

Figure 11.3: Boredom in bed

Source: Press release of Altamura films

Almada notes that when they filmed in the Mexico City subway, no one turned a head, no one noticed a film star was in their midst, Adriana Barraza was so in character (or, alternatively, a 60+ woman generally has the superpower of invisibility). Flor bears a neutral face and glazed look wherever she goes, a victim of dehumanization that we would like to fill with hidden emotion but can't be sure there is any emotion anywhere. When asked to describe the character of Flor and how she was able to connect with it, Barraza says, "she is my aunt, she is the woman I have read about and the woman I pass by [...] the woman who looks lost who I've seen on the subway [...] but seems invisible, she's the person that then becomes invisible."[10] She is off-putting. We want to hug her. We want to ignore her.

The second set of images points to Doña Flor's unrealized dream of floating, the film's main hint of introspection, and its only open show of emotion, in the swimming pool and the shower:

Figure 11.4: Introspection in the pool

Source: Press release of Altamura films

Figure 11.5: Introspection in the shower

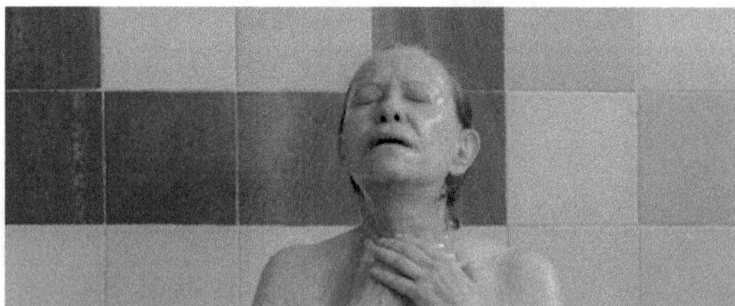

Source: Press release of Altamura films

---

10. Adriana Barraza, "Interview," *altamurafilms*, n.d., http://www.altamurafilms.com/TLD/TodoLoDemas_PressKit_20160929.pdf.

The swimming pool, then, gives us a hint of her interior life. A side note: the pool in this film is one Almada swam in every day in Mexico City, a pool frequented by retired civil servants, some of whom appear in the film. Clearly, the visits to the pool—where Flor haunts the dressing room and stands at the edge of the pool without ever jumping in—are crucial counterpoints to the beige banality of the rest of her life. "The pool becomes the site of Doña Flor's open wound," says the long uncredited synopsis of the film on the Altamura website.[11] Curiously, in contrast, on the same website, Almada says: "I began to see the pool as a symbol of defiance against the institutionalized erasure of the individual."[12] Barraza also describes the character she develops with underwater metaphors, as "soft and still as the surface of a lake...with terrible inner currents."

Many of the reviewers of the film cite the biographical source of this repeated image of Flor at the swimming pool; an image also echoed in the beige painting of water in Flor's bedroom. Doña Flor takes down the painting after her cat dies, though her life otherwise follows its routine. They cite Almada's evocation of her own mother's fear of water after the drowning death of Almada's sister, a topic she addresses in her first film, *All Water has a Perfect Memory*.[13] From my perspective, this unnecessary and reductionist biographical connection is reinforced in some descriptions of the film, including this one on IMDb, which I cite for its perfect stuplimity: "One morning she awakens to find her cat has died. Refusing to accept the loss of her sole companion, Doña Flor tries to continue life as usual, but the loss triggers memories of the drowning of her own child. Doña Flor returns to the water to save herself from drowning in sorrow."[14]

The review of the film in Variety also includes the beige painting of water in Doña Flor's bedroom, with a laudatory remark, "Natalia Almada le apuesta a una perspectiva femenina."[15] The original Variety review cited here is decidedly more mixed than the quote might suggest: "Though the concept of the gendered gaze can be over-pushed in film theory circles, in this case, there's no mistaking Almada's privileging of a woman's perspective."[16] Jay Weissberg, the reviewer, continues: "Festivals are already lining up, though the film's austerity largely

---

[11]. *Todo le demás (Everything Else), altamuraFILMS*, http://www.altamurafilms.com/todolodemas.html.
[12]. Ibid.
[13]. All Water has Perfect Memory, directed by Natalia Almada, Women Make Movies, 2001.
[14]. *Todo lo demás*.
[15]. Jay Weissberg. "Everthing Else," *Variety*, October 16, 2016, https://variety.com/2016/film/reviews/everything-else-review-todo-lo-demas-1201890274/.
[16]. Ibid.

precludes wider play [...] The film also feels overly indebted to theory [...] The camera is as trapped in this intellectual severity as Flor herself."[17]

Like Weissberg, numerous other reviewers have complained that this film is overintellectualized. "How do we make films about violence?" Almada asks. "This is a question at the root of all the films that I have made and one that I have grappled with not only formally, but morally and ethically."[18] In practically every interview she has given, as well as in the press packet for the film, Almada cites major feminist precursors like Susan Sontag, Hannah Arendt, and Simone de Beauvoir as guiding presences in the film, helping her to think about how to understand the slow violence of bureaucracy, how to think about and understand violence in general in a country so wounded and marked by violent death, how to responsibly evoke violence in a filmic context. In Almada's films, the choice has always been to make films about violence without overt violence, to turn away from the sublime and focus her lens on the secondary consequences of violence made banal, stupefying, stuplime.

Bibliography

Almada, Natalia, director. "All Water has Perfect Memory." Women Make Movies, 2001.

Almada, Natalia, director. *El velador*. Icarus Films, 2011.

Almada, Natalia, director. *Todo lo demás*. Altamura Films, 2018. http://www.alta murafilms.com/todolodemas.html

Barraza, Adriana. "Interview," *altamurafilms*, n.d., http://www.altamurafilms.com /TLD/TodoLoDemas_PressKit_20160929.pdf

Fa de Lucas, Jaime. "Review: 'Todo lo demás'." *Culturamas*, May 11, 2017. https://www.culturamas.es/blog/tag/todo-lo-demas/.

Fornoff, Carolyn. "The Case for Slow Cinema: Natalia Almada's Todo lo demás." *Mediático*, November 7, 2016. https://reframe.sussex.ac.uk/mediatico/2016/ 11/07/the-case-for-slow-cinema-natalia-almadas-todo-lo-demas/.

Gutiérrez Segura, Eduardo. "Adriana Barraza agradece trabajar con no actores." *Milenio*, January 18, 2018. https://www.pressreader.com/mexico/milenio/20 180118/282209421268452.

Hwang Carlos, Miriam. "'El Velador': Interiew." *DeCentered*, March 14, 2016. https://blogs.haverford.edu/decentered/2016/03/14/el-velador-interview-with-natalia-almada/.

Mai, Nadin. Art(s) of Slow Cinema. https://theartsofslowcinema.com/.

Ngai, Sianne. *Ugly Feelings*. Boston: Harvard University Press, 2007.

Weissberg, Jay. "Film review: 'Everything Else'." Variety. October 16, 2016. https://variety.com/2016/film/reviews/everything-else-review-todo-lo-demas-1201890274/

---

17. Ibid.

18. Miriam Hwang Carlos, "El Velador," *DeCentered*, March 14, 2016, https://blogs.haver ford.edu/decentered/2016/03/14/el-velador-interview-with-natalia-almada/

Chapter 12

Always explorers, never refugees: Adventure and manifest destiny amongst the stars

Leigh E. McKagen

Virginia Tech; Virginia Military Institute

Abstract

This article explores the adventure narrative of *Star Trek: Voyager* (1995-2001) alongside historical practices of the Euro-American empire to argue that the adventure narrative of *Voyager* enables the continuation of Federation/Starfleet imperial directives and practices throughout the Delta Quadrant. I begin this analysis by exploring how *Voyager* functions as an adventure narrative in ways that normalizes and legitimizes Euro-American imperial ideologies. In particular, I highlight the threads of manifest destiny retained in the *Voyager* narrative, following the American imperial ideology that enabled expansion throughout the continent in the nineteenth century. Manifest destiny—a belief in the 'Providence granted' right to explore and expand—functions in *Voyager* to create and maintain a binary between the Federation explorer/castaway/adventurers and 'everyone else' in the Delta Quadrant. This binary presumes the superiority of Western civilizations, including the belief that Westerners will never be refugees. These practices of storytelling matter, since through this presentation of the crew as always travelers and never migrants or refugees, *Voyager* ultimately projects American post-Cold War Empire and imperial politics and culture into the far reaches of outer space as a possible future.

Keywords: Adventure narratives, manifest destiny, *Star Trek: Voyager*, imperial binaries, mapping

***

A press release announcing the series premiere *of Star Trek: Voyager* (1995-2001) declared that the series "stands as another probing, intelligent and influential component of one of the most popular and successful entertainment franchises in history."[1] The Trek franchise has garnered considerable attention from audiences and scholars in its fifty-plus years on television and the big screen. It is often praised for highlighting a "progressive, liberal vision" of the future.[2] *Voyager* takes the Star Trek universe to the other end of the galaxy in a story that models the directives of adventure and exploration that have been popular Western storytelling tropes for centuries—and served a significant role in normalizing Euro-American imperial expansion for Western audiences. In this paper, I argue that the adventure-castaway traditions present in *Voyager* are modeled on Euro-American adventure narratives steeped in ideologies of empire. These narratives forms perpetuate imperial modes of thinking about exploration and discovery and, in *Voyager*, enable the continuation of American imperial ideologies throughout the Delta Quadrant. Specifically, I examine the adventure narrative of *Voyager*, framed through principles of 'manifest destiny,' to demonstrate the imperial binary retained throughout the series that presumes the superiority of Western civilizations, including the belief that Westerners will never be refugees.[3]

Voyager's focus on exploration and discovery as a means of getting home and laying claim to new territory reflects American imperial practices of 'manifest destiny.' Deployed initially by John O'Sullivan, the term encompasses the belief in a "Providence granted" right of expansion across the North American continent.[4] O'Sullivan's use of the term, and the Democratic Review, in its entirety, of which he was an editor from its inception in 1937 to 1946, created "a national narrative in which America serves as the divinely destined exemplar of human rights, individualism, material, and spiritual progress, and democracy"—principles that elide the overt white supremacy and expansionist rhetoric underwriting those lofty ideals.[5] For O'Sullivan and many Americans of the nineteenth century, manifest destiny was a positive ideology unique to

---

[1]. United Paramount Network Press Release, "*Star Trek: Voyager* Continues the Eminence and Prestige of the *Star Trek* Legacy," 1995.

[2]. Mark Altman and Edward Gross, *The Fifty-Year Mission: Volume One: The Complete, Uncensored, Unauthorized Oral History of Star Trek: The First 25 Years* (NY: St. Martin's, 2016), 5.

[3]. An early version of this chapter was published on the Imperial and Global Forum as part of a roundtable on science fiction and imperial history co-edited by Marc-William Palen and Rachel Hermann. See E. Leigh McKagen, "'To Boldly Go!': Adventure and Empire in Star Trek," *Imperial & Global Forum* (blog), June 14, 2018, https://imperialglobalexeter.com/2018/06/14/to-boldly-go-adventure-and-empire-in-star-trek/.

[4]. John O'Sullivan, "Annexation," *The United States Magazine and Democratic Review* 17 (1845): 5—10, 5.

[5]. Robert J. Scholnick, "Extermination and Democracy: O'Sullivan, the Democratic Review, and Empire, 1837—1840," *American Periodicals* 15, no. 2 (2005): 123—41, 124.

"the nation of many nations [...] destined to manifest to mankind the excellence of divine principles [...]."[6] In actuality, manifest destiny was central to the continued and expanded American settler-colonial project and ongoing imperial violence and oppression.[7] *Voyager* models this ideology through practices that establish hierarchies of difference and superiority between the Federation and new races encountered in the Delta Quadrant. Imperial perspectives continue to normalize and legitimize ongoing practices of the American empire in cultural expectations, which position the Federation (American) travelers as explorers seeking knowledge, rather than refugees seeking sanctuary. In prioritizing the search for knowledge rather than sanctuary, *Voyager* positions Western scientific exploration as superior to seeking aid from others and writes that superior position into possible futures.

The *Voyager's* premiere episode "Caretaker" recounts the events that strand the crew of the USS *Voyager* in the Delta Quadrant of space, over 70,000 light-years—75 years of travel at the fastest warp speeds—from Earth in the Alpha Quadrant.[8] Under the command of Captain Kathryn Janeway, played by Kate Mulgrew, the crew of the *Voyager* spends seven years searching for a quicker way home while traveling and mapping the *unexplored* region of space. This series follows the directives for adventure and exploration laid out in *Star Trek: The Original Series* (1996-1969) and *The Next Generation* (1987-1994) to "explore strange new worlds, to seek out new life and new civilizations, to boldly go where no one has gone before."[9] Janeway emphasizes this directive at the end of "Caretaker," and it underwrites the entire series. In a morale-building speech in the closing scene, Janeway explains to her stranded crew that they will "continue to follow our directive to seek out new worlds and explore space" while they also search for shortcuts back to the Alpha Quadrant.[10] "Our directives" refers to the practices and principles of the United Federation of Planets (UFP), an intergalactic union of peaceful explorers founded by humans in the twenty-second century. The *Voyager* crew are

---

6. John O'Sullivan, "The Great Nation of Futurity," *The United States Democratic Review* 6 (1839): 426—30, 427.

7. See Anders Stephanson, *Manifest Destiny: American Expansion and the Empire of Right* (NY: Hill and Wang, 1996).

8. "Caretaker," directed by Winrich Kolbe, *Star Trek: Voyager* (Paramount Television, January 16, 1995).

9. These words are part of the opening monologue of both *Star Trek: The Original Series* and *The Next Generation*, originally written by Gene Roddenberry in 1966. Herbert F. Solow and Robert H. Justman, *Inside Star Trek: The Real Story* (New York: Pocket Books, 1996), 149.

10. "Caretaker" 1995.

members of Starfleet, the explorative and scientific branch of the UFP, and they take pride in remaining stalwart Federation officers in their unintended exile. Janeway and her crew never consider seeking sanctuary in the Delta Quadrant, and the pilot episode concludes with Janeway's directive to her Helmsman, Tom Paris, to "set a course for home."[11] Audiences watch as the ship—alone in otherwise seemingly empty space—goes into 'warp' (faster-than-light travel) and begins the long journey.

Voyager follows traditions of adventure narratives established in Britain during the eighteenth and nineteenth centuries. In these stories, the main character(s) face challenges in a distant location and must find ways to survive and make their way home. Such narratives have a long and complex literary and cultural history, closely tied to the expansion of the European empire in the classic "Age of Imperialism" and American imperial expansion during the era of manifest destiny to conquer the West. Martin Green traces the broad adventure narrative style back to Daniel Defoe's classic Robinson Crusoe (1719) as one text among many that established adventure as "the energizing myth of empire."[12] Green argues that the mercantilist/capitalist adventure narrative structure of stories like Robinson Crusoe strengthened the expansion of the British and United States empires through disguising the 'civilizing mission' of conquest as stories of adventure and discovery. Building on narratives that permeated British and American imperialism, especially in India and North America, respectively, eighteenth and nineteenth-century novels popularized and reinforced the sense of discovery and manifest destiny utilized by European explorers as a vital component to imperial expansion in the traditional "Age of Imperialism."[13]

Beyond making ideas of empire and imperial expansion popular, stories—adventure and otherwise—normalize and legitimize imperial practices and ideologies. Edward Said observed that cultural texts like novels, operas, and films "do not cause people to go out and imperialize"—instead, these texts normalize empire and imperialistic ways of life.[14] Said explains that, for a text like Jane Austen's non-overtly imperial *Mansfield Park* (1814), "the novel steadily, if unobtrusively, opens up a broad expanse of domestic imperialist

---

11. Ibid.

12. Martin Green, *Dreams of Adventure, Deeds of Empire* (New York: Basic Books, Inc., 1980), xi.

13. Beyond Defoe's classic *Robinson Crusoe*, examples of these texts include Mark Twain's *The Adventures of Huckleberry Finn*, Sir Walter Scott's *Waverley*, Rudyard Kipling's *Kim*, Jonathan Swift's *Gulliver's Travels*, and H.G. Wells *The Island of Doctor Moreau*.

14. Edward Said, *Culture and Imperialism* (NY: Vintage Books, 1994), 12.

culture without which Britain's subsequent acquisition of territory would not have been possible."[15] *Voyager* functions similarly to normalize imperial ways of life, including the presumed superiority of Western principles of Enlightenment, progress, and modernity. Adventure and exploration serve as a central component of these Western principles—a narrative style embraced wholeheartedly in *Voyager*. Rebecca Weaver-Hightower argues that castaway narratives—a subset of adventure narratives—"made imperial expansion and control seem unproblematic and natural."[16] Through the castaway's attempts to lay claim to the island and space—to live, explore, and create in the space—the texts become narratives of possession, and Weaver-Hightower argues that "the castaway (and reading public) could begin to imagine colonization as legitimate."[17] The historical project of imperial legitimization has taken a variety of forms, including militaristic conquest and legal policies.

Moreover, the addition of cultural legitimization through storytelling furthers Said's claims that while imperial storytelling normalizes empire, such stories also legitimize empire and imperial ways of thinking about the world through tropes familiar in castaway-adventure stories. Such tropes include the emphasis on adventure and discovery, especially the mapping of newly 'discovered' areas, and encounters with 'new' worlds and civilizations that position the castaway-explorer as the figure of prime importance and the seeker—and concurrent purveyor—of knowledge. As Stefan Rabitsch argues, the paradox of adventurers seeking knowledge while simultaneously possessing knowledge far superior to the people (aliens) they encounter was popularized and practiced by British maritime explorers, including notable figures like Captain James Cook.[18] Through a unique blend of exploration of the "final frontier" with a "maritime adventure in space," *Star Trek*—and *Voyager* especially—unobtrusively normalizes and legitimizes the imperial icon of the Western explorer/adventurer/traveler who pushes to expand their already superior knowledge and lay claim to more territory through additional knowledge acquisition. For the *Voyager* crew, these projects are wrapped into their "primary mission," as Janeway outlines in "Caretaker" to return home as quickly as possible.

The setting enabled *Voyager's* blend of castaway-adventure, which aligns with Green's first component for adventure stories. Adventure tales are "a series of

---

[15]. Ibid., 95.

[16]. Rebecca Weaver-Hightower, *Empire Islands: Castaways, Cannibals, And Fantasies of Conquest* (Minneapolis: University of Minnesota Press, 2007), ix.

[17]. Ibid, xxi.

[18]. Stefan Rabitsch, *Star Trek and the British Age of Sail: The Maritime Influence Throughout the Series and Films* (Jefferson NC: McFarland, 2018), see especially 55-58 and chapters 7 and 8.

events, partly but not wholly accidental, in settings remote from the domestic and probably from the civilized (at least in the psychological sense of remote), which constitute a challenge to the central character."[19] These distances, both physical and psychological, mark the location and its inhabitants as uncivilized in contrast to the idealized home. The creation of this binary has been vital to Euro-American imperialism for over five centuries, and has become an unquestioned and presumed 'truth' to global international relations.[20] Adventure narratives have played a role in contributing to these differences, even in the basic setting, and *Voyager* is no exception. *Voyager* presents a setting of literal remoteness that constitutes many of the challenges faced by the crew throughout the series duration. The accidental events in "Caretaker" that lead to the Starfleet presence in the Delta Quadrant remove the crew from everything familiar outside of the bounds of their ship. Delta Quadrant native Neelix, introduced in "Caretaker," joins the crew to help them navigate the entirely foreign surroundings. Neelix also serves as the ship's chef, bringing Delta Quadrant food to the crew. Thus, *Voyager* offers reoccurring visual clues of the 'different' Delta Quadrant in a straightforward way. The Federation officers often find the new food strange and unappealing—Tom Paris notes in the fifth episode that "I'm sure the gastrointestinal problems will go away as soon as our systems get used to [Neelix's], uh ... gourmet touch."[21] In the same episode, Janeway asks Neelix for coffee after warily exploring the make-shift kitchen he has fashioned in the officers' mess. She then tries the coffee substitute he has made out of a local "proteinaceous seed." Janeway looks horrified as Neelix pours the thick liquid into her cup, and she flees to the Bridge rather than drink the supposed "better than coffee" substitute.[22]

In line with Green's definition, *Voyager* also demonstrates psychological remoteness. The crew is psychologically removed from their Federation principles, as the narrative will demonstrate time and again: only the *Voyager* crew will adhere to the principles of presumably 'advanced' Western ethics and Enlightenment that mark the Federation as unique—and superior— throughout the galaxy. The season seven episode "The Void" illustrates these distances.[23] Even after traveling for over six years, the crew is still 30,000 light-

---

[19]. Green, *Dreams of Adventure*, 23.

[20]. See Roxanne Lynn Doty, *Imperial Encounters: The Politics of Representation in North-South Relations* (Minneapolis: University of Minnesota Press, 1996).

[21]. "The Cloud," directed by David Livingston, *Star Trek: Voyager* (Paramount Television, February 13, 1995).

[22]. Ibid.

[23]. "The Void," directed by Mike Vejar, *Star Trek: Voyager* (Paramount Television, February 14, 2001).

years away from Earth. Janeway and her crew—while stuck inside a "void" in space with no apparent way out—must once again affirm their commitment to Federation principles. In refusing to raid other ships for supplies, Janeway explains that "[the] Federation is based on mutual cooperation: the idea that the whole is greater than the sum of its parts. *Voyager* can't survive here alone, but if we form a temporary alliance with other ships, maybe we can pool our resources and escape [...] We may lose a little weight, gentlemen, but we won't lose who we are."[24]

"The Void" proposes that the Starfleet crew is not only physically removed from their home but also psychologically removed from any race that prioritizes mutual cooperation in the face of hardship. In the end, through persuasion and bargaining, Janeway manages to form a Federation-like alliance with a group of aliens and escape. This temporary victory reaffirms the crew's desire to return to the Alpha Quadrant, and they once again set a course for 'home.' Their ideal vision of home, and reaching that home, remains the primary motivation for the crew.

Like much of castaway and adventure literature, the idea of 'home' serves a significant and central role in the narrative. Contemporary castaway narratives figure the idea and space of 'home' more prominently than eighteenth and nineteenth-century literature. Explaining contemporary castaway narratives, including the popular *Cast Away* (2000) film starring Tom Hanks, Weaver-Hightower states that in these stories, the castaway "remains [a] perpetual visitor, never owner."[25] The state of perpetual visitation cultivates a "neo-imperial fantasy" that cultivates possession of the island space through indirect forms of colonization, while at the same time idealizing a home to which they all eventually return.[26] Further, Weaver-Hightower explains that "[i]n such endings we can see reflected a popular mythology of the United States as the metaphoric center of the world, the place one would never willingly leave and to which the rest of the world flees in search of a better life."[27] 'Home' is, therefore, both the destination and the ideal standard against which everything in the Delta Quadrant is compared. Michèle Barrett and Duncan Barrett observe that the overall "desire to return to the Alpha Quadrant, [enables] a much broader concept of 'home' that allows us to define it as distinct from a

---

24. Ibid.
25. Weaver-Hightower, *Empire Highlands*, 208.
26. Ibid., 210-215.
27. Ibid., 215.

very other location."[28] This comparison, as in the above example of the "not quite" Federation alliance that Janeway and crew create in "The Void," constantly reinforces the desire to return, and prioritizes humanity—especially the Western civilizations that give the Federation their values and practices— over all 'others.' In reality, of course, *Voyager* itself is their home. In the season four episode "Year of Hell," for example, Janeway explains that "this ship has been our home, it's kept us together, it's part of our family."[29] This dual nature of functional home—the ship—in contrast to ideal home—the Alpha Quadrant)—reachable only with their functional home in working order, continues to strengthen the various ties to 'home' throughout the series.

Beyond distance from home, adventure narratives demonstrate a series of 'advances' on the part of the protagonists that enable their success. These advances normalize and legitimize Euro-American imperial ideologies through reinforcing differences between peoples and civilizations in ways that privilege Western forms of knowledge. Green highlights technologies—specifically "guns or compasses"— and scientific knowledge, including keeping detailed accounts/records and the rationalization for exploration, as the key components the adventurer requires to succeed in the unknown environment.[30] Mapping was one tool used by European imperial explorers and adventures, including well-known figures like Captain Cook and David Livingstone, to solidify difference through scientific and geographic classification—techniques that were also demonstrated in fictional adventure texts. Roxanne Doty argues that in the eighteenth, nineteenth, and twentieth centuries, Western imperial powers utilized tools of naturalization, classification, surveillance, and negation—including extensive map-making—to enable their imperial projects.[31] These practices normalized, legitimized, and enabled imperial and colonial policies through processes that constructed and reinforced hierarchies and divisions, such as civilized/uncivilized. American policies of manifest destiny utilized these practices extensively, including the famous expedition launched by Lewis and Clark in the early nineteenth century to explore land newly acquired by President Thomas Jefferson's 1803 Louisiana Purchase. Numerous native populations already inhabited this extensive tract of land, but Lewis and Clark's expedition presumed to 'discover' the space and

---

28. Michèle Barrett and Duncan Barrett, *Star Trek: The Human Frontier* (Hove: Psychology Press, 2001), 204, emphasis in original.

29. "Year of Hell, Parts 1 and 2," directed by Allan Kroeker and Mike Vejar, *Star Trek: Voyager* (Paramount Television, November 5 and 12, 1997).

30. Green, 23.

31. Roxanne Lynn Doty, *Imperial Encounters: The Politics of Representation in North-South Relations* (Minneapolis: University of Minnesota Press, 1996), 10-11.

map it for the American government. Commonly framed as an expedition to "investigate Indian culture, to collect plants and animal specimens, and to chart the geography of the West," the explorers played a vital role in the classification of land as 'unexplored' until discovered and mapped by Americans.[32] In reality, the Lewis and Clark expedition was a military project that mapped the territory for later American imperial expansion.

Voyager similarly makes use of technologies and scientific approaches to enable and rationalize their exploration of the Delta Quadrant as they journey home. The Captain's Log feature, for example, serves as one form of detailed record-keeping, and functions in the same manner of historical Captains to include information about their explorations.[33] Such record-keeping additionally served to justify their actions and present themselves as successful adventurers, and were often "widely circulated" during the classic "Age of Imperialism."[34] Mapping serves as another technological and scientific advancement that enables *Voyager's* triumphant return home. As noted earlier, Janeway declares the mission of *Voyager* will be two-fold: find a faster way home and map the Delta Quadrant for the Federation. In line with Green's criteria for adventurer success, mapping in *Voyager* utilizes advanced Federation technologies, including *Voyager* itself.

Further, mapping is itself a detailed record of the journey and serves as Janeway's justification/rationalization for exploration. Even though *Voyager's* extensive use of mapping served a practical purpose for the crew, the process enabled the Federation to lay claim to extensive knowledge of a vast region of space. It made the Delta Quadrant less 'foreign' to the Federation crew. Even though practical considerations delimit their map making, the Federation will claim that their map is the only map of the area that contains true knowledge. At the same time, their claim will establish them as 'discoverers' of the area for posterity. The glorification of discovery and the practical process of cartography— and the authority claim of the cartographer—served to normalize imperial projects and legitimize the need for them as efforts to 'civilize' the 'uncivilized' spaces: a tradition *Voyager* taps into through their emphasis on discovery and map-making.

The early season one episode "Eye of the Needle" illustrates how traditions of imperial exploration, adventure, and manifest destiny are infused throughout

---

[32]. James L. Roark et al., *Understanding The American Promise, Volume 1: To 1877: A Brief History of the United States* (NY: Macmillan, 2011), 253-4.
[33]. See Rabitsch, *Star Trek and the British Age of Sail*, chapter seven, for an extensive comparison between these forms of record keeping.
[34]. Ibid, 142-145.

the *Voyager* narrative, including map-making and naming newly discovered territory.[35] The episode details the discovery of a wormhole that Janeway hopes will open into the Alpha Quadrant and offer the crew a way home. They eventually realize that the wormhole opens into the Alpha Quadrant twenty years before *Voyager* left. However, not before Tom Paris suggests that they name the wormhole after Ensign Harry Kim—the 'discoverer' of the anomaly.[36] This comment reflects the monarch-of-all-I-survey feature of popular castaway narratives that itself was rooted in historical imperial exploration. Weaver-Hightower uses this concept to denote the rituals of possession of mapping and naming features of the island or other castaway space, which were also practiced by historical imperial explorers. In typical imperial explorer fashion, both literary and historical, the Federation crew presumes to name and use a 'discovered' feature of their castaway/adventure/explorer space.

Beyond recreating castaway and adventure tropes through mapping and naming newly 'discovered' space, this episode is noteworthy for other traditions rooted in stories and practices of American westward expansion and in reinforcing the *Voyager* crew's refusal to assume refugee status. In a detailed look at the first two years of *Voyager* production, Stephen Edward Poe explained that the first draft of this episode centered on Janeway experiencing a classic Western "holonovel." A version of holographic technology unique to *Voyager*, "holonovels," allow the user to experience a personal narrative where they played the central character. Poe explains of this early draft that,

> When Jeri Taylor wrote the first draft of the teaser [of "Eye of the Needle"], she constructed a scenario in which Janeway was a pioneer woman in a covered wagon, headed out West. She had a husband and children. Day to day living was at a very simple level, often requiring her to do things for which she was unprepared and untrained—such as building a campfire. In short, nothing remotely like her job as a starship captain. Taylor thought it was a great metaphor for the Captain's predicament in the Delta Quadrant, and would also provide a unique method of developing and enhancing Janeway's character.[37]

Even though nothing in the excerpt suggests that the script would have mirrored the historical removal of indigenous peoples that resulted from American practices of manifest destiny, this early draft speaks to the close ties between the tradition of westward expansion. It also shows the creators'

---

[35]. "Eye of the Needle," directed by Winrich Kolbe, *Star Trek: Voyager* (Paramount Television, February 20, 1995).

[36]. Weaver-Hightower, 3.

[37]. Stephen Edward Poe, *A Vision of the Future* (Simon and Schuster, 1998), 11.

understanding of *Voyager* as a castaway-adventure journey. Further, it frames Janeway as a traveler, always pushing forward and—presumably—arriving victorious at her destination. This deliberate allusion, even though it never aired, illuminates the vision of the writers, based on the narrative tropes of castaway-adventure stories themselves founded in historical imperial exploration, to glorify and romanticize traditions of American westward expansion and processes of settler colonialism and imperialism. In doing so, *Voyager* contributes to the normalization and legitimization of methods and concepts of empire as natural ways of seeing and engaging with the world and presents their characters as vaulted travelers and explorers, not refugees seeking salvation. Westerns—and Federation members of Starfleet—can be castaway-travelers: they will never be refugees.

Voyager clarifies the contrast between the castaway / adventurer / traveler / explorer and the refugee, through the former's continued efforts to return home. In doing so, the traveler retains the manifest destiny granted by Providence to explore, to push into the mysterious frontier. The refugee, on the other hand, is presumably less: less favored by Providence, less capable of pushing boundaries, less capable of achieving, and retaining the knowledge and skills needed to make their way in the world. This contrast underwrites the entire *Voyager* adventure narrative and is reinforced each time the crew succeeds against any hardship standing in their way of returning home. Other episodes highlight their drive to return home even when settlement in the Delta Quadrant is an appealing option. The early season two episode "The 37's" provides the *Voyager* crew with an opportunity to settle in the Delta Quadrant with a population of humans.[38] These humans were kidnapped and enslaved by aliens several centuries prior in 1937. The audiences are treated to a resolution to the disappearance of Amelia Earhart, who was abducted and—due to an accident with several cryostasis chambers—is still alive despite the passage of time. Janeway acknowledges that Earhart is one of her role models. The two are quite similar in attitude and ability: Earhart was a world-famous adventurer and explorer who pushed the boundaries of science and her gender in the early twentieth century, and Janeway was the first female Federation Captain to push her ship beyond the known boundaries of the galaxy, in addition to being a scientist herself. The two women are physically similar as well, both with brown hair worn close to their head, a similar height and slim build, and a 'down to Earth' way of addressing those around them. The similarities create a bond between the two women, but they ultimately take different paths. Neither path, however,

---

[38]. "The 37's," directed by James Conway, *Star Trek: Voyager* (Paramount Television, August 28, 1995).

evokes the status of refugees despite the reality of *Voyager*'s (and Earhart's) situation.

Feeling bound by their experiences and a kinship with the human civilization on the planet, Earhart and the other "37's" opt to stay rather than leave with *Voyager.* Janeway offers members of her crew the same opportunity. The Captain struggles with this option, knowing that if any of her crew does choose to stay behind, *Voyager* will have trouble returning home. The final scene shows the results of Janeway's offer for "anyone who wants to stay behind to report to the Cargo Bay at 1500 hours."[39] Janeway tells First Officer Chakotay that she would not blame anyone for wanting to stay, but the Cargo Bay is empty when the two arrive to see who wants to remain. Visibly overcome with emotion, Janeway smiles—her crew will continue whole. Janeway and her crew make a clear choice in this episode that will be repeated throughout the series: they are travelers and explorers on the journey home, not settlers—and indeed not refugees.

Refugee status is firmly eschewed throughout the series, even though the disastrous arrival of *Voyager* in the Delta Quadrant could have easily resulted in that mantel. Through the repeated elevation of the Federation crew as travelers, explorers, and adventures, not settlers—and certainly not presumably disempowered refugees—*Voyager* again reinforces a binary between Western citizens and civilizations as presumably superior. Even in "The 37's," the humans brought to the Delta Quadrant as slaves have freed themselves from bondage, and created an incredible civilization, one where "war and poverty simply don't exist," much like the larger United Federation of Planets.[40] Even here, thousands of light-years away from Earth, humans—and humanity writ large, albeit framed exclusively from a Western perspective with Western values and habits—stand out as unique. Much like the intended comparison between Janeway and a frontier settler in the nineteenth century in the early "Eye of a Needle" script, and in the comparison between Janeway and Earhart as travelers and adventurers par excellence even if the latter does opt to settle and remain behind, the *Voyager* crew will always be adventures, never refugees.

This binary is retained throughout the series. Additional episodes, including the "Scorpion" and "Endgame" sequences, highlight the drive to return home at any cost in ways that continue to prioritize the drive of the Western adventurer rather than someone 'forced' to settle as a refugee. These storylines pit the *Voyager* crew against the well-known Trek villains, the Borg, and reinforce the narrative of castaway-travelers/adventurers who will not settle for

[39]. "The 37's," 1995.
[40]. Ibid.

anything less than home. Doing so privileges the imperial manifest destiny directives of exploration over assuming the status of refugees. "Scorpion" recounts an alliance with the Borg in exchange for passage through Borg-claimed space in an area of space Janeway names the 'Northwest Passage'— going to extreme lengths to continue the journey home.[41] The series finale "Endgame" features a desperate gamble and the sacrifice of Admiral Janeway from the future to return to the Alpha Quadrant.[42] Both of these stories see heroic achievements on the part of the *Voyager* crew, especially Janeway, and cement *Voyager's* manifest destiny to travel and conquer the vast 'undiscovered' territory of the Delta Quadrant to return home. The historical American settler pushing West carved a home out of the rugged 'undiscovered' wilderness, unlike the *Voyager* crew crossing 'unknown' space to return home, but neither ever assumed the status of refugee. In this retelling, the Federation (American) traveler can never be a refugee, firmly establishing the imperial mandate of exceptionalism that threads through American cultural narratives.

Voyager presents the galaxy as a place to be discovered and mapped by the Federation through tropes of adventure and castaway novels—and American imperial actions to colonize the continent. Exploration is presented as an unquestioned right to manifest destiny. Through rituals of possession, including mapping and naming the 'discovered' space, *Voyager* casts those imperial perspectives into cultural narratives of the late twentieth century. Through the continued representation of processes of classification, including map-making, castaway-adventure narratives present Western perspectives as normal and legitimate, and imperial ways of seeing the world are reinforced and strengthened.

Bibliography and Filmography

"Star Trek: Voyager Continues the Eminence and Prestige of the Star Trek Legacy," United Paramount Network Press Release, 1995.

Altman, Mark, and Edward Gross. *The Fifty-Year Mission: Volume One: The Complete, Uncensored, Unauthorized Oral History of Star Trek: The First 25 Years.* NY: St. Martin's, 2016.

Barrett, Michèle, and Duncan Barrett. *Star Trek: The Human Frontier.* Hove: Psychology Press, 2001.

Conway, James, director. "The 37's." In *Star Trek: Voyager.* Paramount Television, August 28, 1995.

---

[41]. "Scorpion, Parts 1 & 2," directed by Winrich Kolbe and David Livingston, *Star Trek: Voyager* (Paramount Television, September 21, 1997).

[42]. "Endgame, Parts 1 and 2," directed by Allan Kroeker, *Star Trek: Voyager* (Paramount Television, May 23, 2001).

Doty, Roxanne Lynn. *Imperial Encounters: The Politics of Representation in North-South Relations.* Minneapolis: University of Minnesota Press, 1996.

Green, Martin. *Dreams of Adventure, Deeds of Empire.* New York: Basic Books, Inc., 1980.

Kolbe, Winrich and David Livingston, directors. "Scorpion, Parts 1 & 2." In *Star Trek: Voyager.* Paramount Television, September 21, 1997.

Kolbe, Winrich, director. "Caretaker." In *Star Trek: Voyager.* Paramount Television, January 16, 1995.

Kolbe, Winrich, director. "Eye of the Needle." In *Star Trek: Voyager.* Paramount Television, February 20, 1995.

Kroeker, Allan and Mike Vejar, directors. "Year of Hell, Parts 1 and 2." Paramount Television, November 5, 1997.

Kroeker, Allan. "Endgame, Parts 1, and 2." *Star Trek: Voyager.* Paramount Television, May 23, 2001.

Livingston, David, director. "The Cloud." In *Star Trek: Voyager.* Paramount Television, February 13, 1995.

O'Sullivan, John. "Annexation." *The United States Democratic Review* 17 (1845): 5-10.

O'Sullivan, John. "The Great Nation of Futurity." *The United States Democratic Review* 6 (1839): 426-30.

Poe, Stephen Edward. *A Vision of the Future.* Simon and Schuster, 1998.

Rabitsch, Stefan. *Star Trek and the British Age of Sail: The Maritime Influence Throughout the Series and Films.* Jefferson NC: McFarland, 2018.

Roark, James L., Michael P. Johnson, Patricia Cline Cohen, Sarah Stage, Alan Lawson, and Susan M. Hartmann. *Understanding the American Promise, Volume 1: to 1877: A Brief History of the United States.* NY: Macmillan, 2011.

Said, Edward. *Culture and Imperialism.* NY: Vintage Books, 1994.

Scholnick, Robert J. "Extermination and Democracy: O'Sullivan, the Democratic Review, and Empire, 1837-1840." *American Periodicals* 15, no. 2 (2005): 123-41.

Solow, Herbert F. and Robert H. Justman. *Inside Star Trek: The Real Story.* NY: Pocket Books, 1996.

Stephanson, Anders. *Manifest Destiny: American Expansion and the Empire of Right.* NY: Hill and Wang, 1996.

Vejar, Mike, director. "The Void." In *Star Trek: Voyager.* Paramount Television, February 14, 2001.

Weaver-Hightower, Rebecca. *Empire Islands: Castaways, Cannibals, And Fantasies of Conquest.* Minneapolis: University of Minnesota Press, 2007.

Chapter 13

Cosmopolitanism in the face of im/migration

Antara Mukherjee

Independent scholar

Abstract[1]

In ancient Greece, cosmopolitanism was a call for all humanity to belong to one world, irrespective of citizenship or social divisions. In ancient India the traditional definition of this concept—Vasudheiba Kutumbakam, translates as: 'we are all members of the family of earth.' However, today this term is open to different interpretations depending upon how cosmopolitanism is conceived, theorized, and practiced.[2] This article attempts to explore how cosmopolitanism becomes a hegemonic narrative when it is appropriated by the affluent to couch a dismissive attitude of arrogant indifference towards the racial and social other. It concentrates on three texts for this purpose: a cover page of the travel magazine *Conde Nast*; the second is an episode of the Trevor Noah comedy show; and the third is a satirical cartoon, by Pikaso. Through its readings of these texts, the present article aims to show that elite cosmopolitanism's 'engagement' with poverty as a social problem is limited to advertised philanthropy or charity, thus exposing its complicity with racism, intolerance, and xenophobia.

Keywords: Cosmopolitanism, nomadic, displacement, im-migrant, discrimination

***

In ancient Greece, cosmopolitanism was a call for all humanity to belong to one world, irrespective of actual citizenship or social division. It is also significant

---

[1]. A shorter version of this paper was presented in an International Conference entitled "Revisiting Cosmopolitanism" organized at the 21st Forum on Contemporary Theory, held in Puri, Odisha during 18-21 December, 2018.
[2]. Jennie Germann Molz, "Cosmopolitanism and Consumption," in *The Ashgate Research Companion to Cosmopolitanism*, ed. Maria Rovisco et al. (New York, Routledge: 2016), 33-34.

to take note of India's ancient traditional definition of this concept as Vasudheiba Kutumbakam, which translates as 'we are all members of the family of earth.' Every civilization has had such philosophers of deep human values such as mutual respect for all, social justice, human dignity, love, and forgiveness. One could name Buddha, Gandhi, Martí, Tolstoy, Freire, Fanon, and Nussbaum to cite only a few who have influenced millions and have often also inspired each other.[3] Today, however, given the increasing scale of trade, economics and changing geopolitics, cosmopolitanism also has acquired new meanings and dispensations very distant from the idealized Universalist idea of global brotherhood. The present paper attempts to look at how another cosmopolitanism is designed and deployed by hegemonic forces to hide racism, xenophobia, and anti-poor feelings. It is an elite cosmopolitanism which is selective, hypocritical and highly problematic. Popular patterns of travel, leisure, touring, and hospitality have completely changed ways of articulation of social etiquettes and consumption in capitalist societies. Service providers are more sharply conscientious of how a client-centric culture is produced by tapping on digital data, controlled surveys of potential consumers, and general studies on desires and pleasures.[4] The consumers also are aware of their rights to access these pleasures, in terms of new destinations and experiences, their preferred modes of travel, and value packages. They have the skills to choose from a global travel menu digitally. At the same time, as the affluent travel, they are aware of politically correct behavior that they would require in high-priced exotic tourist destinations. So, they have to hide their xenophobia, their racism, their casteism, and their intolerance behind the mask of an elite cosmopolitanism.

The article relies upon the Gallorotti's views on soft power to dwell on this issue later. Before that, it engages with a consideration of how capitalist interests exacerbated by global neo-liberal agendas have had to negotiate with glaring domestic and global disparities in wealth distribution as a basis for constructing the other. Generally, governments in developed countries, given

---

[3]. Maria Popova, "Why We Hurt Each Other: Tolstoy's Letters to Gandhi on Love, Violence, and the Truth of the Human Spirit," https://www.brainpickings.org/2014/08/21/leo-tolstoy-gandhi-letter-to-a-hindu/.

Dale Snauwaert, "Social Justice and The Philosophical Foundations of Critical Peace Education: Exploring Nussbaum, Sen, and Freire," *Journal of Peace Education*, Volume 8, (2011): 315-331, https://www.tandfonline. com/doi/abs /10.1080/ 17400201.2011.621371

[4]. Theodor Adorno and Max Horkheimer, "Enlightenment as Mass Deception," in *Dialectics of Enlightenment* (Stanford: Stanford University Press, 2002).

their corporate interests, had to have strong anti-racist laws in order to avoid confrontations with different colored, ethnic, and religious identities.[5] Similarly, in India, the Constitution guarantees protection and dignity to the underprivileged Dalit, the tribal, and women. Hence the affluent of the globalized world are already aware that etiquettes of politically correct behavior are obligatory in order to control situations of encounter with the colored or ethnic or the poor minority.

1. Cosmopolitans and nomads

This article will argue that such state-manufactured, and constitutionally guaranteed arrangements do not wipe out discrimination, and only pushes it down to its underbelly instead. Moreover, the complex re-writings of cosmopolitanism by the privileged and the powerful today have been such that they have served to deny their role in the invisibilizations, marginalization, and ghettoization of refugees, immigrants and other kinds of displaced peoples. For this purpose, the present article proposes to dwell on selected narratives of popular culture such as the cover page of the travel magazine *Conde Nast* that featured an image of the Bollywood star Priyanka Chopra wearing a T-shirt with the words "Refugee Immigrant Outsider Traveler" on it, a political commentary and satire video of Trevor Noah responding to a French diplomat's comments on black football players in the national team, and a cartoon that mocks the media indifference to the plight of Indian migrants walking—often hundreds of kilometers—home after the COVID 19 lockdown by Pikaso, an editorial cartoonist.[6] It will further look at some other popular travel practices involving 'beg packers' and their pleasure trips. Through all of these, the article will explore how popular culture is appropriated to further the alleged 'politically

[5]. Ginger Hervey, "When Britain Exits the EU, Its Diversity Departs Too," *Politico*, November 12, 2017, accessed June 15, 2020, https://www.politico.eu/article/brexit-diversity-exits-the-eu-brussels/.

"Germany Celebrates 10 Years of Anti-Discrimination Legislation," Ilga Europe, September 27, 2016, accessed June 15, 2020, https://www.ilga-europe.org/resources/news/latest-news/germany-10-years-anti-discrimination.

[6]. "Priyanka Chopra Sorry for *Conde Nast* Cover Insulting Refugees," BBC, accessed March 27, 2020. https://www.bbc.com/news/world-asia-india-37676903.

"Trevor Responds to Criticism from the French Ambassador," YouTube video, 08:25, posted by The Daily Show with Trevor Noah, July 18, 2018, accessed July 29, 2019, https://www.youtube.com/watch?v= COD9hcTpGWQ .

Pikaso (@Vikasopikaso), "A responsible media. My cartoon," Twitter, April 8, 2020, https://twitter.com/vikasopikaso.

correct' narrative among the privileged across the world. This stance of the 'politically correct' is perceived as analogous to the use of soft power in international politics.

World politics in the modern age has been undergoing changes that have elevated the importance of soft power relative to hard power. In this transformed international system, soft power will be a crucial element in enhancing influence over international outcomes because it has become more difficult to compel nations and non-state actors through the principal levers of hard power, that is, threats and force. The world stage has become less amenable to Hobbesian brutes, and more amenable to actors that are sensitized to the soft opportunities and constraints imposed by this new global environment. Both domestic and international sources of soft power reflect an emphasis on policies and actions that exude an orientation of justice, collective concern, and rules of fair play.[7] The value of soft power has become useful in negotiating relationships based on political correctness, encouraging myths of global citizenship, peace, and universal brotherhood. However, this article argues how it may actually hide biases against racial and socio-political others and the forces that mount any "brotherhood" facades across them. It argues that the ways of soft power deployed in the present scenario are politically and potentially exploitative to maximize pro-elite interests.

Thus, for example, among the words on Priyanka Chopra's shirt: "Refugee, Immigrant, Outsider, and Traveller," the first three words were struck out in red to foreground an allegedly more dignifying label of "traveler."[8] The image attempted, unsuccessfully, to convey a message against xenophobia. There was a global outrage on Twitter where she was severely trolled for the insensitivity in blurring the plight of refugees, immigrants, and outsiders into a traveler's experience.

---

[7]. Guilio M.Gallorotti, "Soft Power: What It Is, Why It's Important, and The Conditions for Its Effective Use," *Journal of Political Power* 4 (1) (2011): 5 and 22, https://doi.org/10.1080/21583 79X.2011.557886.

[8]. "Priyanka Chopra Sorry for Conde Nast Cover 'Insulting' Refugees," BBC, October 17, 2016, https://www.bbc.com/news/world-asia-india-37676903

Figure 13.1: The controversial cover page

Source: BBC.com

Anum R. Chagani@Anumero trolled her, saying that, "Oh, I am sorry, I wasn't aware that being a refugee is a matter of choice...What were you thinking? Exactly why it's even more hypocritical. You can't equate being a refugee with being a traveler.2/2 It's apples & oranges, and it trivializes their oppression." [9]Another Twitter account of Curious responded, "...for cutting those word....[sic] I have obliged to hate you."[10]An article on this issue in The Indian Telegraph commented on the fiasco of the intended 'political correctness': "Her t-shirt—designed by V Sunil—is evidently meant to fit in with her statements in the interview. However, with the refugee crisis, a pressing global concern, PC's

---

[9]. Anum R. Chagani (@Anumero1), "Oh, I'm sorry, I wasn't aware that being a refugee is a matter of choice...What were you thinking?" October 8, 2016, https://twitter.com/Anumero_1 /status/ 784676798395219968

[10]. Curious (@Curious97351), "... for cutting those word...[sic] I have obliged to hate you," October 18, 2016, https://twitter.com/Curious97531/status/785733718535122944.

t-shirt is being seen as, well, not PC. (That's politically correct for those of us who aren't into acronyms)."[11]

The whole idea here is to remove the very existence of immigrants, to deny the existence of hatred towards outsiders, to deny the politics that create droves of refugees every minute of every day. By labeling them as travelers, one would think that one might be able to 'tolerate' their existence; however, what her shirt did say to those who can afford to buy the magazine is that the entire problem of forced displacement could be solved by using the right words.[12] It trivializes the issue of justice in today's situations of global citizens' movements, which calls for a serious commitment to "strangers both within and beyond state borders."[13]

The second text that this article deals with is Trevor Noah's. When the satirist expressed his delight at seeing "Africa"—actually, a largely black-dominated French team—win the coveted trophy, the response of the French Ambassador to the US, Gerard Araud, revealed the cleavage between the official narrative of French identity and its postcolonially informed cultural understanding. The French football team won the FIFA World Cup in 2018 against Croatia, and Noah's response highlighted the fact that twelve of the twenty-three players in the French team were of African descent. The key point of the debate was how French a person of African descent could be. In fact, people of African descent had quite often to prove their French-ness even when they might have been even born in France. This debate became very prominent when Araud responded to Noah through a letter, where he wrote: "Unlike the United States of America, France does not refer to its citizens based on their race, religion or origin. To us, there is no hyphenated identity. Roots are an individual reality. By calling them an African team, it seems you are denying their Frenchness."[14] Noah's response, in which asked, "Why cannot they be both [French and

[11]. Twinkle Ghosh, "Priyanka Chopra's T-shirt Slammed By Netizens." *The Indian Telegraph*, June 15, 2020, accessed 15 June, 2020, https://theindiantelegraph.com.au/priyanka-chopras-t-shirt-slammed-netizens/

[12]. Priyanka Chopra is a Miss World 2000 pageant, a UNICEF appointed good will ambassador of child rights in 2010 and 2016, and a very popular Bollywood star. See https://timesofindia.indiatimes.com/topic/Priyanka-Chopra for more information.

[13]. Nikita Dhawan, "Coercive Cosmopolitanism and Impossible Solidarities." Vol. 22, No.1. *Qui Parle* 22 (1) Fall/Winter (2013): 139, https://www.jstor.org/stable/10.5250/quiparle.22.1.0139?seq=1.

[14]. "Trevor Responds to Criticism."

African]?" exposed the pitfalls of the assimilationist philosophy, which characterizes the French approach to immigration and identity.[15]

Trevor Noah regarded this answer as problematic, especially because the French Ambassador denied the possibility of a hyphenated identity. What gets highlighted response Araud's response is the pitfalls of French identity issues with respect to integration and identity. It has often been argued that the French model of integration has failed because of socio-economic disparities suffered by colored immigrants who are ghettoized. By asserting that France does not accept hyphenated-identities - which make it possible for American citizens to acknowledge their ancestral origin without giving up their 'Americanness' - Ambassador Araud denied the existence of a large part of his country's population who may have multiple affiliations and even celebrate the plurality in the country. Player Adil Rami defines himself both as French and Moroccan, which does not make him less French than anyone of his fellow citizens.[16] In the context of the present debate, the above arguments highlight "the fragility of non-white Frenchness" [17] in terms of an understanding of cosmopolitanism as an aspiration to belonging on the terms of equality and brotherhood. The question thus is whether cosmopolitanism has been forced by the elite to shed a few of its core values. Elite cosmopolitanism, in this context, deteriorated into a chauvinistic nationalism, which is monolithic and devoid of socio-political and economic sensibilities. Cosmopolitanism ended up being appropriated by those in power (political, financial, and social) to elide real problems that they assume to be unsolvable, or they do not want to solve.

Trevor Noah's sharp criticism of the French Ambassador's comments about black French footballers of African descent is direct, confrontational, and without any inhibition. There is no political correctness that can be absolved of hypocrisy in such selective acceptance of blackness as French while denying their African descent. Referring to the racist colonial history of the French nation, Noah points out that the French-ness of an African becomes indisputable only when he is part of a winning football team. Noah argues against the obligation—tacitly, but clearly, implied in Araud's response—on a French footballer to erase his African legacy. Generally, an African in France,

---

15. Rokhaya Diallo, "On Football, Identity and 'Frenchness': Are Some Members of the French National Team Only French When they Win?" *Al Jazeera*, August 2, 2018, accessed January 20, 2020,https://www.aljazeera.com/indepth/opinion/football-identity-frenchness-1808010802 57299.html.
16. Ibid.
17. Ibid.

immigrant or not, suffers the humiliation of his French identity being easily dismissed, confined forever to being branded as an African immigrant. Noah further reiterates this with another example of an African immigrant who was paternalistically gifted a citizenship because he had saved a child who was dangling from a high-rise building, after the video of the incident went viral on the internet media and social networks.[18] It is as if one needs to be visibly 'useful' to the state to be given basic human rights because otherwise, the immigrants' contribution to society, primarily as low-wage, often exploited, workers, remain largely ignored by the state. Denial and dismissiveness molded by a hyper-awareness of the "immigrant problem" become integral to this new cosmopolitanism, although it also allows for new solidarities across the globe. Chopra apologized haphazardly, almost as if to save face, and Noah never stopped arguing against the French Ambassador's delimitation of Frenchness.

When drawing parallels to the above-mentioned examples, in India, the strains of similarity are obviously visible. The role of the migrant workers and their identities and eventually their political and social fate is decided by their usefulness to the oppressive state. The whole argument of merit that has been powered by oppressive structures rests on the systemic act of keeping the social minorities uneducated, apolitical, and poor. For Dalits, Adivasis, transgender persons, and other minorities comprising a large chunk of the working class, to be given any respect at all, they must conform to the narratives of the oppressor. The filters used to project these minorities as "good citizens" are, in fact, another measure of control that seeps into all spheres of their day-to-day life. For example, the African immigrant who was rewarded with the citizenship of France for saving a French child is very telling of the kind of use the minority must have to be accorded respect. 'Frenchness' is a 'gift' charitably bequeathed by the state on the immigrant. Had the immigrant not saved the child, had the immigrant not been part of such a grandiose show of 'courage', would he be seen as an example of humanity and not as a 'thug'? Likewise, as long as the Dalit migrant sweeps the house of the upper caste employer, as long as s/he is useful, s/he will be tolerated and even shown some patronizing approval. However, the second that the outbreak of a pandemic threatens the upper caste people, the working class cannot be allowed to work anymore, and neither can they be worthy of refuge and shelter in the very cities that they built.

---

[18]. "France Offers Citizenship to Malian Immigrant," Reuters, May 28, 2018, accessed June 23, 2020, https://www.reuters.com/article/us-france-hero/france-offers-citizenship-to-malian-immigrant-who-scaled-building-to-save-child-idUSKCN1IS0UF#:~:text=France %20offers%20citizenship%20to%20Malian%20immigrant%20who%20scaled%20building% 20to%20save%20child,-4%20Min%20Read&text=PARIS%20(Reuters)%20%2D%20France%2 0on,balcony%2C%20President%20Emmanuel%20Macron%20said.

There are no Trevor Noah's in India; there are no John Stewarts or John Olivers in India. Political satire on television channels in India is wishful thinking as there's no scope at all for any criticism given today's situation of surveillance and questionable integrity of the mainstream media. Even the few satirists who have had some success are all upper-caste men, unlike Noah, who is a racially mixed person. Yet they are afraid to make a serious comment against the present power dispensation. But there is no dearth of interest, and some satirists are very active on social media, and political comedy seems to be 'booming' in India.

Right now, satirists cannot even imagine being free enough to speak openly, without the need to 'balance' and criticize all political parties. Akash Bannerjee says, "I work with the knowledge that I might be hounded or shut down any time. You can't do what is being done in the late shows in the US. You will probably be shot dead if you did or said what they are doing."[19] Even though the threat of being persecuted is very much real, mainstream comedians such as Bannerjee[20] are appropriating the fear of persecution as an excuse not to dare take it upon themselves to speak out seriously and prefer to remain compromised. However, there are many young Dalit and Adivasi satirists who, in spite of greater threats to their lives, dare to produce quality content without the support of corporate advertisers. They are reduced to their personal Instagram and Twitter pages as they are not given any space in mainstream media. Divya Kandukari's Twitter account @anticastecat or meme pages like @bahujan_memes produce powerful political satire but are not very popular because they produce disturbing truths which are not packaged in politically correct etiquettes.

Coming to a more recent development, the article examines a cartoon in the context of the Covid-19 pandemic is a global crisis that has affected the affluent as much as the poor. It has cut across class, caste, identities, and there is a call for solidarities across nations, races, and political dispensations. Despite the shared vulnerability, society has remained fragmented. The editorial cartoonist

[19]. Himanshi Dhawan, "Political comedy is booming," *TNN*, March 24, 2019, accessed April 15, 2020, https://timesofindia.indiatimes.com/home/sunday-times/pollitical-comedy-is-booming/articleshow/68544518.cms

[20]. "Akash Banerjee is a political satirist and a social media entrepreneur. He's the founder and host of #TheDeshbhakt - India's largest political satire platform - that uses sarcasm and facts to showcase issues plaguing contemporary India. Akash also runs #SocialBakBak - a Boutique Social Care consultancy, specialising in personal/institutional brand-building and content curation. Akash spent a decade and a half in the world of traditional media too and was most recently Vice President at Radio Mirchi." In https://themediarumble.com/speaker/akash-banerjee

put out an image that portrays the sharp class-divide among the urban elite and the rural subaltern:[21]

Figure 13.2: Cartoon tweeted by the cartoonist

Source: Twitter

In this cartoon, the title referring to a responsible media is actually a critique of the lack of responsibility of the media. Many Indian news channels vehemently criticized, hurled abuses and created a narrative where they blamed the migrant for spreading the virus by not staying put, completely ignoring the fact that the cities where the migrant workers worked had no rooms for them. Social media was abuzz; arguments in support of this massive reverse migration came from civil society, which criticized the state for not preparing a proper plan of action to help such populations. In any event of a disaster, the country's poor, the Dalit the Adivasi and other underprivileged identities are the ones who die first and faster. They get no relief or help, unlike their upper caste and class counterparts. This resonates with Alexandria O. Cortez's recent tweet in which she said, "Inequality is comorbidity."[22] The poor of the country are killed first, often the nation terms it as a 'sacrifice' and thus buries the scandal in an ornate coffin of lies, explanations, and cosmopolitan solidarity.

---

21. Pikaso, "A responsible media..My cartoon."
22. Corey Andrew. Alexandria Ocasio-Cortez Drags Laura Ingraham on Twitter In Response To Nasty Mocking TweetApril 4, 2020 in https://instinctmagazine.com/alexandria-ocasio-cortez-drags-laura-ingraham-on-twitter-in-response-to-nasty-mocking-tweet/

But, for all that, our celebrations of the poor ring hollow. Calling them "heroes" allows those who, unlike them, are privileged enough to remain home to imagine that these workers agreed to serve as human sacrifices, that there is an inherent nobility in the risks they take. It gives the civil society a chance to ignore the rotten, hazardous conditions that have been allowed to fester thanks to capitalist cruelty and governmental malfeasance, and absolve themselves of any complicity. But most of these workers didn't sign up to be first responders, and are now overwhelmed by the magnitude of what is being asked of them. They keep saying that they do not want compliments, they want help, but cosmopolitan 'sympathy' has continued to fail them.[23]

There is a deep fault line in the way the global middle-class comprehends cosmopolitanism and uses it to justify any and all upheavals so long as it does not knock at their own door. Countries like India take pride in having their brethren settle abroad in affluent countries as then it becomes almost a statement of class and prosperity. Yet when migrant workers in India face difficulties due to job losses because of the pandemic, they justify the migrant's job losses as inevitable and then become indifferent to any difficulties faced by him or her. The corporate hub of Gurgaon has built many a high-rise establishment using the labor of licensed refugees from Bangladesh and Myanmar, especially Rohingya and Bangladeshi Muslims. However, in the midst of the Delhi riots[24], when stereotypes and xenophobia gripped the state of Delhi and the country, the political masters were unquestioningly obeyed by firing at the same migrants, despite their usefulness. So, the question of the good migrant or the portrayal of a bad migrant is solely dependent on the oppressor's narrative. It is this very unstable and volatile situation that has rendered the minorities across the nation, homeless, malnourished, vulnerable, and killed.

2. Cosmopolitanism behind charity and glamour

These narratives provoked passionate debates as they seemed to wipe out the political and socio-economic histories of exploitation of refugees and im/migrants who are considered outsiders, undeserving of social justice, safety, and respect or any dignified treatment. By labeling them as travelers, or by giving them a patronizing French identity in an aesthetically pleasing way, or by dismissing poor migrants with a "thank you for the story," elite narratives seem to soothe

---

[23]. Kim Kelly, "Essential Workers don't Need our Praise. They Need Our Help," *The Wasington Post*, April 30, 2020, accessed June 20, 2020, https://www.washingtonpost.com/outlook/2020/04/30/essential-workers-dont-need-our-praise-they-need-our-help/

[24]. "Explainer: What Do We Know about the Communal Violence that Left 53 Dead In Delhi in February 2020?" *Scroll*, May 6, 2020, accessed June 19,2020, https://scroll.in/article/955251/explainer-what-do-we-know-about-the-communal-violence-that-left-47-dead-in-delhi-in-february-2020

the sensitivities of the global rich. Refugees and immigrants packaged as travelers (outsiders), or as French (insiders), or as deserving a polite "thank you", expose the quiet complicity of affluent citizens in the politics of a problematic cosmopolitanism. Does this cosmopolitanism have any purpose other than denying their responsibility and actions that resulted in millions of displaced peoples facing xenophobic, racial, or social discriminatory behaviors across the world?

In recent years, there has been a massive jump in conservative beliefs, politics, and lifestyles. Conversations around #ReverseRacism, nationalism, race, and identities flood social media and politics, generating a definite world vision. The practice of a systemic hierarchy only profits the top-most level and justifies it. Obviously, these conversations are happening around the same time when people are talking about #BlackLivesMatter and race-based discrimination, nationhood and its relation to race and inequality, structural hierarchies, and a clamoring for justice and equality. It is fairly understandable that the former set of conversations happen behind a cloak that is fairly opaque, though they are not entirely hidden. To dull the edges of their—those fueling the Republican, fascist, conservative, xenophobic, casteist fires—divisiveness, they invest to ensure the construction of a narrative that feeds their interests, keeps the common masses complacent and the rest, oppressed. Media houses are bought and sold, and so are their stories and journalistic tendencies as they have become pawns in the political processes of repressive regimes. They are powered by commercial and governmental agendas of race, nationalisms, and identities. The choice of a celebrity such as Priyanka Chopra to model the *Conde Nast*'s 6th Anniversary India edition cover, for example, served such purpose. The nationalistic outburst of the French Ambassador in response to a popular TV show and the cartoon which mocked the insensitivity of the Indian media further heighten this point. Political correctness hides insensitivities of race, xenophobia, and the inequality, and the media is complicit in its moves towards commercializing this for profits.

The rich and the famous parading through beauty pageants, glamour world of sports icons, movie stars, musicians, models, and even politicians and other social media influencers are suddenly trying to become politically correct. They socialize with their corporate overlords, and their names are involved in different kinds of financial scams, and their lifestyles are totally discordant with their politically correct public statements.[25] Such duplicity hides the fact that

---

[25]. The biggest scandal in recent years has been the case of the Panama Papers leak where names of top Bollywood actors have been revealed. For more information see Virendrasingh Ghunavat, "Panama Papers Probe: Bollywood Actors to be Quizzed by ED before December 31, *India Today*, December 5 Decemer, 2017, accessed June 17, 2020,

while one may manufacture a brilliant multi-colored picture of the world, the colors shine only for those who can afford a glossy print.

There are two specific terms that outline the hypocrisy of the affluent when it comes to giving and accepting 'charity'. There is a need to stress the very dubiousness of these words. Poverty Porn, a term that came up in the 1980s, was rebirthed in recent years to define celebrity, almost always white, led 'charity' campaigns in third world countries of Africa and Asia. They usually feature a popular celebrity, standing stark white against a very obviously non-white surrounding, bestowing affection on children, holding them, and tearing up at the sight of poverty, discrimination, malnutrition, and death.[26] With exceptionally deft camera work, the charitable generosity of the celebrity and of the organization that took him/her there is pictographically framed to inspire admiration, which may convince viewers to donate to these charities, purely on visual evidence.

Figure 13.3: The celebrity during a visit to South Africa [27]

Source news18.com

Notwithstanding the genuine emotions that the celebrity may feel when witnessing the horrid conditions that some people are forced to go through,

---

https://www.indiatoday.in/india/story/panama-papers-amitabh-bachchan-aishwarya-rai-ajay-devgn-bollywood-actors-ed-before-year-end-1100548-2017-12-05

26. See https://ifunny.co/picture/bruce-ngwata-1d-v-a-trip-to-africa-is-not-As7O1qEp5 which contains tweets trolling Ellen DeGeneres for doing poverty porn during her trip to Africa, accessed June 17, 2020.

27. "UNICEF's Goodwill Ambassador Priyanka Chopra Shares Photos From Her Recent South Africa Visit," *news18*, May 4, 2017, accessed June 23, 2020, https://www.news18.com/news/movies/unicefs-goodwill-ambassador-priyanka-chopra-shares-photos-from-her-recent-south-africa-visit-1392033.html

one has to also dwell on the very brief, the very disconnected, and un-emotional transaction that the image represents. It documents an event that will usually create no real change for the communities involved. Priyanka Chopra, a UNICEF goodwill ambassador, inadvertently admitted as much in an interview, where she said that Miss World only does "fundraisers, raising money for charities, so she is going to help people who need it, but she is not going to eradicate poverty or change the world."[28]

The donation giver is inspired by the images of the poverty endorsed by the celebrity moves on once the act is done. There is no debriefing period. Usually, there is no afterthought, and the duration for which they probably felt that they are citizens of the world, united in pain and suffering is all too brief. In short, such charities are not responsible activism for change, rather a moment of pastoral confession for the redemption of systemic philanthropy embodied by the celebrities. In his book, *Winners Take All: The Elite Charade of Changing the World*, Anand Giridharadas explores how business elites are taking over the world of change. He specifically dwells on the billion-dollar status that the social change industry has attained, where the practices used for the upliftment of society are rooted in a hierarchical pattern of charity. This allows for the same system to continue to function where the dependency of affected peoples remains just that.[29]

The next term, which also describes the paternalistic attitude of the privileged towards the marginalized, is "Beg-Packers,": a term for a growing number of individuals, again almost always from first world countries, who crowdsource money to be able to take expensive vacations and fund their lifestyle.[30] Furthermore, on numerous occasions, white travelers or tourists have been found begging on the streets of third-world countries, usually asking for donations to be able to travel back home. Once more, the issue here is not the economic stability of those asking for funds, instead, it seems patently unjust that they ask for money from people who probably have none or very little, yet they find nothing wrong in doing so. It is possible to contrast these

---

[28]. "Miss World will Not Change the World," indiatoday, December 14, 2009, accessed April 15, 2020, https://www.indiatoday.in/miss-world--09/india-miss-world--09/story/miss-world-will-not-change-the-world-priyanka-chopra-62978-2009-12-14

[29]. For more on this see, Anand Giridharadas, *Winners Take All: The Elite Changing the World* (New York: Knopf, 2018). Also see his interview in a Trevor Noah show "#TheDailyShow #AnandGiridharadas #WinnersTakeAll" accessed July 15, 2020 in https://www.youtube.com/watch?v=H32z45o0WxA

[30]. Jon Rogers, "Western Begpackers Spark Outrage Across Asia by Rocking up in Poor Countries and Pleading with Locals to Fund Their Travels," *The Sun*, July 5, 2019, accessed June 6, 2020, https://www.thesun.co.uk/news/9448772/western-begpackers-bali-begging-money-travel/.

incidents against the angry choruses of modern-day USA when Obamacare is applauded. Critics of Obamacare believe that 'their' precious money has fed enough undeserving rapists, drug traffickers, no-good-doing Spanish-speaking, Mexicans. The money of the first world is deemed too good to be given to immigrants and others who benefit from social welfare programs. The use of taxes to help the needy is labeled as theft.[31] However, crowdsourcing vacations, first-world tourists begging in the streets of third-world countries where poverty is rampant is not commented upon. This situation has raised many instances of outrage and indignation throughout Asia. Where and how can cosmopolitanism sit in these situations of conflict? There is a need to rethink another kind of cosmopolitanism "in a world of rapid change, war, economic instability, hyperbolic media, and wide-ranging social interaction where we are all, to some degree, itinerants."[32]

3. Conclusion

The trolling of Chopra, the South African identity of Trevor Noah, and the ingenuity of the cartoonist Pikaso call to account big corporations, chauvinistic nationalists, and a dehumanized media for the hidden agenda behind this problematic cosmopolitanism. Given today's situation of planetary catastrophes, displacement, and dehumanization amidst systemic and structural violence, perhaps it is worth the effort to think about how one can visualize any future map to explore possibilities of reclaiming a truly global planetary citizenship for all humanity towards sustainable and peaceful world order. Will cosmopolitanism ever become what it was all about, that is, the Greek and the Indian concepts of human cohabitation and dignity? Or is it necessary to consciously reimagine another cosmopolitanism far removed from its Universalist ideal of global peaceful cohabitation and accept and contend with its nomadic and fractured concoctions?

---

[31]. Michelle Mark, "Trump Just Referred to One of his Most Infamous Campaign Comments Calling Mexicans 'Rapists'," *Business Insider India*, April 6, 2018, accessed June 17, 2020, in https://www.businessinsider.in/trump-just-referred-to-one-of-his-most-infamous-campaign-comments-calling-mexicans-rapists/articleshow/63634728.cms?utm_source=copy-link&utm_medium=referral&utm_campaign=Click_through_social_share

[32]. Jeff Edmonds, "America and Cosmopolitan Responsibility: Some Thoughts on an Itinerant Duty" in *Cosmopolitanism and Place*, ed. Jessica Wahman et al. (Bloomington: Indiana UP, 2017):136-137. It is important to cross-read Jessica Wahman edited book and the tabloid newspaper article by Jon Rogers; "Western begpackers Spark Outrage

Bibliography

Adorno, Theodor, and Max Horkheimer. "The Culture Industry:: Enlightenment as Mass Deception." In *The Dialectics of Enlightenment*, 94-136. Stanford: Stanford University Press, 2002.

Andrew, Corey. "Alexandria Ocasio-Cortez Drags Laura Ingraham on Twitter In Response To Nasty Mocking Tweet." *Instinct Magazine*, April 4, 2020. Accessed June 19, 2020. https://instinctmagazine.com/alexandria-ocasio-cortez-drags-laura-ingraham-on-twitter-in-response-to-nasty-mocking-tweet/.

Dhawan, Himanshi. "Political Comedy is Booming." *Times of India*, March 24, 2019. Accessed April 28, 2020. https://timesofindia.indiatimes.com/home/sunday-times/pollitical-comedy-is-booming/articleshow/68544518.cms.

Dhawan, Nikita. "Coercive Cosmopolitanism and Impossible Solidarities." *Qui Parle*, Vol. 22, No.1. (2013):139-166. Accessed March 15, 2019. https://www.jstor.org/stable/ 10.5250/ quiparle. 22.1.0139?seq=1.

Diallo, Rokhaya. "On Football, Identity and 'Frenchness': Are Some Members of the French National Team Only French When they Win?" *Al Jazeera*, August 2, 2018. Accessed January 20, 2020. https://www.aljazeera.com/indepth/opinion/football-identity-frenchness-180801080257299.html.

Gallorotti, Guilio M. "Soft Power: What It Is, Why It's Important, and the Conditions for its Effective Use." *Journal of Political Power* Vol. 4, No. 1. (2011): 25-47. Accessed March 20, 2020. https://doi.org/10.1080/2158379X.2011.557886.

Ghosh, Twinkle. "Priyanka Chopra's T-shirt Slammed By Netizens." *The Indian Telegraph*. June 15. 2020Accessed June 15, 2020. https://theindiantelegraph.com.au/priyanka-chopras-t-shirt-slammed-netizens/.

Ghunavat, Virendrasingh. "Panama Papers Probe: Bollywood Actors to be Quizzed by ED before December 31." *India Today*, December 5, 2017. Accessed June 17, 2020. https://www.indiatoday.in/india/story/panama-papers-amitabh-bachchan-aishwarya-rai-ajay-devgn.

Giridharadas, Anand. *Winners Take All: The Elite Charade of Changing the World*. New York: Knopf, 2018.

Edmonds, Jeff. "America and Cosmopolitan Responsibility: Some Thoughts on an Itinerant Duty." In *Cosmopolitanism and Place*, edited by Jessica Wahman et al., 123-138. Indiana UP, 2017.

"Explainer: What do we Know About the Communal Violence that Left 53 Dead in Delhi in February 2020?" *Scroll*, March 6, 2020. Accessed June 6, 2020. https://scroll.in/article/955251/explainer-what-do-we-know-about-the-communal-violence-that-left-47-dead-in-delhi-in-february-20.

"Germany Celebrates 10 years of Anti-discrimination Legislation." *Ilga-europe*, September 27, 2016. Accessed June 15, 2020. https://www.ilga-europe.org/resources/news/latest-news/germany-10-years-anti-discrimination

Hervey, Ginger. "When Britain Exits the EU, its Diversity Departs Too: EU Takes 'Color-Blind' Approach While UK Collects Data—and has Strong Anti-Discrimination Laws." *Politico*. Accessed on 15.6.2020 in. January 28, 2018. Accessed June 16, 2020. https://www.politico.eu/article/brexit-diversity-exits-the-eu-brussels/.

Kelly, Kim. "Essential Workers Don't Need our Praise. They Need our Help." *The Washington Post.* April 30, 2020. Accessed June 20, 2020. https://www.washington post.com/outlook/2020/04/30/essential-workers-dont-need-our-praise-they-need-our-help/.

"Miss World will Not Change the World: Priyanka Chopra." *India Today,* December 14, 2009. Accessed June 18, 2020. In https://www.indiatoday.in/miss-world--09/india-miss-world--09/story/miss-world-will-not-change-the-world-priyanka-chopra-62978-2009-12-14.

Mark, Michelle. "Trump just referred to one of his most infamous campaign comments calling Mexicans' rapists'." *Business Insider India,* April 6, 2018. Accessed June 17, 2020. https://www.businessinsider.in/trump-just-referred-to-one-of-his-most-infamous-c.

Molz, Jennie Germann. "Cosmopolitanism and Consumption." In *The Ashgate Research Companion to Cosmopolitanism,* edited by Maria Rovisco et al., 33-52. New York: Routledge, 2016.

Pikaso@pikasotoons. "A Responsible Media. My Cartoon." *Twitter,* April 8, 2020, https://twitter.com/vikasopikaso.

Popova, Maria. "Why We Hurt Each Other: Tolstoy's Letters to Gandhi on Love, Violence, and the Truth of the Human Spirit." *Brainpickings,* August 21, 2018. Accessed June 14, 2020. https://www.brainpickings.org/2014/08/21/leo-t.

"Priyanka Chopra Sorry for *Conde Nast* cover Insulting Refugees." *BBC,* October 17, 2016. Accessed March 27 30, 2020. https://www.bbc.com/news/world-asia-india-37676903.

Rogers, Jon. "Western Begpackers Spark Outrage Across Asia by Rocking up in Poor Countries and Pleading with Locals to Fund Their Travels." *The Sun,* July 5, 2019. Accessed February 15, 2020. https://www.thesun.co.uk/news/944877 2/western-begpackers-bali-begging-money-travel/.

Snauwaert, Dale. "Social Justice and the Philosophical Foundations of Critical Peace Education: Exploring Nussbaum, Sen, and Freire." *Journal of Peace Education* Volume 8, Issue 3(2011): 315-331. https://www.tandfonline.com/doi/abs/10.1080/17400201.2011.621371

The Daily Show with Trevor Noah. "Trevor Responds to Criticism from the French Ambassador- Between the Scenes." July 18, 2018. Accessed July 29, 2019. https://www.youtube.com/watch?v=COD9hcTpGWQ.

"UNICEF's Goodwill Ambassador Priyanka Chopra Shares Photos from Her Recent South Africa Visit," *news18,* May 4, 2017. Accessed June 23, 2020. https://www.news18.com/news/movies/unicefs-goodwill-ambassador-priyanka-chopra-shares-photos-from-her-recent-south-africa-visit-1392033.html.

Wahman, Jessica. "Introduction." In *Cosmopolitanism and Place,* edited by Jessica Wahman, Jose M. Medina and John J. Stuhr Wahman, vi-x. Indiana: Indiana University Press, 2017.

Chapter 14

Chicana Poetry and activism via digital communities in "Poem 25 ~ Giving Voice"

Nicole Crevar

University of Arizona

Abstract

The turbulent sociopolitical climate along the U.S.-Mexico borderland contributes to attacks on Chicanx language and identity. In response, Chicanx artists and activists harness the power of the Internet to form digital communities of resistance. Activism through these communities allows Chicanxs to spread awareness about injustices and to actualize political change in the form of rearticulating their identity and their place in society. Chicana poet and activist Odilia Galván Rodríguez's poem, "Poem 25 ~ Giving Voice," demonstrates how Chicanas extend Gloria Anzaldúa's conception of the politically charged mestiza consciousness into the twenty-first-century terrain of the Internet. As co-founder and contributor of the "Poets Responding to SB 1070" Facebook page, Galván Rodríguez embraces the political potential of social networking sites to disseminate her poetry of resistance. Her poem expresses gratitude for those poet-activists involved in this online digital community who give voice to traditionally marginalized groups. In particular, "Poets Responding to SB 1070" originated in response to police enactment of Arizona Senate Bill 1070, which legitimizes discrimination against Mexican-Americans and immigrants living along the borderland. The poets of this Facebook community work to fight against this racial profiling founded on questioning one's belonging. Aligning with Anzaldúa's definition of the mestiza consciousness, Galván Rodríguez argues for solidarity and education through art as the solutions to combat these human rights violations. These online communities, then, become a new, inclusive digital Main Street for those living along the border to recover their voices and exert their political will.

Keywords: Mestiza consciousness, SB 1070, chicanx, online communities, borders

***

The current, turbulent sociopolitical climate along the U.S.-Mexico borderland contributes to attacks on Chicanx language and identity. In response, Chicana artists and activists harness the power of the Internet to form digital communities of resistance. Activism through these communities allows Chicanas to spread awareness about injustices and to actualize political change in the form of rearticulating their identity and their place in society. Chicana poet and activist Odilia Galván Rodríguez's poem, "Poem 25 ~ Giving Voice,"[1] demonstrates how Chicanas extend Gloria Anzaldúa's conception of the politically charged mestiza consciousness into the twenty-first-century terrain of the Internet. As co-moderator and contributor to the "Poets Responding to SB 1070" Facebook page, Galván Rodríguez mobilizes the political potential of social networking sites to disseminate her poetry of resistance.[2] Her poem expresses gratitude for those poet-activists involved in this digital community who give voice to traditionally marginalized groups, mainly immigrants.

In April 2010, the late Francisco X. Alarcón, Professor at the University of California, Davis, created the "Poets Responding to SB 1070" Facebook page in response to the enactment of Arizona Senate Bill 1070 (SB 1070).[3] He published the first poem on the page, in both Spanish and English, titled "Para Los Nueve del Capitolio / For the 'Capitol Nine.'"[4] This poem recognizes nine Latino Arizona State University students who chained themselves to the Arizona State Capitol building in protest of the proposed bill.[5] SB 1070 legitimized discrimination against Mexican-Americans and immigrants living in the borderlands. This bill encouraged state law enforcement to stop, detain, arrest, and demand proper identification of any individual suspected to be an illegal immigrant.[6] Even legal U.S. citizens who looked "suspicious" or spoke Spanish were subjected to these search procedures. The poets of this Facebook

---

[1]. Odilia Galván Rodríguez, "Poem 25 ~ Giving Voice," self-published on Facebook, April 28, 2011, https://www.facebook.com/notes/poets-responding/poem-25-giving-voice-by-odilia-galv%C3%A1n-rodr%C3%ADguez/200006206702924/. Text references are to line number.

[2]. Poets Responding to SB 1070, "Home," *Facebook*, accessed June 29, 2020, https://www.facebook.com/PoetryOfResistance/.

[3]. Francisco X. Alarcón and Odilia Galván Rodríguez (Eds.), *Poetry of Resistance: Voices for Social Justice* (Tucson: University of Arizona Press, 2016), xiii.

[4]. Alarcón and Galván Rodríguez, *Poetry of Resistance*, xiii.

[5]. Ibid., xiii.

[6]. American Civil Liberties Union, "[Infographic] What's at Stake: SB 1070 at the Supreme Court," accessed January 20, 2018, https://www.aclu.org/issues/immigrants-rights/info graphic-whats-stake-sb-1070-supreme-court?redirect=sb1070-graphic.

community work to fight against this form of racial profiling, founded on questioning one's belonging.

When initially creating the page, Alarcón appointed a team of poets and activists, including Galván Rodríguez, to help moderate posts.[7] In June 2020, the administrative team changed the moderator information to anonymous.[8] The page is a public community, and any Facebook user can "like" the page to follow and comment on its posts; however, only moderators can create content, remove threatening comments, or block users from the page.[9] Because of the public nature of this virtual space, members face the risk of hate trolls responding with the language of violence or reporting suspected noncitizens to U.S. Immigration and Customs Enforcement. The updated anonymity of the moderators reduces the potential threats associated with responding to hate trolls. These threats indicate the community's overlap with the material geopolitical borderland.

Despite these risks, the poet-activists continue to fight, like responders to a crisis, by sharing their poetry of resistance. As a co-moderator and poet of "Poets Responding," Galván Rodríguez's actions align with Anzaldúa's definition of the mestiza consciousness.[10] Galván Rodríguez argues for solidarity and education through art as solutions to combat human rights violations. Her mestiza consciousness poetry advocates building an online community of individuals united in confronting offline injustices. These online communities, then, become a new and inclusive digital Main Street for those living along the border to recover their voices and exert their political will.

Community building as resistance

Borders, as both an ideological and a geographic concept, represent sites of collision and conflict between two or more terrains, identities, and languages.[11] The U.S.-Mexico border proves no exception, as this man-made division remains one of the foremost locations of political violence and resistance

---

[7]. Alarcón and Galván Rodríguez, *Poetry of Resistance*, xiii.

[8]. Poets Responding to SB 1070, "Home."

[9]. Facebook, "What is the Difference Between an Admin and a Moderator in a Facebook Group?," *Facebook*, 2020, https://www.facebook.com/help/901690736606156.

[10]. Gloria Anzaldúa, *Borderlands/La Frontera: The New Mestiza*, 4th ed. (San Francisco: Aunt Lute, 1987).

[11]. Nancy A. Naples, "Presidential Address: Crossing Borders: Community Activism, Globalization, and Social Justice," *Social Problems* 56, no. 1 (February 2009): 2, doi:10.1525/sp. 2009.56.1.2.

throughout North America.[12] The political and cultural violence enacted against those perceived as the "foreign other," however, reinforce dominant Euro-American cultural ideology that indicators of suspicious behavior are one's skin color (i.e., not white) and one's language (i.e., not U.S. English). [13] To combat the barrage of political and social acts of discrimination that make the border an inhospitable zone, Chicanas have developed an identity of resistance through community building. This identity relies on a plural assemblage of individuals asserting their right to be recognized, creating what Hannah Arendt refers to as the "space of appearance."[14] Whereas Arendt believes this space can only exist in the material public sphere, Judith Butler argues in her theory of assembly that when bodies assemble, whether in a physical public space or a virtual one, "the collective actions collect the space itself, gather the pavement, and animate and organize the architecture."[15] The development of this identity tied to assembly undergirds analysis of contemporary Chicanas' migration to digital spaces, such as Facebook, to establish online activist communities.

The community-building aspect of Chicanx identity developed prior to the Internet, during the Chicano Movement in the 1960s and 1970s.[16] The activist-writers of this movement strove to establish a sense of community by rearticulating their place in the United States. Sharing their writing at conferences and national meetings, social spaces that predate Internet platforms, these early activists bolstered ground-level demonstrations. In the political manifesto, "El Plan Espiritual de Aztlán," Chicano poet and activist Alurista evoked the myth of Aztlán, the Aztec mythical homeland of the north that many believe is located in the Southwest United States.[17] Calling upon this cultural heritage, Chicanxs built a sense of community by confirming their ancestral origins in this land. The emerging Chicanx identity thus became what Alurista termed a "force of resistance,"[18] which continues to inform the activist ambitions of contemporary Chicanx writers, such as Galván Rodríguez.

---

[12]. Anzaldúa, *Borderlands*, 25.

[13]. Naples, "Presidential Address," 7.

[14]. Judith Butler, *Notes Toward a Performative Theory of Assembly* (Cambridge: Harvard University Press, 2015), 48.

[15]. Butler, *Notes Toward*, 71.

[16]. Alurista, "Cultural Nationalism and Xicano Literature during the Decade of 1965-1975," *MELUS* 8, no. 2 (Summer 1981): 22, doi:10.2307/467145.

[17]. Roberta Fernández, "*Abriendo Caminos* in the Brotherland: Chicana Writers Respond to the Ideology of Literary Nationalism," *Frontiers: A Journal of Women Studies* 14, no. 2, (1994): 25, doi:10.2307/3346623.

[18]. Alurista, "Cultural Nationalism," 24.

In the late 1980s, Chicana leader and theorist Gloria Anzaldúa furthered this emerging identity by conceptualizing the mestiza consciousness in her foundational text, *Borderlands/La Frontera: The New Mestiza*. Specifically, Anzaldúa gave voice to the gendered realities of mixed-race and queer women living in the borderland.[19] According to Anzaldúa, borders extend beyond the geographic to encompass the inner, ideological borders or restrictions that repress Chicanas into feeling split between two, or more, cultures and value systems.[20] For Chicanas, overcoming this struggle results in a hybridized identity that is malleable and, therefore, resistant to oppressions that attempt to restrict their ethnicity or gender. Confirming the mestiza consciousness as a consciousness of political action, Anzaldúa proposed a vision for Chicanas not just to react, but to act against the social injustices that continue to plague their communities.[21] What remains less well-known in the literature, however, is how Chicanas utilize the mestiza consciousness and take action now, in the twenty-first century.

The dedication to digital communities

Galván Rodríguez's "Poem 25 ~ Giving Voice" evidences a clear response to Anzaldúa's call for action. In 2011, Galván Rodríguez published this poem on the "Poets Responding" community Facebook page to recognize the powerful contributions of the poet-activists protesting an anti-immigration law SB 1070. Galván Rodríguez begins the poem with an epigraph. The poet purposefully dedicates her poem to the poets and activists involved with two specific digital communities: Latinx and Chicanx literary blog, *La Bloga*, and the "Poets Responding" Facebook page. These communities endorse and publicize poetry and news updates in response to human rights violations that occur domestically (the United States) and throughout the world.[22] Considered the world's oldest Chicanx and Latinx literary blog,[23] *La Bloga* partners with "Poets Responding" by publishing selected poems from "Poets Responding" in a monthly "Online Floricanto"[24] on *La Bloga*. Because of *La Bloga*'s prominence as a literary blog, this partnership strengthens the reach of "Poets Responding."[25]

---

19. Anzaldúa, *Borderlands/La Frontera*, 37—45.
20. Ibid., 100.
21. Ibid., 101.
22. Alarcón and Galván Rodríguez, xiv.
23. *La Bloga*, "Homepage," accessed March 24, 2020, https://labloga.blogspot.com/.
24. Michael Sedano, "2017 Best Poems *La Bloga* On-Line Floricanto," *La Bloga*, accessed January 23, 2018, https://labloga.blogspot.com/2018/01/2017-best-poems-la-bloga-on-line.html.
25. Alarcón and Galván Rodríguez, xv.

The concept of floricanto—a term laden with historical significance—also reinforces the collaborative political and literary efforts between these two communities. Denotatively, the Spanish combination of flor y canto translates to flower and song. Etymologically, flor y canto refers to the Nahuatl, or Aztec, word xochicuicatl, which is the phrase for poetry.[26] *La Bloga's* "On-Line Floricanto" was inspired by a three-day, in-person reunion floricanto organized by Michael Sedano at the University of Southern California in Fall 2010.[27] This meeting reunited artists from the original 1973 Festival de Flor y Canto at the same university. The original Flor y Canto celebrated emerging Chicanx artists and writers, including Alurista.[28] Because the in-person Flor y Cantos of 1973 and 2010 relied on a material space, attendees were limited to those in geographic proximity to Southern California or with the means to travel. Sedano adds that because both were live events, only "a tiny representation of artists were invited to read." In contrast, the online Floricantos occupy a digital space that is publicly accessible to anyone, anywhere, with Internet access. The updated one-word spelling of floricanto, with an "i" replacing the "y," reflects the increased inclusivity of access afforded by digital spaces. Regardless of physical or virtual location, these floricantos reveal Chicanxs' collective actions to create a space of appearance. In 2016, Alarcón and Galván Rodríguez acknowledged the need to anthologize a collection of these poems as "a poetic historical record" and published the edited volume, Poetry of Resistance: Voices for Social Justice. [29]

Similar to Alurista adopting the myth of Aztlán for unifying Chicanxs, Galván Rodríguez iterates the importance of an Aztec aesthesis to fuel resistance efforts and to reclaim an identity of belonging in the United States. Reviving the concept of flor y canto, the poet-activists involved in these online communities are practicing what Walter Mignolo and Rolando Vazquez define as "decolonial aesthesis."[30] This term encompasses actions toward healing colonial wounds by unveiling nonwestern aesthetic practices, such as flor y canto, "that have been written out of the canon of modern aesthetics."[31] In "Poem 25 ~ Giving Voice," Galván Rodríguez connotatively defines flor y canto as "poems for

---

[26]. Jackie Cuevas, *Post-Borderlandia: Chicana Literature and Gender Variant Critique* (New Brunswick: Rutgers University Press, 2018), 84.

[27]. Sedano, "2017 Best Poems."

[28]. Ibid.

[29]. Alarcón and Galván Rodríguez, xvi.

[30]. Mignolo, Walter, and Rolando Vazquez, "Decolonial AestheSis: Colonial Wounds/Decolonial Healings," *Social Text,* July 15, 2013, https://socialtextjournal.org/periscope_article/decolonial-aesthesis-colonial-woundsdecolonial-healings/.

[31]. Ibid.

peace" (19) and culminates her poem by declaring that "flor y canto" (21) are the necessary tools to "heal / fear, hatred and yes, to demand / justice" (23—25). Situating poetry as a peaceful apparatus for change, Galván Rodríguez emphasizes the significant role art plays in initiating decolonial healing and advancing the activist agendas of La Bloga and "Poets Responding."

Researchers of social networking sites confirm the unique potential of online communities to advance local, on-the-ground resistance efforts.[32] According to Manuel Castells, a researcher in the field of digital communication, the Internet "provides the essential platform for debate [...] and ultimately serves as their most potent political weapon."[33] Referring to new social movements, Castells argues digital communication through online platforms builds broader networks of social actors and increases the frequency of interaction compared to traditional forms of social organizing.[34] Still, such efforts are rooted in the local. "Poets Responding" provides a prime example of how local resistance efforts have traversed to digital social spaces. Initially formed in reaction to the nine Latino university students who protested SB 1070, the Facebook page was an extension of ground-level political demonstrations. [35] The following year, the "Poets Responding" community organized a symbolic Floricanto rally that included a poetry reading and a press conference at the U.S. Capitol.[36] This live event gathered writers attending the 2011 AWP Conference & Bookfair in Washington, DC.[37] The assembly brought attention to immigration and civil rights issues under review by Congress and state governments. Such demonstrations evidence an online-street connection between virtual and material forms of protest. The momentum generated by these acts of organized civil protest, coupled with the online activism of the "Poets Responding" community, did lead to significant changes to the initial bill.

In 2012, the U.S. Supreme Court weighed in on SB 1070 and reduced the original provisions from four to one.[38] The original provisions included,

---

32. Manuel Castells, "Communication, Power and Counter-Power in the Network Society," *International Journal of Communication* 1 (2007): 250, http://www.ijoc.org/index.php/ijoc/article/view/46/35.

33. Ibid., 250.

34. Ibid.

35. Alarcón and Galván Rodríguez, xiii.

36. Ibid., xiv.

37. Ibid., xiv.

38. American Civil Liberties Union, "[Infographic]."

1. Police demand "papers" and investigate immigration status if they suspect a person is undocumented.

2. Police arrest individuals without a warrant if they believe they are deportable immigrants.

3. Immigrants who fail to carry federal registration papers are guilty of state crime.

4. Immigrants who seek or accept work without authorization are guilty of state crime.[39]

This final ruling upheld Provision 1. The strike down on the other three provisions reinforced that state and local law enforcement were not legally allowed to conduct warrantless arrests to verify a person's citizenship status. This ruling proved a major victory for offline and online protestors alike. Although some argue the difficulty in distinguishing a direct link between the resistance efforts of online communities, such as "Poets Responding," and policy change, researchers Anastasia Kavada[40] and Clay Shirky[41] confirm online activism is a contributing factor.

Shirky asserts social media provide complementary forms of communication to traditional, offline modes of public protest.[42] The organized rally by "Poets Responding" in Washington, DC, exemplifies this assertion. However, to determine the political power of social media, Shirky argues the impact of these tools should be considered in long-term timeframes (e.g., years instead of weeks).[43] The researcher reasons change in society can only occur after "the development of a strong public sphere,"[44] which social media help strengthen over time. Further explaining this point, Shirky references sociologists Elihu Katz and Paul Lazarsfeld's discovery that mass media influence public political opinions through a process of first transmitting a particular political opinion and second having that opinion repeated by family and friends.[45] This latter step reinforces the valuable social aspect of social media. Shirky affirms, "Access

---

[39]. Ibid.

[40]. Anastasia Kavada, "Engagement, Bonding, and Identity Across Multiple Platforms: Avaaz on Facebook, YouTube, and MySpace," *MedieKultur: Journal of Media and Communication Research* 52 (2012): 28, https://doi.org/10.7146/mediekultur.v28i52.5486.

[41]. Clay Shirky, "The Political Power of Social Media: Technology, the Public Sphere, and Political Change," *Foreign Affairs* 90, no. 1 (Jan.-Feb. 2011): 38, Gale.

[42]. Ibid., 29.

[43]. Ibid., 30.

[44]. Ibid., 32.

[45]. Ibid., 34.

to information is far less important, politically than access to conversation."[46] The collaborative partnerships between La Bloga and "Poets Responding" demonstrate these online groups engage in digital democracy by their very nature of facilitating a conversation.

Social media researcher Kavada also explores the crucial link between social networking sites and political activism. Kavada's research informs the analysis of the "Poets Responding" Facebook page because this community specifically functions as a digital social space with the goal of promoting on- and offline political activism. Kavada delineates social media do not only increase opportunities for interaction but also they "build ties of solidarity."[47] In particular, grassroots movements, such as "Poets Responding," harness the community-building potential of social media by providing new "entry points for activism."[48] Such entry points, according to Kavada, become ideal avenues of political participation for individuals with "limited political experience."[49] These individuals include immigrants who fight for their freedom to appear. According to Butler, this freedom is "central to any democratic struggle," and even political actions that occur "from the shadows or the margins,"[50] such as through anonymous Facebook profiles, are still effective. "Poets Responding" and La Bloga, therefore, establish more inclusive ties of solidarity among all individuals, regardless of citizenship status, who are united in confronting social injustices.

Both digital communities, La Bloga and "Poets Responding," are also highly active. *La Bloga*, with a growing list of associated authors including Norma E. Cantú and Ana Castillo, has attained a page view of more than 4.5 million since its inception in 2004, indicating a steady volume of traffic to the blog.[51] Likewise, although "Poets Responding" began in response to SB 1070, its community continues to grow, now ten years later. The Facebook page has more than 12,000 followers engaging with the posts as of June 2020.[52] As these numbers illustrate, the easy and free access to conversations afforded by the Internet[53] enables more individuals to join, and participate in, these communities. Kavada

---

[46]. Ibid., 35.
[47]. Kavada, "Engagement, Bonding, and Identity," 31.
[48]. Ibid., 31.
[49]. Ibid., 31.
[50]. Butler, 55.
[51]. La Bloga, "Homepage."
[52]. Poets Responding to SB 1070, "Community." Facebook, accessed June 29, 2020, https://www.facebook.com/pg/PoetryOfResistance/community/?ref=page_internal.
[53]. Castells, 250.

confirms social media assist activist groups in reaching new audiences by increasing "production, collaboration, and interaction,"[54] which leads to broader political participation. This participation ranges from anonymous actors, such as noncitizen immigrants who may only feel comfortable participating online, to actors who attend the in-person events organized or promoted by "Poets Responding." Although all forms of participation help spread awareness about "Poets Responding" and its mission, it is the poetry that directly engages in digital democracy by challenging the institutional values of society.

The poem

Transitioning from a meta-analysis of the groups to which Galván Rodríguez dedicates her poem, the body of the poem speaks to the harsh reality of life in the borderland. Contextualizing what these poets are responding to allows Galván Rodríguez to both inform readers and to inspire them to act against these injustices. Researcher Arnab Chatterjee explains, "Poetry can always act as a vehicle for protest and change in two ways:" to highlight social injustices and produce alternative directions, or to highlight and challenge previous modes of representation. [55] "Poem 25 ~ Giving Voice" aligns with Chatterjee's two avenues of poetic protest by identifying three groups linked to the issue of immigration along the U.S.-Mexico border: the voiceless immigrants, Chicana artists and activists, and those in the U.S. dominant culture who establish the prevailing modes of representation (e.g., Euro-American white males, the media, and political decision-makers).

Galván Rodríguez draws attention to the violence and oppression along the border by referencing those immigrants who "must hide" (4), who "have no voice," (4) and who "live silently in fear" (9). As SB 1070 exemplifies,[56] U.S. lawmakers and law enforcers attempt to hold power over Chicanas and immigrants by continuing to question their identity and belonging in the country. The demand for papers propagates the restrictive ideology that only those who align with specific racial designations are 'free' from stop and search procedures. Those who are not 'free,' Galván Rodríguez explains, "hide / while being used / by people who speak lies" (6—8). In these lines, "they" likely refers

---

54. Kavada, 28.

55. Arnab Chatterjee, "Poetics as Resistance: Exploring the Selected Poetry of Pablo Neruda and Sachidananda Vatsayayan Ajñeya," *Journal of Comparative Literature and Aesthetics* 39, no. 1-2 (2016): 133, Gale Academic Onefile.

56. American Civil Liberties Union, "[Infographic]."

to those illegal immigrants who are taken advantage of by corrupt politicians and the media—or those who "speak lies" (8)—for personal or political gain.

Throughout history, those who "speak lies" (8) have used immigrants and minorities as scapegoats for the cause of broader social issues.[57] From President Nixon to President Trump, politicians have consistently used fear-mongering tactics, such as the need for stricter border control, to win voter support.[58] Yet this limiting "us vs. them" mentality further perpetuates a national acceptance of discrimination against those voiceless immigrants who, as Galván Rodríguez describes, "work, live silently in fear/waiting" (9—10). Galván Rodríguez is not arguing that these immigrants have no voice, but rather that their cries and protests seem to fall on deaf ears. The recent overcrowding and sanitation crises in U.S. immigration detention centers along the border, for example, present appalling conditions for migrants.[59] Despite the many literal cries by migrants for clean water and sanitary living conditions, let alone the cries from children not to be separated from their parents,[60] the Trump Administration and State politicians have done little to remedy these human rights violations.[61] Therefore, Galván Rodríguez's reference to "those who must hide have no voice" (4) remains applicable ten years later to current social injustices along the border.

Interestingly, Galván Rodríguez adopts a similar "us vs. them" binary rhetoric in her poem, as exemplified through her juxtaposition of "those who must hide" (4) with "those who speak lies" (8). This reductive language demonstrates the poet's attempt to use the colonizer's rhetorical devices as a form of resistance. Again, her tactic does not essentialize that all immigrants are voiceless or that all persons in the dominant culture speak lies. Instead, this reduction adds a dramatic effect to understanding the severity of law enforcement's identity surveillance of the racialized "other." For those whose visibility is a crime, their freedom to appear depends on collective action.[62] Supporting this need for an alliance, Galván Rodríguez writes to dismantle the dominant culture's oppressive social institutions by "giving voice" to the muted realities of

---

[57]. Peter Andreas, Chapter Seven: "Borders Restated," in *Border Games: Policing the U.S.-Mexico Divide*, 2nd ed. (Ithaca: Cornell University Press, 2009), 141.

[58]. Ibid., 141.

[59]. Jim Sergent, Elizabeth Lawrence, Elinor Aspegren, and Olivia Sanchez, "Chilling First-Hand Reports of Migrant Detention Centers Highlight Smell of 'Urine, Feces,' Overcrowded Conditions," *USA Today*, July 17, 2019, https://www.usatoday.com/in-depth/news/politics/elections/2019/07/16/migrant-detention-centers-described-2019-us-government-accounts/1694638001/.

[60]. Sergent, Lawrence, Aspegren, and Sanchez, "Chilling First-Hand Reports."

[61]. National Immigrant Justice Center, "Immigration Detention & Enforcement," last modified 2016, https://www.immigrantjustice.org/issues/immigration-detention-enforcement.

[62]. Butler, 52.

marginalized immigrants at the border. The poet acknowledges all of the poet-activists of La Bloga and "Poets Responding" who, despite the risk of death threats and cyber abuse, also give voice to those who "hide" (6) and feel they have "no voice" (4). Although primarily referring to illegal immigrants, Galván Rodríguez's stress on "those who must hide" (4; emphasis added) extends to legal Mexican-American citizens, as well. As SB 1070 indicates, even legal U.S. citizens who spoke Spanish or looked 'suspicious' (e.g., not white) experience their identity under fierce scrutiny. Therefore, many Chicanas may also feel forced to "live silently in fear" (9) and only speak their native tongue in private spaces.

Galván Rodríguez depicts this attack on language, and therefore on culture and identity, with the image of "slashed tongues" (5). This visual depiction evidences the dominant culture's insistence on maintaining a hegemonic language by restricting languages other than English to the private sphere, behind closed doors.[63] Flores and Yudice explain this struggle over language, stating, "language, then, is the necessary terrain on which Latinos negotiate value and attempt to reshape the institutions through which it is distributed."[64] Galván Rodríguez's image of "slashed tongues" bears a graphic wake-up-call that Chicanas—and by extension all traditionally marginalized groups—need to take back their voices and assert their right to appear in the public sphere. Through a bilingual affirmation, Latinx and Chicanx communities continue to create a space of appearance. Butler confirms these collective actions, which occur in both private and public spheres, represent "a bodily demand" for equality. [65] The Internet represents an advantageous medium for such public dissent because of its ease of use, low cost, instant communication, and accessibility from the private sphere.[66] This increased opportunity for political action, however, remains open to similar threats of violence that occur at the material geopolitical border.

Galván Rodríguez illustrates her political activism against language hegemony by using both English and Spanish in her poem. Her bilingual approach stresses that both languages should be recognized as valid codes of communication in the United States. Galván Rodríguez thus attempts to reshape the more extensive social institutions that value English over Spanish, such as the U.S. education system.[67] However, the poet does not just use

---

[63]. Juan Flores and George Yudice, "Living Borders/Buscando America: Languages of Latino Self-Formation," *Social Text* 24 (1990): 61, doi:10.2307/827827.

[64]. Ibid., 61.

[65]. Butler, 11.

[66]. Castells, 252.

[67]. Anzaldúa, 80—83.

Spanish as a form of resistance. Galván Rodríguez also aspires to educate her readers to learn Spanish by including English translations. In the final stanza, the poet translates the Spanish "poder" to the English "power" (22). These translations emphasize the poet's belief that education and solidarity are necessary tools for society to heal from social injustices and to bring forward "peace" (19).

In the theme of healing, Galván Rodríguez acknowledges the continued efforts of the poet-activists who "dedicate [...] poems for peace" (19) to those "muted voices" (17) who experience discrimination based on their spoken language. The poet indicates the writers in these online communities turn pain into art, "sweet medicine to heal" (23), with the hope of letting those victimized immigrants in their borderland communities know they are not alone. Researcher Nancy Naples asserts that women activists are "especially skillful in building bridges across different issues, diverse communities, and varied political perspectives."[68] Contemporary Chicana poet-activists align with this assertion as they use art to build bridges between diverse groups of individuals who join these online communities. This aspect of bridge-building correlates to Anzaldúa's explanation that Chicanas' role is "to link people with others [...] It is to transfer ideas and information from one culture to another."[69] Galván Rodríguez's poetry and activism validates how Chicanas are extending the mestiza consciousness of political action into the twenty-first-century context by creating digital communities of resistance.

To build bridges despite lack of unanimity, Galván Rodríguez challenges those in the dominant culture to join Chicanas "in solidarity" (14) against social injustices. Galván Rodríguez writes, "who then / will speak for us / when others turn away / who joins in solidarity ~ / speaks up" (11—15). The rhetorical questions in this stanza force readers, particularly those in the dominant culture, to reflect on their own conscious or unconscious biases that have led many to "turn away" (13) from helping others. This direct confrontation of those who turn a blind eye parallels the corruption of those who "speak lies" (8) referenced in the second stanza. Alarcón and Galván Rodríguez further enumerate the importance of solidarity, declaring "Poets Responding" are united by a "commitment to express solidarity" and to "advocate civil and human rights for all."[70] Galván Rodríguez's poem, therefore, aligns with the "Poets Responding" mission as she urges readers to help stop the lies, "unearth/muted voices" (16—17), and "demand/justice" (24—25).

---

68. Naples, 9.
69. Anzaldúa, 106-107.
70. Alarcón and Galván Rodríguez, xiv.

Because the interplay between art and activism within digital spaces increases the accessibility and the reach of their message, the work of these poet-activists has a tangible impact on promoting public policy changes. Specifically, the artist-activists of these communities showcase what Castells believes is the powerful contribution of online social movements—to propagate "purposive collective actions aimed at changing the values and interests institutionalized in society."[71] An example of this collective action appears in the comments on the "Poem 25 ~ Giving Voice" Facebook post. Many commenters of the poem acclaim Galván Rodríguez for her truthful and inspirational rhetoric. Her poem has spurred others to join in the conversation about political injustices, particularly within the U.S. government. One commenter wrote,

> I believe your poem has a great message that most people in this country must listen to and consider. There is a great injustice when our leaders, our civil, elected representatives lie to us. Yet, there is a greater injustice being done if people who have the power to "vote" don't do anything to hold these representatives accountable for their lies. Thanks for sharing this inspiring and well-crafted poem.[72]

This comment reveals how members of "Poets Responding" engage with the poetry, have a voice in the community, and take an active role toward spurring political change. Kavada explains social media promote community building among members because users are active contributors to the conversations and posts, as opposed to mere consumers of content.[73] Through these "spaces of interaction,"[74] the "Poets Responding" community of moderators, writers, and commenters publicly demonstrate their collective actions toward change through political conversation.

By speaking up and challenging the dominant culture to join "in solidarity" (14), Galván Rodríguez writes to rearticulate a new reality in which Chicanas' "demand" (24) that "justice" (25) is heard. The first step in this demand, according to the poem, is to "unearth/muted voices" (16—17). The word choice of "unearth" depicts a digging up, or unburying, of something hidden, ignored, or out-of-view. Through this language, Galván Rodríguez refers to the past and current atrocities that have occurred in the borderland, such as land rights not being honored, and citizenship status being called into question. Because an assimilationist agenda has pervaded the experiences of U.S. immigrants,

---

[71]. Castells, 249.

[72]. Galván Rodríguez.

[73]. Kavada, 31.

[74]. Ibid., 33.

Chicanas have experienced the constant threat of their language and history being erased. To overcome this silencing, Galván Rodríguez urges all who care about human rights to take a stand and "speak out - / loud about injustice" (2—3). The enjambment between lines 2 and 3 strengthens the poet's message. The inserted pause between "out -" and "loud" emphasizes the need for all to not just speak out, but to speak loudly and publicly so that their voices are heard. Compounding Galván Rodríguez's encouragement for public protest, the lack of end punctuation throughout the poem evokes a sense of urgency that the time to act is now.

As part of this urgency to speak out, Galván Rodríguez underscores the importance of education to increase awareness about the harsh reality of life at the border. Galván Rodríguez writes, "teach them new songs to sing" (18), with "them" broadly encompassing Chicanas, those in the dominant U.S. culture, and all minorities who feel oppressed. The poem reflects Galván Rodríguez's view that education is a tool for social justice. Specifically, the poet educates readers about injustices by calling attention to "muted voices" (17) and inspires activism by encouraging solidarity. Galván Rodríguez's mestiza consciousness poetry thus strives to dismantle the larger social institutions that strip Chicanas of their voices. For example, Galván Rodríguez's question, "when others turn away / who joins in solidarity," challenges the reader to determine what kind of person they want to be—one who ignores or one who takes action?

The theme of education in the final stanzas also encompasses the role of art to liberate "muted voices" (17) and to begin the healing process for those who "live silently in fear" (9). From the creation of "new songs" (18), Galván Rodríguez informs that "peace ~ / flowers" (19—20) will follow. Because flowers are a symbol of growth and vitality and because songs are a form of cultural expression, these concepts together—flor y canto—have what the poet sees as the "poder ~ [power]" (22) to inspire the construction of a new, inclusive world for Chicanas.

The Aztec aesthesis of flor y canto represents both a rejection of colonial ideologies that question Chicanxs' belonging and represents how art can heal the broader history of oppression along the U.S.-Mexico border. Galván Rodríguez concludes that education through art provides the means to heal the wounds of injustice, both for Chicanas and for U.S. society as a whole. Galván Rodríguez's "Poem 25 ~ Giving Voice" thus exhibits how Chicanas are healing Anzaldúa's original conception of the borderland as an "open wound."[75]

---

75. Anzaldúa, 25.

Concluding Remarks

Galván Rodríguez's online activism and mestiza consciousness poetry serve as testaments to Chicanas' unwavering ability to assemble and develop communities of resistance. By spreading awareness about injustice and actualizing political change, the artists and activists involved in these digital communities meet Anzaldúa's vision for Chicanas to challenge the oppressions of society and establish a new culture wherein Chicana voices are heard and respected. However, future implications exist for the survival of activist digital communities, such as "Poets Responding." First, in the era of fake news, the moderators of this Facebook page must ensure the community remains a reputable source of information. Spreading false news may threaten the survival of this community, as members may decide to "unfollow" the page. Second, scholars and politicians need to recognize these digital communities as valid, fertile grounds of resistance demonstrations that accompany offline activism. Likewise, the community-published poems should be viewed as legitimate academic texts worthy of study. Still, although this poetry engages in decolonial healing and defies the limitations of capitalistic publishing companies that often exclude minority voices, the potential deletion of "Poets Responding" may lead to the erasure of this poetry. Last, future researchers should continue to investigate the powerful role of social media in broadening resistance agendas—whether through national or global organizing or by establishing public platforms for dissent that lead to real, actionable changes in society.

Bibliography

Alarcón, Francisco X., and Odilia Galván Rodríguez, eds. *Poetry of Resistance: Voices for Social Justice.* Tucson: University of Arizona Press, 2016.

Alurista. "Cultural Nationalism and Xicano Literature during the Decade of 1965-1975." *MELUS* 8, no. 2 (Summer 1981): 22-34. doi:10.2307/467145.

American Civil Liberties Union. "[Infographic] What's at Stake: SB 1070 at the Supreme Court." Accessed January 20, 2018. https://www.aclu.org/issues/immigrants-rights/infographic-whats-stake-sb-1070-supreme-court?redirect=sb1070-graphic.

Andreas, Peter. "Chapter Seven: Borders Restated." In *Border Games: Policing the U.S.-Mexico Divide,* 140-52. Ithaca: Cornell University Press, 2009.

Anzaldúa, Gloria. *Borderlands/La Frontera: The New Mestiza.*San Francisco: Aunt Lute, 1987.

Butler, Judith. *Notes Toward a Performative Theory of Assembly.* Cambridge: Harvard University Press, 2015.

Castells, Manuel. "Communication, Power, and Counter-Power in the Network Society." *International Journal of Communication* 1 (2007): 238-66. http://www.ijoc.org/index.php/ijoc/article/view/46/35.

Chatterjee, Arnab. "Poetics as Resistance: Exploring the Selected Poetry of Pablo Neruda and Sachidananda Vatsayayan Ajñeya." *Journal of Comparative Literature and Aesthetics* 39, no. 1-2 (2016): 133-141.

Cuevas, T. Jackie. *Post-Borderlandia: Chicana Literature and Gender Variant Critique.* New Brunswick: Rutgers University Press, 2018.

Facebook. "What is the Difference Between an Admin and a Moderator in a Facebook Group?." Facebook, 2020, https://www.facebook.com/help/90169 0736606156.

Fernández, Roberta. "Abriendo Caminos in the Brotherland: Chicana Writers Respond to the Ideology of Literary Nationalism." *Frontiers: A Journal of Women Studies* 14, no. 2, (1994): 23-50. doi:10.2307/3346623.

Flores, Juan, and George Yudice. "Living Borders/Buscando America: Languages of Latino Self-Formation." *Social Text* 24 (1990): 57-84. doi:10.2307/827827.

Galván Rodríguez, Odilia. "Poem 25 ~ Giving Voice." Self-published on Facebook, April 28, 2011. https://www.facebook.com/notes/poets-responding/poem-25-giving-voice-by-odilia-galv%C3%A1n-rodr%C3%ADguez/200006206702924/.

"Immigration Detention & Enforcement." National Immigrant Justice Center. Last modified 2016. https://www.immigrantjustice.org/issues/immigration-detention-enforcement.

Kavada, Anastasia. "Engagement, Bonding, and Identity Across Multiple Platforms: Avaaz on Facebook, YouTube, and MySpace." *MedieKultur: Journal of Media and Communication Research* 52 (2012): 28-48. https://doi.org/10.7146/mediekultur. v28i52.5486.

La Bloga. "Homepage." Accessed March 24, 2020. https://labloga.blogspot.com/.

Mignolo, Walter, and Rolando Vazquez. "Decolonial AestheSis: Colonial Wounds/Decolonial Healings." Social Text, July 15, 2013. https://socialtext journal.org/periscope_article/decolonial-aesthesis-colonial-woundsdecolonial-healings/.

Naples, Nancy A. "Presidential Address: Crossing Borders: Community Activism, Globalization, and Social Justice." *Social Problems* 56, no. 1 (February 2009): 2-20. doi:10.1525/sp.2009.56.1.2.

Poets Responding to SB 1070. "Home." Facebook. Accessed June 29, 2020. https://www.facebook.com/PoetryOfResistance/.

Poets Responding to SB 1070. "Community." Facebook. Accessed June 29, 2020. https://www.facebook.com/pg/PoetryOfResistance/community/.

Sedano, Michael. "2017 Best Poems La Bloga On-Line Floricanto." *La Bloga*, January 23, 2018. https://labloga.blogspot.com/2018/01/2017-best-poems-la-bloga-on-line.html.

Sergent, Jim, Elizabeth Lawrence, Elinor Aspegren, and Olivia Sanchez. "Chilling First-Hand Reports of Migrant Detention Centers Highlight Smell of 'Urine, Feces,' Overcrowded Conditions." *USA Today*, July 17, 2019. https://www.usatoday.com/in-depth/news/politics/elections/2019/07/16/migrant-detention-centers-described-2019-us-government-accounts/1694638001/.

Shirky, Clay. "The Political Power of Social Media: Technology, the Public Sphere, and Political Change." *Foreign Affairs* 90, no. 1 (Jan.-Feb. 2011): 28-41.

Chapter 15

Chambal as nomadic in global and local narratives on Putli and Phoolan

Sanghita Sen

University of St. Andrews

Indrani Mukherjee

Jawaharlal Nehru University, India

Abstract

The myth of the Chambal is surrounded by its unholy origin from the blood of thousands of cows sacrificed to appease the gods. It is also a land cursed by Draupadi, the female protagonist of the ancient Indian epic, The Mahabharata. No civilizational forces have been able to overcome the real or imagined fear associated with this wild geophysical spatiality. Yet the Chambal Valley (henceforth the Chambal) has been a site of refuge for the most deprived castes, for victims of social injustices and fugitives of the law. It hence becomes an alternative home to such peoples that the nation-State does not accommodate. Tarun Bhaduri's *Abhishapto Chambal/ The Cursed Chambal* (1960), Galeano's "Phoolan" in *Mirrors* (2009), and Shekhar Kapur's *Bandit Queen* (1995) retell the Chambal valley as a nomadic space traversed by women dacoits. In this essay, we propose to explore the geo-political and eco-sociological logical spatiality of the Chambal, through Deleuze and Guattari's theorization of a nomad space, and Walter Mignolo's agenda of "location" of enunciation, thus de-privileging the human, using the three texts above as case studies. The Chambal thereafter becomes an enabling space of border thinking through and beyond coloniality of power, as the women-dacoits perform embodied counter-narratives here. This counter-narrative dislocates a processual culture of a competitive patriarchal assemblage of sympathetic inclusion by the media, the condescending government institutions, and popular culture. The Chambal valley and its nomad occupants become a perfect example of a Deleuzean War Machine.

Keywords: Caste, Chambal, women dacoits, cursed, border thinking

***

Introduction

We grew up in Bengali middle-class households in the 1980s, hearing stories of the dreaded Chambal Valley being heavily populated by dacoits who proudly called themselves as baghi, literally meaning the rebel. Indian literature and folklore, mainstream Hindi and Bengali cinema, and other forms of popular culture are replete with stories of dacoits of Chambal—while some of them are Robinhood-like figures on the side of the disenfranchised, others are ruthless plunderers creating havoc in adjacent villages. There are innumerable oral recountings of myths based on our epics, especially the Mahabharata. Such myth of the Chambal is surrounded by its unholy origin from the blood of thousands of cows sacrificed to appease the gods. On her way to heaven, Draupadi, the female protagonist of the Mahabharata,[1] cursed the Chambal valley because it was the site where Yudhishthira, the eldest of her five Pandava husbands, wagered her as the stake in a game of dice played against their rival cousins, the Kauravas in which the former lost. This loss led to her public humiliation and molestation in the court. This land was assigned with such ill omen as it belonged to the kingdom of Shakuni—the unscrupulous uncle of the Kauravas and the arch-enemy of the Pandavas—who enticed the royal cousins to the game of dice to strip the Pandavas of their kingdom and to win it for his nephews.

The Chambal remained a space beyond either the State or the nation. No civilizational forces have been able to overcome the real or imagined fear associated with this wild geophysical spatiality. Neither the powerful Mughal Empire nor the British colonial rule could tame this space. As a space left unknown generally by the regular human habitation and contact, it became a safe space for wild animals and birds, which thrived there. The river, after which the valley is named, remained clean and unpolluted for this very reason. The isolation created a sanctuary of crocodiles, gharials, jackals, river dolphins, birds, and wolves. Besides serving as a sanctuary for nonhuman life, the Chambal has also served as a site of refuge for the most deprived castes, for victims of social injustices, and fugitives from the law. Such people found an alternative home outside the society in the valley. However, the understanding of home in the context of this valley is contentious, given its liminality within the nature-society-savage-civilization paradigms of multiplicity. The Chambal valley and its occupants have been mutually comprised as an assemblage in a random possibility of the givenness of its spatiality, which is constantly being

---

[1]. Our *knowledge* of the epic *Mahabharata* comes from oral rituals of story-telling, folklore such as *jatra* (an open air theatre), folk arts and craft, songs and other popular culture such as comics, television and movies.

produced, changed, and dissipated on a plane of immanence or possible lines of flight.

Nomad Space

A nomadic space is characterized by its subversive and disruptive potential to unsettle power and authority, in a relationality of becoming. Deleuze and Guattari describe the nomad space as constituting the War Machine.[2] This idea is based on an insight of nomad intrusions into affairs of the State, where the conceptual pairing of States and War-Machines involves an understanding which is primarily relational and processual, as the State is under constant threat of disruption by the nomads, who are considered as outsiders. In this essay, we propose to explore one such geo-political-socio-ecological spatiality, which is gendered and completely deterritorialized through the transitory occupancy of the Chambal valley by an assemblage of women dacoits and their nonhuman allies of an inhospitable topography - the scrublands, intractable ravines, predatory animals, and inclement weather.

We use Deleuze and Guattari's theorization of nomad space and Walter Mignolo's agenda of location of enunciation as potential lines of flight to explore the Chambal as nomad space comprising the War Machine which contests and combats any submission to grammatical performatives of any State. It is wild, violent, and vastly inhuman in its dimensions and dispositions. Its bodily ravines demonstrate Mignolo's notion of a "brewed spatiality," which is a performative leading to another way of thinking, which he calls "border thinking."[3] Mignolo argues that local histories and global designs have been brewed in a location of power.[4] However, one may recognize that the nature of power also may be nomadic and unstable, given its enabling potential of another thinking. It is as much epistemological as it is ethical. Borrowing from Khatibi, he explains: "it is not inspired in its own limitations and is not intended to dominate and to humiliate; a way of thinking that is universally marginal, fragmentary and unachieved; and, as such, a way of thinking that, is not ethnocidal."[5]

---

[2]. Gilles Deleuze and Félix Guattari, "Treatise on Nomadology-The War Machine," in *A Thousand Plateaus: Capitalism and Schizophrenia*, trans. Brian Massumi (Minneapolis and London: University of Minnesota Press, 2014), 351-423.

[3]. Walter Mignolo. *Local Histories, Global Designs Coloniality, Subaltern Knowledge, and Border Thinking.* (New Jersey: Princeton University Press, 2000), 68-69.

[4]. Ibid., 68-69

[5]. Ibid., 68-69.

Taking cognizance of his argument on alternative thinking, Mignolo also borrows from Enrique Dussel, who explores the potential of another thinking by problematizing modernity itself as pretending to become a rationale of emancipation as it hides a justification for genocidal violence.[6] Another thinking is thus both a proposal of an alternative thinking in its multiplicity and a rebuttal of a rationale of emancipation through the myth of modernity, thus opening up possibilities of new epistemologies of becoming. The woman dacoit of the valley is a unique kind of nomad given her relationships with her 'geophysical-ecological-political' ontologies in terms of her location and her potential to reclaim some agency, hitherto denied, through this nomadic terrain. This means that her possible agency as much as her location-occupation, de-privilege the human spatiality, favoring the nonhuman, History favoring Nomadology. The geophysical and its animal occupants become prominent as her allies in these narratives of the Chambal.

The interspatial cracks seen by Deleuze and Guattari, and Walter Mignolo enable another way of thinking, taking full cognizance of the danger of the contradictions of the above-mentioned paradoxes. As case studies for our essay, we explore how Tarun Bhaduri's book *Abhishapto Chambal/* or The Cursed Chambal (1960), Galeano's vignette on "Phoolan" in Mirrors (2009), and Shekhar Kapur's film *Bandit Queen* (1995) sojourn through a territoriality that evades any affiliations to institutions, borders or programs. Moreover, the river Chambal flowing through the valley across a desert of ravines, constantly changing its course according to the seasons, fits the Deleuzean articulation of a becoming river. As mentioned earlier, the space carries the heavy legacy of myths and histories as well as a presence in time, in a relationality of rhizomatic becoming with every bit of whatever surrounds it, including dust, flora, mud, fauna, dacoits, air, and water in its ecosystem. The rhizomes stretch and connect horizontally through these matters so that the human privilege in the Anthropocene imagination becomes diffused. Consequently, the Chambal stretches beyond its own course and embankments, small villages along its flood plains and beyond; she often swallows up large tracts of paddy fields, leaving behind huge mounds of ravine mud and road track beneath and between them. Entire battalions of police have been known to get lost in these ravines while chasing a dacoit on the run. The dacoits, on the other hand, know every nook and corner of these inhospitable territories like the back of their hands.[7]

---

6. Ibid., 68-69.

7. Tarun Kumar Bhaduri, *Abhishopto Chambal/ The Cursed Chambal* (Kolkata: New Age, 1960), 28-32.

The Chambal and its dacoits always escape any scope of control by the landlords, the tehsildars (revenue officers), or any other forces of the State who seek to domesticate its savage wildness. The nomads (women dacoits) who occupy this space also perform such evasion, thus comprising the spatiality of the landscape in its relationality of becoming.[8] While upper caste male dacoits indulge in caste wars—"by giving a share of the loot to their handlers from the same caste who live in the village so that they protect the dacoits from the police" —A band headed by a woman or by a Muslim man are truly nomadic as ethnicity, cultural identity, caste, and gender are overlooked for them as shown vividly in Kapoor's *Bandit Queen*. As a result, they remain fiercely on their own. The Muslim dacoit becomes an important ally of Phoolan, as portrayed in Kapoor's film. Putlibai or Gauharbano was also a Muslim courtesan who took the name of Putli. She was a very beautiful, slim, and almost petite woman who used to dance at weddings and other social events of the rich and affluent as a notch girl. On one such occasion, the dacoit Sultana kidnapped her so she could perform in his den. Soon after, however, Gauharbano fell in love with him and married him. She became a dacoit and the gang leader of his group after Sultana fell to police bullets. She reigned for six years, from 1950 to 1956, and was the first woman dacoit of independent India. Stories of her inhuman violence and terror continue even today. Yet she was also known for her kindness to the poor and the depraved whom she helped in every way she could.[9]

The rhizomatic links of the Chambal with its landscape and its occupants has been extensively explored here. Bhaduri traces the historical origins of the caste wars, especially between different sub-castes of the Rajput, result of their loss of power due to their defeat by Sher Shah.

[8]. Karen Barad, "Posthumanist Performativity: Toward an Understanding of How Matter Comes to Matter," in *Signs: Journal of Women and Society*, no. 3 (2003): 814.

Appertaining to the de-privileging of the human who fixes stable subjects/objects amidst essential Cartesian perceptions. Relationality is on the contrary, a mode of perception of everything in a dynamic relationship with everything else. Karen Barad refers to a "relational ontology" as the basis of her understanding of posthuman perceptions of material bodies.

[9]. Very little is known about Putlibai. The only photograph available is of her dead body in police records. Bhaduri gives some details of her life throughout the two volumes, *The Cursed Chambal* 2012. Kolkata: New Age, 1960 and *Behar, Bagi, Bandook*. (Kolkata: Anand Publishers, 1991). Besides these, there are two articles on Putali that appeared in *Patrika* and *Jansatta*, two Hindi newspapers, published from Lucknow and Delhi, respectively, that provides some information about her.

See https://www.patrika.com/kanpur-news/story-of-chambal-bandit-queen-putlibai-latest-news-in-hindi-1594731/ and https://www.jansatta.com/crime-news-hindi/story-chambal-bandit-queen-putlibai/806108/.

In this essay, we argue that the inhospitable terrains of the Chambal as nomadic is honed by its occupancy by women dacoits as nomad rebels as much as by the wild animals and plants. A relational ontology of a posthuman performative of material bodies will serve as the trajectory of this endeavor. The Deleuzean becoming-woman and becoming-animal are literally played out here in the Chambal valley. Over time, Putlibai and Phoolan have become synonymous with the untamability and notoriety of the valley, as the heart of darkness of the Indian subcontinent. As we referred to above, this landscape has never been domesticated because the river constantly changes its course as do the ravines and the surrounding landscape.[10] The women-dacoits, who peopled the valley, were socially disadvantaged, domestically and sexually abused, battered occupants of this nomad space. Thus, the image of the so-called "heart of darkness" becomes a possible site of deterritorialization, especially for the Dalit woman as the baghi. This rebel outlaw has taken to the behad. Popular versions, however, submit to the myth of its being an inhospitable and terror-laden space needing modernization and mainstreaming. It is this position that we find in Bhaduri, Kapoor, and Galeano problematized as they work as a counter-narrative, exposing them as sites of ongoing caste and gender struggles shunning domestication and modernization. These texts serve to deterritorialize both the competitive patriarchy of control and power on the one hand and its combative contestations and resistance, on the other. It is in this sense that Bhaduri's Putlibai and Kapoor and Galeano's Phoolan Devi work toward a stuttering/stammering of a performative History towards Nomadology. Bhaduri portrays a vivid description of the Chambal as a raging, vindictive, and violent waterbody.

---

[10]. Sudhir Singh et al., "Socio-Economic Impact of Reclamation of Chambal Ravines Through Afforestation," *Indian Journal of Soil Conservation* 46, no 2 (2018): 225-232, http://indianjournals.com/ijor.aspx?target=ijor:ijsc&type=home.

Tim Sullivan, "Curses Protected Indian River, but Now it Faces Modern World," *AP NEWS*, February 23, 2015, https://apnews.com/18cd00f3950345648c162bd308515ab2

Only recently the Chambal has indeed been taken over by security agencies thanks to google earth maps. The valley is completely sanitized of dacoits as well as of their upper caste handlers living in the villages along the river. Roadways through the valley have brought remote villages within access of communication and surveillance systems. In 1979 the National Chambal Sanctuary was put in place to reclaim vast stretches of wasteland and include it in its state tourism package. This was followed by the state government of Madhya Pradesh' attempt to ravine reclamation projects with World Bank aid in 1980 and under Anti-Dacoity programme during 1988-92. Thereafter in 2007-2008 the Department of Forestry took to afforestation Programmes in the Chambal valley.

The cursed Chambal.

The erstwhile Charmavati has today become the Chambal. It has been flowing away at its own pace since time immemorial, not from north to south, rather from the south to the north. On the western side of MP is Mhow, where the river originates. After that, it gushes down across 300 miles, meandering through Uttar Pradesh and Rajasthan. This sojourn ends at Itawa, Uttar Pradesh, just a few miles further down. She disappears thereafter into the blue waters of the Yamuna.

The wrathful Chambal.

Her thirst is never quenched. Allegedly, her waters used to be red. Many battles were fought on her banks. Chambal's blue waters had become red with blood. Blows of sharp-edged swords had cut off many human heads which had rolled into the river, reddening the waters even more. Yet the Chambal hadn't attained any placidity.[11] (Our translation)

Taking a cue from Deleuze and Guattari's distinctions of smooth-striated and nomad-space, the State works to reclaim terrains by building walls, enclosures, and roads between enclosures. The nomads, on the other hand, do not try to tame the earth; instead, they try to populate its expanse, inserting themselves into the continually shifting nature of the desert, tundra, etc.[12] Nomads, therefore, with their deterritorialization—a result of their destructive and disorganizing effect—undermine and destabilize any domestication by means of the oppressive organizational power of the States. Women dacoits in their entanglements with the Chambal valley thus additionally refuse to submit to the laws and mapped orderliness of dominant narratives. In his book, Bhaduri stretches this occupancy further, through people, animals, objects, and spaces.

She wants more and more blood. In her rage and revenge and in her thirst for blood, the Chambal keeps racing for miles in fire and fury, devouring everything that comes her way. She has dragged, destroyed, drowned, and completely devastated villages and paddy fields on her banks, year after year.[13]

Galeano moves in the reverse gear: locating Phoolan Devi on the tumultuous fringes of the State walls and enclosures, he writes, "Phoolan Devi had the terrible idea to be born poor and female and a member of one of the poorest

---

11. Bhaduri, *Abhishopto Chambal*, 29.
12. Deleuze and Guattari, "A Treatise on Nomadology," 381.
13. Bhaduri 1960, *Chambal*, 29, our translation.

castes of India."[14] This line of the vignette re-digs the nation and the caste out from burdens of significations and controls of a grammar of language to an ungrammaticality of bodily performative or a body affect. "Phoolan had the terrible idea [...]" is ungrammatical just as her choice of caste or status is. However, they are conditions of the materiality of her birthing into a caste and a social status. Thus, what plays out in the vignette is a competing and contesting force of representation (or its crisis, deconstruction) on the one hand and that of the performativity of the material body on the other.[15]

It is the materiality of the body of Phoolan—which gains attention instead— in its relationship with other bodies and non-bodies as an assemblage. Woman, rape, and patriarchy are bodily encounters, which are vertical and continuous formations of an oedipal space that sustain each other, fixing a constant that is patriarchy. Deleuze and Guattari's prescription that all becoming must submit to a becoming-woman is understood as surrendering to other things, both animate and non-animate, implying connections and horizontal rhizomatic networking.[16] Contrary to this suggestion, however, in the present context, Galeano's vignette on Phoolan exposes a blockage of rhizomatic linkages because it re-members a striated space outside any nomad space, as in:

> In 1974, at the age of eleven, her parents married her to a man from a caste not quite as low and gave him a cow for a dowry.
> Since Phoolan knew nothing of conjugal duties, her husband taught her by torture and rape. And when she fled, she went to the police, and the police tortured and raped her. And when she returned to the village, the ox, her ox, was the only one who did not accuse her of being impure.
> And she left. And she met a thief with a long and impressive record. He was the only man who ever asked if she was cold and if she felt alright.
> Her thieving lover was shot down in the village of Behmai, and she was dragged through the streets and tortured and raped by a number of landowners.[17]

Enclosures engineered to sedantarized spaces of caste, home, jail, and panchayat cannot accommodate a subject like Phoolan. The ox and the thief

---

[14]. Eduardo Galeano, *Mirrors: Stories of Almost Everyone*, trans. Mark Fred (London: Portabello, 2009), 317.

[15]. This idea of representation as problematic is borrowed from Barad 2003, "Posthumanist Performativity," 802. She argues about how it implicates a laziness of the unexamined habits of mind that grant language and other forms of representation more power in determining our ontologies than they deserve.

[16]. Deleuze and Guattari, 352.

[17]. Galeano, *Mirrors*, 317.

are Phoolan's partners in crime. The politics of this becoming rests in a critique of the salvation paradigm of coloniality/modernity dualism, which occludes the genocidal side of humanist rationalism as observed by Mignolo.[18] The notion of a bodily encounter fits perfectly with the bodily performatives of Galeano's text on Phoolan Devi's rape by her husband, the police, and upper caste men as an accident or chance at intersectionality, an event potential. A Deleuzean accident is an encounter rather than a representation. Representation can be a laid-back comfort zone of thought. Still, an accident or an encounter is something which is like a violent outside force, pushes us out of a situation of habit towards an exiled and orphaned spatiality of discomfort of thought. This could be a becoming of our thinking as nomad readers, from a passive consumer of texts and images to that of reading itself as a bodily performative in/from another nomad space. The ox and the thief in Galeano's text encounter the striated space of the State to confront an epistemic package of modernity, rationalism, secularism, democracy, thus rendering them also as nomadic.

Nomad space as the loci of enunciation

Borrowing Barad's issue with representationalism as explained above, our attempt at a posthumanist reading is to evoke an awareness of our own entanglements and understanding of everything else into a relationality of becoming. Deleuze and Guattari refer to a nomad space as an assemblage which rests upon a condition of possibility or a plane of immanence, interspersed by lines of flight.[19] It potentiates unmapped spatial dispositions that are open to occupation and extension into any possible outsides or retraction into its insides at random. Likewise, Walter Mignolo's Seeing—as against the colonial blindness of an all-seeing-schizophrenic-subject-centered kind of seeing—bears an important potentiality for participating in a non-Oedipal gendered ontology of becoming. It is a performative act that can negotiate with "seeing" the Chambal Valley as a narrative and practice—in journalism, literature, and film— and as an assemblage, a body without organs. We also use the idea of seeing in the sense of being aware of one's location amidst possibilities of lines of flight, very conscientiously, and very responsibly. Such an act of seeing is aimed at overcoming what Mignolo calls "colonial blindness."[20] Far from being the act of seeing through or staring at—that the

---

[18]. Walter Mignolo, *Local Histories/Global Designs: Coloniality, Subaltern Knowledges and Border Thinking* (Princeton, New Jersey: Princeton University Press, 2000), 12, 68-69.

[19]. For more on this concept see Deleuze and Guattari, *A Thousand Plateaus*, 88-89 and 266-267.

[20]. Mignolo, *Local Histories*, 56-57. This blindness refers to how a brilliant enlightenment thinking may be totally blind to coloniality of power.

gaze of the splintered subject position is privileged with—the act of seeing, in fact, becomes a performative towards decoloniality by aligning with the seeing and the seen while engaging with them. The materiality of the ravines comprised of jagged cuts across striated surfaces, create fractures in the continuous territory, resist human presence, but enable spaces for flow of the nonhuman. This kind of seeing activates delinking, as Mignolo proposes, a paradigmatic shift from the Cartesian subject location towards an epistemological break of geopolitics of location—"I am where I think."[21] This "I" is not an individualized subject of the humanistic tradition, rather a processual one in a relationality of becoming. In the present context, the Chambal is that potential space of processual geopolitics of another thinking, an assemblage.

> Bhaduri speaks from his real sojourns through the Chambal valley, where the immense desolation of the ravines pushes him to think how the Chambal waters produce bravery among its dacoit occupants.
> I have roamed through these terrains many times. Holding my heart held in my hands, I have traversed the territory extensively, miles and miles across, on foot, on my bicycle, on horseback, or in a jeep. I attempted to understand why they become dacoits. How do they become dacoits? I have some answers while I am yet to get some. I don't know what it is about the Chambal's waters, but I have been astounded by the courage of these people. One can't measure their bravery against any criteria of our age-old understanding of civilization. Their courage is their own. It is rooted in their traditional rituals of avenging blood with blood. Murder for revenge is the prime proof of courage in their social set-up. A wailing mother while putting her son to bed, says, "my dear little one, my dear son, grow up boy, grow up big and grow up fast, be tall and strong and avenge your father's death."[22]

Galeano writing Phoolan takes us to another rhizomatic plateau which networks through multiple cultures, the Latin American and the Indian, among many others. La Malinche, Penelope, Cleopatra, Hypatia, Phoolan, and many other power women find a space in his writings. Although there are two different kinds of postcolonialities in Galeano's narrative appertaining to India and Latin America—a post-enlightenment northern and a post-renaissance Iberian respectively—an interesting issue plays out in this nomad space: an-Other postcoloniality. It is possible to posit this third postcoloniality with reference to Soja's notion of the Third Space. This third space is a hybridized

---

21. Ibid., 89.
22. Bhaduri, 32, our translation.

spatiality comprising of an-Other conception of spatiality cutting across binary oppositions and inclusive of Lefebvre's social space, Foucauldian Heterotopia, and bell hooks' margins as open space.[23] These are real and performative spaces that produce "what may at best be called a cumulative trialectics that is radically open to additional otherness to a continuing expansion of spatial knowledge."[24] Ghost of the Malinche, the Virgin Guadalupe—the goddess, and the conquistadores stain Galeano's force of the encounter with Phoolan. In the case of Phoolan, the father, the husband, and the several men of upper caste 'map' an old legacy of becoming through a political takeover of her body. While upper caste women were domesticated into a private space, Dalit women were increasingly subject to cultural and sexual violence. The situation has not changed much, even in contemporary times. For example, popular responses to women's education, affirmative action for the Dalit, and inter-caste marriages have exposed the threat that upper caste men feel with respect to their privileges of control of land through control of the Dalit bodies. No amount of punitive action seems to be able to stop the spate of gang rapes and other heinous acts of violence against women in general and the Dalit woman in particular. Galeano has to wriggle himself out of any 'Orientalist' culpability, while also pushing himself out of any prescribed academic blame game suggested by the notion of "official dissent" that Nandy has articulated:

> Today, when 'Westernization' has become a pejorative word, there have reappeared on the stage subtler and more sophisticated means of acculturation. They produce not merely models of conformity but also models of 'official' dissent. It is possible today to be anti-colonial in a way that is specified and promoted by the modern world view as 'Proper,' 'sane' and 'rational.' Even when in opposition, that dissent remains predictable and controlled. It is also possible today to opt for a non-West, which itself is a construction of the West.[25]

Galeano traverses the brink of nomad space to contest and expose the designs of patriarchal discourse in India as he reckons with official discourses of permissible dissent and also negotiates with his own western-ness. Elsewhere, he has written about the caste system in India, about female feticides, and the practices of Sati.[26] Through such a cliff walk, he argues that while Phoolan's perpetrators think that they are just making her, they are also

---

23. Edward Soja, *Third Space: Journeys to Los Angeles and other real and imagined spaces* (Oxford: Blackwell, 1996).
24. Ibid., 61.
25. Nandy, *The Intimate Enemy*, 11.
26. "Origin of the Division of Labor" and "Hindus," in Galeano 2009, *Mirrors*, 8 and 34.

making themselves into a rhizomatic phobia by blotching her map. Removing her body effects from the burdens of language, family, and the nation of 'salvation,' untying herself from her makers, enabling the rhizomatic blockages to breathe again and "re-territorialize" as possible lines of flight led towards nomadic becoming. The salvation paradigm of the colonial humanist tradition is hijacked and deployed by nationalist discourse in postcolonial contexts, which we address below.[27] Galeano's forces out the centered root-tree as structured power towards a de-centered system of horizontal transduction. The fact that only Phoolan's ox and her thieving lover did not behave like tree-subjects is a case in point. Here India becomes the tree, deeply centered, hierarchical, and upright/vertical while Galeano's force becomes the eastern steppes or gardens or the oasis, and the desert, that is, smooth space. Deleuze and Guattari's argument of kinship practices, which are sustained by alliances of the male members is constitutive of micro-fascistic rhizomes that shape political discourse in the Indian context of patriarchy that we engage within this essay.[28]

Spaces and bodies of humans, animals, and objects in the smooth and striated spaces of the Chambal are more open to rhizomatic visibility in *Bandit Queen* compared to either Bhaduri or Galeano's printed text, by virtue of the moving image's mimetic capacity, the potential of enactment, and enabling a process of witnessing subsequently.[29] Cinema in general and this film, in particular, uses both movement and time images so that the viewer also becomes a mutually intertwined mirror of events in the film and the movie screen in a "free indirect discourse" (FID).[30] FID materializes in cinema when the viewer is unable to differentiate between characterological subjectivity and narratorial objectivity. This creates the polyvocality or polyphonic character in narrative cinema, paving the way for aesthetic ambiguity and trigger 'différance' and 'deterritorialization.' Language separates the human from other creatures and things. Still, the film performs a presence, enabled by an assemblage of the spectatorial 'we' and the represented 'they' in a slice of

---

[27]. Rajeswari Sunder Rajan, "Outlaw Woman: The Politics of Phoolan Devi's Surrender, 1983," *The Scandal of the State: Women, Law and Citizenship in Postcolonial India* (Durham, NC and London: Duke UP, 2003) 212-35.

[28]. Timothy Laurie, "Epistemology as Politics and the Double-bind of Border Thinking: Lévi-Strauss, Deleuze and Guattari, Mignolo," *PORTAL Journal of Multidisciplinary International Studies* 9, no. 2 (July 2012), 8.

[29]. Leshu Torchin, *Creating the Witness: Documenting Genocide on Film, Video, and the Internet* (Minneapolis: University of Minnesota Press, 2012), 10.

[30]. Giles Deleuze, *Cinema 1: The Movement Image*, trans. Hugh Tomlinson and Barbara Habberjam (Minneapolis: University of Minnesota Press, 1986), 72.

time/movement image with its fleeting past and an event potential future. For example, in Kapoor's *Bandit Queen*, the Chambal valley is 'seen' —and shown— from an aerial bird-view camera angle depicting the depths of the bottom of the mud hills of the ravine by a long shot. Its rugged beauty and vastness are exposed, in an unimaginable expanse of the unfertile desert-like landscape through which the river gushes in unforeseen stormy turbulence, or becomes uncanny in its sleepy calmness, blending with the color of the muddy valley. From a spectatorial position, the long aerial shots render overwhelmingly immersive affective contexts to transform the audience into becoming the mirror of the screen, oblivious of the violence that the space hosts or the ones that the screen would soon unfold.[31] Kapoor's Chambal—depicted through such long shots of the valley and its violent inhabitants—brings to the fore our own locations in the text as colored bodies also claiming a presence in the nomadism of the Chambal valley. Kapoor himself appears briefly with a grin on his face as a truck driver who is about to be looted by Phoolan and her gang. Thus, Bhaduri and Kapoor stare out of their own narratives through the mirror of our minds, like Velazquez' Las Meninas.[32]

The loci of enunciation in texts of Bhaduri, Kapoor, and Galeano are re-territorialized in local and global nomad spaces embedded in the wilderness of the Chambal ravines; the authors' engagements with either of the dacoits are fraught with risks as they also work as stone cutters who carve out material stone irrespective of an approved engineer's blueprint, that is in a randomness of figurations.[33] It is anarchy directed against the smooth flow of power through spaces of docile regulated and governed bodies. They are nomad workers who

---

[31]. The 2019 film *Sonchiriya/ The Golden Bird* (directed by Abhishek Chaubey) depicting the Chambal and its dacoits of the 60's, however, fails to capture the temporal context as the ravines and the riverbank are completely green in this film. The river water is so transparent and calm that a gharial which attempts to eat off a girl's hand hanging out of a boat is highly visible as it swims through in stealth towards the boat and then swims away. This is the result of a Chambal valley which has been completely taken over by the State through afforestation programs supported by international monetary bodies since the 1990's, as mentioned earlier. However, the biopic, *Paan Singh Tomar* (directed by Tigmanshu Dhulia, 2012)—based on the life of an Indian athlete and a soldier of the Indian Army who by turning into a baghi went into the Chambal to fight against the formidable feudal system—depicts the Chambal in its untamed and unknowable territoriality similar to *The Bandit Queen*, as a nomad space, and becoming to the subalterns.

[32]. Foucault's reading of Las Meninas in *The Order of Things: An Archeology of the Human Sciences*. London and New York: Routledge

[33]. Delueze and Guatarri, 352-353.

Delueze and Guattari provide example of the game of Go as a contrast to chess.

enable a retelling of Putlibai and Phoolan Devi across multiple postcolonialities to propose a subaltern becoming between different worlds of border thinking while potentiating a possible south-south dialogue, rendering exposed cultures of nomadic deterritorializations as a spatiality of violent event-potentialities hidden under heterotopias of normative paradigms of postcolonial law and orderly societies.

Thus Bhaduri, Kapoor, and Galeano talking about Putlibai and Phoolan are not falling into the trap of any potential danger of authority while speaking on cultural others. It is possible to read this talking as articulations of' border thinking,' which reinstates the scope of retelling and theorizing from the outside of coloniality of power.[34] Such recounting highlights colonial-patriarchal blindness of privileging either writing or history as measures of civilization, a kind of phallogocentrism. This is so because both writing and history, have been known to belong to the Weberian arrogance of flaunting writing of history as a justification for colonization.[35]

The warring machine

Before inhabiting the Chambal valley, both Putlibai and Phoolan Devi were subject to repeated brutal cultural, domestic, and sexual violence. The Chambal river valley becomes a potentially enabling space as it became occupied by the nomadic baghis, who also redeem the river of its accursed terrritoriality. When the security forces poison the water of the river to force her to surrender, she still hopes that the womb of the Chambal would protect her. This is a classic example of the nomadic subjectivity, which is ontologically non-humanist, and "a subjectless individuation that constitute collective assemblages."[36]

Bahaduri's Putli and Kapur and Galeano's Phoolan translate their bodies in the Chambal valley as event potentials of violence. Phoolan's surrender was a result of a staging by competing patriarchal units like political parties, the police, and the media. That she surrendered before thousands of onlookers and television spectators as well as before the image of Durga and Gandhi is emblematic of the nationalist salvation paradigm as she moved from one kind of patriarchy—feudalism—to another one, the nation-State, packaged as modern, democratic and inclusive. Putli, however, was shot dead and mostly forgotten, though the myths of terror built around her survived. Women dacoits are never remembered as Phoolan has been, precisely because they were never

---

34. Mignolo, 64-71
35. Ibid., 4-5
36. Deleuze and Guattari, 266.

salvaged by the State. Mignolo's critique of the salvation paradigm in a politics of coloniality of power is significant in the present context of a staged surrender. Galeano had written his piece before this surrender happened, and expectedly this story of surrender does not occur in his text. However, Kapoor shows this surrender in an amazing voice-over of Phoolan Devi, while she is struck mute by the visual evidence of her overwhelming fame and acceptance by a huge crowd of spectators. The attempt of hijacking the War Machine for its own use involves both the stuttering/stammering of a culture of sympathetic inclusion by the media and condescending government institutions as well as spectacularizing the subjugation of the rebellious other as content for mediatization and fodder for popular culture. In all these retellings, the forbidden, the foreboding, and the formidable entailed a rhizomatic linkage with an arrogant, misogynist, and gynophobic patriarchy that imagines itself to be the rightful "saviors" of the unknown and potentially dangerous subjects.

Ghosts of competitive patriarchy remain pervasive in all these narratives, locally and globally, within the striated realm of the State. Thus, the Malinche's negotiation with Cortes before setting out for the Honduran conquest assured her of "salvaging" her dignity and legitimacy through marriage to Alonso Jaramillo.[37] Likewise, Phoolan's surrender—stage-managed by different political parties keen to claim responsibility for her "salvation" into Indian politics—delivered her into her "own saving." She did not trust the Uttar Pradesh Government and hence wanted to surrender to the Madhya Pradesh police. Different political parties wanted to become visible through the light of her salvaging. V.P Singh, the chief minister of the State, had to resign, as there was friction between UP Police and MP Police. Competitive patriarchy had been at its prime manifestation in this surrender in postcolonial India. It packaged how an illiterate, lower caste, untouchable third-world female subjectivity is produced for "consumption" by a national and a globally wired readership/spectatorship.[38]

What we illustrated in this essay so far involves potential alliances of nomad interests or what Deleuze and Guattari call the War Machine with gendered sexuality, caste, nation, and class enclosures of the State apparatus. Bhaduri, Kapoor, and Galeano, in this sense, have taken to the Behad, as the saying goes, without becoming dacoits, but from a position of empathy as they simultaneously uncover the weird situation of the War Machine and the patronizing salvaging missionary zeal of the State. The War Machine is a

---

[37]. Camilla Townsend, *Malintzin's Choices: An Indian Woman in the Conquest of Mexico (Diálogos)* (Albuquerque: University of New Mexico Press, 2006), 152-156.
[38]. Anuradha Ramanujan, "The Subaltern, The Text and The Critic: Reading Phoolan Devi," *Journal of Postcolonial Writing* 44, no.4 (2008): 367-378.

nomadic assemblage, a result of creative minds, that is designed to fight with clandestine and surprise attacks as opposed to organized, hierarchical, and a trained and weaponized State. There are no ranks and files in the War Machine as they flow through breaking grounds in innovative ways without "conquering" them by names, flags, or any other labels. They operate through an organizational tension rather than any ideological or moral outlook. Hence, they resort to stealth, secrecy, and cunning. Unlike the striated space of the former, the nomadic Chambal leaves no references of landmark or address or any paper maps. It is cartography that carries on its performativity in the nomadic memories of its occupants that is human and the nonhuman, women, eco-geography, animals, water, and mud.

Bibliography

Barad, Karen. "Posthumanist Performativity: Toward an Understanding of How Matter Comes to Matter." *Signs Journal of Women and Soci*ety (3) (2003): 801-832.

Bhaduri, Tarun Kumar. *Abhishopto Chambal.* Kolkata: New Age, 1960.

Deleuze Gilles, and Félix Guattari. *A Thousand Plateaus: Capitalism and Schizophrenia*, translated by Brian Massumi. Minneapolis and London: University of Minnesota Press, 1987.

Devi, Phoolan, with Marie-Therese Cuny and Paul Rambali. *I, Phoolan Devi.* London: Brown and Company, 1996.

Foucault. "Las Meninas." In *The Order of Things: The Archeology of the Human Sciences*, 3-18. New York and London: Routledge, 1970.

Galeano, Eduardo. *Mirrors: Stories of Amost Everyone*, translated by Mark Fred. London: Portabello, 2009.

Kapoor, Shekhar, director. *Bandit Queen.* Kaleidoscope for Channel Four, 2004.

Laurie, Timothy Nicholas. "Epistemology as Politics and the Double-bind of Border Thinking: Lévi-Strauss, Deleuze and Guattari, Mignolo." *PORTAL Journal of Multidisciplinary International Studies* vol. 9, no. 2, July (2012): 1-20.

Lorraine, Tasmin. *Deleuze and Guattari's Immanent Ethics: Theory, Subjectivity, and Duration.* New York: State University of New York Press, 2011.

Mignolo, Walter. "Delinking: The Rhetoric of Modernity, the Logic of Coloniality and the Grammar of De-Coloniality." *Cultural Studies* 21 (2-3) (2007): 449-514.

Mignolo, Walter. *Local Histories/Global Designs: Coloniality, Subaltern Knowledges and Border Thinking.* Princeton, New Jersey: Princeton University Press, 2000.

Nandy, Ashish. *The Intimate Enemy.* New Delhi: Oxford University Press, 1983.

Puar, Jasbir. "I Would Rather be a Cyborg than a goddess." *philoSOPHIA: A Journal of Continental Feminism* 2 (1) (2012): 49-66.

Puar, Jasbir. *Terrorist Assemblage: Homonationalism in Queer Times.* Durham and London: Duke University Press, 2007.

Ramanujan, Anuradha. "The subaltern, the Text and the Critic: Reading Phoolan Devi." *Journal of Postcolonial Writing* 44 (4) (2008): 367-378.

Singh, Sudhir, Y.P. Singh, R.B. Sinha, A.K. Singh, S.K. Dubey and G.P. Verma. "Socio-economic impact of reclamation of Chambal ravines through anicuts and afforestation." *Indian Journal of Soil Conservation* 46 (2) (2018): 225-232. http://indianjournals.com/ijor.aspx?target=ijor:ijsc&type=home.

Soja, Edward. *Third Space: Journeys to Los Angeles and Other Real and Imagined Spaces*. Oxford: Blackwell, 1996.

Sullivan, Tim. "Curses Protected Indian River, but Now it Faces Modern World." *AP NEWS*, February 23, 2015. https://apnews.com/18cd00f3950345648c162bd3085 15ab2.

Torchin, Leshu. *Creating the Witness: Documenting Genocide on Film, Video, and the Internet*. Minneapolis: University of Minnesota Press, 2012.

Townsend, Camilla. *Malintzin's Choices: An Indian Woman in the Conquest of Mexico (Diálogos)*. University of New Mexico Press: 2006.

Afterword:
Nomadic theory, again?

Didier Coste

Université Bordeaux-Montaigne, France

I return to a critique of Deleuze and Guattari in my provisional conclusions, and investigating the positions of Luce Irigaray and other post-Deleuzian feminist thinkers, such as Rosi Braidotti, I try to outline how a more rigorous, anthropologically, and historically informed approach to senti/mental and spatial human mobilities, whether individual or collective, could be methodologically fruitful and designed to circumvent the traps of various postisms as well as the paradoxes of a universal anti-universalism.

It would be a daunting and an unfair task to try to summarize Deleuze and Guattari's massive but "molecular" *A Thousand Plateaus* (thereafter *ThP*). But, although it was published after the revival of multiple notions of mobility, *dérive*, interminable interpretation, infinite semiosis, and questioning of identities between the rise of existentialism and the aftermath of the 1968 insurrectional moment, this book and its "nomadology" mark a turning point in postmodern western thought and remains influential in certain feminist and postcolonial circles as well as in experimental, late avant-garde aesthetic creation and theory. I will therefore limit myself here to collecting some significant occurrences of the [nomad] signifier in this work and clarifying to what strains of thought it is associated, thus trying to sketch the dynamics of its uses in context. After this, I will briefly compare this process with some later manifestos of mobility.

Mappamundi of A Thousand Plateaus

Let us note first that "nomadism" is initially associated with "rhizomatic" and that the old East-West dualism is still convoked to oppose the sexed verticality of trees and seed plants (the West) to the non-sexed horizontality of horticultural cloning (the East) or the steppe. This other form of orientalism, a priori anti-West, divides in two a world limited to Eurasia, and, if one thinks of the diversity of South Asia, for example, it is impossible to understand where the limit between East and West has ever run. From the start, it would be preferable to accept that if "it is true that the nomads have no history; they only have a geography,"[1] their "smooth," "non-striated" space cannot be mapped or located on any existent panoptic mapamundi. It is also clear that, if the authors repeatedly evoke early Mesopotamia, the Huns, the Great Invasions, the successive Chinese Empires, etc., not 'having' a history cannot mean that the nomads are not locatable in History, from outside their culture, but maybe that their perception of themselves is a-historical, or at least that their temporality is non-linear. The choice of composing a "non-molar" book, a quasi-non-book made of chapters referring to/dated from non-sequential and dis-located historical moments, purports to be an application to the flesh of discourse of a spatio-temporality proper to "nomadic thought." However, the dating and locating themselves are foreign to nomadic consciousness as represented by the authors, and the nomads find themselves doubly othered once again, by their figural use and by their location outside the discursive apparatus and global knowledge mastered/wielded by the book. We can see that it is not any easier for a philosopher and a psychoanalyst of the late 20th century to leave the "old man" behind when 'traveling to the other side,' as Le Clézio would put it than it was for Victor Segalen or Isabelle Eberhardt at the turn of the century.

Secondly, the key symbolic object in Deleuze and Guattari's nomadology is the "war machine". The war machine is that nomad invention that, in fact, has war not as its primary object but as its second-order, supplementary, or synthetic objective, in the sense that it is determined in such a way as to destroy the State-form and city-form with which it collides. [...] When the State appropriates the war machine, the latter obviously changes in nature and function, since it is afterward directed against the nomad and all State destroyers, or else expresses relations between States [...][2]

Anthropologists tell us that "absence of war has been reported for quite a few small bands of nomadic hunter-gatherers living at very low population densities, [...] with few or no possessions worth defending or acquiring, and relatively isolated from other such bands."[3] However, the invention of the war machine is "assigned" to "the nomads" "only in the historical interest of demonstrating that the war machine as such was invented [...]"[4] It is not easy to pinpoint what the war machine "as such" can be unless it is not understood as a material artifact (pictured as a wooden chariot) but as an agonistic function of

---

[1]. Gilles Deleuze and Félix Guattari, *A Thousand Plateaus*, trans. Brian Massumi (Minneapolis: University of Minnesota Press, 1987), 393.

[2]. Ibid., 418.

[3]. Jared Diamond, *The World until Yesterday: What Can We Learn From Traditional Societies?* (New York: Viking, 2012), 276.

[4]. Deleuze and Guattari, *A Thousand*, 422.

nomad life (nomad thought) itself, and unless "historical" means an actual event, without implying precedence: "the nomads do not precede the sedentaries; rather, nomadism is a movement, a becoming that affects sedentaries, just as sedentarization is a stoppage that settles the nomads."[5] Furthermore

> The nomad exists only in becoming and in interaction; the same goes for the primitive. All history does is to translate a coexistence of becomings into a succession. And collectivities can be transhumant, semisedentary, sedentary, or nomadic, without by the same token being preparatory stages for the State, which is already there, elsewhere or beside.[6]

As movement (as such) becomes the criterion for becoming, which is true exsistence (while the State *is* in its striated space and *is it*, a hierarchized space with formal boundaries, a fortress), additional differentiations are needed, such as the ones above, or those between nomads proper and migrants, or barbarian invaders, or yet, among the sedentary, the inhabitants of the fortress and the peasants around. One might think that, with all this fragmentation, the war machine of the now minoritarian nomads ('now' in the logical rather than historical process) loses its efficiency and is bound to be appropriated and turned inside out by the State, but it is not so according to the figural strategy of *ThP.*

> Being "between" also means that smooth space is controlled by [...] two flanks, which limit it, oppose its development, and assign it as much as possible a communicational role; or, on the contrary, it means that it turns against them, [...] affirming a noncommunicating force or a force of divergence like a "wedge" digging in.[7]

This strategy, projected on a (non-sequential) history of the nomads, is very similar to the position of some radical left intellectual groups in Europe from the 1950s to the 1970s, among them Guy Debord's Situationism.

Thirdly —it is striking—, the discriminating factors between individuals, such as gender, sexuality, education, skills, age, and/or between groups of all sorts, such as language(s), modes of solidarity or dependence, collective world views, are largely absent from *ThP.* Undercover of a nomadic model opposed to sedentariness, the kind of liberation/emancipation that was already invented in the 1960s and 70s by Herbert Marcuse, Monique Wittig, and others, and whose roots could also be found in some "non-western" philosophies (Tagore), is not

---

5. Ibid., 430.
6. Ibid., 430-431.
7. Ibid., 384.

explicitly considered. A desirable "becoming-woman," or better "becoming-girl", is presented as having its primary locus in writing:

> Writing should produce a becoming-woman as atoms of womanhood capable of crossing and impregnating an entire social field, and of contaminating men, of sweeping them up in that becoming. Very soft particles—but also very hard and obstinate, irreducible, indomitable.[8]

ThP describes an effective queering of this kind, "sparing no man," in the modern English novel, due to "the rise of women" in this genre, but it does not investigate the conditions, far from "nomadic," that made this rise possible as early as the first half of the 19th century (the Brontes, Jane Austen, George Eliot). The various becomings are all becoming-minoritarians (i.e., non-dominant), so that, insofar as nomads "die" when they conquer, a becoming-nomad would be the most general theoretical model for other becomings, further reducing the specificity of gender difference that "Deleuze and Guattari do not go very far in mapping."[9]

Finally, with all the good-will shown to revive, philosophically and politically, the myths or mirages of nomadism and turn them into a progressive war machine, we are sadly obliged to conclude that high *metaphoricity* and high abstraction nourish each other to the point of fabricating magic oxymorons that have little more impact on the ethics of thought than that of poetic bewilderment:

> But nothing completely coincides, and everything intermingles or crosses over. This is because the differences are not objective: it is possible to live striated on the deserts, steppes, or seas; it is possible to live smooth even in the cities [...]We can say of the nomads [...] they do not move. They are nomads by dint of not moving, not migrating, of holding a smooth space that they refuse to leave [...]. Voyage in place: that is the name of all intensities, even if they also develop in extension. To think is to voyage.[10]

It is certainly reassuring that you don't need to drive all along US Route 66, or do whoring and binge drinking in Mexico like Kerouac or the criminal tramps of *In Cold Blood*, or do drugs in Goa or young boys in Tangiers to "become-nomad." However, we would love to associate *real*, not just imaginary/intellectual mobilities to a program of divergence (as *ThP* puts it) or dissidence, a program of

---

[8]. Ibid., 276.

[9]. Tasmin Lorraine, *Deleuze and Guattari's Immanent Ethics* (Albany: Suny Press, 2011), 184.

[10]. Deleuze and Guattari, *A Thousand*, 482.

discovery far from the well-trodden circular tracks of labor and consumption, obedience and authority, difference and reproduction.

Nomadology after Deleuze and Guattari

If the figure of the nomad is to help to break fences or to prevent their erection, impeding foreclosure, relaxing the rigidity of desiccated concepts and categories, serving creative differentiation, (re-)inventing a non-possessive, non-destructive *jouissance*, a few questions should become answerable (or reformulatable) that have been kept at bay so far, below the horizon of the metaphor. At least these two questions:

- How can we "mobilize" the other's mobility, or produce "one's own" mobility through otherness(es) without appropriating, enslaving, essentializing mobility?
- How can we live and enjoy differentiation, or even let non-sameness, non-repetition *happen*, if we posit that difference is always already there?

Luce Irigaray, philosopher, linguist, psychoanalyst, feminist, and, finally, adept at the practice and theory of yoga, is one thinker of the same generation as Deleuze and Guattari, but still alive and whose writings have both co-existed with theirs and developed later in somewhat unexpected directions. Turning to her at any moment of her work can be disconcerting in our perspective. On the one hand, gender difference (not differentiation, or becoming) is the foundation of all relatedness, a woman is always already a woman, and a woman should not be seduced, diverted outside herself, from her womanhood, a normative view that has often been criticized as essentialist:

> Exiled from yourself, you fuse with everything you meet. You imitate whatever comes close. You become whatever touches you. In your eagerness to find yourself again, you move indefinitely far from yourself. From me. Taking one model after another, passing from master to master, changing face, form, and language with each new power that dominates you.[11]

Without naming it, in the guise of autonomy and self-protection, there is an underlying implication of authenticity, of an inherent identity (both as sameness to the same and as ipseity) to be preserved from the risk of an outside: "There is no need for an outside; the other already affects you. It is

---

[11]. Luce Irigaray, *An Ethics of Sexual Difference*, trans. Carolyn Burke and Gillian C. Gill. Ithaca (NY: Cornell U. P., 1993), 210.

inseparable from you."[12] Alison Stone observes that, if we follow Irigaray, "women should not pursue the expression of any forces or capacities which might conflict with those which constitute them as women."[13] On the other hand, constant moving, especially in discourse, speaking lips to lips, is a requirement to "embrace oneself."

> It's not that we have a territory of our own, but their fatherland, family, home, discourse imprison us in enclosed spaces where we cannot keep on moving, living, as ourselves. Their properties are our exile. Their enclosures, the death of our love. Their words, the gag upon our lips. How can we speak so as to escape from their compartments, their schemas, their distinctions, and oppositions? [...] You know that we are never completed, but that we only embrace ourselves whole.[14]

Not a territory? But mobility restricted to the limits of the Deleuzian smooth space, supposing that such a space has ever existed, can never exist unspoiled by its others, happily spoilt by its non-dwellers, non-owners only. Is this why, besides the pressing appeal for/to a woman language, Luce Irigaray manifests some nostalgia for figures of communication between fixed, hieratic, static entities above (a God, the Gods) and people below arrested in the economy of their social roles? They could be angels, or Iris, the other messenger of the Gods, male or female. Supposing that the mobility of womankind is of the same type as that of the nomads, its timelessness, its "immemoriality" (a constant feature from Loti to Duras[15] and Le Clézio through Lemonnier[16] and many others), would entail a mechanism of repetition that would probably be no better than the corseting of invention and (re)creation by the imperative of reproductive sexuality. Some other figures (not to be found in the real) would be needed to restart time:

> Angels would circulate as mediators of that which has not yet happened, of what is still going to happen, of what is on the horizon. Endlessly reopening the enclosure of the universe, of universes, identities, the unfolding of actions, of history. They are not unrelated to sex.[17]

---

12. Ibid., 211.
13. Alicia Stone, *Luce Irigaray and the Philosophy of Sexual Difference* (Cambridge: Cambridge University Press, 2006), 216.
14. Irigaray, *An Ethics*, 212.
15. See Marguerite Duras, *The Vice Consul*. New York: Pantheon books, 1987.
16. See Camille Lemonnier, *Au cœur frais de la forêt*. Paris: La Renaissance du livre, 1900.
17. Irigaray, *An Ethics*, 15.

One wonders why the nomads themselves, women-as-nomads, or their nomadic thought always in the movement do not take up; in reality, the role of angels in myth.

In most of the general essays, fictions, travelogues, and philosophical speculations I have examined or mentioned, it seems that memory, in the sense of an archive of words and images from which straightforward or less obviously relevant items are retrieved in certain states and situations, is not a feature of the nomads. They are not amnesiac or even oblivious, but, not "having a history," they are presented as activating past emotions, sensations, bodily experiences in an almost instinctual manner rather than consciously separating the present from the past and the future to compare data belonging to each of these temporal categories. Tamsin Lorraine quotes Rosi Braidotti on this topic: "Nomadic memory reconnects to the virtual totality of a continuously recomposing block of past and present moments," and comments: "The pure past of the virtual whole is a past that is always being affected by the passing of time." [18]

A good summary of Braidotti's intervention on the questions of nomadism and feminist thought, that she has made 'intersectional' with the postcolonial question, can be found in her article "Les sujets nomades féministes comme figure des multitudes" published in the journal *Multitudes* in 2003.[19] She immediately situates herself in the framework of what she calls "late postmodernity": this moment, marked by the "crisis of the modern subject" requires to respond to the insufficiency of "dialectic oppositions and structuring dualisms," "rethinking the relationship to otherness in a nomadic sense" because "nomadic otherness is not one, it is multiple."[20] Multiplicity becomes a feature of nomadism, almost synonymous with it, and links it tightly to the deconstructed postmodern subject, to the female subject as not-One, and to the diversity and hybridity of postcolonial cultures.[21] With capitalist globalization moving merchandise around, the locus of (deterritorialized) mobility is no longer a free or temporarily autonomous zone outside; it is the subject's bodily existence where categories are displaced: "Our roots move, and our subjectivity becomes nomadic. [...] our bodily matter is caught in a system of circulation and exchange, at the local level as well as at the planetary level."[22]

---

[18]. Rosi Braidotti, "Les Sujets nomades féministes comme figure des multitudes," *Multitudes*, 2003/2, n° 12, (2003): 28, https://www.cairn.info/revue-multitudes-2003-2-page-27.htm.

[19] Ibid.

[20]. Ibid., 29.

[21]. Ibid., 34.

[22]. Ibid., 31.

Beyond the destabilization of logocentrism and the necessity of "creating new forms of thought," mobilities here labeled "nomadic" remain more ambiguous than ever, particularly when the author talks of mapping her own hybridity. This mapping would be "nothing more in the end than a descriptive genealogy [*généalogie raisonnée*, as in *catalog raisonné*]."[23] Geography converted back into history? A space in-between (not just two but several) in which "productive interconnections" are multiplied is very much unlike the anthropological nomadic space, and, if "being a nomad in the sense of undocumented migrant, exile or refugee [...] has nothing of a metaphor,"[24] it is a semantic extension that was rejected, rightly, by Deleuze and Guattari, but exploited without limits by Maffesoli or Attali, with the unfortunate result that the word "nomad" would lose at the same time its denotative efficiency and its metaphorical power.

Alternatives to nomadic identities

To conclude this survey on a softer note, let me call on two contemporary, bi- or pluricultural/ plurilingual writers who never use the word "nomad" in their meditations on their own displacement and other mobilities. Despite this discretion, I dare say that the intellectual, sensitive, and ethical space they have constructed for themselves and try their best to share resembles more a nomadic space and the hospitality that it can sometimes offer than the extreme amplitude taken by the nomadic metaphor in other writings I have discussed in this essay.

Akira Mizubayashi is a Japanese writer, translator, and Professor who wrote his Ph.D. on Rousseau in Paris and now writes in French as well as in Japanese. In his *Petit éloge de l'errance* ("A Little Apology of Wandering"), he uses a scene from one of Akira Kurosawa's samurai films to explain the ethical and emotional situation of the *ronin*, the renegade samurai who will no longer serve any lord, belong to a troop, a team, a caste, a tribe. A samurai is a wandering warrior, a nomad, but he goes by the strict laws of his condition, his rank, his place in the feudal society. The *ronin* is a solitary wanderer on his own, who no longer accepts pre-established codes, career plans, institutional violence. He is also a nomad, but one who will write his own story, invent his own law, elaborate his individuated identity (even if it's a desperate one), turning his back on "the lies that bind," to use Anthony Appiah's formula in the title of his latest book. The *ronin*, as perceived by Mizubayashi, is not an anarchistic runaway, an ordinary bandit; he is the one who has drawn the line between the crushing authority of discipline, an enrolment coming from before and from above, and self-discipline that goes hand in hand with self-knowledge and the

---

23. Ibid., 32, 35.
24. Ibid., 35.

recognition of chance, of the share of randomness that makes us what we become and determines where we are heading. The *ronin* is a nomad-as-dissident, in the most positive, politically, and ethically effective sense of the last word. And the most elegant expression of insubordination is, according to Mizubayashi, "silent and inflexible."[25]

Ying Chen is a Chinese Canadian Francophone writer who now lives mainly in British Columbia. Her fiction and her essays have always been, but have become more and more thoughts and images (of) in-between. Seeing how she and her Canadian-born children are classified along racial stereotypes that, moreover, mix up all the different cultures of Asia, returning to Shanghai after many years and noticing that the "cultural difference" in everyday life, tastes, attitudes with regards to the family and family values, etc., between Shanghai and Canada, has shrunk to the point of being hardly perceptible, she is now trying to find more meaning in the sense of place than in personal mobility itself. Time, rather than movement, is the great operator of change, outside us and consequently in us. "Change is an absolute law in a world without absolute," she writes. Consequently, she "has decided that [she] cannot limit herself to anything local, that [she] will drink the water of all seas, breathe the air of the whole universe, receive the teachings of the masters of all times without being a disciple of any of them."[26] A "nomadic" wandering across continents, languages, philosophies, and aesthetics (in her case, across East Asia, North America, and Western Europe) turns inevitably into an actual cosmopolitanism across time as much as physical, geographical space. The ever-migrant is today the closest kin of the historical and mythical nomad. In an interview that takes the form of a correspondence with a friend and critic, Ying Chen writes:

> Your letter to me started in Umbria and was sent from Normandy, I received it a few days ago, almost instantly, on Pender Island, and by the time my letter reaches you, I might already have left the island. Feelings and perceptions might already have been altered during this jetlag, at least from my side, because many things are happening every day, every moment, in the world, at home, in the natural environment, within my own body and mind.[27]

---

[25]. Akira Mizubayashi, *Petit éloge de l'errance* (Paris: "Folio" Gallimard, 2017), location 393, Kindle edition.

[26]. Ying Chen, *La Lenteur des montagnes* (Montreal: Boréal, 2014), 12, 14.

[27]. Chen, *Le Lenteur*, np.

Nomads are ceaselessly redefined when the world moves about/around them. If they are real, positive cosmopolitans, dwellers of a human world, they will re-invent the wisdom of living in any place for any length of time as if it were one's abode, where one belongs. Which does not involve developing a nomadic identity (as Bedouins do): "I was wondering […] if one has to claim for or bear an identity, for that could imprison a mind and a soul to be made, to be reshaped, in a changing age and environment."[28] Nomadism, reworked from an experiential and experimental shifting position that, being a dynamic situation, will never make itself pass for an origin (emanating from a mouth that was there before it spoke), could thus become a proper figure for the kind of cosmopolitanism that listens to and dialogues with the "whole earth" in each of its particular manifestations, lasting or ephemeral; in this sense, it would not be very different from an interactive humanism that requires at the same time participation in the general otherness of the defamiliarized real, and speculative seclusion.

Bibliography

Braidotti, Rosi. "Les Sujets nomades féministes comme figure des multitudes". *Multitudes*, 2003/2, n° 12, 27-38. https://www.cairn.info/revue-multitudes-2003-2-page-27.htm.

Chen, Ying. "Letters from Umbria and other places." Interview with Christine Lorre-Johnston, Fall 2019. Forthcoming in *Migrating Minds*, Didier Coste, Christina Kkona and Nicoletta Pireddu, eds, 2021.

Chen, Ying. *La Lenteur des montagnes*, essai. Montreal: Boréal, 2014.

Deleuze, Gilles, and Guattari, Félix. *A Thousand Plateaus.* Translation and foreword by Brian Massumi. Minneapolis: University of Minnesota Press, 1987.

Diamond, Jared. *The World until Yesterday: What Can We Learn From Traditional Societies?* New York: Viking, 2012.

Duras, Marguerite. *The Vice Consul*, translated by Eileen Ellenbogen. New York: Pantheon Books, [1966] 1987.

Lorraine, Tamsin. *Deleuze and Guattari's Immanent Ethics.* Albany: Suny Press, 2011.

Irigaray, Luce. *An Ethics of Sexual Difference.* Translated from the French by Carolyn Burke and Gillian C. Gill. Ithaca, NY: Cornell U. P., 1993.

Irigaray, Luce. *This Sex which is not One*, translated by Catherine Porter with Carolyn Burke. Ithaca, New York: Cornell U. P., 1985.

Lemonnier, Camille. *Au cœur frais de la forêt.* Paris: La Renaissance du livre, 1900.

Mizubayashi, Akira. *Petit éloge de l'errance.* Paris: "Folio" Gallimard, 2017. (Kindle edition)

Stone, Alison. *Luce Irigaray and the Philosophy of Sexual Difference.* Cambridge: Cambridge University Press, 2006.

---

28. Ibid.

Contributors

Dr. Prantik Banerjee

Associate Professor of English, Hislop College, Nagpur, India. His areas of interest include cultural studies, medical humanities, trauma theory, gerontology, and disability studies. His publications include a book and over forty articles and research papers in anthologies and peer-reviewed journals. His new book titled *Cultural Studies: Texts and Contexts*, is due for publication.

Swagata Basu

Assistant Professor, Doon University, Dehradun, India. She has an M.A. and M.Phil. in Spanish from Jawaharlal Nehru University. Her research interests include contemporary Spanish literature and culture, immigration in Spanish cinema, language policy, and minority Integration. She has been a Visiting Researcher at GRITIM, UPF, Barcelona, and Resident at the thematic program on Linguistic Diversity at Faber, Olot.

Dr. Debra Castillo

Professor, Cornell University. She is Emerson Hinchliff Chair of Hispanic Studies and Professor of Comparative Literature, Director of the Latino/a Studies Program and former director of the Latin American Studies Program. She is the author of *Talking Back: Towards a Latin American Feminist Literary Criticism* (Cornell UP, 1992) and several other books.

Dr. Didier Coste

Professor Emeritus, Université Bordeaux-Montaigne. He has been a professor of Comparative Literature for seventeen years at the same university. He has taught in nine countries across the world. Specializing in Poetics, Aesthetics, Narrative Theory, and Translation Theory, he is the author of *Narrative as Communication* (Minnesota UP, 1989) and several other books.

Nicole Crevar

Graduate Teaching Assistant and Research scholar in English Literature, University of Arizona. She holds an M.A. in Multicultural and Transnational Literatures from East Carolina University. Her research is focused on contemporary Chicanx literature, social justice literature, and critical and cultural theory.

Tonisha Guin

Researcher, Forum on Contemporary Theory. She has an M.A. with a specialization in Literary and Cultural Studies and a Ph.D. from The English and Foreign Languages University, Hyderabad, India.

Hamza Iqbal

Researcher in Comparative Literature at the South Asia Institute, the University of Texas at Austin. His research interests include the long-nineteenth century, Urdu Poetics, French literature, and Continental Philosophy. He also holds an M.A. in Philosophy from the University of St. Andrews, Scotland.

Olivia Kurajian

Olivia Kurajian holds two degrees (BA'19, MA'20) from McGill University, Montreal. She is currently pursuing a degree in Law at Michigan State University. She is a multidisciplinary scholar interested in international and comparative histories, anthropology, and gender studies. While her research spans multiple areas of study, she concentrates upon representing marginalized voices in the academic literature.

Dr. Leigh McKagen

Leigh McKagen holds an M.A. in English Literature and an interdisciplinary Ph.D. from Virginia Tech. Currently, she is an Adjunct Professor at the History Department at Virginia Tech and the English Department at the Virginia Military Institute.

Dr. Indrani Mukherjee

Professor, Centre for Spanish, School for Literature, Language and Culture Studies, Jawaharlal Nehru University, New Delhi, India. Her most recent book is *Gendered Ways of Transnational Un-belonging* (Cambridge Scholars Publishing, 2019). She has published extensively in international journals.

Antara Mukherjee

Antara Mukherjee is an independent scholar who is interested in Social Work and Academics. She has a Master's degree from the Tata Institute of Social Sciences, Mumbai. She has worked with Delhi Forum (NGO) on advocacy campaigns for various social movements across the nation, as a Programme Associate. Later she worked in Deepalaya, a Delhi-based NGO, for the right to education and women's empowerment. At present, she continues to work as a freelancer for different organizations such as ANHAD, PIPFPD, and JAN SAROKAR.

Ruth Prakasam

Instructor in the Department of English at Suffolk University, Boston. Her research interests include 19th Century British Women's Travel Writing and Novels about India and Colonial and Postcolonial Literature in the Anglophone Tradition.

Sushmita Sihwag

Independent scholar. She holds an M.A. in English from Ashoka University, India. Her master's thesis was titled, "Memory, Narrativity, and the Struggle for an "I": Issues of Identity in the Tibetan Memoir." Her research interests include exile and diaspora literature, narratology, and memory studies.

Dr. Sanghita Sen

Sanghita Sen, an independent film researcher, has a Ph.D. in Film Studies and another in Comparative literature. Her research interest includes Cultural Studies, Marxism, feminism, Bengali literature, film history, Third Cinema, and documentaries. She writes on political cinema, gender and cinema, film history, and decolonization. She curates film programs and does English subtitling of films in Bengali and Hindi languages. She also teaches in the department of Film Studies, University of St Andrews, Scotland, UK.

Dr. Java Singh

Lecturer in the Spanish department at Doon University, India. She has a Ph.D. from Jawaharlal Nehru University. She also holds an MBA from the Institute of Management, Ahmedabad. She co-edited *Gendered Unbelonging* (Cambridge Scholars Publishing, 2019). The topics of her publications include Spanish and Latin American Cinema, immigration, works of Southern Cone women writers, and myth and postcolonial criticism.

Dr. Shelby Ward

Lecturer, Virginia Tech, and Tusculum University. She holds a Ph.D. in Social, Political, Ethical, and Cultural Thought. She is a transdisciplinary scholar with backgrounds in critical, feminist, and postcolonial theories, her most recent publications have been in *Pivot: A Journal of Interdisciplinary Studies and Thought*, *Interdisciplinary Political Studies*, and *Otherness: Essays and Studies*.

Index